The God Experiment

Can Science Prove
the Existence of God?

RUSSELL STANNARD

Foreword by
PAUL DAVIES

HiddenSpring

Jacket design by Mark Horton

Jacket photo by Adam Chinitz

First published in Great Britain in 1999 by
Faber and Faber Limited
3 Queen Square London WC1N 3AU

Library of Congress Cataloging-in-Publication Data

Stannard, Russell.
The God Experiment : can science prove the existence of God? /
by Russell Stannard ; foreword by Paul Davies.
p. cm.
Originally published: London : Faber and Faber, 1999.
Includes index.
ISBN 1-58768-007-6 (cloth)
I. Title.
BT102.S68 2000
212′.1—dc21
00-057249

Published in North America by
HiddenSpring
an imprint of Paulist Press
997 Macarthur Boulevard
Mahwah, New Jersey 07430

www.hiddenspringbooks.com

Printed and bound in the United States of America

Contents

"I came to know God experimentally"

George Fox, a leading figure in the founding
of the Quaker movement

Foreword

Imagine a faraway planet on which a species of intelligent beings had evolved. Over time, communities of these beings developed organized societies and rudimentary technology. Somewhat later, a group of bright aliens stumbled across the basic laws of physics. Soon what we would call science began to flourish. The aliens realized that with this new knowledge of the world they could improve their technology and understand more and more about the physical universe.

Some centuries passed, and the scientific project reached its culmination. The aliens understood just about everything in their environment, near and far, in terms of scientific principles. A complete "theory of everything" was formulated, involving elegant and abstract mathematical expressions that embodied all fundamental physics. To be sure, some systems remained too complex to study in detail, but the aliens were confident that all the basic principles of nature were thoroughly understood.

Much later, historians would regard this scientific golden age as the easy phase in the attempt by the aliens to make sense of the world. With all the formulas established and all the experiments completed, some curious aliens began asking altogether harder questions. Why, for example, were the laws of nature what they were, rather than something else? The beautiful laws of physics, captured so succinctly within the theory of everything, clearly could have been different. What determined, from among the set of all possible laws of physics, those laws that actually applied to the real world? And where did these laws come from anyway? In addition to asking "Why this Universe?" and "Why any universe?" the aliens began wondering about where they themselves fit in. Did the emergence of life, consciousness, and understanding of the physical world signify a profound link between the nature of the universe and their own abilities to unravel the secrets of nature, or was it just a lucky fluke? Was there any deeper meaning to physical existence? How could the remarkable coherence and consistency of the natural order be explained? Might the universe be unfolding according to something like a scheme? Could concepts such as purpose and design be applied to nature as well as to alien activity? A new project was duly begun to tackle these thorny issues.

Most of the aliens were highly skeptical about the new project, not because they thought the questions were pointless or stupid, but because they were hard - much harder than the scientific questions. In approaching them, scientists had to go beyond physics, rooted as it was in experiment and observation, into the realm of metaphysics. Progress was likely to be slow, consensus difficult. Even the best alien minds were baffled in the face of such daunting mysteries. My description of a hypothetical alien community serves the purpose of contrasting with the history of human civilization. In our case, metaphysical questions were tackled long before science arose. Early human communities constructed a wide range of mythologies, superstitions and religions to make sense of their world. To modern eyes, many of these early attempts at explaining reality look childish and fanciful. Later, when the great world religions developed, more intellectual rigor was brought to bear on these fundamental questions of existence. Leading thinkers in the monotheistic tradition, such as Augustine and Thomas Aquinas, developed a systematic approach to metaphysics and attempted to relate features of the physical universe to theology. Scholars in Judaism and Islam pursued similar projects.

Then, in the seventeenth century, modern science began to flourish. Scientists had an altogether different agenda. Their methods could, with effort, lead to explanations for physical phenomena, but they were ill suited to dealing with metaphysical questions. To be sure, most early scientists were deeply religious, and they saw their scientific investigations as a way to reveal God's handiwork in the cosmos. The laws of nature that underpin the scientific enterprise they regarded as God's way of ordering the world. But principally scientists were preoccupied more with how than with why questions. Over the succeeding three hundred years, science became so successful that its theological underpinnings were largely abandoned. Many scientists began to regard the ancient questions of existence as either misguided or unanswerable, and therefore pointless. They looked back with derision at mankind's early fumbling attempts at metaphysics and presented the scientific enterprise as an antidote to such primitive musings. Once the public was properly educated in the scientific method, it was claimed, they would stop asking meaningless why questions and simply accept the physical universe, with its manifold wonders, as a brute fact.

It is fascinating to speculate whether, had human history resembled that of my hypothetical alien community, this contempt by scientists for matters metaphysical would have been so strident and entrenched. I suspect that had it been the scientists rather than the priests who first addressed the great metaphysical puzzles, then the topics concerned would have been regarded as extremely difficult but entirely respectable to contemplate. Such is scientific hubris! In fact, something of a sea change is occurring in the scientific community. Perhaps it is inevitable that those scientists working at the frontier on topics like the origin of the universe cannot avoid encountering the age-old metaphysical questions that were formerly the exclusive preserve of theologians and philosophers. Those scientists have been drawn, through their scientific work, to revisit the earliest and deepest riddles of existence: why the world is as it is and what the place of human beings might be in the great scheme of things.

Russell Stannard epitomizes this new breed of thinker. He is a physicist by profession, with a long-standing interest in deep problems such as the origin of the universe, the nature of time, the fundamental structure of matter, and the role of conscious observers in nature. He approaches the subject of God and science through the Christian tradition, although his work will be of interest to adherents of all religions and none. In this book he sets out a comprehensive agenda to bring scientific methods and concepts to bear on theological and religious issues, and also to help science rediscover its theological roots. He argues that with the benefit of our scientific understanding of the world, it is now profitable to go back and reexamine those early prescientific attempts at explaining the universe in God-related terms. Remarkably, in spite of their more limited knowledge of the physical universe, many early religious thinkers nevertheless seem to have identified profound and enduring truths.

Stannard does not restrict his analysis to abstract theological and scientific topics. Indeed, he is not afraid to confront mainstream religious problems head-on. He begins his account with a critical assessment of miracles and goes on to consider the significance of Biblical narratives, especially those that relate to the life and death of Jesus Christ. Nor does he shy away from thorny problems, such as the existence of evil, human free will and life beyond death, which have exercised the minds of some of the world's greatest thinkers over the centuries. He brings a refreshing new scientific perspective to bear on these contentious issues, and while he makes no claim to have solved them, readers will discover many fresh analyses.

Unusually for a scientist, Stannard strives to build bridges between ancient religious traditions and modern science. Rather than dismissing many of the Biblical stories as myths, he reexamines them in the light of modern science and finds much of enduring value. One of his key themes, which I strongly endorse, is that theology is not a static discipline, but continually evolving in the light of new knowledge. Thus the concept of God in the Old Testament develops chronologically. He starts out as a tribal warrior deity and gradually evolves into the Christian God of love and forgiveness. But who is to say the process ends there? As Stannard points out, the universe revealed by science opens up whole new vistas that went unnoticed by the Bible writers. There is an urgent need for theological reevaluation in the light of discoveries about the birth and death of the universe, the genetic revolution, and the possibility of extraterrestrial life, to name but a few fashionable areas of research. We should not just look backward to the remote past for religious inspiration and neglect future developments.

The idea of progress in religion may seem strange to some people, but to a scientist it is natural to think of our understanding advancing with the aid of new discoveries. One can still respect the Bible and other sacred texts for building the foundations of faith, but that does not mean they should be the last word on the subject. Stannard's achievement is to garner the core message of the Bible and move on to enrich it with scientific insights.

One of the most exciting areas of theological enquiry at this time concerns the reemergence of what used to be called natural theology - the belief that God is revealed through the workings of nature as well as through personal religious experience. For example, vigorous debate is taking place between scientists and theologians about the significance of the so-called anthropic principle - the discovery that the existence of conscious organisms depends rather sensitively on certain delicate features in the basic laws of physics. Does this point toward some sort of design in the structure of the universe or to the existence of an infinite variety of alternative universes - a multiverse - in which just a tiny fraction possess by chance the favorable circumstances for life to emerge? In universities and at conferences around the world, theologians can be found talking to computer scientists and mathematicians, physicists and cosmologists, geneticists and evolutionary psychologists, discussing complexity theory, the foundations of mathematics and logic, the evolution of altruistic behavior, and many other challenging topics.

Perhaps it is too soon to talk of the new theology, as one does of the new physics or the new biology, but there is certainly a new theological agenda, and this book by Russell Stannard provides an excellent guide to the sorts of issues likely to engage theologians and religious organizations in the coming decades. Einstein once wrote that science without religion is lame and religion without science is blind. I can think of no better emblem for the chapters that follow.

Paul Davies

South Australia

The Prayer Experiment

Does prayer work?

You are suffering from heart disease – in need of coronary artery bypass surgery. At the hospital someone asks whether you are prepared to take part in an experiment. Not, I hasten to say, an experiment involving some novel surgical technique; the operation will be perfectly standard. No, it is an experiment to test whether prayers for the sick are effective.

On agreeing to participate, your name is to be randomly assigned to one of two groups. Patients in one group will be prayed for by special teams of intercessors drawn from a variety of religious denominations, each team being given a particular batch of patients. Patients in the second group will *not* be prayed for. The second group is identical in all respects to the first, with the sole exception of its not being the subject of prayer. There will, of course, be the inevitable statistical differences between the groups, but these should be small, given that each group consists of 600 patients drawn from the five major hospitals participating in the experiment. The second group is the *control* group.

Over a period of two to three years, the patients' case histories will be followed up to see if there are any differences in recovery rates between the two groups. Indicators will include measurements of the physical functioning of the heart, the frequency of death from all causes, length of stay in hospital, and whether patients discharged from hospital return to their homes or enter a nursing home.

As a participating patient you will not know to which of the two groups you have been assigned. You might be prayed for, or you might not. That is all you know. Likewise, the medical staff tending you will have no access to this information. Those doing the praying will know only the Christian names of the people assigned to them, together with some details of their condition – not sufficient to reveal the identity of the individual. Only at the very end of the experiment will all the data be collated. The project has been designed as a rigorously controlled scientific experiment.

I first came to learn of this experiment through being a trustee of the John Templeton Foundation, a charitable organization devoted to supporting projects promoting progress in religion. It was our foundation that agreed to fund this experiment. When I recently spoke of the project in a radio broadcast in the UK, I was inundated with queries from newspaper reporters and radio and TV interviewers; the telephone did not stop ringing for a week. Everyone seemed totally amazed – and intrigued – at the thought that one might apply scientific principles to investigate a religious question.

But why? Several other fields of academic activity have tried – admittedly, with varying degrees of success – to turn themselves into sciences. We have seen, for example, the rise of the social sciences; we have heard Sigmund Freud and Carl Jung claiming on behalf of psychology that it too was a science. So why not theology?

One objection stems from the idea that theology is fundamentally rooted in Scripture. The starting-point is that one accepts, in faith, that the Bible, or some other set of sacred writings, is the inerrant Word of God. This set of writings, interpreted in a literal manner or in some more liberal way, is the ultimate authority on all matters relating to God.

If that is the stance adopted, then it is clearly unlike anything that holds in science. Science is fundamentally based in experimentation and observation. It is an approach where one's theories are in a constant state of flux as they adapt themselves to new empirical findings. No matter how cherished one's hypothesis might be, it must always yield in the face of contrary evidence. The ultimate authority lies with the data. The idea that the truth was set in stone at some earlier time, and is not to be questioned, has no place in science.

But that is just one approach to theology. There is another – one that resonates much more closely with the scientific approach. One of the tasks of this book is to explore to what extent this second approach to theology can be regarded as a science.

I suppose most people's idea of the way scientists go about their work is of an investigation conducted under carefully controlled laboratory conditions. A situation is set up in which, as far as possible, the particular effect under investigation is isolated, and all other extraneous background effects are reduced to a minimum. That is indeed the aim in many scientific studies. As regards religious investigations, the best attempt to apply such a methodology is to be found in the experiment I was talking about just now – the so-called *prayer experiment*. That will be our starting-point. So let us take a closer look at it.

The prayer experiment

Belief in the power of prayer is widespread. One hears the claim, for example, that the collapse of atheistic communism was an answer to prayer. It had long been held that, because of the totalitarian nature of communism – the lack of free elections – once a country went communist there could be no going back. Religion in those countries would become a thing of the past. And yet it was not to be. Against all the odds, communist regimes have toppled, and the churches in those countries, suppressed for decades, are now coming back into their own once more.

Or take the case of South Africa. It was an almost universally held belief that apartheid in South Africa could end only in a bloodbath. In the event, the transition to majority rule occurred relatively peacefully. This is also claimed to be an answer to prayer.

Though such examples might strike believers as highly persuasive, they are not, of course, conclusive. We are unable to rerun history – once with the benefit of prayer, and once without – to see if it makes a difference. No, to try and see whether prayer "works," one has to turn away from the big one-off world events, and concentrate on situations that are repeatable – frequently occurring situations where we have a chance of varying the conditions.

Prayers for the sick appear to offer just such an opportunity. If miraculous healings happen, then this would seem on the face of it to be evidence for God – God directly intervening and having an effect in the world. There is a widespread acceptance of the efficacy of intercessory prayer. This might be evident in the spectacular, highly charged, emotional rallies held by the evangelist Maurice Cerullo, or in the more sober practice of making pilgrimages to holy places such as Lourdes in France or Guadelupe in Mexico. More commonly, faith in miracles manifests itself in the intercessions for the sick offered up in every church on a Sunday, or in the daily private devotions of millions when praying for the recovery of sick loved ones. But do such prayers work? That is what the prayer experiment hopes to discover.

The project's chief investigator is Dr. Herbert Benson of the Mind/Body Medical Institute, New England Deaconess Hospital, Boston. This is not the first time an experiment of this sort has been carried out. Results published in 1988 of an intercessory study at the San Francisco General Hospital performed by R. C. Byrd appeared to show a significant difference between the two groups of patients. Those who received intercessory prayer appeared to have a less complicated hospital course and required fewer medications and procedures than those belonging to the control group who did not receive prayer. However, the results have not been widely accepted, in part because of concerns over the details of the methodology involved.

The current project is a considerable improvement on the original in a number of respects. The sample sizes have been increased from the 200 characteristic of the first study to the 600 involved in the present experiment. Secondly, whereas the Byrd study included anyone admitted to the coronary care unit, the patients involved this time are more homogeneous in that they are all undergoing the same surgery (thus facilitating tighter medical definitions of evaluation points or endpoints of treatment). The follow-up period has been extended from one year to two/three years. Five sites are involved instead of one. More sophisticated statistical techniques will be employed to analyze the data.

In addition, the Benson study includes a third group of 600 patients. Like those in the first group, these are prayed for, but unlike the first, they *are* informed that they are to be the subject of prayer. The intention here is to examine whether there is any additional benefit to be gained (of a psychosomatic or placebo nature) from knowing that one is the subject of prayer. This part of the study will test hypotheses to do with "patient expectation."

Possible outcomes and interpretations

And what of the results? It is too early to say. Final results are not due out before 2002. Meanwhile, there will be no interim progress reports. This is to ensure that early indications do not feed back into the experiment and possibly affect its outcome. So, you might be wondering, why bring up the subject now? Are we not being premature? The reason is that, long before it was agreed to go ahead with the experiment, much thought had been devoted to considering the possible outcomes, and what significance might be attached to them. Even without knowing the actual outcome, it is highly instructive to think through the various options.

As regards the first two groups – those unsure whether or not they are being prayed for – should the project eventually yield a statistically significant positive correlation between prayer and good recovery from the operation, that would of course be fascinating. Doubtless such a discovery would trigger a whole series of follow-up experiments. In the first place one would want to establish, beyond all reasonable doubt, that the positive correlation was no mere statistical freak. Different prayer techniques would be tried to see whether some were more effective than others. One would want to investigate whether other medical conditions yielded to this form of treatment – cancer, perhaps. Clearly an important field of study would open up.

However, it must be noted that none of this would amount to proof of God's existence; persuasive evidence in favor, maybe – but not out-and-out proof. Both the investigators themselves and the funding agency make it clear from the outset that the project is *not* to be thought of as an attempt to prove God's existence. An alternative explanation of a positive correlation might involve, for example, some form of direct transference of thought between the mind of the person praying and that of the patient, presumably of a telepathic nature. There would accordingly be no need to invoke God as an "intermediary" in the process. The beneficial effect would pass directly from intercessor to patient.

As for the other possible result – *no* measurable difference between the two groups – what might be the implication of that?

Doubtless many will jump to the "obvious" conclusion: intercessory prayer does not work – perhaps because there is no God. But again one must be careful. In the same way as a positive result does not necessarily vindicate belief in God, so a negative result does not have to be damaging to belief. There are alternative explanations of a null result:

For instance, when it is said that one of the groups will not be prayed for, that simply means there will be no special prayer team at work on their behalf. That of course will not stop the patients praying for themselves, nor their loved ones and friends from praying. The investigators refer to this (somewhat tongue-in-cheek) as the "unwanted background noise." What the experiment is trying to do is to measure whether there is any *additional* benefit coming from the prayers of the special team. It could well be that the efforts of these strangers will be swamped by the heartfelt prayers of those directly involved with the patients.

There is another concern: when scientists investigate the physical world, provided they ask the right questions and adopt good, sound scientific methodology, nature has no alternative but to yield up its secrets. But applying that methodology to God (or to anyone else with a will of their own) is *not* a guarantee of success. God might simply decide not to cooperate. It could be argued that a loving God might indeed be reluctant to penalize patients merely because some strangers deliberately choose not to include them in their prayers.

Not only that, God might well appreciate better than we ourselves some of the drawbacks of allowing us to probe too deeply into his* manner of working. By the very nature of the clear-cut way in which the experiment has been designed, the result will be a quantitative one. That means it becomes possible to put a price on whatever benefit might be gained from this type of prayer exercise. Do we *really* want some treasury official to use a positive result as an excuse to close down hospital wards – because vicars can be hired to pray more cheaply? While we are doubtless all in favor of a cost-effective Medicare system, it seems a far cry from what many would regard as the true nature of prayer: a natural expression of a loving, trusting, personal relationship with God. For this reason, it would not altogether be surprising if God decides to frustrate the best efforts of the investigators – for their own good. We would do well to recall that it does say in the Bible: *Thou shalt not put the Lord thy God to the test.* So, we can't say we haven't been warned!

Important and intriguing though this experiment might be, it is necessary to keep it in perspective. The experiment is concerned solely with intercessory prayers; there are many other aspects of prayer. Moreover, it deals only with prayers offered up on behalf of strangers. Like many others, I reckon the central core of intercessory prayer has more to do with the agonizing, involved prayers of loved ones and intimate friends – the so-called "noise" – than with those of distant strangers.

Nevertheless the Benson experiment has aroused enormous interest, it has been beautifully designed, and it deserves to be done. I for one await with great interest both the outcome itself, and the heated discussions that are bound to ensue as to what interpretation should be put on the result – whatever that turns out to be.

Limitations of solitary investigations

In view of the ambiguities that will inevitably attend the result of this experiment, you may be wondering why I have chosen it as the starting-point for our discussion of the evidence for God. The reason is simple. It is to bring home that even when we are able to set up conditions of our own choosing, under thoroughly scientific constraints, it becomes surprisingly difficult to arrive at any firm, incontrovertible conclusion as to whether or not a supernatural intervention has taken place. If we cannot get knock-down proof when we are controlling everything, it is surely unreasonable to expect *any* single, decisive proof of God's existence, and of his influence in the world. Those who make such a demand are likely to be disappointed.

So does that mean that the whole idea of trying to apply scientific thinking to the study of God is ill-conceived? Is it doomed to failure from the outset? No. It is important to recognize that the kind of difficulties encountered over the interpretation of the outcome of the prayer experiment are nothing unusual; they are to be found all the time – even in hard-core physical science.

Take, for example, my own field of research: high-energy nuclear physics. This is the study of the behavior of sub-atomic particles. These particles are so small they cannot be seen directly (under a microscope, say). They are to all intents and purposes invisible – much like an invisible God. Instead, one has to observe their *effects*, and from these draw inferences. The usual effect is that they leave a trail or track behind them marking where they have been. (The track might be in the form of a string of tiny bubbles in a transparent liquid, or a series of small sparks in a gas subject to a high electric voltage.) As the sub-atomic particles collide with each other, or as they spontaneously disintegrate, so they leave behind characteristic patterns of tracks marking out the paths followed by the various particles involved.

The trouble is that for any given pattern of tracks, there might be a number of competing interpretations. If all one has is a single event, there might be very little that can be deduced from it. Many examples might have to be collected, perhaps using a variety of detection techniques; statistical analyses have to be carried out as to the likelihood of the various rival explanations. Only after a period of time might a consensus emerge as to which is the more likely interpretation. Throughout this process there will not be any well-defined point at which the interpretation is *proved* correct. Rather, the evidence progressively accumulates; the odds become stronger in favor of one particular explanation. Eventually, the controversies die down, and the scientific community as a whole finds that it is no longer seriously questioning the conclusion.

As another example, we can look to cosmology. This will figure prominently in our discussions later, in Chapter 9. There we shall be examining the evidence for the Big Bang origins of the Universe. According to this theory, the Universe began with a great explosion. Why do we think that? For a start, we find that the Universe is expanding; it is still expanding in the aftermath of that explosion. At least, that is the interpretation put on it. But there is another possibility. According to a rival theory, new matter is continually being created throughout space. As fast as matter moves away, the gaps left behind are filled by the newly created material. Thus, the overall picture remains essentially unchanged over time: in particular, there was *no* explosive beginning. This "Steady State" theory used to be a serious rival to the "Big Bang" theory. And that is how the situation would have remained, had not other indications come along.

As we shall be seeing later, the Big Bang theory holds that the initial conditions in the Universe would have been very hot; the explosion would have been accompanied by a fireball. It is argued that the cooled-down remnants of that fireball ought still to be about in the Universe today. Indeed, this radiation has now been discovered. At least, it has all the hallmarks expected of it. But of course there are many sources of radiation in the Universe. It could well be argued that, just as the expansion of the Universe on its own was not proof of the Big Bang hypothesis, neither is this form of radiation, on its own, clinching proof. Rather, it is to be seen as helping to strengthen the overall case.

The expected conditions of the Big Bang also allow one to calculate what kind of atomic particles were likely to emerge from it. The calculated abundances of the different kinds of atom are found to be in good agreement with those of the atoms that make up the gases from which the stars formed. This constitutes yet further confirmatory evidence.

Finally, we note that it takes time for light to reach us from the far depths of space. Examining distant objects through a telescope is like looking back in time. We are able to see directly how the Universe was long ago – and it looked different then to what it does now. The density of matter throughout space appears greater then than it does now – in agreement with the Big Bang theory, and contrary to what would be expected on the basis of the Steady State theory. But in saying that, it has to be recognized that there are difficulties involved in trying to estimate distances to far-off astronomical objects. Systematic errors could creep in, and if present, would distort one's estimates of density. For this reason, the evidence, once again, is not by itself conclusive.

What one discovers from a discussion like this is that acceptance of the Big Bang theory does not rest on any single decisive piece of evidence. Instead, the case has to be based on the examination of a range of indicators, all of which point to the same conclusion. The Big Bang hypothesis is an economical and elegant way of accounting for a wide variety of disparate phenomena. The evidence is cumulative; it is *persuasive* rather than clinching. And different scientists need different degrees of persuasion in order to be won over.

One lesson we can draw from this is that, when trying to establish the reality of God, rather than looking for one decisive experiment –

say, the prayer experiment – we perhaps ought to be broadening our horizons. We need to examine a wide variety of indications to see whether, *taken together*, they add up to a compelling case.

When conditions are not under our control

A further reason one might have for believing it inappropriate to associate scientific methodology with studies of God is that, apart from the prayer experiment, it is hard to think of situations that would lend themselves to the establishment of controlled investigations into God.

This, in fact, is not a problem peculiar to theology. An inability to control the circumstances of an investigation is quite common in science too. Take, for example, cosmology – the study of the Universe on the largest scale. We have just been discussing the scientific evidence for the Big Bang. But, of course, there was never any question of us controlling the circumstances of the Big Bang. The cosmos cannot be contained in a laboratory. In fact, the whole subject of cosmology and astronomy is one where we control virtually nothing. We are reduced to observing, in a purely passive manner, whatever radiation signals happen to come our way.

And yet no one would deny that cosmology and astronomy are "sciences." They gain that status from the systematic and scrupulous way the data are gathered, and the manner in which the theories are always open to modification in the light of those empirical findings.

The same holds in certain branches of the biological and earth sciences. In Chapter 10 we shall be examining Darwin's Theory of Evolution by Natural Selection. We shall see how we humans, in common with the other animals, have descended from more primitive ancestors – stretching all the way back to the inanimate chemicals to be found on the surface of Earth soon after it formed some 4,600 million years ago. This is the generally accepted scenario for human origins.

But how has this assessment been made? The evolution of humans is not a repeatable process. Indeed, we shall later be pointing out that if evolution has taken place on other planets in the cosmos, giving rise to intelligent life-forms, these are most unlikely to end up looking like us humans. And yet evolutionary biology is most definitely a "science."

The reasons are the same: the systematic collection of a wide range of different types of data (the fossil record, anatomical comparisons between species, genetic comparisons, etc.), together with a willingness to allow the weight of that empirical data to be the final arbiter on the success or otherwise of the theoretical hypotheses. Nor is it necessary for that data to be so overwhelming as to convince everyone. There are many professional biologists, let alone lay persons, still unhappy about various aspects of the conventionally accepted evolutionary theory.

Finally, we might mention the earth sciences. These have been transformed in recent times by the theory of plate tectonics – the manner in which various parts of the Earth's crust move about the surface of the globe causing earthquakes, and the building of mountains. Once again, these are processes that are not under our control.

Thus, the ability to control the circumstances under which an experiment is conducted, together with the possibility of repeating the experiment under the same or different conditions, though desirable, is not a necessary prerequisite for that field of study to be regarded as scientific. For that reason we speak of the social sciences – despite the strong limitations that exist on the extent to which it is acceptable to manipulate social groupings. We might also speak of psychology as a science, even though there are strict ethical limits on the degree to which a therapist might seek to "experiment" on his/her clients.

Opening out the prayer experiment

The same kind of situation confronts us over the study of God. God is not some object we can control. We cannot expect God to submit to repeated experimentation under conditions of our choosing. There will be no single, definitive proof of his existence and of his manner of working. Instead, we have to examine, as objectively as we can, a whole range of experience – a multitude of diverse indications – whatever happens to be on offer. We have to ask: given the totality of the data presented to us by our experience of life, does it make better sense in the light of the God hypothesis? Does it all hang together better if we assume there is a God? If so, what kind of God are we dealing with?

Thus, the line of investigation that began with a narrow experiment into the effectiveness of intercessory prayer is opened out. The prayer experiment becomes just one piece of the jigsaw puzzle. The whole of life – every aspect of our experiences – has to be drawn into what I call: *the God experiment.*

Note
*Occasional usage of "his" and "he" not to be taken as implying the assignment of a specific gender to God.

2

Do Miracles Happen?

The prayer experiment is investigating requests for God to intervene in the normal course of events. Essentially the prayers are asking for a miracle. But, of course, there have been many, many claims of miraculous happenings – especially in the Bible. So, is this where we ought next to be looking for evidence of God's intervention? Indeed, were we wise to begin our investigation with examples of healing? Perhaps less ambiguous evidence is to be found in other types of miracle – nature miracles – those that do not involve the complicated inner workings of the human body, with all its psychological ramifications.

The Bible appears to lay claim to many such miracles; it is to these that we now turn for our second source of evidence for God. But note that in so doing, we are *not* looking to the Bible as an authority – a source of unquestioned integrity. We examine it in exactly the same critical frame of mind as we would any other potentially fallible written record.

Definition of miracles

But first we need to clarify what exactly we mean by the term "miracle."

Originally a "miracle," or a "marvel," was meant to refer to *any* event that was held to be especially revelatory of God. God is revealed in various ways. On a starlit night one might sense an awesome presence and power; on contemplating the physical laws some would claim to glimpse a divine sense of order; God's purpose might be discerned through the history of a nation (such as the Jewish nation), as well as through the pattern of one's own individual life. Perhaps even more importantly, God is felt to be revealed to the individual through the medium of prayer and meditation.

But having said that, certain events stand out as being especially revelatory of God. For example, a plane crashes, there is no loss of life, a newspaper headline reads "miracle escape." To say that it is a "miracle escape" does not necessarily imply that a law of physics has been violated. The newspaper reporter is merely saying it is an amazing occurrence. Some would put this down to luck; others would say it was God's providence – evidence that one was under divine protection. Such events can be regarded by the faithful as so revelatory of God that they have the power to change the whole course of their subsequent life.

Clearly, there is no difficulty in accepting miracles if this is all we have in mind – events that are out-of-the-ordinary, but do not violate any law of nature. But this is *not* what most people mean when they question the possibility of miracles. For them, a miracle is specifically a violation of a law of nature – God interrupting the smooth flow of the working of nature by a one-off, supernatural input.

From now on we shall stick to this narrower definition of a "miracle." We ask: are there such exceptions to the laws of nature? Do miracles of *this* kind happen?

Biblical miracle accounts; a variety of explanations

Many religious believers regard miracle stories as a package deal; you either accept them, or you don't. But most Biblical scholars would hold that this is too simplistic. It is certainly not the case that in order to be a religious believer you have to accept all the miracles lock, stock, and barrel. The miracle accounts are a very mixed bag.

In the first place, some of the events described can be covered by the normal laws of nature: they are not miraculous in the narrow sense in which we are defining the word "miracle." For example, Moses feeding the Israelites on manna in the desert. Manna is a syrupy secretion given out by insects called *Trabutina mannipara*. It forms in sugary drops the size of peas which harden on the leaves of tamarisk plants overnight and then fall to the ground in the morning. Bedouin Arabs use manna as part of their normal diet between the months of May and July. So, although the faithful might well offer thanks to God for his providence in supplying such needed sustenance in unlikely circumstances, there is nothing here that is against any law of nature.

Similarly with the casting out of devils. Today these might be regarded as the work of a good psychiatrist rather than a miracle-worker.

Next, we note that one or two miracle stories appear to have been generated by mistake. Compare, for example, the following two stories:

(i) The disciples are in a boat on the Sea of Galilee. They see Jesus walking on the water. Impetuous Peter gets out of the boat to go to him, but sinks into the water;

(ii) The disciples are in a boat on the Sea of Galilee. They see Jesus walking on the seashore (this being soon after his resurrection). Impetuous Peter gets out of the boat to go to him, swimming in the water.

Essentially the same story – apart from Jesus in one instance walking on the sea, and in the other walking on the seashore. It is at this point we note that, on going back to the original Greek, there is an ambiguity between the phrases meaning "walking *on* the sea" and "walking *by* the sea." This observation gives rise to the theory that originally there was but a single story – one in which Jesus was walking by the sea. In the repeated tellings of the story, someone got hold of the wrong end of the stick. Through a simple mistranslation, they unwittingly created the story of Jesus walking on the sea. This explanation appears to me to make a lot of sense. It has always been difficult to understand why Jesus would refuse the temptation in the wilderness to defy gravity by throwing himself off a building, but would then, to no particular purpose, defy gravity by walking on water.

So, we are able to dispose of a few miracle stories either as naturalistic occurrences, or as mistakes in translation. But not many succumb to such easy explanation. What of the others?

A miracle-story-telling culture

We need a background against which to judge them. This is provided by the books that did *not* get into the Bible – such as "The Infancy Gospel of Thomas," or "The Arabic Gospel of the Childhood." In such writings we find a wealth of miracle stories. For instance, Jesus as a schoolboy supposedly got bored during his lessons and made clay models of birds; these then promptly flew out of the window. Again at school, Jesus on one occasion cursed a boy who had run into him by mistake, and the boy fell down dead. We read of a young man who had been turned into a mule by witchcraft. Mary placed the infant Jesus on the back of the mule, whereupon the mule was transformed back into the young man.

Similar extraordinary stories are told of the apostles in writings such as "The Acts of Peter," "The Acts of John," and "The Gospel of Peter." On one occasion, for example, a contest took place between Peter and a magician. The magician had at one stage managed to levitate himself to a great height above the city. Peter pointed out to God that this feat was not doing the cause of Christianity much good. God cut off the magician's power; he fell to earth and broke his leg in three places. Everyone present was converted – and celebrated their conversion by stoning the magician to death!

Clearly such stories are blatant invention; we do not believe a word of them. It is no wonder they were excluded from the canon. But these stories are instructive. They show us that people in those days delighted in miracle stories and tales of wondrous happenings. For us, brought up in a pragmatic culture largely dominated by scientific thought, we find this hard to comprehend. For us, miracle stories can be something of an embarrassment. But for those living in a culture dominated by story-telling, they were a source of delight. They were a recognized and accepted way of conveying to others something of the exceptional nature and quality of the person being referred to.

If this invention was going on in the books lying outside the Bible, can we be sure that the same influences were not at work *within* the canon?

The accretion of miracle accounts in the Bible

We answer this by looking at stories that are dealt with in more than one gospel; we compare the earlier version with the later one.

Firstly, we look at the call of the fishermen to become disciples. In

Mark (the first of the gospels to be written), Jesus simply says to the fishermen, "Follow me and I will make you fishers of men." In the later gospel of Luke, we have the same words of Jesus – but only after a miraculous haul of fish has taken place.

As a second example, we take the arrest of Jesus in the garden of Gethsemane. Mark describes how one of Jesus' followers cuts off the ear of the high priest's servant. That is all that happens: the ear is cut off. By the time we get to the later writing of Luke, however, Jesus performs a miracle: he puts the ear back on and heals it. If this truly happened, it is difficult to understand why Mark, telling the same story, omits the punch-line. Luke's version seems to betray evidence of accretion.

Further indication of the proliferation over time of miracle stories comes when we make a general comparison of the gospels and Paul's writings. Paul's epistles are the earliest writings in the New Testament. Apart from the resurrection, he mentions *none* of Jesus' miracles. This raises questions. For example, in trying to convince people that Jesus was the Son of God, why did he not refer to the Virgin Birth? Surely this is the "proof" beyond all others that Jesus was uniquely divine. It makes for a strange omission – assuming of course that he had heard of the Virgin Birth. If he hadn't, why was that? Could it be that at the time he was writing, the story had not yet come into circulation?

By the time we get to Mark, the first of the gospels, we read of the stilling of the waters, the raising of Jairus's daughter, the feeding of the multitude, the walking on water, and various healing miracles. Most of these are to be found in Matthew and Luke (who used Mark as a source), but in addition there are now to be found the miraculous haul of fish, the ear of the high priest's servant being healed, the raising of the young man of Nain, and the Virgin Birth. Finally, when we come to the last of the gospels to be written, that due to John, we find for the first time the raising of Lazarus, the healing of the man born blind, and water being turned into wine.

We cannot be certain, but there does appear to be a process at work whereby miracle stories were increasingly coming into circulation with time. So, what is going on? Are these attempts to deceive us?

The nature of a miracle story

We can answer this only by coming to grips with the true nature of a miracle story.

The Jews lived in a story-telling culture. What does that mean? In ancient times, stories were much used to convey the wisdom of a nation, including timeless spiritual truths, from one generation to the next. One thinks here of the great myths of Genesis: the creation myths and the story of Adam and Eve. As we shall be seeing in more detail later in Chapters 9 and 10, what matters in these mythical stories is not the six days of creation, or the making of Eve from a rib taken from Adam's side, or the serpent, but the deep spiritual truths that lie behind the stories: the dependence of ourselves and of the world upon God; the nature of marriage as uniting a husband and wife as one flesh; our relationship to planet Earth and how we are to tend it; our potentiality as having been made in the image of God; our tendency to fall short of that potential and to succumb to our desires rather than be obedient to the will of God. It is these deep spiritual truths that matter to us, and the conveyance of such truths was the original intention of those who put these stories together in the first place.

The same idea of conveying truths through stories was continued by Jesus much later in his parables. There might well have been a man on the road from Jerusalem to Jericho who fell among thieves; there might have been a Good Samaritan. But possibly not. It does not matter. The point of the story was to get across to Jesus' questioner the message concerning whom he should regard as his neighbor, and how he ought to behave towards that neighbor.

The prevalence of story-telling in ancient cultures leads us therefore to ask the question of whether the conveyance of deep spiritual truth was the prime motivation underlying the miracle stories.

To answer this question, we turn to John's gospel. John wrote mainly for Gentile readers – those who could perhaps not be expected necessarily to be in tune with Jewish thought, and therefore required the underlying truths to be spelt out rather more explicitly than we find them in the other gospels. Let us take a look at some of the miracles recorded by John:

(i) *The feeding of the multitude.* It is an occasion where Jesus describes himself as "the Bread of Life." Although he is feeding people physically, what he is talking about is spiritual hunger.

(ii) *The raising of Lazarus.* Jesus says on this occasion, "I am the resurrection. If anyone believes in me, even though he dies, he will live, and whoever lives and believes in me will never die." Thus eternal life, we are being told, is not something we have to wait for, as Martha had thought when, earlier in the story, she had replied to a question from Jesus on the subject. Again we are presented with a spiritual truth.

(iii) *The cure of the man born blind.* Jesus, on this occasion, says, "I am the Light of the World." Here the thrust of the incident is the truth about spiritual blindness, as Jesus makes abundantly clear in his subsequent conversation with the Pharisees who were looking on.

(iv) *The miraculous haul of fish.* This is a gloss on the idea of the disciples being fishers of men.

(v) *The Virgin Birth.* Jesus' uniqueness as both God and man is what this story is about – the joining together of the divine and the human in one seamless union. What more graphic imagery could there be to illustrate this truth than a virgin being overlain by the Holy Spirit?

A miracle-story case study

To bring home just how complex a Jewish miracle story can be, let us look at a particular narration in more detail. We ask: what might be the spiritual content of the story of Jesus turning water into wine?

It is an account that appears in John's gospel alone (*John* 2). It speaks of a transformation involving wine – water changed into wine. For Christians, the transformation of something lowly into something higher – involving *wine* – has about it an unmistakable allusion to the Holy Communion service. Such services were well established at the time John was writing. So, is reference being made here to that form of service? The answer is almost certainly yes. We read (in English translations) how Jesus told the servants to bring him water – the water that was later to be turned into wine. However, if we go back to the original

Greek, the word he uses is *not*, in fact, that meaning "servant"; he uses the word for "deacon." He told a *deacon* to bring him water. The deacon is the person in the Holy Communion service who brings the water and wine to the celebrant in order for them to be transformed into the blood of Christ. So there definitely is an allusion here to the Holy Communion service.

What is the function of the water that is brought to Jesus? We are told in the story that it is water used for purification – ostensibly for washing the guests' hands and feet before the feast. But in the Jewish mind the only way one can truly be purified is through the Law of Moses. So, symbolically the Law of Moses is being brought to Jesus. What is Jesus' relation to that Law? He himself was to declare that he had come to fulfill it. It was not a case of him setting aside the Law, but of him fulfilling it, or transforming it. And that is what he does to the water; he transforms it – elevates it.

We next read that the guests are already well drunk. So how much wine does Jesus produce? Between 120 and 180 *gallons*. That is the equivalent of 60 to 90 watering-cans full – and for people already well and truly over the legal limit! And, naturally, it is the very best wine – the steward affirms this. This is meant to symbolize God's *overwhelming* beneficence – the sheer extravagance of his response to our requests.

Let's go back to the beginning of the story. It gets off to a strange start. When Mary comes to Jesus pointing out that the wine is running out, Jesus replies, "Why turn to me? My hour has not yet come." On the face of it this sounds as though he is saying, "Sorry, but I don't want anything to do with this, my time for doing that sort of thing isn't here yet." But then he goes straight ahead and does it. How are we to understand that?

The occasion is a wedding. Jesus sometimes referred to *himself* as the bridegroom. He was once asked, "Why don't your followers fast in the same way as those of John the Baptist?" He replied by saying that when the bridegroom is with them that is the time for feasting. But when the hour is come for the bridegroom to be taken away, then is the time to fast. So it appears that when Jesus says to Mary in our story, "My hour has not yet come," he is speaking as that bridegroom. In effect he is saying, "My hour to be taken away has not yet come, and therefore it is indeed a time for feasting and celebration." In other words, he is saying "yes" to Mary.

We close this study of the story by noting its very first words: "On the third day. . . ." Supposedly this refers back to a conversation with Nathanael. But nobody living in the post-resurrection period could possibly fail to get the allusion of the "third day." The reference is obviously to the resurrection, and to the joy and celebration that attends the resurrection.

Thus, what at first sight might appear to be a rather trivial, fanciful story, is revealed under closer examination to be nothing of the sort. It is in truth a remarkably complex account, encapsulating within it an abundance of spiritual meanings.

In summary, there can be no doubt about the spiritual content of Biblical miracle stories. In this they contrast starkly with the silly, empty stories in the New Testament Apocryphal books about clay birds, the cursing of schoolmates, and the transforming of mules into young men. But this still leaves open the question of whether these spiritually deep stories also refer to physical events that actually happened. Are at least some of these stories also meant to be read as accounts of events that literally occurred as described? Or can we, without delay, summarily dismiss such a possibility?

Can miracles be ruled out as impossible?

Remember we are defining a miracle in the restricted sense of an event that violates a law of nature. But what do we mean by "a law of nature"?

The world presents us with a seemingly breathtaking array of phenomena. Controlled experimentation and close observation, however, reveal that behind this rather bewildering facade, a few general rules of behavior are at work. The situation is not as chaotic as it might at first seem. Given enough information, and a knowledge of the rules of behavior, the future course of events can be anticipated.

This in itself need not mean that everything, under all circumstances and at all times, *must* obey these rules. Certainly it is an empirical observation that those events we happen to have studied do appear to obey them. But it has to be an article of *belief* that the laws apply under *all* circumstances. It is not something a scientist can prove as such.

Of course, this is a belief we all tacitly subscribe to most of the time – even those who entertain the possibility of the occasional miraculous exception to the general rule. But there are those who take it on trust that the laws of nature are without exception inviolable. If they are right, then there is no possibility of miracles.

Others have a different starting-point. They begin from the premise that the rules have to come from somewhere – they can't just happen. There has to be a reason why the world is run on these particular lines, rather than some other. A choice has to be made, and the one who makes the choice is the Creator God. They are *God's* rules; they owe their existence to a divine origin. That being so, there seems little problem in accepting that the originator of the laws could suspend their operation, given sufficient motive for doing so. It is not a question of whether God *can* perform miracles; more, it is a question of whether, as a matter of historical fact, God *chooses* to perform them.

A possible hierarchy of laws

Suppose we tentatively accept that miracles might, from time to time, happen. Does that mean we have to regard such occurrences as "violations" of physical laws?

Jesus, in his temptations in the wilderness, declined to use miraculous power for turning stones into bread, or, as already noted, for defying gravity by throwing himself off tall buildings. In working out what form of ministry he should undertake, he seemed to be choosing one that showed respect for the laws of nature. Some would claim that this in itself was a reason for dismissing subsequent accounts of his supposedly performing miracles.

But we have to bear in mind that Jesus was bound by a higher obligation. He was to be the embodiment of God's perfect love for humankind. At various points in his ministry he was to be faced with people who were ill or in distress. In similar circumstances we know what we would do; out of our love for those people we would do whatever we could to alleviate their suffering. Jesus, as the perfect embodiment of love, could do no less. What was he capable of doing for them?

As the Son of God, he could cure them – miraculously if necessary. It can thus be argued that it would have been less than perfect love wilfully to have withheld such healing power.

Might he have had to decline to perform the miracle because the exercise of such power would have forced the recipient into belief in him – a form of coercion incompatible with freely offered love? Not necessarily. Most of the people involved in these incidents had already declared their faith in him verbally, or had demonstrated it implicitly by coming to him in the expectation of a healing.

Thus, it could be argued, in obedience to the all-embracing law of love, he was *bound* to perform miraculous cures. Such cures would not have been in accordance with the physical laws, but they would have been in accordance with the *higher* law of love.

Something similar to this already happens within physics itself. When it comes to looking at our laws of physics, we find them arranged in a hierarchy. In Chapter 13, I shall be introducing you to Einstein's theory of relativity. There we shall discover that at high speed, time slows down and space contracts. A mission controller at Houston would conclude that an astronaut in a spacecraft traveling at nine-tenths the speed of light would be ageing at half the normal rate; his spacecraft would be reduced in length to half its normal size. The mission controller and the astronaut each have their own space and their own time.

Such seemingly bizarre conclusions are totally beyond the power of classical Newtonian physical law to describe. According to Newton, we all inhabit a common space and a common time, so we ought always to arrive at the same measurements for times and distances. Does that mean whenever a spacecraft travels fast, it "violates" Newton's laws of motion? That, in fact, is *not* how we would customarily describe the situation. Rather we would say that Newton's laws have limited validity, and in particular do not apply to circumstances involving excessive speeds.

It is at this point we have to recognize that the laws of physics are arranged in a hierarchy. The laws characteristic of relativity theory are hierarchically superior to those of Newton. It is not that Newton's laws apply at low speed, and Einstein's at high speed. Einstein's law applies at *all* speeds, including everyday speeds of, say, thirty miles per hour. *All* observers in uniform relative motion occupy different spaces and times. It is just that at speeds low compared to that of light, the differences between the various times and spaces are so small as to make them indistinguishable. Under those conditions, it is far simpler to treat the situation as if there were only the one space and time, and hence use Newton's laws. For most purposes they are a more than adequate approximation. But in our present context, it is important to recognize that they are nevertheless but an approximation to the more comprehensive and superior laws of relativity – laws that cover not only the realm where Newton's laws are useful, but also those situations that the classical laws are powerless to handle.

In the same spirit, one might postulate that, although relativity rules the roost as far as the hierarchy of physical laws is concerned, it might not be the last word. It could be argued that even that set of laws is subservient to a further law: the truly all-embracing law of *love*. According to the religious point of view, love is the very reason for the existence of ourselves and the Universe. As we shall be seeing in Chapter 7, one of the prerequisites for being able to lead a meaningful, purposeful life based on love, is that one lives in an environment that, by and large, operates in a predictable manner – hence the need for physical laws. But the absolutely *strict* observation of those physical laws, at *all* times and in *all* circumstances, is not necessary. In particular they might not necessarily cover untested situations like those involving the actions of the Son of God in human form.

In this way, one could argue that miracles are not maverick occasions where God capriciously and arbitrarily intervenes in the working of the world. Instead, when due regard is paid to the all-embracing law of love, and the exceptional circumstances that sometimes obtain, they can be regarded as part of a law-like, orderly approach to everything that occurs within the world. The physical laws are not "violated"; it is simply that their domain of applicability does not embrace all situations.

When is a law a law?

A further thought: you might – quite understandably – feel uncomfortable over the idea of mixing up laws of a physical nature with a so-called "law" of another kind. I would therefore like to conclude this discussion by pointing out that it is not always clear what one means by a "physical law."

Suppose, for example, you have dropped something, a book or a cup, on the floor and there it lies at your feet. On an impulse you declare, "I command you to rise." Lo and behold, the object jumps off the ground and lands in your hand! Would that be a miracle – a violation of a physical law?

It would certainly fly in the face of the evidence of countless observations that when objects have fallen to the floor they stay put until they are picked up. But in fact, it would not be impossible. We can understand why when we consider that the floor upon which the object lies is made up of atoms. Atoms jiggle about and vibrate by virtue of the heat energy they possess. Normally these motions are in random directions. But imagine for a moment, by some weird coincidence, they all happened to vibrate in unison. This is highly unlikely, given that it would require billions upon billions of atoms all to do this purely by chance. But just suppose it did. And suppose this briefly coordinated motion happened to be in the upwards direction. The cup would be flung into the air. No law of physics would have been violated – only a so-called law known as the *Second Law of Thermodynamics*. This states that such events are so improbable, we can for all intents and purposes say that they never happen. But note, it is only a statistical statement involving probabilities. And because it is statistical, given enough opportunities, you would expect the unusual occasionally to happen – in the normal course of events. So I ask: is the Second Law of Thermodynamics a physical law? If one can envisage situations where, in the *natural* course of events, it could be disobeyed, then it is clearly not a physical law with the same status as the others. (Unless, of course, we are mistaken in according *any* physical law more than a statistical significance.)

Incidentally, the idea that statistical fluctuations could lead to violations of the Second Law of Thermodynamics is one of the explanations that have been advanced to try and explain certain of the miracles. God, at the time he created the world, set up the initial conditions such that at some later point in time, the atoms in the Sea of Galilee, for example, were due to vibrate preferentially upward for a while, so allowing

Jesus to walk on the surface. I personally prefer the explanation I gave earlier for that so-called miracle.

Conclusion

In summary, it can be held that miracles are not intrinsically impossible. Which is not to say they necessarily happen – merely that belief in miracles is not irrational. Such a view does not, of course, entail accepting all the Biblical miracle stories as having a literal content – for the reasons I have given. For us today, the prime importance of the Biblical miracle accounts lies in the deep spiritual truths they illustrate – truths that are applicable and relevant to our own lives. Perhaps we can remain agnostic over whether these accounts did, in addition, refer to actual physical events.

Personally, I am inclined to accept certain acts of healing, and others that are clearly motivated in accordance with what I have been calling the higher law of love. But at this distance in time, we are never going to be able to prove one way or the other what happened. If the "prayer experiment" described earlier, conducted in our own time, and under controlled conditions, is unlikely to come up with an unambiguous interpretation of its outcome, we can hardly expect a firmer conclusion regarding events that occurred long ago and in a culture markedly different from our own. In the end it has to be a personal conviction. For some people, reports of miracles in the Bible will be taken as indicative of the work of God, and thus as evidence for his existence; others will not see it that way.

3

Life Beyond Death

A non-literal understanding of the resurrection

The greatest miracle story of all is that concerning the resurrection of Jesus. It lies at the very core of Christianity. The gospel – or good news – is precisely this: Jesus has risen from the dead. Paul says that if Christ is not risen then our faith is futile. It is to the Biblical accounts of the resurrection we must now turn.

As with the other miracle accounts, it is possible to take this purely as a story illustrating a deep spiritual truth: the idea that death is not the end of everything; there is life beyond. The story of the empty tomb and of the subsequent appearances of Jesus are to be taken as allegories – something concrete for the mind to get hold of as it tries to come to terms with an eternal life that is really beyond human imagining.

With the resurrection occupying such a central place in Christian belief, such an interpretation of the resurrection accounts is bound to stir up controversy. This was famously demonstrated over the sermon by the former Bishop Jenkins of Durham when he spoke on an Easter Sunday of a "conjuring trick with bones." Some would hold that it is impossible to regard oneself as a proper Christian unless – unlike Bishop Jenkins – one does accept that the tomb was physically empty.

I certainly would not say that. The importance of Easter is that it testifies to Jesus having conquered death, that he is in some sense alive now, and present everywhere. He is aware of what we are saying and thinking. His presence is as real as the presence of you and me. Christianity is all about having a loving relationship with that living Lord Jesus. As far as I am concerned, anyone who believes that, believes in the resurrection – at least the resurrection as it affects us who live here and now. This being so, such people can rightly claim to be fully Christian.

As with the other miracle accounts, it is of secondary importance whether the tomb was literally empty – whether Jesus rose physically.

And yet it is a fascinating question. As we shall be seeing, the Biblical accounts of the resurrection provide us with probably the most persuasive documentary evidence for a supernatural occurrence. For that reason, I propose to examine the evidence in some detail.

The structure of Jewish miracle stories

The first question to address is whether the accounts of the resurrection are to be read in the same way as one might approach a more mundane miracle (if *any* miracle can be regarded as "mundane"!).

Jewish miracle stories traditionally conformed to a pattern. They were divided into three parts:

(i) *An introduction.* The purpose of this was to set the scene, ensuring that what was to follow was indeed regarded as a remarkable event. Thus, for example, the man who was to be cured of blindness is described in the introduction to that story as having been *born* blind, i.e., this was no temporary attack of blindness which might have worn off in the normal course of events.

(ii) *The main part of the story.* This is the account of the miracle itself. Often it involves a description of actions taken and words spoken. Thus, for instance, Jesus spits on the ground and makes a mud pat which is then applied to the blind man's eyes. He tells the man to go and wash at the Pool of Siloam.

(iii) *An epilogue.* This usually describes the onlookers as being astonished, and there are often actions on the part of the person cured demonstrating that something wonderful has indeed happened.

Such then is the overall pattern of the typical Jewish miracle story. As one might expect, the most prominent and important section is the middle one – the description of the miracle itself.

With this in mind we turn to the account of the resurrection of Jesus. What do we find?

The first part of the story is there: we have a description of all the events leading up to Jesus' arrest, trial, scourging, crucifixion, and burial. And it is exceedingly detailed: what Jesus was wearing at various stages, who said what, his being offered a drink while on the cross, etc.

The third part of the story is there: the accounts of the many resurrection appearances, which in themselves purport to demonstrate that Jesus had risen from the dead.

But what of the all-important middle section – the very heart of the narrative – the description of the actual miracle itself? It is entirely missing. This alone alerts us to the fact that this is no ordinary Jewish miracle story. No Jew would have dreamt of concocting a miracle story without describing the event itself. If the whole point of the story was to give hearers a concrete image of Christ's victory over death – a picture to carry in the mind – why is there no picture?

We get a hint as to how "scandalous" this omission must have seemed to the early church, through the way attempts were made to fill in the missing details. Mark's account of the discovery of the empty tomb mentions the presence of a man dressed in a white robe. In Matthew he is called an angel (perhaps not too surprisingly as, in those days, angels were not thought of as having wings). Then, in Luke and John, this angel is joined by a second. Matthew goes in for further embellishment; whereas the other gospels describe the stone as already having been moved, Matthew describes the angel in the act of coming down from heaven, and to the accompaniment of an earthquake, rolling aside the stone – with the women onlookers there. The writer seems to be giving way to a temptation to fill in the gap in the narrative – the missing details which his readers would undoubtedly be expecting.

But this is small beer compared with what we find in the New Testament Apocrypha – those books that didn't quite make it into the canon of accepted writings. In the Gospel of Peter, for instance, the writer really goes to town. He describes how two men encircled by a great light descend and roll the stone aside. In full view of the assembled throng, three men are seen coming out of the tomb, one being supported by the other two, with a cross following them, "and the heads of the two reached as far as heaven, but that of him that was led overtopped the heavens. And they heard a voice from heaven saying, 'Hast thou preached to them that sleep?' And the response was heard from the cross, 'Yea.'"

In *The Book of the Resurrection of Christ* by Bartholomew it is claimed that Philogenes witnessed the whole act of resurrection (Philogenes being the father of the Simeon who was cured by Jesus when he came down from the Mount of Olives). He had been to the tomb at midnight to find the heavens opened and filled with Cherubim, Seraphim, Powers and Virgins. The sight was so tremendous, if he had not been supported by the apostle Peter (who was also supposed to be there) he would have died. In this version of the resurrection, Jesus appears in a chariot!

It's obvious what's going on here. The writers are desperately trying to fill in the missing center portion of the narration – so as to force it to conform to a traditional Jewish miracle story. But from our point of view, what matters is that in the earlier versions – the more authentic ones that we find in the Bible – the center section was absent. This alone tells us we are dealing with something radically different.

Characteristics of eyewitness reports

The Biblical narratives are supposed to be based on a set of eyewitness accounts of events that actually happened. So let us now change tack, and examine whether they do indeed have that quality about them. A good deal of work has been put into examining the authenticity of accounts describing events that are alleged to have taken place. These form the basis of psychological tests, and the procedures for sifting through testimonies given to the police regarding crimes and accidents.

The first thing to note is that eyewitness evidence is rarely presented in a neat logical sequence. Rather, one tends to get a kaleidoscope of impressions with irrelevant details mixed up with the important facts. One is left wondering whether the witness will ever get to the point!

Secondly, moments of shock or surprise are remembered particularly vividly. It is almost as though the unexpected scene has been indelibly imprinted on the witness's mind.

Thirdly, one expects there to be aspects of what people have witnessed that they are unable to explain – perhaps even aspects of the way they themselves reacted at the time. Typically one has them saying, "I don't know what came over me. I don't know why I didn't think to call the police straight away. It seems sensible now, but at the time – I don't know, I just didn't."

Lastly, if more than one witness is involved, then it is highly unlikely that their various accounts will agree in all details. In broad outline, yes, you would expect a general consensus – but not over details. It is when the schoolchildren march into the principal's office and trot out exactly the same story, word for word, that one knows their testimony needs to be taken with a pinch of salt.

The resurrection accounts as eyewitness statements

So, with those criteria for assessing the authenticity of eyewitness accounts in mind, let us examine the accounts of the resurrection as we find them in the gospels.

We begin with the two disciples going to the tomb. They start out together, but one outruns the other and gets there first. But he doesn't go straight in; he waits for the other to arrive. And it is the second disciple who enters first. This in itself is quite unimportant; it has no bearing on anything. Why bother to mention it? Presumably because that's just the way it was; witnesses do throw in extra information for no good reason.

They enter the tomb, and to their surprise it is empty. But that's not how it is described. They don't just say, "The body's gone." Instead we get a description of the way the cloth that had been round Jesus' body was still lying there, and the smaller cloth that had been round his face was also there but lying separate from the first one. Why mention this detail? Because it is a moment of shock. The scene is etched into the mind. They are describing a picture they can still see.

How about the followers of Jesus who were walking along the road to Emmaus? They are joined by the risen Jesus. They don't recognize him. They walk together and talk together; they still don't recognize him. They go in the house together and eat together. They still don't recognize him. Not until he breaks the bread. Then their eyes are opened. Why? Something particularly characteristic in the way Jesus did it – some mannerism? Perhaps they had been told by the disciples how Jesus, on breaking the bread at the last supper, had spoken of the bread being his body and the wine his blood. Now, in this house on the road to Emmaus, they see exactly the same action, the breaking of the bread – a very special moment, recalling for them those strange words. But it still must have left those disciples feeling foolish when later they related the story of their encounter with the risen Jesus, and had to admit that, for some unaccountable reason, they hadn't recognized him. It was an aspect of behavior that the genuine witness is unable to explain. It doesn't make for a neat, tidy, rehearsed exposition. It's just the way it happened to be.

We get exactly the same kind of thing with Mary Magdalene's encounter with Jesus. At first she mistakes him for the gardener, and she enquires whether he knows where Jesus' body has been put. Then comes the flash of recognition – when he speaks her name. What was so special about him uttering her name? Mary had been a prostitute. Men had used her; she had been a sex object. Then Jesus had come into her life, and had treated her, not as a thing, but as a person; he took a personal interest in her. He had called her by name. We can imagine what her feelings must have been on hearing for the first time this remarkable man address her by name. She would never have forgotten that – how he said it, the tone, the inflection of the voice. It all came back to her when Jesus once again spoke her name in that garden.

Next, we address the inconsistencies in the different gospel accounts. Matthew and Mark would have us believe that all Jesus' post-resurrection appearances were confined to Galilee; Luke has them occurring in and around Jerusalem; John has them happening in both locations. It is a small thing; it could easily have been sorted out. And if it were a made-up story, a conspiracy, doubtless the gospel writers would have taken the trouble to get the details straight – so everyone was telling the same story. But they didn't; one suspects because they were simply relaying fallible, somewhat careless eyewitness accounts, rather than some carefully crafted invention.

Perhaps of more concern is the description of Christ's body after his resurrection. An obvious question on everyone's lips on hearing about Jesus' appearances would have been, "What kind of body did he have? Could you touch it?" This would have been important in establishing whether it was merely a vision, or something more substantial.

We note in this connection that doubting Thomas was encouraged to put his finger into the imprint of the nail marks in Jesus' hands, and to thrust his hand into the wound in Jesus' side. Then we recall that Jesus broke bread – he could exert physical pressure – and on occasion he ate. These incidents point to a tactile body.

That being so, what are we to make of Jesus' injunction to Mary in the garden, "Touch me not; for I am not yet ascended unto my Father"? Does this constitute a serious inconsistency? Actually, no. The original Greek can be translated either as "Do not attempt to touch me," which is the sense that has usually been given to it, or alternatively as "Stop touching me," implying that Mary was already touching him – perhaps clinging to him. The latter translation would be consistent with the descriptions of other encounters with Christ's body. Our preference for the latter translation is enhanced when it comes to the phrase "for I am not yet ascended unto my Father." It would be a curious state of affairs if embracing were not allowed now, but would be later on. According to the latter interpretation, this phrase could simply mean that there will be plenty of opportunity and time for loving embraces in Heaven, but for now he has other things in mind for her; he has an urgent errand for her to run; she is quickly to go and tell the disciples what has happened. It is the second translation, "Stop clinging to me," that modern versions of the Bible prefer.

Mention of the women who were first to find the tomb empty raises a further point. They were *women*. Women lacked the status of men in society. They were regarded as not being qualified to act as legal witnesses. If the resurrection were a made-up story, and the disciples wanted people to take it seriously, they would never have had women as the principal witnesses. Another thing: how do the men fare in this story? Why weren't they at the tomb alongside the women? Because they were in hiding – behind locked doors – for fear of their fellow Jews. They were cowards. The only courageous people in this story – the only ones to emerge with any credit – were the women. Can one really imagine Jesus' disciples sitting down and concocting a story which cast themselves in such a bad light?

In short, one can conclude that the gospel narratives pass the tests expected of eyewitness accounts of actual events. They are clearly meant to be taken at face value.

Alternatives to a resurrection

That of course, still leaves us with the problem of whether or not to believe them. So, finally, what are the alternatives to a resurrection?

The tomb was empty; about that there can be little doubt. If it weren't, the chief priests could simply have produced the body and instantly put a stop to the rumors of a resurrection. Some people have conjectured that perhaps there was a muddle over which tomb had been used. But again, the motives for the priests to find the body were too great for it to be plausible for them simply to have "lost" the tomb.

So, with the tomb empty, who could have taken the body? The priests? Yes. But they had no motive. Suspicion therefore has to fall upon the disciples. But what might their motive have been? What could they have gained from such a deception? A dead leader shamefully martyred would have been a much more powerful rallying cry than a silly made-up story of a resurrection. Sure enough, there had been stories of temporary resuscitations (for example, that of Lazarus), but these people died again. Resurrection to eternal life was a totally different matter. Though some people in those days believed there would be a resurrection, that was to be at the end of time. It was certainly not expected to take place within the course of history, in one's own day. Not surprisingly, even some of Jesus' closest followers could not at first accept the report that Jesus had risen.

Such a theory of theft and deception calls for a conspiracy of massive proportions. Not only were all Jesus' closest friends involved – the twelve disciples and all the women – but a crowd of five hundred. And it was not as though Jesus' supporters were the kind of people who were habitual liars. They would all have had to have acted totally out of character. It would have to have been a conspiracy which held up even in the face of torture and death. Such tremendous pressures were brought to bear, but not one of the supposed conspirators ever confessed to a plot.

The subsequent behavior of Christ's followers

Finally, we look at the transformation wrought in the disciples. At the time of the crucifixion, they were a defeated, demoralized rabble, hiding for fear of their lives. A few days later, they were unrecognizable. They were *triumphant* – ready to lay down their lives for the cause. There is not a hint of anger or indignation against the terrible wrong done to their leader; instead there is unalloyed joy. This is *not* the natural reaction of people who are supposed to have just come out of a meeting where they have devised some cock-and-bull story, that no one is going to believe anyway, and moreover is going to land them in trouble with the very authorities from whom they had previously been hiding. Clearly, something dramatic must have happened. Could it be they were telling the truth?

Conclusion

In the end, of course, it has to be a matter of personal conviction – based either on an analysis of the weight of the evidence – or on one's own personal experience of the risen Christ. As with the other Biblical miracle accounts, it is not possible at this distance to arrive at any universally acceptable evaluation. Even if we ourselves were to witness a resurrection today, how would we convince others who had not seen it? Suppose some figure from the past, such as Winston Churchill, were suddenly to materialize in the room where you are at present sitting. The two of you talk together, you eat together. Then the manifestation disappears. How would you go about offering proof of what had happened to others? You wouldn't be able to. That being so, it is unreasonable for a skeptic to expect proof of Jesus' resurrection. All we can note is that the evidence in favor of a physical resurrection of Jesus is as strong as it could conceivably be – given the circumstances. It can be regarded as a further incremental corroboration of the God hypothesis.

For the record, I myself accept that there was a bodily resurrection. But I do have to add that if somehow it could be proved that I am mistaken, it would not to any significant degree adversely affect my faith. Regardless of what exactly happened 2,000 years ago, I still find the presence of Jesus today a very real presence – and that is what I believe to be crucial.

4

Staying Within the Law

What if one finds it quite impossible to accept that there might be exceptions to physical law? Does that mean God has no effect on anything happening in the world? If that were to be the case, it would be largely immaterial whether there is a God or not, and we could draw our "God experiment" to a premature conclusion. Even if one does believe that God can, and does, intervene on occasion in miraculous fashion, we are still left with the problem of whether that is God's *only* type of interaction. If so, it would appear to be a very occasional, intermittent type of interaction.

So it is we now turn to the question of whether the physical world can provide intimations of God's presence – through its *normal* operation.

God as the ground of existence

We begin with the question: "Why is there something rather than nothing?"

Normally we take the existence of the world for granted. It is simply *there*. Given that there is this world, it is the job of the scientist to investigate what kind it is. But a theologian would say this is jumping the gun. Before examining the details of the world, we ought to be enquiring why there is a world at all. What is *responsible* for its existence? What can be said about the ground, or source, of all being?

Some are inclined to dismiss this as a meaningless question. But to many of us, it appears perfectly sensible and reasonable. The fact that it might be difficult, or impossible, to answer conclusively need not affect the validity of the question itself.

The theological answer is that the world and ourselves owe our existence to God. In saying that, we do not have in mind a God who created the world long ago, and since then has had no further part to play. God's responsibility was not limited to a single act of creation – the world from then on being able to continue in existence on its own. Theologians customarily couple talk of God the Creator with that of God the Sustainer. It has long been held that God's creativity is required equally at all points in time.

If that is the picture one has in mind – God continually upholding the world in existence – then, in a sense, God is involved in absolutely everything that goes on in the world. It is not that God performs this miracle and that miracle, but is otherwise not involved – when nature is running smoothly. Rather, it is the case that nothing at all happens without his direct involvement.

That then is one sense in which God is thought to have an effect. It is not something that can be experimentally tested, of course. We cannot momentarily switch off God's sustaining power – if there is such a thing – and see whether, in fact, we promptly disappear! So it remains a defensible position to claim that no such influence is required; existence is just a natural state of affairs calling for no explanation. But for the faithful, it is a way in which they see God relating to the world.

Stacking the cards

Secondly, there has been the suggestion that God brings about effects through the way he originally set up things at the very beginning. The effects we see at later times come about through their causal links to those initial conditions. According to this idea, God could have fixed the motions and positions of all the fundamental particles initially so that, through the natural outworking of the laws of nature, the divine purpose was achieved.

We have already mentioned a possible example of this: Jesus walking on the Sea of Galilee. From the very start, God could have arranged things so that, by the time Jesus later stepped on to the water, the atoms in its surface were all due to vibrate synchronously in the same direction at the same time. In this manner, Jesus could have been prevented from sinking. Such an occurrence, in the normal course of events, would be exceedingly unlikely, relying as it would on pure chance. But in the present context we are not dealing with chance; we are envisioning God deliberately tampering with the initial conditions to ensure that "the unusual" actually did happen.

Nor does this procedure have to be confined to miraculous events. It could account for any normal event where God wanted to have an input. In fact, we can liken the situation to that of the card player who deals a pack that has been prepared in advance to ensure the desired outcome.

Although it is an interesting idea, it strikes me as being somewhat contrived. Devising the unique set of initial conditions necessary for bringing about a detailed multitude of desired outcomes, occurring at widely different locations, and at different times throughout history, all interlocked and needing to be coordinated – that would surely be a monumental task, even for God!

The missing links in the causal chain

The approach just described relies on the idea that from any given cause it is possible to predict what its effect will be. That effect, in its turn, then becomes the cause of the next effect – and so on down the causal chain. All the events linked by this chain are fully determined by what has gone before. It is a picture of events that appears to be fully confirmed by our everyday experience, and indeed much scientific experimentation is based on that belief.

But such a state of affairs does not always apply. When scientific studies are extended to include the behavior of matter at the sub-atomic level, it is discovered that, from any initial behavior of the particles at a given point in time, it is *not* possible to predict what will happen next – at least, not with certainty. Why should this be?

In order to predict the future, one needs to have precise information on both the position and the motion of every particle taking part. Given such information, and knowing the forces between the particles, one would then be able, in principle, to calculate the future positions and velocities of the particles. The problem is that the constituents of the sub-atomic world are exceedingly small and delicate. It is impossible to have any interaction with them without disturbing them. One cannot even *look* at them without destroying features of what one is trying to see. This arises because in order to see something one obviously must illuminate it. But light itself carries energy. As the light strikes the tiny sub-atomic particle, some of that energy is transferred to the particle, thus altering the very motion one is trying to observe.

This is the realm of quantum theory. Later on we shall be saying a good deal more about it. But for the time being we simply note that, according to quantum theory, one is denied simultaneous knowledge of both the precise position and precise velocity of any particle. To have precise knowledge of position, say, one must be prepared to sacrifice all knowledge of its velocity; alternatively, precise knowledge of velocity can be bought only at the price of loss of all knowledge of position. In between, there are the intermediate cases where *some* knowledge can be obtained of both the position and the velocity, but not precise knowledge of either. This is all summed up in Heisenberg's famous uncertainty relation.

(If you are interested, the relation is: $\Delta x.\Delta p = h$, where Δx denotes the range of uncertainty in position, Δp the range of uncertainty in momentum [momentum being the mass times velocity], and h is a constant called the Planck constant.)

For example, we might know that the position of an electron lies between, say, 23 centimeters and 29 centimeters. The uncertainty of position is therefore 6 centimeters. Corresponding to this, the relation specifies a range of possible values for the velocity (or momentum) of the electron. In order to improve on the determination of the electron's position, one would have to use a different form of illumination. This might, for instance, allow one to reduce the uncertainty from 6 centimeters to 2 centimeters. However, because that new illumination would have to be of a more energetic type, it is liable, on bouncing off the electron, to give it a more severe knock; this will increase the uncertainty in momentum. Heisenberg's Uncertainty Relation tells us that a reduction in position uncertainty to a third of what it would otherwise have been, must necessarily be compensated by an increase in momentum uncertainty by a factor of three. Alternatively, any improvement in the precision of the momentum determination must be accompanied by a corresponding increase in the uncertainty of position.

Thus, according to the uncertainty relation, we are denied all the information that would be necessary to predict the future precisely. The best we can do is state the probabilities of a variety of possible outcomes.

Now, you might be wondering what all this might have to do with God's action in the world. Earlier we raised the possibility of God setting up initial conditions such that the tight chain of cause and effect would eventually produce the desired outcomes. This second approach is quite different. It makes use of the fact that there is no such thing as a tight chain of cause and effect – at least, not at the sub-atomic level. One *cannot* be absolutely sure what is going to happen next. That being so, it is argued, God could take advantage of these quantum gaps in our knowledge – the missing links in the causal chain. God could use the quantum uncertainty to push things in the required direction – while still staying within the probability limits allowed by the uncertainty relation. By making use of what would appear to us to be merely statistical fluctuations, God's input would remain undetectable.

An apparent problem with this approach is that we are talking of very small uncertainties – those significant only on the scale of individual sub-atomic particles. What possible effect could that have on the macroscopic scale of normal everyday life? John Polkinghorne, ordained minister and former Professor of Physics at Cambridge University, invokes chaos theory. Chaos theory alerts us to the fact that there are many circumstances where the slightest alteration to the initial conditions can lead to marked changes in the final outcome. How a situation develops on the large scale can depend sensitively on the smallest details of how it was originally set up. An often quoted example of chaos theory in action concerns the weather. If a butterfly in Britain decides to flap its wings, this could conceivably set in motion a whole train of events eventually culminating in a hurricane in Florida. This arises because weather patterns are exceedingly unstable.

So it is we form this picture of God using random quantum probabilities at the atomic level, these slight effects being subsequently magnified by the chaos theory mechanism to produce significant changes at the macroscopic level where we humans operate.

Nor do we have to regard chaos theory as the only way of magnifying the effects of the underlying quantum events. Think, for example, of biological genes. The physical characteristics of our bodies, and those of other animals, are largely dependent upon the genes inherited from parents at conception. The genes are based on a molecule (a particular combination of atoms) called the DNA molecule. DNA is, if you like, the blueprint design for our bodies. Changes, or mutations, to the DNA – perhaps affecting but a single atomic constituent – can have profound effects on the overall structure of the resulting body. As we shall be seeing later, it is these random changes to the physical characteristics of animal bodies that provide the variations upon which the process of evolution by natural selection gets to work. Thus, the development of the different species we see today can be attributed in the first instance to what was happening at the atomic level. So, again, minimal inputs at the quantum level can give rise to significant effects at the macro-level.

The idea that God might make use of quantum uncertainty as a means of having an effect on the world is an intriguing one. But it has to be admitted, such a proposal raises a niggling concern. Such a mechanism, so subversive and undercover, might strike one as being unseemly and inappropriate. Are we really supposed to believe that the great Creator God has been reduced to this somewhat sneaky, half-apologetic mode of operation?

Ourselves as agents in the world

If one likes neither the idea of a fixed causal chain based on specially set-up initial conditions, nor the use of the flexibility allowed by a probabilistic quantum chain of events, what else is left to God?

At this point we turn to the question of how we ourselves, as human agents, have an influence on the world. If we could sort that out, perhaps it would give us a clue as to how God operates.

We influence things through the actions of our physical bodies. These in turn are governed by impulses coming from the brain. There is some relation between what goes on in the brain and the mental experiences one has as a *conscious* human being. We know that following the mental experience known as "making a decision" (for example, to raise one's arm), this is followed by the appropriate physical action (the raising of the physical arm). What the connection, or the relationship, is between what goes on mentally in the mind and what goes on physically in the brain, nobody knows. Perhaps we shall never know. The so-called mind/brain problem has proved so elusive, many have come to regard it as a mystery of ultimate significance.

One of the features we encounter in mental experience is that we appear to possess free will; we arrive at freely chosen decisions. We do not regard ourselves as automatons blindly having to follow the dictates of our fate. But how does this arise? After all, if we are asked how the brain works, I suppose most of us would be inclined to describe it as operating like any other physical assembly of atoms – in accordance with the laws of nature. But if that is so, doesn't that mean that the future flows of chemicals and of electrical currents in the brain are predetermined? From that, one would expect that whatever conscious thoughts might be associated with those particular physical flow patterns would also be predetermined. On that picture, there is no need of any conscious decisions – what will be, will be.

But that is not how we live out our mental lives. Even if we were intellectually convinced that our brains operate in a deterministic fashion, and hence our thinking is determined, none of us conducts our lives on that basis; we do not *behave* as though there is no need to make decisions. Even were we to try to follow such a policy, the mere fact of deciding in future not to make conscious decisions would in itself be a conscious decision.

Here we come across an extraordinary dichotomy. In many ways the life of the mind closely mirrors the life of the physical body. Thus we get the physical raising of the arm being accompanied by the mental sensation of feeling it go up; the physical act of taking aspirin with the alleviation of a mental headache; the racing of the heart with the experience of fear; the burning of the skin with the feeling of pain, etc. But the apparent "openness" of mentally taken free-will decisions does not seem to be reflected in a corresponding openness in what we presume is happening at the physical level in our brains.

This raises the issue of whether quantum theory has anything to contribute here. We have already noted an openness, a quantum indeterminism, at the atomic level. The future progress of brain events is *not* expected to be determined on the micro-scale. Could this be the answer?

The trouble with invoking quantum uncertainty is that one is not replacing determined outcomes by chosen ones. Quantum processes are based on random chance, not conscious decisions. When in ordinary life an issue is settled by the toss of a coin, we are not making a decision; we have in fact abandoned the conscious decision-making process and left the matter to chance instead. So, I for one do not see how invoking quantum uncertainty can offer a satisfactory account of decision-making as we know it.

Free will as an illusion

Of course, what this might be telling us is that we are not as free as we like to think we are. Our thoughts *are* determined in the same way as the physical processes in the brain are. We are under the illusion of being free and unconstrained in our decisions simply because the part of the brain associated with thinking is not fully aware of what else is going on in the brain; the so-called "openness" is just another name for ignorance.

One might at first object to this idea on the grounds that if our thinking, like the corresponding physical processes, were required to run along predetermined lines, we would be aware of having to operate under such a constraint; there would be a tension between what we *wanted* to think and do and what we *had* to think and do. But this does not necessarily follow. Just as the physical outcome arises in a perfectly natural way from what physically went before, so the corresponding mental outcome (the "decision") will arise in a perfectly natural way out of what mentally went before (the mind-set). The mind-set and the resulting decision will be wholly compatible with each other. The outcome is identical to the "choice" such a mind would have made had it had "free will" in the normally accepted sense. There is therefore no reason why there should be any perceived sense of having to act under constraint.

Alternatively, if it is the quantum realm that is relevant to decision-making, then our so-called decisions are in truth derived from pure chance. Once an outcome is realized, the mind immediately "owns" it – in other words, feels responsible for it in some way. But this sense of "ownership" is a delusion; the outcome has not arisen from any deliberate decision made freely and consciously.

Thus, we have the possibility that free will is an illusion – either because the outcome of the supposed decision was determined all along, or because it was a result of mere chance – without our knowing it.

Mind over matter

One way to defend the notion of a genuine free will is to adopt an interventionist approach – the mind, as an entity in its own right, intervenes in the working of the brain.

Unlike less complicated physical structures, the brain is accompanied by consciousness. As we said earlier, we do not know why this should be. For the time being at least, we must simply accept it as a brute fact. This leads to the suggestion that when the mind reaches a decision on a certain course of action, there is an interruption to the normal flow of activities in the brain. A mental decision to raise the arm is accompanied by a physical change in the brain state that is different from what it would have been had the mind reached some other decision, or taken no decision at all. That altered brain state then leads to a chain of events throughout the body resulting in the arm being raised.

What this means is that if, at the time the decision was made, a scientific study had been in progress on the behavior of the subject's brain, the investigators would have observed a change in the processes that was completely unpredictable on the basis of a knowledge of what had been going on immediately prior to the decision's being made. The processes occurring in the brain would be observed not to follow the same rigid pattern as that which governs the behavior of inanimate matter. In effect, they would have witnessed a "miracle" – an interruption to the normal running of the laws of nature. This is the so-called "dualistic" approach to the mind/body problem. The mind is thought to be capable of acting on the brain in a manner not too dissimilar to that of some external physical agency.

It has to be said that this is a solution that is currently out of favor (not that there are any scientific investigations of brain processes to disprove it). It is a widely held assumption that nothing goes on in the brain that is markedly different from what happens in inanimate matter. Although the processes occurring in the brain are undoubtedly more intricate because of the extreme complexity of the physical structure, they are nevertheless all to be held accountable for – in principle – through the operation of the well-established laws of nature. As I say, whether this is so or not, we simply do not know. In the absence of any decisive studies, the interventionist solution to the free-will problem remains an option.

The holistic approach

One final assault on the problem I wish to mention is that based on quantum "wholeness." From the outset, it has to be admitted that this is something not at all well understood. But briefly the situation is this:

Imagine two electrons approaching each other, colliding and then separating. They end up so distant from each other that there is effectively no longer any physical interaction between them. It is natural to suppose that with no physical force operating between them, we are now dealing with two separate and distinct physical systems – each consisting of an isolated electron.

And yet it is not so. This can be demonstrated in the following way: All electrons spin like miniature earths rotating about their north/south axes. Once the electrons are well separated from each other after the collision, we arrange for an experimenter to carry out a measurement of the "north/south" direction in which one of the electrons spins. The extraordinary thing is that, whatever the result of this measurement, it immediately affects what a second experimenter will discover on carrying out a similar measurement on the orientation of the spin axis of the second electron.

But how is this influence conveyed across space from one location to the other? It cannot be by any known physical force, electrical or gravitational; the two electrons are physically isolated from each other. Not only that, since the advent of Einstein's theory of relativity, we have come to accept that nothing can travel faster than the speed of light – be it matter or energy. And yet, the "information" about the direction of the spin axis appears to be conveyed instantaneously from one electron to the other; it is not subject to the same restriction. As "Dame Edna Everage" might put it – this action at a distance is all rather spooky!

The resolution of the problem (if indeed it can be regarded in any sense as a resolution) is that, contrary to appearances, we are not dealing with two separate isolated physical systems, each consisting of a single electron. Instead we are dealing with a *single physical system* consisting of two electrons. When the measurement of spin is made on the first electron, it is in reality a measurement made on the entire two-electron system. The whole system is simultaneously affected. In this way, the second experimenter, although situated at a distant location, operates on the *same* physical system as the first experimenter. The results of this second measurement will therefore be dependent on what the first experimenter has already done to that system.

I have to say the situation reminds me somewhat of a form of witchcraft practiced long ago. It was customary for those fearful of witchcraft to take very good care to keep their possessions to themselves. This was in the belief that a lock of hair, or nail clippings, or worn clothing, or a used menstrual pad, were they to fall into the wrong hands, could be used to inflict what was called "contagious magic." Thus it was held that things that had once been physically connected to a person, in some sense *remained* connected to that person. Contagious magic was then founded on the idea that what was done to the part was done to the whole.

Of course, today we would regard such beliefs as the fanciful superstition of the ignorant. But somewhat to our embarrassment, we find exactly the same kind of thinking has now been incorporated into respectable modern quantum theory! The two electrons we have been considering are subject to "quantum wholeness." Although there is no longer any recognized physical force operating between them, they are nevertheless components of an integrated system. All this because, for one instant in the past, they fleetingly encountered each other. That brief, casual meeting, long ago, continues to hold them fast with invisible bonds, their destinies mutually entwined.

With this being true of the simplest combined system one can imagine – two electrons that are so far separate from each other that no physical force operates between them – how much more must this apply to a system consisting of the human brain, the most complex object in the known world. Can anyone seriously imagine that we can account for the workings of the brain without taking into account the "spooky" effects that *must* be going on up there?

I hasten to say that quantum wholeness does not in any discernible way provide an explanation of how we come to have free will. There could conceivably be a connection, but what that might be is beyond us at present. No, the reason for raising the subject is to sound a warning – a warning against trying to apply simplistic methods of reasoning to an understanding of the brain. And if an understanding of the brain in purely physical and chemical terms is likely to remain beyond our grasp for a very long time, what hope have we of widening that study to include the phenomenon of consciousness?

Conclusion

Our discussion of how we, as conscious agents, have an effect on the world – either through the exercise of free will, or in its absence – has ended inconclusively. Given the state of current knowledge on the subject, this is inevitable; we are bound to feel dissatisfied with the outcome. For the time being, there simply is no intellectually or philosophically competent explanation.

So, where does that leave us? I believe there is nothing for it but to adopt a more pragmatic approach. This holds that, even though we have no coherent understanding of what goes on in our physical brains, and how this relates to what goes on in our minds, we nevertheless have to get on with our lives. In that context, at least, we can safely assert that it makes no sense to assume anything other than that we do possess free will. Day-to-day living can only be conducted on the basis of having to make a stream of decisions, each of which affects the world we live in, and for which we are to be held responsible. Furthermore, if we do not see ourselves as supernatural miracle-workers – our decision-making minds intervening miraculously in the working of our

47

brains – then presumably we believe that somehow or other we are able to bring our influence to bear on the physical domain in a manner compatible with the smooth running of the laws of nature.

That being so as regards ourselves in relation to the world, then it does not strike me as sensible to rule out the possibility that God could have a somewhat analogous relationship to the world. If we humans do not make use of supernatural interruptions to the running of nature whenever we wish to exert our influence, then I don't see why God should have to rely on such means. This is not to say that miracles *never* happen. But miracle-working would not have to be God's exclusive, or indeed main, ongoing interaction with us and the world.

5

A Meeting of Minds

Looking inward

The physical world is not the only place where one might search for evidence of God. Indeed, many would say that the main focus of the God experiment ought to be on the mental, rather than the physical. After all, one asks, "Is there a God?" not merely to satisfy some disinterested academic curiosity, but as a prelude to entering into a personal relationship with that God – a relationship founded on love. The most convincing evidence for God, therefore, is likely to be found in the exercise of that relationship. Religion is nothing except outward show and ritual if it is not accompanied by a deeply felt inner religious experience. This being psychological in character, it directs us to examine the life of the mind, and in particular, the nature of prayer.

Earlier we discussed an experiment investigating the effectiveness of prayers for the sick. But, as we noted then, there is much more to prayer than intercessions. Prayer in its totality is multifaceted, consisting as it does of worship, thanksgiving, contrition, self-dedication, contemplation, meditation, etc. Intercession is but one component. These different forms of prayer are various aspects of the relationship with God. It is in these acts we are confronted with the sense of the numen – a great power that is other than ourselves. We become exposed to a wisdom that is not our own – a wisdom that can take us by surprise. These experiences have an "otherness" about them – we are encountering another mind.

Or are we? Is the perceived "otherness" of this experience genuine evidence of God impacting directly on the human mind? Perhaps we should be seeking some other explanation. For example, might not the sense of "otherness" derive from the unconscious – the unconscious mind impacting on consciousness in a way that mimics an input from a supposed God?

Ideally, of course, we would like some scientific means of deciding the issue. But from the outset, the prospects do not look hopeful. The contents of an individual's mind are not open to direct public scrutiny, in the way a biological specimen, say, can be jointly examined, and experimented upon, by a group of scientists. Except that Sigmund Freud, the founder of modern psychology, did in fact regard his work as a science.

In his defense, it can be argued that open access to the data is unnecessary, provided that the description given by the individual faithfully and truly relays to others the nature of the psychological experience he/she has had. Again, when it comes to the repeatable nature of scientific investigations, there is no problem; the psychological experiences reported by many individuals can be collected and compared, these leading to the identification of reproducible, repeated patterns of common experience. Of course, one does on occasion come across aberrant experiences – perhaps of individuals convinced that they are Napoleon or God. Rogue results are to be expected in any scientific study. But these are easily sifted out, leaving a reproducible set of psychological experiences common to large sections of the population, and hence requiring some universally applicable, overarching explanation.

As with many other scientific investigations, it is the *interpretation* of the raw data that can prove problematic. To illustrate the problems encountered over the interpretation of religious experience, this chapter is devoted to presenting the conflicting views of two great psychologists: Sigmund Freud, whom we have already mentioned, and Carl Jung. As we shall be seeing, they came to markedly differing assessments as to the origin and significance of the inner religious experience.

Sigmund Freud

Freud was not the first to discover the unconscious, but he certainly played a major role in systematically uncovering many of its contents and its workings, and how it can impact and affect conscious experience.

Freud drew attention to how, in childhood, we repress shameful, disagreeable, painful, alarming thoughts. We push them out of our conscious thinking, and from there they lodge in the unconscious.

Freud held that these thoughts were mostly of a sexual nature.

Though repressed, they can yet express themselves. They give rise to neurotic behavior – that is to say, behavior arising when one is at odds with oneself because of some conflict between basic instinctual urgings and the demands of one's perceived individual and collective obligations. Such behavior can give rise to unreasonable fears and compulsive actions. One of the aims of psychoanalysis is to bring the repressed features into consciousness where they can be identified for what they are and dealt with.

As regards religious belief, Freud was of the view that it arose from wish-fulfillment. This is a process whereby the unconscious takes something that is devoutly wished for, and causes the conscious mind to believe that the wish has indeed been fulfilled. In particular, Freud claimed that as one grows up, one becomes anxious and fearful of losing the fatherly protection one has enjoyed in childhood. One wishes that it would continue into adult life. So the unconscious invents a heavenly father-figure to take the place of the earthly father. The idea of there being a God out there is thus just a projection arising out of this unacknowledged infantile fear.

Wish-fulfillment has a second effect. We fear death, and would like to have life prolonged. So, again, the unconscious gets to work and convinces us that there is indeed life beyond death.

Freud accepted that there was within us an inner moral authority, or ethical complex, monitoring the individual's behavior. He called it the *superego*. (We might loosely think of it as conscience.) But whereas a religious person would think of this as originating with God – the promptings of the Holy Spirit, if you are Christian – Freud claimed that it was nothing more than whatever code of behavior was instilled into one by parents and society during early childhood.

Thus, according to Freud, belief in God and in eternal life is an illusion. It is immature and mentally unhealthy. Far better to face up to the realities of life, harsh though these might be, and learn to stand on one's own feet. One should spurn the false comfort and support of this fictitious figure in the sky, with his empty promises of life beyond death.

Such then are Freud's views on religion. They are set out in his books *Moses and Monotheism*, *Totem and Taboo*, and *The Future of an Illusion*.

When they first appeared, some regarded them as having conclusively explained away religion. Today, among professional psychologists, they are among Freud's most neglected works. Why should this be?

In the first place, the theory appears to be based on straight, dogmatic assertion, with no evidence offered. The philosopher of science Karl Popper was among those particularly scathing about the *ex-cathedra* statements Freud so often made.

Secondly, it has to be said that those of us familiar with the *quality* of the religious experience – the sense of awe and wonder, the sheer beauty and nobility of the numinous – find it quite impossible to understand how something of that nature is supposed to have arisen out of the dustbin morass of repressed shameful and frightening responses to feelings of sexual inadequacy, which is what Freud would have us believe are the main contents of the unconscious. There seems to be no connection between the two.

Thirdly, it is obvious that simply because one wishes for something to be true does not in itself say anything about whether the thing wished for is the case or not.

Next we note that if Freud were correct, we would expect all religions to be based on a father-figure God. This is far from the case. Such a figure is not there in Buddhism. You would expect it to have been there at the start of the Judaeo/Christian/Islamic tradition, but it was not. As we shall be seeing in the next chapter, the idea is almost non-existent in the Old Testament. It takes on its prominent role only in relation to Jesus and *his* Father – we being merely "sons by adoption." Indeed, traditional Christian theology then goes far beyond the simple Heavenly Father idea of God with its doctrine of the Trinitarian nature of God (more of that in the final chapter).

As for dismissing religious practice as a manifestation of neurotic behavior, here Freud seems to have been misled by a superficial similarity between compulsive actions of certain neurotics, and religious ritual performed in church services. But this is to neglect an important distinction between the two: neurotic behavior consists of actions performed unconsciously; religious ritual is performed consciously and deliberately.

This is not to say that there aren't neurotic people whose obsessions have a religious content. There are. But this is not surprising. Neuroses can be associated with anything and everything. There are people with scientific delusions. For example, they might be obsessed with the idea that there is some force field adversely affecting them, or they might claim to be getting telepathic messages from space aliens. There can be delusions with a political content, where the victim believes he is being hounded by government spies and agents. And there are those delusions of a broadly social nature, where the subject believes that everyone is involved in a plot against them. The fact that a small minority have delusions of a religious nature is only to be expected.

Another point to note is that the idea of religion being just a prop, a comfort for the weak, is far from the mark. Though it can indeed be a comfort in that sense – and there is no harm in that – when one speaks of the Holy Spirit as the Comforter, that designation carries an altogether different connotation; it means the Strengthener. The Holy Spirit gives one the wherewithal needed to stand up to the challenges and demands of the religious way of life. The religious life is one of self-denial and self-discipline – not self-gratification. It can in some circumstances even lead to martyrdom. There is so much in religion that could not possibly have anything to do with wish-fulfillment. Note that, among the great religious figures such as Moses, Elijah, Jeremiah, and Jonah, none wanted to assume the roles chosen for them by God. They knew that such vocations would inevitably embroil them in dangerous confrontations with the authorities of the time.

Yet another point about wish-fulfillment. Wouldn't one expect religion to be more prevalent among the poor and needy – those denied the most in terms of worldly goods and esteem, and therefore with the greatest scope for wishing? But survey after survey reveals this not to be the case; one has only to compare the well-attended churches in relatively affluent suburbia with the empty ones in the inner city to know this.

As for the desire to prolong life, is that wish really a potent factor in promoting religious belief? For early Judaism it was not. References to descending into Sheol seem to refer to an unpleasant state of non-existence rather than to fullness of life. This lack of anything much after death was one reason why for Jews it was so important to have male children as a means of perpetuating the family name. Buddhism seeks annihilation rather than life eternal. And even many Christians, if closely questioned, do not actually believe in life beyond death, despite their recitation of the creed on a Sunday morning.

In fact, the whole thesis of wish-fulfillment can be turned on its head. If the religious life can be so demanding, cannot one claim that it is atheists who are more prone to indulge in wish-fulfillment – through their wish to avoid religious obligations and duties to God.

Finally, why don't we probe into the possible workings of Freud's mind – given what we know about *his* childhood – in the same way as he attempted to psychoanalyze others? What do we find in his background, and what would we expect his subsequent attitudes to be – based on his own theories?

Freud came from a free-thinking, non-observant Jewish family. In Vienna 90 percent were Catholics and there was much anti-Semitism. Freud's father, Jacob, once told of how he was walking down a street wearing a new fur hat. "A Christian came up to me, and with a single blow knocked off my cap into the mud and shouted, 'Jew, get off the pavement!'" Freud asked his father what happened next. "I went into the roadway and picked up my cap," he replied. At the age of forty-three, when Freud recalled that incident, it was clear that he was still overwhelmed with feelings of shame at his father's passive behavior. He wrote:

> I contrasted this situation with another which fitted my feelings
> better: the scene in which Hannibal's father . . . made his boy
> swear before the household altar to take vengeance on the
> Romans. Ever since that time Hannibal has had a place in my
> phantasies.
>
> (*The Interpretation of Dreams*, SE IV, p. 197)

He had earlier written:

> Hannibal, whom I had come to resemble in these respects, had
> been the favourite hero of my later school days . . . . To my youth-
> ful mind Hannibal and Rome symbolized the conflict between
> the tenacity of Jewry and the organization of the Catholic Church.
>
> (ibid., p. 196)

We can but guess what part the passive response of his father to an overt act of anti-Semitism, by a supposed Christian, played in shaping his attitude toward religions based on father-figures, and toward Christianity in particular. Jacob was never able to provide adequately for his family; they were desperately poor. Freud dismissed him as "always waiting for his boat to come in." His contempt for his father came to be incorporated within his psychological theorizing:

> In the second half of childhood a change sets in in the boy's relation to his father – a change whose importance cannot be exaggerated. From his nursery the boy begins to cast his eyes upon the world outside. And he cannot fail now to make discoveries which undermine his original high opinion of his father and which expedite his detachment from his first ideal. He finds that his father is no longer the mightiest, wisest and richest of beings; he grows dissatisfied with him, he learns to criticize him and to estimate his place in society.

(*Some Reflections on Schoolboy Psychology*, SE XIII, p. 242)

Freud's first encounter with religion came through his nanny, the maid-servant of the household, Thérèse Wittek. He was later to describe her as "the prehistoric old woman," and "an ugly, elderly but clever woman." She was always taking him to church and instructing him about God and hell. But then, with Freud still only about two and a half years old, she was dismissed from the household for stealing money and encouraging Freud to do the same. She was jailed for ten months. Again one can but conjecture what lasting impression this "Christian" woman's hypocrisy left on the boy.

Given the poor example of the nanny, the general anti-Semitism of so-called Christians in Vienna, and the low esteem Freud had for his father, it is little wonder he grew up wishing to reject religion and anything that smacked of adulation of father-figures. He became an atheist from his earliest years.

So much for the deficiencies of Freud's attempts to explain away religious experience. But before leaving the subject, one ought to sound a brief conciliatory note. Though his theory of religion was unsound for a number of reasons, it would be foolhardy to dismiss it entirely. Wish-fulfillment projections based on childhood experience might not be the explanation of belief in God, but they nevertheless do have a part to play. Surveys reveal that the view held by religious people as to the nature of their heavenly father can be significantly colored by the relationship they have had with their own earthly parent. If one has had a severe upbringing, then one is inclined to emphasize the sterner, more judgmental aspects of God. On the other hand, if one has enjoyed a more free-and-easy relationship with one's father, the inclination is to think of God as being correspondingly more benign. In general, it seems true to say that the old Victorian idea of a strict disciplinarian type of God has now given way to a contemporary notion that in some cases borders on the idea of a God who takes the line: "Let's talk this thing over together man to man, shall we?" The emphasis now is on love and forgiveness rather than punishment. It is rare indeed today to hear a sermon on hellfire and damnation.

Clearly, what is going on in these different perceptions of God is projection – one is projecting on to the figure of God aspects drawn from one's own personal experience of earthly relationships. It is unavoidable. But that by itself is not to say that belief in a heavenly father is *nothing but* a projection of one's earthly father – as Freud would have had us believe.

So much for Freud. It is now time to turn to the work of our other psychologist – one who came to radically different conclusions.

Carl Jung

Carl Jung studied under Freud, and was always generous in acknowledging his debt to him. But in time they fell out. Jung grew disenchanted with what he regarded as Freud's dogmatism – his authoritarian stance. He did not think Freud was right to place so much emphasis on the unconscious as being just a repository for the unconscious repression of shameful thoughts – mostly those regarding sex. He thought of the unconscious as containing much more besides that. In general, he was not so much interested in the first years of life and in how repression dating from those years affected one's later psychological development; he was more concerned with the second half of life, and the achievement of a fully rounded personality.

While accepting that the unconscious does indeed contain repressions of thoughts derived from one's own individual experience of life – what he called the *personal unconscious* – he held that there was in addition a *collective unconscious* that we all share from birth. To understand what he meant by the latter, it is perhaps best if we approach it from the standpoint of genetically influenced behavior.

We saw in the last chapter how our genetic make-up is contained in a molecule called the DNA molecule. Essentially it consists of a chain of smaller base molecules, the sequence of which constitutes a set of codes. These determine our physical characteristics, but also certain behavior traits – what one might loosely regard as inherited instincts. As we shall be seeing in more detail when we come to consider evolution by natural selection in Chapter 10, these were fashioned in the so-called struggle for survival. According to Darwin, certain individuals by chance acquire codes leading to either physical characteristics or behavior traits that enhance their chances of survival. These individuals are the ones more likely to live to an age where they can mate. In mating, they pass on the newly acquired beneficial genes to their offspring. Those individuals, on the other hand, with characteristics that are less beneficial, are not so likely to survive and mate. This means the less beneficial genes tend to die out over time. Thus, genes that confer some survival advantage are selected in preference to others that do not. It is through this process of evolution by natural selection that we have arrived at today's range of species adapted to survival in their various habitats.

For our present purposes we concentrate on behavior traits. These might include, for instance, what we might loosely call the "killer instinct" of today's domesticated cat. Even though it is not hungry, it will automatically stalk and try to kill a mouse or bird. This is an inbuilt tendency that was essential to the survival of the cat's ancestors; without it the prey would have been likely to get away, and the ancestor would have starved. We see genetically influenced behavior in the way a baby kangaroo, on being born, will automatically head up its mother's fur to find the pouch that is to become its new home; the animal is "pre-programmed" to do this; its behavior is not something it has to be taught. Then we have the mothering instinct, whereby a mother will go to any lengths to protect her offspring.

Recognizing this genetically influenced behavior at work in other species, it is only reasonable to expect that, as evolved animals ourselves, we humans are also subject to similar tendencies. Confronted by a certain set of circumstances, we have a natural inclination to behave in a certain manner – one that did not have to be consciously learned because it was pre-programmed into us.

As with the other animals, such behavior traits are encoded into our DNA, and this was done from the moment of conception as our DNA was being compiled from that of our parents. Over succeeding generations, such survival codes have become a common feature of all members of our species.

Now, if all this is going on in the physical, biological world, we would expect there to be a correlate in the psychological realm of the mind. And this is what Jung discovered. It is called the collective unconscious – the tendency all of us members of the human species share of adopting thought patterns that are common. We have a predisposition to think and act in certain ways when presented with appropriate stimuli from the environment.

Jung, of course, knew nothing of our modern understanding of genetically influenced behavior based on what happens at the biological level of DNA molecules. He arrived at his conclusions by carefully studying the responses of his patients, and identifying from them continually repeated patterns of thought and attitude to given situations. He supplemented this by also examining recurring themes in traditional fairy-tale literature, ancient practices, alchemy, myths, legends, dreams, etc. In this way he identified certain elemental tendencies which he called *archetypes*. Together these archetypes made up our collective unconscious. The archetypes are to be regarded as unseen organizing principles that shape our conscious thoughts and attitudes. One way is to think of them as jelly moulds. In themselves they are empty. But when filled by conscious experience, they shape the form that the experience takes. The word "archetype" in fact means "imprint." And because the archetypes are possessed by us all, we find our thoughts being shaped in similar ways, these in turn yielding common behavior patterns.

Thus, for example, Jung identified a mother archetype and a father archetype – these leading to instinctive attitudes toward parents. There is the "wise old man" archetype, resulting in a tendency to look to some person as the fount of wisdom and authority. Closely allied to that is the "hero" archetype inclining one to worship and follow a leader, perhaps blindly according him allegiance. This can turn out to be very dangerous when the object of this hero-worship is a man like Hitler, or a leader of a fringe religious cult that eventually ends up committing mass suicide. In the man there is the "anima" archetype – the unconscious feminine side of his personality, and in the woman the corresponding masculine "animus" archetype. Then there is the "shadow" archetype. This is the sum of all the personal and collective elements which, because they are incompatible with the chosen conscious attitude, are denied expression in life and therefore coalesce into a relatively autonomous "splinter personality." The shadow personifies everything that the subject refuses to acknowledge about him or herself. These traits nevertheless keep resurfacing; they constitute the dark side of oneself.

In summary, there are, it seems, as many archetypes as there are recurring typical situations capable of engraving themselves on the collective psyche.

And among the archetypes there is a "religious" archetype. The evidence for this is that it appears that all peoples everywhere and at all times have acted religiously. Admittedly, on occasion there have been reports of ancient tribes that were not religious. But on further investigation, these claims invariably have been proved unfounded. Traces of religious involvement manifest themselves in found artifacts, and particularly in the manner of burial adopted in these ancient societies. We thus conclude that there is an all-pervasive tendency to be religious.

In parenthesis, I might mention that Richard Dawkins, well known as a crusader against religious belief, has taken every opportunity to promote the idea that religion is to be likened to a computer virus infecting the human race. Computer viruses are self-replicating; they are based on pieces of software that keep saying "duplicate me." In this manner they proliferate and spread across the internet system from one computer to another. Dawkins sees this as being similar to the way religion is passed on from one generation to another through parents telling their children about it, and instructing them, in their turn, to pass it on to the grandchildren, etc. After a while it gets a firm hold and, like a computer virus, disrupts the normal running of things.

Although superficially persuasive, Dawkins's argument is flawed. What he does not take into account is that religion has been in evidence at all times and in all places throughout the history of the human race. In fact, there is nothing more *normal* than to be religious. If religion is to be regarded as a contagious infection, then most people have for most of the time been sick. No, what is *abnormal* is the current rise in atheism. Why is it that atheism, which initially got a hold in the industrialized West, is now spreading? Would it not be more appropriate to regard atheism as the virus?

The religious archetype is enormously influential. Jung held that if this inner drive did not manifest itself in the worship of God, then it would come to rest on some other object. It is rather like the way experiments have shown how the mother archetype of the newly born gosling can be deflected towards some bizarre alternative object. If, instead of being presented with its real mother, the gosling immediately encounters some human being or a piece of painted wood, then all its pent-up feelings of devotion to a mother will get displaced. The human or the piece of wood is treated as though it were the real mother.

So it is with religion. The religious archetype can get deflected to some object other than God. The individual might come to devote all his or her energies to nationalism, racism, feminism, support for a political party or a football team, campaigning against blood sports or highway bypasses, support for environmental pressure groups, fighting AIDS, and so on. Not that some of these activities in themselves are not worthy and deserving of support and action. What we are talking about here is when a person gets things out of proportion – when the whole focus and rationale of his/her life centers on the cause in question, to the exclusion of other considerations. When that is the case, the cause has become the person's religion.

Above the door of Jung's house, he had carved in Latin a sentence attributed to the Delphic Oracle. When translated it reads, "Invoked or not invoked, the god will be present." Even though we ourselves live in what seem to be particularly irreligious times – in the sense of declining church attendance and formal observance – one has only to go into a bookshop and see the proliferation of books on the occult, to realize that the deep-rooted religious archetype will find its expression somehow.

Again we see its all-pervasive influence at work in attitudes toward death. A person might assert the finality of death, and deny all possibility of life beyond the grave, but will nevertheless feel compelled to speak well of the dead. Or take the way the British people reacted to the death of Diana, Princess of Wales. What could possibly have triggered such an overwhelming display of grief? Jung would surely have had a field-day explaining it to us – in terms of the religious archetype.

Jung, perhaps somewhat confusingly, spoke of this archetype as the *self*. Why should it be given such a name? Let me try and explain. Earlier I mentioned how it was a particular characteristic of Jung that he concentrated on the second half of life; this contrasted with Freud and his special concern for the early years. As Jung saw it, each of us comes under pressure to behave and conform in certain ways. We take on responsibilities for running a house, and supporting a family. This means having a job. Work is time-consuming; it is normally of a highly specialized nature, perhaps requiring lengthy training. Because of the need to specialize in order to become good at one's vocation, there are other aspects of one's potential that have to be neglected.

I myself well remember how at school I had first to give up art, which I had enjoyed, in order to concentrate on studying for the exams I was to take at age sixteen. Then came further specialization as I had to drop English to concentrate on my scientific studies at advanced level. And by the time I got to university, I was doing nothing but physics and the mathematics needed to support the physics. At each stage it was something of a toss-up which way the decision went – which subject got dropped, and which was retained.

We all have similar stories to tell. These life-affecting decisions might be made for quite arbitrary reasons – perhaps related to the personality of a particular teacher, or what one's friends have opted to do.

This means that by the time one reaches mid-life, there are large aspects of one's initial potential that have never been tapped; they remain stunted, while other parts of one's make-up have been excessively nurtured to the extent that they have taken over one's whole life. Each of us reaches the halfway stage of life unbalanced.

Thus, according to Jung, it becomes the task of the second half of life to redress this imbalance. We are to return to the neglected parts of our personality and encourage them to give belated expression to themselves. The overall aim is to become a fully rounded, whole person. This process Jung called *individuation*. It was the process of fully realizing oneself as an individual – not being formed and shaped by largely incidental and accidental outside restrictions and pressures – but being true to one's real self. As such, the process begins in one's earliest years, and carries on in our working career, marriage, bringing up a family, etc. But it is in danger of being left half-done. In the second half of life one must consciously strive to attend to those neglected parts of one's potential; one must learn to give expression to the totality of one's personality – expression to the all-important archetype known as the "self."

Jung then went on to say that just as a round object – like a ball – has to have a center, so the well-rounded person has to have a center. And that center is to be God. The process of discovering the real you is indissolubly bound up with the process of getting sorted out over your relationship to God. For that reason, the self archetype becomes synonymous with the religious archetype. In fact, Jung would speak of the religious archetype as the "God-image." We are reminded that the Bible tells us that we are made in the image of God. So the process of discovering your true self is one where you are confronted with the God-image. The very core of your being, its very center, defines for you the meaning of life – where you stand. That meaning is rooted in God – or if not in God, then in some God-substitute. It is what colors and gives meaning to your whole life, and for that reason all other archetypes relate to this self archetype or God-image – hence its position at the very center of the psyche; the psyche being the sum total of all that is conscious and unconscious.

We saw in Freud's psychology that religion was to be regarded as a sign of immaturity, an inability to stand on one's own feet and realize that there is no protective father-figure. Religion was a neurosis – the state of being at odds with oneself because of unresolved conflicts. Psychologically it was unhealthy and needed to be treated. For Jung it was quite the opposite. A well-sorted-out religion was an integral part of psychological maturity – the epitome of psychological well-being. It was something one should actively seek to cultivate. Jung said:

> Among all my patients in the second half of life – that is to say, over thirty-five – there has not been one whose problem in the last resort was not that of finding a religious outlook on life. It is safe to say that every one of them fell ill because he had lost that which the living religions of every age have given to their followers, and none of them has been really healed who did not regain this religious outlook.

> (*Modern Man in Search of a Soul*)

For Jung, the moralistic God was not a projection of a superego that had been instilled by parents and society. Rather, the superego was to be regarded as an introjected God or, as Jung put it, "a furtive attempt to smuggle in the time-honored image of Jehovah in the dress of psychological theory."

Which brings us finally to the question of the *origin* of the religious, or self, archetype.

I introduced the subject of archetypes by drawing on what has recently been learned concerning genetically influenced behavior fashioned by the process of natural selection. And there is no doubt that we see in the life of the mind the counterparts of those inherited external behavior patterns we all share.

But that is not to say that this is all there is to the archetypes. It does not exclude the possibility that there are mind-sets in the psyche that have little if anything to do with the survival of the fittest. Take, for example, this religious archetype.

One might at first try to dismiss it as simply a chance genetic aberration, which once it came into existence, was subsequently perpetuated because it happened to confer a better chance of survival. After all, a gene that encouraged people to act cooperatively could indeed have survival value.

But there are problems with this suggestion. One is the obvious disadvantage of having, as the rallying point for the shared loyalty, a belief in an invisible God whose existence could not be indisputably demonstrated. Why not make the rallying point a charismatic leader (which of course does happen – in response to the hero archetype we mentioned earlier), or alternatively a shared devotion to a particular country or race – which is also commonplace? What is not good for survival is a belief in a God that leads you to love your enemies, and to care for the sick and disabled – those who, in terms of the harsh dictums of evolutionary theory, one would presumably have to brand as the "unfit."

Certainly Jungian psychologists would be reluctant to accept that the archetypes are limited only to those that are clearly the psychological counterparts of the genetic traits to do with survival.

How the others might have arisen, however, is not clear. With genetically influenced behavior fashioned by evolution through natural selection, we know that the mental character traits relate to a physical sequence of base molecules; those traits can be altered by altering the sequence. But this does not exclude the possibility that there might be additional mental traits associated with other features of the DNA molecule, such as for example its overall helical structure. This presumably did not arise through the same selection process; it is there because the chain of base molecules has to have an overall structure of some kind. Could it be that this overall structure is the physical analogue of the self archetype to which all other archetypes relate? Such an idea would be pure speculation, very hard to prove or refute. Suffice it to say that psychologists might well be right in seeing more to the archetypes than just the mental correlates of the physical features fashioned by natural selection.

These considerations are of particular interest when it comes to the origins of the God-image or self archetype. Jung, having explained that the term "archetype" derives from the word meaning "imprint," once wrote:

> ... thus an archetype presupposes an imprinter. Psychology as
> the science of the soul has to confine itself to its subject and

guard against overstepping its proper boundaries by metaphysi-cal assertions or other professions of faith. Should it set up a God, even as a hypothetical cause, it would have implicitly claimed the possibility of proving God, thus exceeding its com-petence in an absolutely illegitimate way . . . we simply do not know the ultimate derivation of the archetype any more than we know the origin of the psyche. The competence of science as an empirical science only goes so far as to establish, on the basis of comparative research, whether for instance the imprint found in the psyche can or cannot reasonably be termed a "God-image." Nothing positive or negative has thereby been asserted about the possible existence of God, any more than the arche-type of the "hero" posits the actual existence of a hero.

("Introduction to the Religious and Psychological Problems of Alchemy," *Psychology and Alchemy*, Collected Works 12, paras 1–43)

So what Jung is saying here is that psychology of itself cannot make claims about the existence of God. In the final analysis, we are left with the problem of whether the source of the otherness of religious experi-ence is God (acting either directly on consciousness, or through the intermediary of our unconscious) or whether, alternatively, that source lies solely in our own unconscious.

What makes this a particularly difficult problem to unravel is that, in talking of prayer, we do not have in mind some ghostly telepathic transfer of thoughts from a source physically situated outside. God is thought to be *in* oneself as well as outside. It is the God within that stirs up thoughts in one's mind. We are called to be at one with God. As we approach that ideal, it becomes increasingly difficult to draw a hard-and-fast distinction between the mind of God and that of the believer.

None of this prevented Jung himself, as a private individual, from having his own personal views on the subject. In a famous TV inter-view with John Freeman, he was asked whether in fact he did believe in God. He replied: "Difficult to answer. I *know*. I don't need to believe; I know."

Conclusion

This draws to a close our study of what two leading psychologists had to say about religion. Confronted by essentially the same data on recurring types of religious experience, their studies led to diametrically opposed views on how they should be interpreted. Clearly it remains for us as individuals to decide for ourselves where, within this broad spectrum of interpretation, our own response lies. Sufficient to say that, for many, the inner religious experience lies at the very heart of the God experiment, providing the most compelling evidence for God.

6

Getting Acquainted with God

What is God like?

If prayer is to be seen as a meeting of minds – our mind and God's mind – then presumably God has some kind of personal nature. So, what kind of personality – if we can call it that – does God possess?

As in any other type of investigation, including scientific studies, no one is expected to discover everything for themselves; there is no point in reinventing the wheel. Each of us benefits from the experience of others – particularly from that of the acknowledged leaders in the field. When it comes to finding out what kind of God we are supposed to be dealing with, if one is of the Judaeo/Christian/Islamic tradition, then an important source of information has to be the Bible. There we expect to find the accumulated wisdom of the great religious figures of the past. Unfortunately, the picture of God it presents seems, at first sight at least, to be a confusing one.

For a start, we are assuming there to be just the one God. And much of the Bible points to that conclusion. It affirms God as the creator and ruler of the whole world. But elsewhere it refers to other gods, for example, the Canaanite baals. The God of the Israelites was jealous when his people worshiped these other gods.

Next we note that God is supposed to be a God of love and mercy. But there is much in the Old Testament about a God of wrath and vengeance. His anger could be so great as to bring him to the verge of destroying his people.

Then again, God is supposed to be the god of all peoples – loving them equally. In that case, how are we to account for what happened to the Egyptians? We can understand God wanting the Israelites to be freed from slavery, but killing off the Egyptians' first-born children and drowning their army seems somewhat extreme.

I repeat: what kind of God do we think we are dealing with?

Progressive theology

Much of the confusion is resolved once it is realized that theology, not unlike science, is a progressive subject.

All too often we are inclined to think of theology as static – fixed in stone. Our understanding of God was formulated once and for all at some point in the past. Since then, all that has been required is for that original conception to be faithfully preserved and passed down to succeeding generations. Thus, it is held, theology stands in marked contrast to science which is a dynamic endeavor, constantly moving forward, progressively refining and improving its understanding of the world.

Such a view of theology could not be further from the truth. One has only to place the writings of the Bible in chronological order to see this. The Bible, of course, is no ordinary book; it is a whole library of books, written by different people at different times. And, for whatever reason, they are not presented to us in the order in which they were written. Indeed, the chronology is even more complicated than that. Genesis, for example, is not in itself a single book; it is a collection of writings which themselves are not in chronological order. Take the two creation stories: the one beginning at verse 4 of Chapter 2 was written in the eighth century BCE, 200 years *before* the one we find earlier in Chapter 1.

It is no easy matter for Biblical scholars to sort out the correct chronology. But when this is done, to the best of their ability, a truly fascinating pattern emerges. What we discover is that the conception of God (in the Judaeo/Christian/Islamic tradition) has changed and evolved dramatically over the ages. These developments took place largely through the insights of great leaders and prophets. There follows a brief sketch as to how these ideas about God gradually took shape over the course of history.

Originally there were thought to be many gods. They were largely territorial, each being in charge of a particular country or tract of land. On crossing the border from one country to the next, one was expected to worship the god of the country that had now been entered. Much like an earthly king, it was he who was in charge of everything going on in that territory. The god of particular interest to the Bible is one called Yahweh; the god who lived on Mount Sinai. He was a fearsome god; put a foot on his land, and one ran the risk of instant death.

Moses belonged to the Israelite nation, which at the time was enslaved in Egypt. But he had escaped and found his way across the desert to Mount Sinai. He strayed on to the mountain, and met Yahweh in the form of a burning bush. Not only did he survive the encounter, he was told to return to Egypt and lead his people out of slavery. When Moses protested that the King of Egypt was unlikely to grant freedom to the Israelites, Yahweh offered help. He sent plagues and all manner of troubles upon the Egyptians, including the slaughter of their first-born. Eventually the Egyptians capitulated and gave the slaves their freedom. They then had second thoughts and went after them to bring them back. In the course of the chase, their army was drowned in the Red Sea.

Yahweh was a tribal god; he was the god of the Israelites, and only the Israelites. To that extent he was conventional. Where he was *not* conventional is that he had exercised power in a country that was not his own. How was it possible for the god of Mount Sinai to perform acts in Egypt?

Yahweh was different in another respect. Normally one belonged to whatever god was in charge of the land where one's people lived. There was no choice in the matter, any more than one could choose one's parents. But with Yahweh and the Israelites it was not so. They entered into a contract, a covenant. Yahweh proposed that if they conformed their lives to his ways – as embodied in the ten commandments brought down from Mount Sinai by Moses – then he would afford them his protection, and guide them to a land of their own. The Israelites were to become an adopted people. It wasn't to be a matter of birth, but of choice.

The next development was that Yahweh went with his people on their wanderings through the desert. He was no longer exclusively tied to Mount Sinai. We see here a further loosening of the link between a god and his particular territory.

They reached the promised land, but it was already occupied. This posed no problem, however, because Yahweh was still at this stage a tribal god concerned only for the interests of his adopted people, the Israelites; he cared no more for Canaanites than he had done earlier for Egyptians. He installed his people. The worship of the Canaanite gods, the so-called baals, was to be discontinued. Yahweh was now in exclusive control of the country.

And yet old habits die hard. King Solomon had many wives, some of whom were foreign. They wished to continue to worship their own gods, and Solomon permitted this – even building altars to them in the great temple in Jerusalem he had originally dedicated to Yahweh. Not only that, but the people in general surreptitiously took up the worship of other gods. After years of wandering the deserts with their flocks, they had become settled. It was now worthwhile to turn to agriculture and grow crops – because those who planted them would still be around later in the year to collect the harvest. But crops require rain. To whom should the Israelites pray for rain? Yahweh had supplied them with manna to eat in the desert, sure enough, but basically he was a warlike god – good at fighting Israel's enemies. No, the experts at making it rain were the old Canaanite baals.

Here we get another strand of thought contained in old ideas about gods. There was not only the notion that they could be territorial, but also that different gods were associated with different functions. We see this particularly with the ancient Roman and Greek gods – Mars the Roman god of war, Aphrodite the Greek goddess of love, Bacchus the Roman and Greek god of wine, and so on. Yahweh was regarded by the Israelites at this stage as being particularly good at fighting. It was up to the prophet Elijah to demonstrate that Yahweh's powers and influence extended beyond merely waging war. In a time of drought, he went up a nearby mountain and prayed to Yahweh for rain. A cloud appeared. Tiny at first, it grew and grew – and it rained. So it became clear to the Israelites that Yahweh was not simply a god of battle; he could look after their needs in times of peace also.

And note that Yahweh could make clouds in the sky; he controlled the sky. But the sky stretches everywhere. His domain of influence was spreading.

Elijah was prominent in calling the people back to exclusive worship of Yahweh. Under the bidding of the vengeful, jealous Yahweh, Elijah instigated the slaughter of 450 priests of Baal that Queen Jezebel had set up throughout the country.

But then we see a new side to Yahweh. The prophet Hosea had a wife who was repeatedly unfaithful to him. He ought to have done away with her – had her stoned to death. But he could not bring himself to do it. He found that no matter how often she deceived him, when she returned to him he could not help but forgive her. Hosea saw in this a parallel with Yahweh's relationship to the Israelite people. They too were repeatedly unfaithful to him, chasing after the other gods. Although Yahweh would punish them for their wrongdoing – as for example in the way he set the people against each other to the extent that the kingdom became split into two halves, at enmity with each other – he did not destroy them. Why? Because he was not purely a god of justice and vengeance; he had the capacity to forgive. He was a god of mercy.

Then we have the contribution of Amos. He lived at a time when the people had become polarized: the rich and the poor. With the cultivation of the land, some landowners had become very rich. Most were singularly uncaring of the plight of the starving masses. As long as they went through the motions of making sacrifices on the temple altar, they reckoned they had done as much as was needed. It was Amos, a poor shepherd, who had the task of denouncing the excesses of the rich. Yahweh was not a god simply interested in the good of the Jewish nation as a whole, and therefore particularly interested in the leaders of that society – the rich and influential. He took a personal interest in everyone – as individuals. Again this was to be seen as fresh insight.

The next prophet on the scene was Isaiah. He came from a very different background to Amos; he was one of the ruling class. He spent much of his time in the palace of the king. He was used to nobility and splendor. He had a vision of Yahweh in which his glory filled the heavens; he was god of the whole Earth. It was not that he ruled the land of the Jews, and in addition had considerable influence beyond its boundaries: he ruled everything.

And yet the Jews had difficulty focusing their worship on this god. They set up altars to him in each village and town, which was fair enough, but then they got to talking of "the Yahweh of our town," as distinct from "the Yahweh of your town." They had in fact regressed once more to the worship of local deities. King Josiah decided to put a stop to this once and for all. He ordered all altars to be smashed except the one in the great temple at Jerusalem. From then on, there was only one place where sacrifices could be offered. With just one altar it became clear that there was just one god the Jews should worship.

All of this meant that sacrifices could only be made by journeying up to Jerusalem. These pilgrimages were very significant occasions for the faithful. Unfortunately, King Josiah's plan had its down side. Whereas people got a special thrill coming up to Jerusalem to the one and only altar, when it was time to quit Jerusalem and head for home, they felt as though they were leaving Yahweh behind. Although this had never been Josiah's intention, the people got to thinking that Yahweh lived exclusively in the temple at Jerusalem. Out of sight, out of mind. Once they were home, they felt free to live their lives however they wanted to, Yahweh supposedly being none the wiser.

It was against these excesses that the prophet Jeremiah railed, warning the people that if they did not mend their ways Yahweh would punish them by sending in the Babylonians to lay waste their country. The authorities tried hard to stop Jeremiah upsetting the people with his predictions of gloom and doom. His warnings went unheeded, however, and in due course the Babylonians invaded. They captured Jerusalem, and razed the temple to the ground. After 350 years, there was nothing left of it. The rulers and leading citizens were taken into exile to Babylon. It seemed the end of the Jewish nation, and of their god. Having got used to the idea that Yahweh lived in the temple, they had now to come to terms with the idea that their god had been made homeless, or indeed had been destroyed along with the temple.

At that stage, Jeremiah ceased castigating the people and became their comforter. He assured them that after a period of seventy years, Yahweh would bring them back home from exile and they could make a new start; they would be forgiven. As for the loss of the temple, that was not the disaster they had assumed it to be. It was not the case that Yahweh lived in a specific building. He made his home in the hearts of people – wherever they might be – even in exile in Babylon. It is difficult to overestimate just how significant was this particular shift in thinking about Yahweh. He was a god who made his home *inside* the individual person.

Then we have Ezekiel. He had a wild vision that left him in a state of total shock for seven days. He had glimpsed the wonder, the power, and the awesome nature of Yahweh. It was so breathtaking and tremendous, he could not put it into words. Here we have the realization of how pitiful it is to try and describe Yahweh by making analogies with earthly images such as kings. Yahweh is so great, so beyond human imagining, that our descriptions have no chance of doing him justice. Contrast this with earlier accounts of him as someone who walks in the garden in the cool of the evening, or engages in a wrestling match with Jacob – portrayals of him that barely extended beyond a somewhat larger-than-life man.

Then we have the most remarkable revelation of all. Toward the end of the Book of Isaiah (beyond Chapter 40), another writer takes over. We know nothing of him; he is simply known as Second Isaiah. According to him, Yahweh declares:

> As the heavens are higher than the earth, so are my ways higher than your ways, and my thoughts than your thoughts.

> (*Isaiah* 55:9)

This was confirming the message of Ezekiel that we have no way of comprehending fully the nature of God. But then he also says:

> I am the Lord, and there is no other;
> apart from me, there is no other god.

> (*Isaiah* 45:5)

There we have it – at last. There is only the one god. From now on one can refer to him as God with a capital "G" because there is none other with which to confuse him. We can now seen that when in the past Yahweh was spoken of as being jealous, it was not that he wanted the people to worship him in preference to the others. It was more the case that he didn't want his people wasting their time addressing gods that weren't even there.

From this perspective it now becomes possible to understand why he was able to exert influence in Egypt and leave his mountain; he was the God of all the Earth. He not only owned it all, he created it in the first place. Only now, at this late stage in the story, does it become possible to think of God as being the sole Creator God.

Moving on to the New Testament, Christians see there yet further insight into God. He sends his own Son to live the life of a human, to share in our sufferings and to be the ultimate sacrifice on our behalf. We see in Jesus the perfect human life; what we ourselves are called to be. That God would humble himself in this way is the most eloquent testimony there could possibly be as to the inexhaustible depths of his love for us. Christ's prayer for the soldiers who were nailing him to the cross that God would forgive them because they knew not what they were doing, again shows the extraordinary extent to which he is prepared to forgive.

Summary

Reviewing these changes, we find we have progressed:

• from the god who was tied to his mountain retreat – to the creator of the whole world;

• from one god among many gods – to the one and only God;

• from the god of the Israelites who cared nothing for Egyptians and Canaanites – to the one who is God of all people equally;

• from a warlike god of wrath and vengeance – to the God of love and mercy;

• from a god who would strike people down dead if they approached too closely – to the God who dwells in our hearts;

• from the lofty God of the heavens – to the one who comes to Earth and suffers alongside us.

Earlier I warned that this would be but a sketchy, broad-brush approach to the development of theology down the ages. It is crude in the sense, for example, that I have presented the changes as building up toward the climax of monotheism. This is fair enough in terms of the generally accepted religion of the times. But that is not to deny that there had been certain schools of thought that had arrived at that position long before it became the consensus. In a subject this complex, the true story-line splinters down more than one path, some ending in blind alleys, others undergoing a number of detours. But the overall picture that emerges is one of general progression.

Progress still to come

Nor is this progress in theology something that took place solely in the distant past. Before leaving his disciples, Jesus told them that he would send them the Holy Spirit:

> When he, the Spirit of truth, comes, he will guide you into all truth. . . . He will bring glory to me by taking from what is mine and making it known to you.
>
> (John 16:13–14)

One way of understanding this passage is to see it as hinting that there was still more that God could reveal about himself, but the people of those days were not prepared for it.

Take, for example, the way we in our own time have begun to recognize and take an interest in the feminine side of God. We are coming to see God not only as our Heavenly Father, but also as our Heavenly Mother. In earlier times, when all positions of power and influence were occupied exclusively by men, it was only natural to think of God in masculine terms. But social change has meant that today the superiority of the male no longer applies – at least not to the same extent. This affects how we can think of God. Our minds have been prepared; we are now able to enrich our conception of God by exploring female analogies as well as male ones. For instance, I am rather taken with the analogy of the created world springing from the womb of God. The act of giving birth can be a useful complementary model to the more usual one of the world being fashioned much as a potter shapes a pot.

Again, with our modern understanding of astronomy we see just how vast and prolific the Universe is. This enhances our sense of the unimaginable power of God, far exceeding what was possible in the past. On planets out there, going round distant suns, are there other civilizations? If so, how does God relate to them? Are they more advanced than we are? Are they more valued by God than we are? How does the Son of God relate to them in terms of salvation?

Then comes the recognition of all the chance processes that are going on in the world, whether we are thinking of the formation of planets with only a few capable of supporting life, or the random mutations to DNA upon which the process of evolution by natural selection gets to work. It is an interesting way for God to achieve his purposes. So what is this telling us about God?

Then we have the aeons of time that the Universe existed before life developed within it, and the infinity of time that lies in the future when the stellar fires will have run their course and all becomes cold – the Heat Death of the Universe – the end of all life. What does this tell us about how God relates to the physical world itself? Are we right in seeing it as nothing more than a home for life, or in the eyes of God does it have a worth of its own – regardless of whether there is life in it?

Make no mistake about it: theology is an ongoing activity; it is far from static – far from being stuck in the past.

Marrying the new and the old ideas of God

If we think of our understanding of God as being so much better these days than it was in the past, you may ask, why do we retain "out-of-date" ideas? Why do we still read those passages in the Bible that refer, for instance, to there being other gods?

One reason is that there often remains a kernel of truth in them; religious people of the past were never entirely wrong in their conception of God. Agreed, we no longer think of there being other gods in the sense of supernatural beings. But as we saw in the last chapter, the psychologist Carl Jung warned that we have a natural inborn tendency to be religious, and if that drive is not consummated in the worship of God, then it will be deflected on to some other object or cause. Some different passion will absorb our energies; it will become a "god" for us, and those passages in the Old Testament about the Israelites chasing after other gods still provide us with salutary warnings of the consequences of chasing after modern "gods."

Or you might wonder why one continues to read passages describing Yahweh as a severe, indeed vengeful, God of justice. Surely we now know him to be a God of love, and mercy, and forgiveness. True, but the element of justice is still there. In the Christian tradition, the price of sin had to be paid by someone – it couldn't just be swept under the carpet as though it had never happened. And the price – a terrible one – was paid by Christ. What happened to Christ on the cross was not the work of the "Big Old Softie" kind of God some people seem to believe in these days. He is made of sterner stuff than that – and references to Yahweh as the God of justice act as an important reminder to us that there is another side to the "gentle Jesus, meek and mild" type of God.

So, on balance, it is right for us constantly to remind ourselves of the earlier ideas of God, provided we do this in the context of the overall development of theology, and don't read into them a significance and interpretation that is no longer deemed appropriate.

Genuine progress in theology?

From the above it would appear that our understanding of God has undergone changes and development as radical as any that have taken place, through science, in our understanding of the world. Moreover, that ongoing progress, as in science, continues in our own time.

But are we sure that it is genuine "progress"? I believe so. One would no more wish to revert to past understandings of God than one would wish to go back to earlier notions of science. In the philosophy of science, it has become customary to speak of "critical realism." This term acknowledges that we can never expect at any stage to be absolutely certain that our scientific theories are correct and will never need further amendment. But at least we are convinced that there is a real world out there (we are not making it up) and that our current descriptions of it are superior to those they have superseded.

I reckon the term "critical realism" can be applied as appropriately to theology. Modern theology does not have to be dogmatic in the sense of its supposedly providing the last word on the ultimate truth about God. Our understanding of God is fallible; it is open to correction and refinement in the light of greater experience. The fact that theology is, and always has been, in a state of flux, is a sign of strength rather than weakness and indecision. Scientists and theologians alike must approach their respective data with humility, fully prepared to change their theories in the light of new evidence and insights.

A dissenting view

Before concluding, it is only fair to point out that there is, of course, a quite different way of accounting for the continually changing conception of God. According to this alternative viewpoint, the changes do not represent genuine increases in our understanding of God; God is not progressively revealing to us more and more of his true nature. Rather, it is a case of people continually recreating God in their own image, and in accordance with whatever might be the current prevailing tendencies in society.

Recall how, in the last chapter, when we were dealing with the psychological inner religious experience, we saw that it was difficult to put it all down to wish-fulfillment – the unconscious tricking us into believing that our wish for a protective father-figure had been fulfilled in terms of a Heavenly Father. This could not be the whole explanation. And yet we noted that there was indeed a *certain amount* of projection going on.

So we have to ask questions like: is it the case that God is a forgiving God, and the only way he could get that message across was through a person who knew, from personal experience, what forgiveness was all about – Hosea in relation to his unfaithful wife? Or was Hosea simply creating a forgiving God in his own image?

Again, is it the case that God wanted to get across to us something of his splendor and majesty, and could only do that through someone used to pomp and ceremony – the rich Isaiah at the king's court? Or again was Isaiah simply projecting into the heavens a God in his own image?

If God is a God who cares for the individual – the poor as much as the rich – does it mean that such a message has to be entrusted to someone who is himself interested in the poor, because that is what he himself is – the humble shepherd, Amos? Or was Amos indulging in wish-fulfillment?

There is no easy way to resolve such dilemmas. In the end it is up to each of us as individuals to make up our own minds on which side of the fence we come down: genuine revelations of God's nature coming to us through minds that are prepared and sensitized to the transmission of that particular message; or those self-same minds projecting on to an imaginary god their own likeness.

As you will guess, I myself side with the first interpretation – that these are genuine revelations of God. Why do I think that? Because if we are to put it all down to making God in one's own image, then only forgiving people would think of God as forgiving, only rich people would think of God as powerful and magnificent, etc. But that is not how it is. Once the prophets said what they did, it was not long before their messages gained *universal* acceptance. One doesn't have to be poor to accept that God loves the poor as much as the rich; one doesn't have to have an unfaithful wife in order to accept that God can forgive. Certainly it takes the soil of a prepared mind for the seed of the idea to germinate in the first place. But once germinated, it could be propagated. Consensus formed around those particular ideas concerning the nature of God that were judged to have the ring of truth about them. It is the same in science. It took the prepared mind of an Einstein to cultivate the theory of relativity. But once this insight had been articulated, it quickly gained universal acceptance in minds that could never have originated it.

7

Why Evil and Suffering?

Does our conception of God make sense?

So much for how we come to have our present-day understanding of God. We can sum it up by saying that there is just the one God; the Creator of the Universe and of ourselves; all-powerful; all-loving; all-good. Because God is everywhere, even within our very minds, he is also all-knowing.

But does such a portrait of God, assembled from the accumulated insights of past ages, tally with our own experience of life as we find it today? All-powerful? All-loving? All-good? How can that be compatible with the evil and suffering we find in the world, to say nothing of death? For many people, the existence of evil and suffering poses an insuperable problem to belief in a benign God.

It is no good us calling our investigation "the God Experiment" if it is aimed solely at finding evidence *in favor* of God's existence. Science doesn't operate like that. Science takes on board *all* the evidence – whether or not it appears to be in favor of, or contradictory to, one's chosen hypothesis. So we too must be even-handed over the evidence; we cannot in all intellectual honesty sweep the problem of evil and suffering under the carpet just because, on the face of it, the evidence does not seem to fit. It is to that problem we must now turn.

But before doing so, I should perhaps make it clear from the outset that I have no ready answers. Anyone who thinks they have cracked this perennial problem once and for all should, I suggest, imagine themselves face to face with someone terminally ill, suffering intense, unremitting pain; or someone who has just lost a loved one; or a survivor of the Nazi Holocaust; or someone whose life has been blighted by the sexual abuse they suffered as a child. Under any of those circumstances, would an intellectual argument about the problems of evil and suffering be of any help? Of course not. In those situations, what is required is the exercise of compassion, understanding, sympathy, and offers of practical assistance.

But that is not to say we just throw up our hands in helpless resignation, declaring it to be a mystery. A mystery it certainly is – using that term in the sense that we are confronted with something that we shall never comprehend in its entirety. But that is no excuse to remain silent. We must at least provide pointers as to where the truth might lie – some measure of rationalization.

Various approaches to the problem of evil

One generally hears talk of the problem of evil and suffering – "problem" in the singular. But I think it helpful to break this down into the problem of evil, and the problem of suffering. Inasmuch as evil can lead to suffering, there is clearly a link between the two. But not all suffering derives from human, moral evil; it can also come from natural causes – floods, fire, earthquakes, etc. For that reason, suffering merits separate treatment.

The first question we have to ask about evil is whether it is *real?* That sounds fatuous, I know. But it is a genuine concern. After all, it could be that the all-good God simply creates goodness, and evil is merely the absence, or comparative absence, of goodness – in certain places at certain times.

An absence can be experienced as something real in its own right. On a cold day, for example, we wrap up in lots of clothes. Why? To keep the cold out. But what do we mean by that? Cold is nothing but the absence of heat. It is not a case of "cold" getting in from outside; rather, it is heat being lost to the outside.

An objection to the notion that evil is nothing more than an absence of goodness is that such a proposed solution does not do justice to the sheer power and depth of evil in some of its manifestations. Can one really account for the deaths of millions of Jews in the Nazi concentration camps as simply an absence of goodness? When a crowd of soccer fanatics meets a handful of rival supporters, and mob hysteria takes over, to the point where they positively relish kicking and beating up the helpless victims, are we to put that down to an absence of goodness?

It has to be said that in extreme cases, an absence can indeed give all the appearance of something highly active in its own right. In the case of coldness, under severe conditions we talk of "frostbite" – the cold actively *bites* our toes. We talk of the scourge of poverty and the ravages of disease – even though these could equally, if not so forcefully, be described as due to an absence of money and an absence of health.

Nevertheless, it is customary to accord to evil a metaphysical status on a par with that of goodness. That being so, we must enquire as to its possible origins.

One solution is to postulate a rival divine power – an evil spirit challenging the goodness of God. The Bible in various places refers to the Devil. Satan is not to be thought of as a rival god, but as an angel created by God who subsequently rebelled against its maker. Though there have always been people who believe this to be literally true – that Satan is as real in the spirit world as God, others see the Devil as more in the nature of a useful fiction. By thinking of the power of evil personified, actively seeking to tempt and lure people into sin, one is placed on one's guard against such backsliding tendencies. It is when we laugh at the Devil, depicting him with red cape, horns, and a tail, that we are in danger of not taking genuine evil as seriously as we ought.

An alternative to thinking of two rival spiritual beings is to postulate that goodness and evil are both to be found within the one deity. In other words, the assumption that God is wholly good is not, in fact, correct. Just as there is a dark side to each of us, there is a dark side to God – a "shadow" side to him, as Carl Jung put it. Indeed, this was the solution to the problem of evil that Jung himself advocated. Goodness and evil both originated with God.

It is a possibility, but one that has commanded little acceptance. It is an understanding of God that appears to be at odds with the kind of God one personally encounters in one's prayer life – the kind of God personified for Christians in Jesus.

Which leaves us with one final possibility: God is wholly good – as traditionally believed – but he is placed in the position where he is somehow forced into allowing evil to have a place in his created world. It is not that he *wants* evil to be present; rather it is the case that there is some logical imperative that demands that it be there.

Is this not doing away with another of the supposed findings about the nature of God, namely that he is all-powerful? Not necessarily. When we say that God is all-powerful, that does not imply he is able to do logically impossible things. An omnipotent God is no more able to form four-sided triangles than we. So, the question is whether there might be some *logical* constraint under which God has to operate.

Love as the supreme principle

If one were to be allowed just one word to describe God's all-important characteristic – just one word – it would have to be *love*. His purpose for making us was that we might enter into a loving relationship with him.

This in itself is somewhat surprising. I don't know about you, but if I were a god intent on creating a world, I suspect my first consideration would be to ensure that the inhabitants of that world were happy and content; everyone would have a good time. The key word to describe my world would have to be "happiness," rather than "love." I would doubtless have been a very popular god!

On mature reflection, however, I might find myself regretting that policy. After all, it is common experience that people who have everything handed to them on a plate – those who live solely for the pursuit of pleasure – become insufferably spoiled and self-indulgent. So, perhaps God got it right when he elevated the concept of love to be the greatest good, rather than human happiness.

In any event, it is not up to us to choose what kind of God we deal with – any more than the scientist is called on to decide how the physical world "ought" to have been. Theologians deal with whatever God they are given, just as scientists are stuck with whatever world they find. Both have to try and understand what is presented to them. And what we are saying is that, for whatever reason, God's prime reason for creating us has to do with the concept of love rather than happiness or pleasure. That being the case, certain conclusions follow.

The necessity of freedom – and evil

One is that God must give us free will. Love is not something that can be forced, or coerced, or programmed into us. By its very nature – in order for it to have any value – it must be freely offered.

So far, so good. But if that will is to be really free, then there must be the possibility of us exercising it in a manner that is not in accordance with God's will. There must be the possibility of our withholding that love. This is a risk God has to take. Nor can it be just a *theoretical* possibility. When dealing with billions upon billions of people, if nobody in practice ever did reject God, then there would be grounds for doubting the reality of this "freedom." In order for free will to be genuine, there must surely be actual examples of people who do decline to respond to God's love; they turn their backs on God. And, in doing that, they turn their backs on the source of all goodness; they embrace evil.

The very manner in which we, as humans, evolved through natural selection, in itself almost inevitably ensures that some will not enter into a right relationship with God. In Chapter 5, we saw how we have inherited built-in genetic tendencies to behave in certain ways. These behavior traits evolved through their being able to confer some survival advantage on our ancestors. It is only to be expected that among these instinctive tendencies will be one inclining us toward selfish, self-centered behavior – a behavior trait likely to be conducive to the survival of our ancestors when food and shelter were in short supply. Note: we have a tendency to be self-centered rather than God-centered; we start life at a distance from God. This being so, it takes a positive, conscious decision on our part to recenter our lives on God in place of ourselves. In religious terminology, this is the act of repentance – the principal meaning of which is "a change of mind."

There are those who will not take that step. Indeed, *all of us* – believers and non-believers alike – from time to time turn our backs on God; we do our own thing; we misuse the freedom God has given us.

But, you might say, why does God make it so hard for us? Why not give us a natural tendency to love him and do his will, rather than the reverse? Just as a hypnotist might place a post-hypnotic suggestion into a subject's mind that on waking she will find herself infatuated with him, so God could have created us with an irresistible tendency to love him. True. But would such a contrived form of "love" be of value? Would the hypnotist think he had genuinely *won* the woman's love?

Obviously not. The same would be true of a falsely induced "love" of God.

In similar vein, one cannot have a God who makes us free, but is constantly overwhelming us with manifestations of his presence and power – for instance, through a never-ending succession of spectacular miracles. That would be another form of coercion. No. For our freedom to be genuine, God *must* adopt an approach to us that is veiled, that is somewhat hands-off. It is an approach that is clear to those of the faith – those who have eyes to see and ears to hear – but one that is open to other interpretations for those who exercise their freedom differently.

Thus, the so-called "free-will defense" of the all-good, all-loving, all-powerful God, is that in order for love to be given a chance, God has to permit the possibility of evil. This is something that is logically required. It is not *God* who creates the evil. The evil we find in the world is *our* responsibility; we create it whenever we decide to rebel against God.

Various approaches to the problem of suffering

Much suffering is caused by the evil we do. Indeed it almost becomes part of the definition of what constitutes an evil act: a deliberate act that knowingly and wilfully leads to someone suffering. But this addresses only part of the problem. Even without anyone perpetrating deliberate evil acts, there would still be much suffering from *natural* disasters – earthquakes, floods, tornadoes, etc. – as well as from disease and disability. How are we to account for suffering that comes from such sources?

One approach is to regard suffering as a punishment for sin. Accordingly, those who suffer most must have sinned most. From earliest times, this seemed an obvious way of trying to make sense of why some are called upon to suffer more than others. In the great Biblical exploration of suffering, this was the answer given to Job by his friends: all the calamities which befell him must be God's way of punishing him for having been particularly wicked. But Job would have none of it. He knew he wasn't perfect, but he wasn't *that* bad.

The idea of suffering as a punishment for sin was still around at the time of Jesus. But, like Job, Jesus rejected any such explanation. And in our own times, it seems perfectly obvious to us that those who suffer most are in no way more wicked than the rest.

In order to build a more constructive approach to the problem, we return to the question of free will. We have seen how free will is an essential prerequisite for being able to love God or love each other. But free will can only be exercised in an environment that is predictable. One must be able to anticipate the likely outcome of any course of action we might choose to take. That means the environment must be law-like – it must obey set rules. It must be a neutral environment – one that can be used for good or ill.

Not only that, it must be a *common* medium – one through which we can interact with other individuals. We make ourselves known to others through physical bodies operating in an environment that is jointly shared. It must be a world that does not bend its rules to meet the passing whim of any individual – an occurrence that might infringe the interests of some other individual who has just as much, or as little, right to have things *their* way. A gardener might want it to rain; a vacationer might prefer fine weather: there is no pleasing everyone. So the environment has to be even-handed. The world we jointly inhabit has to have a *nature of its own*. And that is how we find it.

But having said that, it follows that the inexorable working out of those laws of nature is bound from time to time to lead to some unfortunate consequences. One of the prices we have to pay for our freedom is that we are liable on occasion to fall foul of those laws.

Another point regarding the integrity of the world and its laws is this: just because we have declared that the greatest good is love – love between conscious living creatures – we must not immediately assume that this has to be the one and only purpose behind creation. Quite apart from its being a home for conscious, living beings like ourselves, the Universe might *in itself* be a source of delight to God. Just as God extends to us a measure of independence so that we can be ourselves, so he extends a measure of autonomy to the world – he lets it be. Natural disasters appear evil only when seen from *our* perspective. They might not be so regarded from God's perspective. They are but the natural outworkings of creation – creation doing its thing – and as such could be seen as good.

Of course, it might be objected that if God *really* loved us the way he is supposed to, he would not let terrible calamities, such as earthquakes and floods and volcanic eruptions, cause havoc to innocent people. He should on such occasions intervene. This brings us up against all the difficulties we encountered when dealing with the question of miracles. How for instance is God to stop an earthquake, or volcanic eruption, without it being obvious that some spectacular intervention to the smooth running of nature has taken place? If God were to intervene on a scale like that, it would not be long before everyone was forced to accept his existence. One would be coerced into a relationship with God, whether one liked it or not; the conditions necessary for freely offered love would be compromised. As we have noted before, it seems incumbent on God to have a somewhat hands-off approach. While he might offer a sign to someone who already has faith in him, and so is not *relying* on such a sign, it is a different matter performing signs and wonders on such a scale that unbelievers are likely to be forced to reconsider their position regarding their relationship to a possible God.

One has also to point out that sometimes – by no means always – but *sometimes*, when people fall victim to a natural disaster, they are not entirely innocent of responsibility for what happens to them. I am as guilty of this as any. As a young research physicist, I took up an appointment at the Radiation Laboratory, Berkeley, near San Francisco in California. Journeying out on the old Cunard ship *Mauretania*, I saw on the wall of the ship's library a photograph of San Francisco in the aftermath of the 1906 earthquake. It was a scene of total devastation – hardly a building left standing. What was I doing going to a place like that!? Geologists at the time were warning, as they do today, of the Big One to come. So, I knew the dangers involved – but still I went and stayed. The work opportunities were too tempting, the climate was inviting, the life so good. But throughout my time there I never completely shook off the sense of unease. I could not help thinking, if I get caught up in an earthquake, I cannot honestly blame the San Andreas Fault; it will be *my* fault, and mine alone. The same goes for anyone who settles in that area; the same goes for anyone who makes their home in Naples, under the shadow of Vesuvius, or in many other locations known to be dangerous.

Of course, it would be glib to say that people should simply avoid such places. Those living in Bangladesh know all about the dangers of living in a place prone to flooding, but they simply cannot afford to move – there is no other place for them to go. Similarly, the inhabitants of Assisi could be pardoned for thinking that the risk of an earthquake in that location was too small to worry about – until it happened in 1997. No, despite the fact that some people can be held responsible for a measure of contributory neglect of the potential dangers, we are still left with the problem of totally undeserved suffering.

The necessity of suffering

At this stage I find that a useful approach to the problem is to ask: what if there were *no* suffering in the world – no suffering whatsoever? What would be the knock-on consequences of such a seemingly idyllic world – the kind of world most people think God *ought* to have set up?

When one talks of "no suffering" one would, of course, have to include mental suffering as well as the physical kind. (Most suicides occur as a result of mental rather than physical suffering.) In such an imaginary world, everyone would have to have everything they could possibly want, otherwise they would suffer feelings of deprivation and inadequacy.

In such a world, how would one demonstrate one's love for another?

A moment's reflection reveals that this would be extremely difficult, if not impossible. Certainly one could have good times together – sex, and that sort of thing. But sex is enjoyable. How is the partner to know that one is doing it out of genuine love, and not just for the sake of one's own enjoyment? The same holds for any other activity that is pleasant.

Proof of love can come only from the way one reacts to the other's *needs* – the way one person puts himself or herself out for the other – how they *suffer* and *sacrifice* themselves in order to alleviate the suffering, and tend to the needs, of the other. In order to be convincing, the loving act has to be costly.

This can be seen in little things: for example, the way a mother will get up in the middle of the night – even though she is herself desperately tired – in order to feed and change the diaper of her baby. Or it is to be found in big things, like the way someone might devote his or her life to the care of a housebound wife or husband suffering from the ravages of multiple sclerosis, rather than going off to seek some other partner. One sees it each time someone gives a big donation (often one they can ill afford) to a charity devoted to the relief of refugees or victims of famine. Such self-denial is a demonstration of brotherly love for people one does not even know and has never met.

These, and countless other examples we can all bring to mind, serve to confirm that, in order for love to be manifest, there has to be self-sacrifice and suffering on the part of the giver, in response to the need and the suffering of the person to whom the love is offered. In a world without *any* suffering, there would be no needs to attend to, no suffering to alleviate, and no one would, in any case, be allowed voluntarily to take on any measure of suffering on behalf of another.

Earlier we saw that in order to have love as the highest principle, there had to be free will – and hence evil. Now we discover that a second condition to be satisfied is that the world must be such as to permit suffering.

The good side of pain

The next point to be made is that, although we naturally do all we can to avoid and alleviate suffering, there are circumstances where a measure of suffering may not in itself be a bad thing.

Take pain, for example. It would be simplistic to think of pain as if it were something *totally* bad. In fact, in its origins, it is a thoroughly positive, good thing – a vital part of our ability as an evolved animal to live and survive in an environment that can sometimes be hostile. Pain is a warning of danger and injury. The pain of placing a hand on a hot object is a warning to withdraw the hand to avoid injury. It needs to be unpleasant so as to make the avoidance of danger immediate and instinctive. Likewise, the prolonged headache we get when we bang our head on an overhanging tree branch provides us with an unpleasant memory to encourage us in future to take greater care to avoid such encounters. Internal pain, like that of appendicitis, is similarly a warning that something is wrong inside and needs attending to; without the pain we might be unaware of the condition.

Certain people have a medical condition that prevents them from experiencing pain. They lead a most hazardous life. Even we in our own small way know that when we have been to the dentist and had a local anaesthetic, it can be difficult, in the absence of feeling, to escape biting our tongue or cheek. Pain does have its uses.

But of course that does not go for *all* pain. Why, for instance, do we have to go on suffering the pain once the warning has been heeded? One grasps a hot object, then in response to the pain signal, lets go as quickly as possible. But if it was not quick enough and one gets burnt, the pain continues long after it has served its useful function. Or take the case of arthritis. What is the point of being continually reminded by the pain that the joints are swollen – when there is nothing that can be done about it?

As for the *degree* of pain, this can often seem out of proportion to the severity of the condition for which it acts as a warning. Toothache can be agonizing – but it is hardly life-threatening. On the other hand, many fatal diseases give no discomfort at all – at least not until the terminal stage. And what good comes from the suffering and pain of childbirth?

Then one is bound to ask questions about the suffering endured by animals – particularly that which arises in the course of evolution by natural selection (which we examine in Chapter 10). This is a process often dependent on predators catching and killing prey. If producing humans by this means is what God had in mind from the beginning, couldn't he have chosen some other way of doing it?

Of course, when talking about suffering in the animal kingdom, we have to be careful that we are not projecting too much of our own human experience on to the lower animals. Is a worm in pain when it writhes about, having been accidentally cut in two by the gardener's spade? Are both halves in pain (they are both writhing about)? Does the worm now have *two* minds – both in pain – or is it not mentally experiencing anything at all? Does the wriggling fish on the end of the hook feel pain? If we think that, why isn't angling banned?

How much of pain is in the *anticipation* of it? Is it not curious that a soccer player can come off the field at the end of a game to discover his leg grazed and bleeding – an injury he cannot even remember sustaining – and yet the same person recoils at the prospect of having a needle stuck in him at the doctor's? In one case the attention was distracted; in the other it was focused on what was happening. If we ourselves respond so differently to injury, depending on our state of mind at the time, can it not be argued that animals – possessing as they do a mental capacity far lower than ours – might feel very little? It is impossible to say. But the problem of suffering in the animal kingdom might not be as pressing as it is generally portrayed.

Other good things from suffering

We have seen that there are circumstances where pain can be a positively helpful warning of danger – not always, but in some cases. There are other good things that can arise out of suffering.

We have already noted that it provides others with the opportunity for ministering and showing love and concern. Suffering can be effective at bringing people together. As Paul says, we "weep with those who weep." People assist each other in all sorts of ways, whether it's helping out at the local hospital, raising money for a hospice, getting in the shopping for the housebound, etc. All these activities forge links between people.

One of the interesting aspects of the prayer experiment we spoke of at the beginning, is the group of patients that *know* they are being prayed for. Regardless of whether such prayers can be shown to bring about physical benefits in terms of improved recovery rates, it is already widely acknowledged that people derive much comfort and inner strength from knowing that they are being upheld in their troubles by the prayers of others.

Or take someone you don't particularly like, or indeed someone who is an adversary of some kind. On learning that they have fallen desperately ill, or that they are dying from some incurable disease, one's feelings toward them immediately change; one feels closer to them – more sympathetic. Suffering, to say nothing of death, can be a great reconciler.

As for the people suffering, there can be additional benefits for them too. If the highest good is to be in a loving relationship with God – that is what we are intended for – then evil is whatever keeps us from such a relationship with God. That being so, we cannot simply conclude that suffering of itself is necessarily evil. Certainly there are those, worn down by suffering, who become bitter, cynical, disillusioned, and turned in on themselves. These are the ones who lose their faith in the face of calamity. Suffering in these cases is truly an evil – a separation from God. But it does not have to be. Setbacks and difficulties can, and often do, lead to a *strengthening* of ties with God – a deeper realization of one's dependence on God, a more profound appreciation of his ultimate protection. That being so, the suffering that brought about this enriched relationship with God can surely not be called "evil." In itself, suffering is neither good nor evil; it is what we *make* of it, how we *use* it that determines whether it works for good or evil – whether we end up closer to, or further away from, God.

I would go so far as to say that all that is best, most valued, longest lasting, is born out of pain and suffering. Human suffering can destroy – or ennoble. Under the pain of suffering, one either becomes a bitter person, or a better person.

Pottery must be fired. Unless the clay pot is subjected to extreme heat, it will remain soft clay – no use to anyone. It has to pass the test of fire before it is transformed into something useful and valuable. Not all clay pots survive this test. An unsuspected flaw – a trapped air bubble – will cause the pot to explode and be destroyed.

So, too, must we be submitted to the test. One speaks of this world as a "vale of soul-making." It is through trials and tribulations that we develop our spiritual souls. And just as every piece of pottery that has ever been fired is still around today, in some form or other, so it seems to me our souls need to be fired in the kiln of suffering in order to become immortal.

Jesus uses the alternative metaphor of the vine being pruned. Just as the gardener prunes the vine to make it even more fruitful, so God prunes every fruitful branch with the pruning knife of suffering, in order that it too will yield yet more fruit.

All of us, from time to time, become so distracted by our daily activities, so wrapped up in the pursuit of our goals and ambitions, that we fail to keep things in perspective; we lose sight of the bigger picture – what life should *really* be about. We need to be jolted out of our routine. Often the only way this can happen is by our being made to suffer in some way. Many a life has been transformed – for the good – by a long, enforced spell in a hospital, or a brush with death. As C. S. Lewis put it:

> God whispers to us in our pleasures, speaks in our conscience, but shouts in our pains – it is his megaphone to rouse a deaf world.
>
> *The Problem of Pain*, C. S. Lewis

If things go well we are inclined to be complacent; it's human nature. It is so much harder to attend to one's devotions when all is well with our world. It is more likely to be in times of trouble that we are driven to our knees in prayer. Too many people regard God in the same way as a jet pilot regards the parachute – something to be called on in emergencies. So be it; if that is the only way God can jolt us out of our ill-considered self-satisfaction, let there be emergencies.

Too much suffering?

There are those who are quite happy to accept that good can come from suffering in the ways I have described. That is not the problem. The problem is the *degree* of suffering that some are called upon to endure. It is all very well saying there has to be suffering in order for there to be a demonstration of love. But why *so much* suffering? Particularly one thinks of the Holocaust; of the appalling suffering and death of many innocent children. Why did God not set *limits*?

In a sense he *has* set limits. Under great pain and torture, the victim is at some stage likely to pass out – to become unconscious. Secondly, there is the limit set by death. The sufferings of this mortal life will come to an end when we pass to the life beyond. We suffer, yes; but only for a time. Thirdly, there is the possibility that he has set limits we do not even recognize. For all we are aware, the "natural" state of affairs – that which would exist in the absence of a loving God – might have more in common with a never-ending, all-pervasive holocaust than the life we know. Only through God's influence is suffering contained within the limits found.

Such suggestions, valid though they might be, nevertheless carry little consolation. In the end, we simply have to face the fact that we are dealing with a God who never does things by half. We shall encounter further evidence of this in the next chapter when we have to come to terms with the vast scale of the Universe, and the seemingly unending stretches of time that had to pass before intelligent life put in an appearance. To our limited human minds, these defy the imagination. It is the same with suffering; what we on our restricted human scale would regard as excessive suffering might not seem so to God.

What we have to learn to accept is that this is no toy world. It is not a playschool, pretend type of world; it is the genuine article. We are not God's pets. As a general rule, pet-owners pamper and spoil their animals; they make sure they come to no harm, and never want for anything. But that is not how God is with us. He has something more challenging in mind. He wants us to be strong, to stand on our own two feet, take responsibility for our own destiny, and to some extent be independent of him – so that we can, of our own free choosing, respond to him in a loving relationship. This is not to claim a loving relationship between equals, but certainly something much richer than the dependence of a pet on its owner. However, in order to acquire this distinctive individuality, we must expect to go through tough times and suffer hard knocks. If a little sacrifice and suffering is a small indication of love, then profound suffering is a sign of a deep love.

In this context, it is important to recognize that there are two distinct types of evil: the sort that causes suffering, and a second sort that leads to *triviality*. We humans are wonderfully complex beings, capable of great depth and spirituality. But it has to be said that many of us live our lives at a very superficial level. Few ever come close to fulfilling their true potential. This has to be seen as a waste of the life that has been given us, and as such it is an evil – an affront to our Creator.

A measure of suffering might be the only way to trigger an exploration of this potential, and hence avoid the evil of the trivial, misspent, wasted life. The greater the intensity at which one lives, the greater the love one has to offer. The other side of the coin, of course, is that an intensely lived life could result in a deeper exploration of one's potential for causing harm – evil of the first kind. The two go hand in hand. But living an *intense* life, rather than a trivial and superficial one must, in itself, be good.

Instinctively we know this to be the case. We have only to think of the way we are prepared to take risks in order to enjoy a more fulfilled life. One cannot ski without running the risk of a broken leg; one cannot learn to ride a bike without the risk of falling off; one cannot climb a mountain without the risk of a fall; one cannot enjoy foreign travel without the attendant dangers of possible plane or train crashes, or the boat sinking. These risks we voluntarily undertake. Why? We do it in order to add zest and depth to our life. A rich life exacts a price – the richer the life, the higher that price.

Take marriage, for instance. There are many advantages to living alone. One can have the house or apartment just the way one wishes; eat what one likes, go out and do whatever one wants. There is no need to fit in with anyone else's plans. One can simply do one's own thing. But that is not what most people choose. Instead, they prefer to be involved in a loving relationship with someone else – even though that entails self-sacrifice, compromise, difficulties, and conflicts of interest. It is a price most of us are prepared to pay. Even having gone through the traumatic upheaval and unhappiness associated with divorce, people are still liable to seek out a new partner with whom to share their lives. This surely testifies to there being something about a loving relationship that is far more rewarding than a life of private self-indulgence – it is something worth suffering for.

In considering whether the suffering in this life is excessive, another point to take on board is that all suffering is relative. If it were all to be scaled down – in response to our protests that at present it is too severe – we would quickly readjust our sense of what was, and was not, "severe" suffering. We would soon end up convinced that the higher levels of suffering, even on this reduced scale, were excessive. Take a small child and the way it yells and screams when it falls down and grazes its knee. To hear it crying one would think it was the end of the world. It is only later, when in adulthood we have been visited with greater pains, that the severity of a grazed knee is viewed in a different perspective.

One final point about the severity of our sufferings. A few unfortu-nate people are driven to commit suicide. But for most people, this way out of suffering is never a serious option. Indeed, it is our natural reac-tion to fight tooth and nail to stay alive. For many people the greatest fear is the fear of death – the end of this life. Surely that in itself says something powerful about how we really value this life – despite the many complaints we make about it.

Where lies justice?

The problem of suffering is seen in its starkest form when it involves the plight of children:

> One day when we came back from work, we saw three gallows rearing up in the assembly place, three black crows. Roll call. SS all around us, machine guns trained: the traditional ceremony. Three victims in chains. . . . All eyes were on the child. He was lividly pale, almost calm, biting his lips. The three victims mounted together on to the chairs. The three necks were placed at the same moment within the nooses. . . .
>
> The child was silent.
>
> "Where is God? Where is he?" someone behind me asked.
>
> At a sign from the head of the camp, the three chairs tipped over.
>
> Total silence throughout the camp. . . .
>
> The two adults were no longer alive. Their tongues hung swollen, blue-tinged. But the third rope was still moving; being so light, the child was still alive. . . .
>
> For more than half an hour he stayed there, struggling between life and death, dying in slow agony before our eyes. And we had to look him full in the face. He was still alive when I passed in front of him. His tongue was still red, his eyes were not yet glazed.
>
> Behind me I heard the same man asking:
>
> "Where is God now?"
>
> And I heard a voice within me answer him:

"Where is he? Here he is – He is hanging here on the gallows."

(E. Wiesel, *Night*, trans. S. Rodway, Fontana/Collins, 1972, pp. 76–7)

We are reminded here of the God who dwells inside each and every one of us – the Holy Spirit; the God who suffers when we suffer.

The suffering and death of small children is the single most powerful piece of evidence our God experiment has come up with that appears to refute the idea of an all-loving, all-powerful God of Mercy and Justice. In such cases, there is manifestly no justice to be seen. It strikes at the very heart of the God hypothesis.

At least, it strikes against the God of "half-baked" Christianity. By that I mean a belief that is basically Christian – Jesus was the best man who ever lived, and we all ought to follow his example – but a form of Christianity without the resurrection, without a belief in life beyond death. That kind of religious belief, so popular these days, so apparently reasonable, simply does not stand up to close examination; to me it makes no sense. It is manifestly clear that some people are subject to manifold injustice in this life. I am at a loss to see how a belief in a loving God – one who is supposed also to be a God of justice – can be sustained without there being something beyond this earthly life. God has to have the means whereby he can compensate for all that is wrong with this life. It is for this reason I devoted a whole chapter to sifting the evidence for the resurrection of Jesus. It really does play a key role in the whole scheme of things.

Now, it will be objected that this is simply the "jam tomorrow" scenario – a product of wishful thinking. Remember how Freud claimed that if you wished for something hard enough, your unconscious could trick you into believing it's true. But why shouldn't it be "jam tomorrow"? What kind of pessimism is it that assumes that happy endings must by their very nature be an illusion? If God is all-powerful, and all-loving, and a God of justice, then this is something he *can* do, and indeed is *bound* to do.

How can a life hereafter adequately compensate for the intense suffering that some individuals have to undergo? Intense their suffering might be, but one thing is certain: it is finite; it comes to an end. The life beyond death is *infinite* – and there is no comparing the finite to the infinite.

One point that puzzles many over this Christian belief in resurrection is the way the creed declares: "I believe in the resurrection of the body." How can this be? How are all the pieces of a person's body to be gathered together again once it has decomposed and been eaten by worms and gone to make up the bodies of the worms now – or, alternatively, when it has been reduced to ashes and gases in the fires of the crematorium?

This is to misunderstand what is meant by that credal statement. It is not a question of gathering together the atoms of the old body. When it says that we believe in the resurrection of the body it is not talking about the *physical* body. It means that in the life to come, each of us will retain our *individuality*; we shall not be lost in some kind of anonymous, homogenized spiritual "soup." We shall still be recognizable as ourselves.

Why then talk about "resurrection of the body" like that? It is here we need to remind ourselves that, in this earthly life, it is only through the possession of physical bodies that we distinguish one person from another. We recognize each other from our physical appearance, the sound of the voice, and so on. To some extent that is how it must be in the next life; we shall need a "body" of sorts. Not *this* body – not a physical body, but a body of some kind.

As an analogy, take an encyclopedia. One might conjure up a mental picture of a whole shelf full of books. Alternatively it could be in the form of a CD-ROM disk. All that information – exactly the same information – repackaged in different form. That is what one means by the resurrection of the body. Each of us is to be likened to a bundle of information. At present that information is packaged as a physical body. But it doesn't have to be. It can be passed on and repackaged in a different form – a spiritual body.

I have spoken specifically of Christian belief. Other religions, of course, differ in varying degrees with regard to what, if anything, lies beyond death. Hinduism, for example, speaks of reincarnation – coming back to this world in a different form – rather than resurrection. What *is* remarkable is that all the major religions – East and West – are agreed that there is something about us as individuals that continues beyond death – a persistence of identity – and the quality of that exten-

sion of life depends to some extent on how we live *this* life. Death marks
a transition, rather than an end. As such it is not to be feared.

God's involvement in suffering

So far we have tended to confine our thoughts to our own engagement
with suffering, how we cope with it, and the possible effects it has on
us. But that extract from Wiesel's book raises the question of God's
involvement.

In the first place it has to be said that God is not one to stand back
and let us get on with it alone. Religious believers are convinced that
God hears our prayers. That's why we pray to him for the sick. The
prayer experiment we mentioned at the start might be able to throw
some light on this when the results become available. It is not that we
expect such prayers for recovery always to be answered in the way we
would like. God is the only one who knows the full circumstances. In
his greater wisdom he might realize that the long-term well-being of
the person might better be served some other way than by a straight
"yes" to our request. Regardless of how he might respond, however, we
are convinced that God is not impervious to the suffering. Either he
alleviates it, or he strengthens us to help us get through the trial – if
there is no other way.

For Christians, the ultimate evidence for God's involvement in, and
concern for, human suffering is to be found in the life and the sufferings of
Jesus. If Jesus truly were the Son of God, as is claimed, then God has first-
hand experience of what we are going through. We look at the figure of
Christ on the cross, and we ask: "If that isn't love, what is?" God is not a
God who just offers encouragement from the sidelines; he's in the thick of
it with us – assuring us, through the resurrection of Jesus, that this is the
way to ultimate victory and the accomplishment of his purposes.

Ultimate mystery

That really is as much as I can say about how one might begin to try
and make a little sense out of the mystery of suffering. All it amounts
to is a few pointers as to where a hint of a solution might lie – why the

existence of evil and of suffering is not *necessarily* against the idea of an all-good, all-powerful, all-loving God. The God experiment remains intellectually viable.

But let us be clear, no matter how hard we strive to come up with answers, we are faced with mystery – something that lies ultimately beyond the power of human reasoning. This much is made clear in the story of Job we mentioned earlier. Job, the good God-fearing man upon whom befalls a series of terrifying calamities, in the end comes face to face with God. He has demanded an explanation for his troubles. We are thinking, "At last we are to receive the answer straight from the mouth of God." But no. Instead of an answer, Job is bombarded with a whole succession of questions from God:

> Where were you when I laid the earth's foundation?
> Tell me if you understand.
> What marked off its dimensions? Surely you know!
> Who stretched a measuring line across it?
> On what were its footings set, or who laid its cornerstone –
> While the morning stars sang together, and all the angels
>   shouted for joy? . . .
> Can you bind the beautiful Pleiades?
> Can you loose the cords of Orion?
> Can you bring forth the constellations in their seasons or lead
>   out the Bear with its cubs?
> Do you know the laws of the heavens?
> Can you set up God's dominion over the earth?
>
> (Job 38)

And so the questions come, thick and fast – over fifty of them – all designed to expose how little humans know about anything. Job can do nothing but humbly accept that in the final analysis, suffering is beyond understanding; it is something we must bear patiently, trusting that the loving, all-powerful God will, in his own time and in his own way, ensure that all will be well.

We are like children in the face of God. How often are children bewildered by, and resentful of, the rules laid upon them by their parents? In later life they might be able to look back with the benefit of hindsight and see the good that came out of being forced to do home-work, being made to acquire tidy habits, clean their teeth, not live on a diet of chocolate, take nasty-tasting medicine when ill, go to bed at a set time, and so on. But at the time, it was simply a case of getting on with it, trusting that one's parents were acting in a loving, caring way.

So it is with us and God. A God who was fully comprehensible to the mind of man would be a product of the mind of man. The fact that we do *not* fully understand God strikes me as the mark of his indepen-dence – his independent reality. He is not the sort of God anyone would have been inclined to dream up out of their own imagination. He is too problematic for that.

8

Our Place in the Scheme of Things

We have seen that a key feature in the defense of a loving, good, and all-powerful God is that the rationale for our existence is founded on a loving relationship with God. Once that premise is granted, we begin to see how there might have to be a measure of evil and suffering. Without them, love would be unable to flourish.

But that in turn raises another difficulty: are we really expected to believe that the Creator of the entire world takes that kind of personal interest in each and every one of us? To put it bluntly, given all that has been revealed to us about the world through modern astronomical investigations, can we possibly regard ourselves as *that* important?

It is interesting that in the answer to Job we quoted just now, God began by directing Job's attention to the heavens. It was God's way of cutting him down to size. So it must be with our God experiment. It is time to resume our study of the physical world, but now to expand its scope to take in the Universe – the grand overall stage on which we live out our lives. What kind of place is it? What are the implications of modern astronomy for the significance of human life?

A quick guide to what is out there

On looking up at the sky we see the Sun, Moon, and stars. They appear to be revolving round us once a day. But looks are deceptive. As is well known, it is really the Earth that is revolving on its axis once a day. Only the Moon actually orbits us. It is our satellite, the Earth having eighty-one times the mass of the Moon. As heavenly bodies go, the Moon is not of great interest.

Much more important is the Sun. Although it looks about the same size as the Moon in our sky, apparent size is affected by the distance of the object from us. The Sun is much farther away than the Moon – 400 times farther. In fact, the Sun is so large, one million Earths would fit inside it. It is we who orbit the Sun, not the reverse.

The Sun is mostly made up of the two lightest elements, hydrogen and helium. It is a ball of fire, its heat being derived from the nuclear fusion of its hydrogen into helium (as happens in nuclear-fusion bombs), followed by the progressive fusion of the helium and other products to produce yet more complex nuclei. The Sun has been burning like this for the past 5,000 million years. It has about another 5,000 million years to go before eventually running out of fuel.

Turning our attention to the stars, we find that a few of them continually change their position against the general star background. These "wandering stars" are not really stars at all; they are planets. Like the Earth, these eight other planets orbit the Sun, and shine by light reflected from the Sun. The planets and the Sun together make up the Solar System.

Stars (as distinct from planets) are balls of fire just like the Sun. In fact, the Sun is itself a star – a medium-sized one. The reason the others look so small is on account of their great distances from us. On a scale where the distance from the Earth to the Sun is represented by one meter, and that to the most distant planet in the Solar System (Pluto) is forty meters, the nearest star to us (Proxima Centauri) would be at 250 kilometers. Putting it another way: light travels at 300,000 kilometers per second (or 186,000 miles per second). At that speed, sunlight takes eight and a half minutes to reach us, whereas starlight from Proxima Centauri takes just over four years.

Recognizing that stars are in themselves suns, it becomes natural to enquire whether any of them have planets going round them in the same way as the Sun does. From our understanding of how the Solar System originally formed out of a gas cloud (more of this later), it would seem that other stars, forming in the same way, would also be likely to have planets. In fact, at the time of writing, about forty planets going round other stars have now been detected.

How many stars are there? A hundred thousand million, gathered together in a great flattened, swirling disc called a galaxy. That's twenty stars for each man, woman, and child on Earth. We are positioned about two-thirds of the way out from the center of the disc. On a clear, dark night, away from the glare of street lights, one can see a faintly glowing band stretching across the sky from one horizon to the other, called the Milky Way. This is the Milky Way Galaxy seen end-on from our position lying in the disc. Looking away from the Milky Way one is directing one's line of sight out of the plane of the disc where there are fewer stars.

What lies beyond the Galaxy? Other galaxies. How many? A hundred thousand million – the same number as the average number of stars in each galaxy. So that is 20 *galaxies* for every man, woman and child on Earth. Adding together all the stars of all the galaxies, the total number in the Universe is approximately the same as the number of grains of sand in a sandcastle five miles high by five miles wide and five miles long. (I had to do some messy experiments on the kitchen table, sub-dividing piles of sand and counting individual grains in order to arrive at that estimate!)

The galaxies occur in clusters. Our own galaxy belongs to one called the Local Group – a collection of about thirty galaxies gravitationally bound to each other. On a larger scale still, clusters are associated into even larger superclusters. These are thought *not* to be gravitationally bound to each other, though clearly their close positions relative to each other must have arisen from their mutual gravitational influence.

Clusters and superclusters of galaxies are found at very great distances from us. Some lie so far from us, it takes almost 12,000 million years for their light to reach us. The Universe is BIG.

The place of humans – the Galileo affair

So much for our whistle-stop tour of the Universe. Where do we humans fit into it?

There was a time when it was thought that we were at the center of the Universe – it had been created exclusively as our home. Just as each newly born baby starts life thinking that everything revolves around it, and has subsequently to learn better, this was a misconception that the human race as a whole had to grow out of. It was a painful transition – one associated above all with the name of Galileo.

Throughout this book I have been at pains to point out that the religious quest has more in common with a scientific investigation than most people suspect. Yet in the case of Galileo, it appears their approaches could not be more different – one doggedly holding on to a traditional, outmoded viewpoint, the other open-mindedly adapting to whatever new data are found. And that is not all. Here we have the church actually trespassing on the other's preserve – in outright opposition to the advance of science. The story is gleefully peddled of how Galileo was imprisoned and tortured for stating that it was the Earth that went round the Sun, rather than the reverse. Some versions of the legend even have it that, having been forced to recant his views, he stamped his foot on the ground, defiantly declaring, "And yet it moves!" Whereupon he was cast into the dungeons and had his eyes put out.

But what *really* happened?

It had been Copernicus who in 1543 had originally come up with the new cosmology based on the Sun being at the immovable center of the cosmos. His ideas did not catch on because they did not seem to make much sense according to the science of his time. For example, if the Earth were moving, why didn't all the loose things on its surface, to say nothing of the clouds, get left behind? Not only that, where was the force keeping the Earth going? We have to recall that in those days, they did not have the benefit of a good understanding of mechanics – something that was later to come from Galileo himself and from Newton. At that time it was not appreciated that no force is needed to keep something moving – provided there is no friction or air resistance. In addition it has to be said that, in terms of mathematical simplicity, the new theory offered no advantage over the old one. Copernicus was still wedded to the idea that the planets had to move in circles. However, the experimental data on planetary motions did not fit with the idea of each planet moving in a simple circle about the Sun as center. So Copernicus proposed instead that each planet moved in a circle, the center of which moved in a circle about the Sun. This motion based on composite circular motions was complicated. Only later was it replaced by the simpler idea of planets moving in ellipses – an insight due to Kepler. For these reasons the ideas of Copernicus caused little stir at the time.

Then in 1609, Galileo built one of the newly invented telescopes, trained it on the sky, and started gathering data on the moons of Jupiter, the phases of Venus, etc. These observations lent weight to the Copernican world-view. At this stage, Galileo's problem was not the reaction of the church, but that of his scientific colleagues. Some of them were so deeply suspicious of the distorting glasses in the newfangled telescope, they refused even to look through the instrument. They were also concerned that the mechanics they had been teaching all their lives now appeared to be jeopardized.

The response of the clerics on the other hand was altogether more favorable. The Jesuit mathematicians of the Roman College were quickly convinced. Galileo, a devout Catholic himself, was delighted with this. Inevitably some church officials were worried that the authority of Scripture was being called into question. They required of Galileo that he speak of his theory as a hypothesis, rather than as an incontrovertible established fact. Galileo had no trouble going along with this. The Pope himself had a great interest in natural philosophy. He wrote a letter of congratulation to Galileo, and even a poem celebrating the discoveries made by the telescope.

With Galileo now getting on in years, his friends, including the Pope, encouraged him to write a book setting out his findings – the very book that was later to get him into hot water. The Pope even asked Galileo to include in it an argument of his own. This was to the effect that God, being all-powerful, could arrange to make it *look* as though the Earth went round the Sun, whereas in reality, the Earth was fixed and it was the Sun, and everything else, that went round it. A rather silly argument, and one that Galileo must have been reluctant to include, but he dutifully complied.

The book, *Dialogue Concerning the Two Principal Systems of the World*, passed the church's censors. In fact two lots of censors were involved, one in Florence, the other in Rome. Unusually, it was written in the vernacular Italian rather than the academic Latin that would have been conventional for such a work. This made it instantly accessible to the public at large. It was published in 1632, and immediately caused a sensation. Everyone was talking about it.

But within a year, Galileo was on trial for heresy. So, what went wrong?

In the first place it has to be said that while Galileo managed to get his book passed by the censors, it was only with difficulty. Galileo was a persistent man. He had badgered the censors unremittingly, winning more and more concessions. He had worn them down. But more importantly, although he had presented the Copernican view as a hypothesis – as had been required – it was hardly a balanced discussion. The spokesman for the theory, a character called Salviati, completely overwhelmed his rival in the dialogue, Simplicio, who had the admittedly unenviable task of defending the earlier cosmology based on the ideas of the Greek philosophers.

Worse than that, though, was the manner in which Galileo had chosen to deal with the argument advanced at the request of the Pope. This he had put into the mouth of the discredited Simplicio. Simplicio introduces it by saying that this was "a solid doctrine that I once heard from a most eminent and learned person, and before which one must fall silent. . . ." No reader could have failed to recognize that this must be the Pope himself. Salviati goes on to demolish the argument with scorn – thus holding the Pope up to ridicule. This was not sensible. From what we know of the character of the Pope – a rather vain and conceited man – this was too much. Not only was he personally being lampooned, but he was doubtless advised that his very Papal office was being treated with contempt. Hence the trial.

Galileo was himself in no doubt as to why he had suffered this reversal of fortune. Years later he wrote in a letter:

> I hear from Rome that His Eminence Cardinal Antonio and
> the French Ambassador have spoken to his Holiness and
> attempted to convince him that I never had any intention of
> committing so sacrilegious an act as to make fun of his Holi-
> ness, as my malicious foes have persuaded him and which was
> the major cause of all my troubles.

As for the later stories of imprisonment and torture, these were but gross distortions. Galileo never saw the inside of a prison; even during his trial he lived in a comfortable five-room suite with a servant provided to attend to his needs. Admittedly, there had been a nominal threat of torture – but this had been merely an archaic form of words, since it was actually illegal for someone of Galileo's age to be tortured. His punishment was merely that of having to recite the penitential psalms. In the event, he was even excused this when his daughter, a Carmelite nun, was permitted to say them on his behalf.

Nevertheless, it has to be said that the church emerged from the whole sorry business with little credit. No one can today read without anger the words of the infamous abjuration by which Galileo was forced to renounce his support for the Copernican view:

> I, Galileo, son of the late Vincenzio Galilei, Florentine, aged seventy years, arraigned personally before this tribunal and kneeling before you, Most Eminent and Lord Cardinals Inquisitors-General against heretical pravity throughout the entire Christian Commonwealth . . . with sincere heart and unpretended faith I abjure, curse, and detest the aforesaid errors and heresies. . . .

But having said that, it is important, nevertheless, to keep things in perspective. The important lesson we learn from this account is that the Galileo affair was not the science-versus-religion conflict it was later cracked up to be. It arose more directly out of a private, personal conflict – one in which a headstrong, tactless Galileo had bruised the feelings of a rather vain, self-important Pope – the latter feeling, with some justification, that his trust had been betrayed by a one-time friend.

The fact that the Copernican shift in understanding of the structure of the world did *not* have any crucial theological significance is more than adequately borne out by the fact that there had already been an *earlier* shift in cosmology. It had been just as significant as that introduced by Copernicus, and yet it had produced no clerical backlash whatsoever. I refer to the fact that the cosmology being defended by the church at Galileo's trial was not in any case the cosmology of the Bible. Interpreting the Bible literally we are presented with a three-tiered Universe. It consists of a flat Earth; above it is the Heavenly realm; below it is Hell. But what the church came later to defend was a cosmology in which the Earth was a sphere, around which circled the Sun, Moon, and stars. It was a cosmology taken over from the Greek philosophers when the new religion of Christianity came into contact with Greek culture and ideas. How did this happen? When did it happen? It is hard to say. It was a process of natural assimilation and gradual change. Of one thing we are sure: it was a change of cosmology that took place without any fuss or bother. This being so, one cannot help but wonder whether, given men of different temperaments, the whole unfortunate Galileo affair might never have happened – thereby making this diversion into history unnecessary.

The place of humans – the present day

What was learned from Copernicus and Galileo, and what has since been confirmed and extended by modern astronomy, is that we are emphatically not at the center of the Universe. We live on one of nine planets circling the Sun. The Sun is just a medium-sized star. It occupies an undistinguished position in the outer suburbs of the Milky Way Galaxy. Our Galaxy is an ordinary galaxy – one of a cluster of galaxies called the Local Group. That, in its turn, is a not very important member of a supercluster – the supercluster being one of many others. These have been observed out to a distance of 12,000 million light years (a *light year* being the distance traveled by light in a year). This is called the *observable Universe*. For all we know, the observable Universe might be but a small part of the *overall Universe* – with galaxies lying beyond the present reach of our telescopes – perhaps out to infinity.

In the face of such immense numbers and size, it is understandable that we ourselves should feel small and unimportant.

We have to accept that on an astronomical scale we have virtually no effect on anything – it is we who go round the Sun; the Sun does not go round us. For all the effect we have on the motion of the stars and planets, we might just as well not exist – we are not important.

But "importance" is a slippery concept. It derives its significance from its context. . . .

The thinking reed

Consider the following question: "We have just agreed that physically the Sun is more important than us. Most of us would like to think of ourselves as being important. Does that mean we would prefer to swap places with the Sun?"

It does not take much thought to realize that the answer is emphatically "No." It is all very well being important, but if you do not *know* that you are important, what's the point? And of course, the Sun does not know that it is important; it does not *know* anything; it is not conscious (at least, we strongly suspect that it is not!).

It is when we introduce the notion of *consciousness* – our ability to be aware of things, and to have thoughts and feelings – that the whole understanding of what counts – what is and is not important – gets overturned. No one put this better than the French mathematician and philosopher, Blaise Pascal, when he wrote:

> Man is the feeblest reed in existence, but he is a thinking reed . . .
> though the universe were to destroy him, man would be more
> noble than his destroyer, for he would know that he was dying,
> while the universe would know nothing of its own achievement.

> (*Pensées*, 1, 6)

We noted earlier that no one understands how consciousness comes about. All we can say is that it appears to have something to do with the complexity of the brain. Our brain is admittedly not big on the astronomical scale, but it is probably one of the most complex structures to be found anywhere in the Universe. In view of the accompanying consciousness which comes about at some level of complexity, it would seem that in physical terms what is more relevant than size is *degree of complexity*. As far as organized complexity is concerned, the Sun must count as an extraordinarily simple object compared to the human brain.

If the size aspect is to be discounted in favor of complexity and accompanying consciousness, then it is perhaps not so absurd after all that God would take a particular interest in us.

Our importance in relation to life elsewhere in the cosmos

We are, nevertheless, still faced with the vast number of other stars and planetary systems, and the possibility that they too sustain life. Here it is not being suggested that they are populated by humans – with two legs, two arms, two eyes, height between five and six feet, etc. As already mentioned, it is most unlikely that evolution would have traced out exactly the same steps there as it has done here on Earth. But many scientists believe that other planets are likely to be home to life forms that, although they may look nothing like us, are at least as advanced in intellectual terms as we are.

This is not a consensus view among scientists. As we shall see in Chapter 10, there were many hurdles to be overcome before evolution could produce us out of what was originally inanimate chemicals on the surface of Earth. It might be that the chances of life forms as advanced as ourselves emerging are exceedingly remote – even given the vast number of locations throughout the Universe where theoretically it could have happened. Indeed, it might have happened only once in the history of the Universe.

The only way to settle this issue is to make direct contact with alien civilizations. To this end searches are being made of the heavens under the SETI (Search for Extra-Terrestrial Intelligence) program for signs of intelligent radio signals being beamed at us – to date without success. Some would argue that there is unlikely to be intelligent life very close to us or we would have evidence of their having visited our planet – despite the fact that even our neighboring stars could hardly be called "very close." (Here I am discounting UFO claims, crop circles, alien abductions, and so on.)

My own view is that although, for all we know, intelligent life in the cosmos might be unique to planet Earth, that smacks of arrogance – the kind of arrogance that led us initially to think that we were at the center of the Universe. I am quite happy to accept that the cosmos is teeming with life forms as intelligent as we are – *as* intelligent, but probably not much more so (for reasons I shall be explaining later when we deal with evolution).

Proof of the existence of other intelligent life forms would somewhat downgrade one's own sense of significance in the grand scheme of things. But not especially so. One can already feel the sense of being lost in a crowd walking down Oxford Street in London. If, in ways unknown to us, God is able to take a personal interest in every man, woman, and child on Earth, then clearly God's mind does not work in the same way as ours; he is not subject to the same limitations. Granted he can perform this feat, it is hard to see what would set a limit on his ability to accord individual attention to everyone – including those living on other planets – no matter how astronomical the number might be.

That said, the thought that there might be lots more intelligent life forms out there in the cosmos is a sobering one. But then again, when did a little humility do any harm?

9

How It All Began

Having seen what the Universe is like, it is only natural to ask how it got to be like that. Where did it all come from? This is where our investigation turns the spotlight on God as the Creator of the world. We take a look at modern cosmology to see what insights it might provide on that particular aspect of God's supposed relationship to the world. In particular, we need to examine recent claims that the Universe could have originated itself spontaneously – of its own accord. Were that the case, would we need a Creator at all?

Evidence for the Big Bang

It is generally accepted that the Universe began with a Big Bang. I have already briefly pointed out the various types of evidence that led to that conclusion. Let us examine them in somewhat greater detail:

(i) *The recession of the galaxies.* On looking at distant clusters of galaxies, we note that they are receding from us. We can deduce this from the color of the light they give out. We find that it is systematically shifted toward the red end of the spectrum, i.e., toward light of lower frequencies. This is somewhat similar to the way the siren noise emitted by a speeding police car or ambulance is heard to have a lower pitch when the vehicle is receding from us than when it is stationary or approaching us. The lower pitch is due to the sound waves being stretched out by the vehicle's recessional speed from us, and stretched out waves correspond to lower frequencies. Light is subject to an equivalent effect: if a source of light is receding from us, then the frequencies will be reduced by a ratio dependent on the speed of recession – in other words, the light appears to be redder. And this is what we find with the light received from the stars belonging to distant galaxy clusters. It is known as the *cosmological red shift*.

Combining our knowledge of how far away the galaxy clusters are, with the estimate of recessional speed based on the measured red shift, we come across a remarkably simple relation: the red shift is proportional to distance. Thus, for example, a cluster that is ten times further away than another will be receding from us ten times faster. This proportionality of recession speed with distance is called *Hubble's Law* – after its discoverer, the American astronomer Edwin Hubble.

It is not difficult to see that a world obeying Hubble's Law has a remarkable feature: namely, that at some time in the past, all the contents of the Universe were together at the same point. To see this, imagine a video recording has been made of the movements of the galaxy clusters over time. We now play the tape backward. In doing so, we note all the clusters coming toward each other. One that is ten times farther away than another has ten times farther to go to reach us – but it is going at ten times the speed. This means it arrives at exactly the same time as the other. And the same holds for all the galaxies – they all arrive at the same time. Now playing the tape the correct way we find that all the contents of the Universe start out from the same place. Suddenly, it all expands away – the faster material traveling the farthest distance from us in any given time. And that is precisely what we find today – the clusters obeying Hubble's Law.

The recessional motion of the galaxies, with its characteristic dependence on distance, is therefore the first piece of evidence pointing to the violent beginning of the Universe.

(ii) *The cosmic microwave background radiation.* The second argument in favor of the Big Bang theory comes from another quarter. It was argued by the Russian-born physicist George Gamow that the violent Big Bang ought to have been accompanied by an intense burst of electromagnetic radiation (in much the same way as a nuclear explosion is accompanied by a blinding flash of light). Moreover that radiation should still be about in the Universe today – there being nowhere else for it to have gone. By now it would have cooled down and become a form of radiation our eyes cannot pick up – hence we do not get blinded by the light from the Big Bang every time we look up at the night sky. Nevertheless there are types of equipment capable of detecting it. Two American physicists, Arno Penzias and Robert Wilson, were the first to observe it. They did so with equipment developed for radio communication rather than as a device for investigating cosmology. It was a discovery made by accident. They found that, regardless of where they pointed the antenna in the sky, they were plagued by an annoying "background signal." This turned out to be Gamow's predicted radiation.

Indeed, to pick up this radiation it is not necessary to own the specialized type of equipment used by Penzias and Wilson. A domestic TV set makes a good "Big Bang detector." When not tuned to the dominant signal of a broadcast station, it displays the familiar "snowy" picture. One in 100 of those "snowflakes" is due to the TV aerial picking up the remnant of the Big Bang fireball. (That snowy picture could well be more interesting than some of the programs broadcast.) The radiation is now called the *cosmic microwave background radiation*.

(iii) *Primordial nuclear synthesis*. A further piece of evidence in favor of the Big Bang hypothesis comes from a study of the chemical composition of interstellar gas. In order to see how this comes about, let me begin by introducing some basic atomic physics:

An atom consists of a particle, the *nucleus*, surrounded by smaller particles, *electrons*, moving outside it. It is sometimes likened to a miniature Solar System with the nucleus taking the part of the Sun and the electrons being the planets. But that is not a particularly appropriate analogy; the electrons do not actually move in smooth continuous orbits like planets. Suffice it to say that they are situated outside the nucleus. The nucleus itself is made up of smaller particles: the *neutron* and the *proton*. These are very similar to each other, apart from the proton carrying a positive electric charge whereas the neutron has none – it is electrically neutral. It is the attraction between the positive electric charge on the protons and the negative electric charge on the electrons that keeps the electrons close to their nucleus rather than drifting off somewhere else.

The different kinds of atom in nature differ in two ways: the number of electrons they contain (hydrogen has one, helium two, carbon six, oxygen eight, etc.); and also the number of protons and neutrons in their nucleus (hydrogen has a single proton, helium two protons plus one or two neutrons, and so on).

Turning to the Big Bang, we note that, at an early stage in its development, conditions were exceedingly hot, with everything moving about fast and violent collisions taking place. Under those conditions, matter was in the form of isolated protons, neutrons, and electrons. No sooner did neutrons and protons fuse together to form a heavier nucleus than they were smashed apart in some subsequent collision. And of course there were no atoms as such because no sooner did an electron form an attachment to a particular proton than it too was sent flying by a later impact.

But eventually (meaning about one minute after the instant of the Big Bang) things cooled down somewhat. Protons and neutrons that fused together could now stay together – later impacts not being violent enough to disrupt them. The newly formed nucleus could then undergo further fusion, adding more protons and neutrons. In that way more complex nuclei could form.

But the synthesis of the heavier nuclei was a race against time. The temperature was continuing to decline. This meant that eventually a point would be reached where the newly formed light nuclei would have insufficient energy to overcome the repulsive force between the positive electric charges on their constituent protons – and so would not be able to get in close enough to form further fusions. Not only that, with the expansion of the Universe, the density of particles was declining, and the chance of coming into collision with another nucleus was reducing. For a combination of both these reasons, the fusion processes came to an end after about 20 minutes. This yielded what we call the *freeze-out mix* of nuclei.

Three hundred thousand years later, conditions had further cooled to the point where the delicate bonds between nuclei and electrons could be established, thus forming the first atoms. These were atoms corresponding to the nuclei that made up the freeze-out mix.

Now one of the remarkable features of Big Bang theory is that it is able to calculate what the freeze-out mix should have been. This comes from information gained in laboratory experiments about the different types of nuclear reactions, and from a knowledge of the average density of matter in the Universe today. The latter tells us what the density must have been at any past epoch, and in particular what the frequency of the collisions must have been during the period of time available for the nuclear fusions to take place. The calculations indicate that the final mix issuing from the Big Bang should have consisted of 77 percent hydrogen and 23 percent helium (by mass), with traces of heavier nuclei.

What is found in practice? Here we have to be a little careful because in addition to the nuclear synthesis we have been considering – the so-called *primordial nuclear synthesis* – there has subsequently been further nuclear synthesis occurring in stars. Some of the products from *stellar nuclear synthesis* have been recycled into interstellar space and so, for our present purposes, form a contaminant. Nevertheless, when care is taken to examine regions of space thought not to be significantly contaminated, one finds almost exact agreement with theory.

(iv) *Time development of the Universe.* Finally, we note that when we view a distant object through our telescopes, the light being received by us today was actually emitted a long time ago. The further away the object, the longer it has taken for the light to reach us, and the further back in time we are effectively looking. What we find is that the Universe has developed and changed in character over time; it has not always been as it is today. These observations are consistent with the Big Bang hypothesis.

So, summing up our findings we can say that on the basis of (i) the Hubble recession of the galaxies, (ii) the cosmic microwave background radiation, (iii) the primordial nuclear synthesis, and (iv) the time development of the Universe, the Big Bang hypothesis has gained universal acceptance. As was explained in Chapter 1, any one of these indications, considered in isolation, might not in itself have been regarded as clinching proof. Rather, it is the combination of different, independent forms of evidence that makes for the convincing case.

When did it happen?

How long ago did the Big Bang take place? Knowing how fast the galaxies are receding from us, and how far distant this motion has taken them from us, we can work out how long they must have been traveling to have reached that distance by now. This simple calculation yields a figure of about 15,000 million years. But such an estimate needs to be handled with caution. The mutual gravity acting between everything in the Universe tends to slow down the expansion. A distant galaxy will not be receding from us today as fast as it was in the past. And having traveled faster in the past, it would have taken less time to reach its current distance from us. That in turn leads to a lowering of the time to the Big Bang. A figure of about 12,000 million years is probably more realistic.

The Big Bang as the origin of the Universe

The Big Bang was such a cataclysmic event, it is natural to suppose that it marked the origin of the Universe – the moment when it all came into being.

But it does not have to be that way. I have just said how, under the influence of mutual gravity, the recessional motion of the galaxies is slowing down. It is possible that there is enough material in the Universe to bring it all to a halt one day. What would happen then? Gravity will still be operating, so now all the matter of the Universe will be drawn together – everything being squashed down to a point. We call this possibility a *Big Crunch*.

What happens after the Big Crunch is anyone's guess. The Universe might go out of existence. The alternative is that it rebounds – we get a *Big Bounce*. What we have so far been referring to as the Big Bang might in fact be no more than the most recent of the Big Bounces. The Bounces might have been going on for ever. In that case, the Big Bang would *not* have marked the origin of the Universe. In fact, such an oscillating Universe might never have had an origin – it might always have existed.

But as I said – for reasons that will become clearer later, we do not accept the oscillating Universe scenario (there is not enough material in the Universe to pull everything back together again). As for the Steady State theory – an alternative way of having a Universe that has always been in existence – we dismissed that possibility in Chapter 1. So it is we come to regard the instant of the Big Bang as marking the beginning of the Universe.

The cause of the Big Bang?

That being the case, it seems only reasonable to ask what *caused* the Big Bang.

The religious response is to say that God created the world. But, as indicated at the opening of this chapter, that is not the only possibility. There are those who argue that the world might have created itself – spontaneously. For this to have happened, two problems must be addressed:

(i) *How to get something for nothing.* This is not as difficult as one might at first think. Let me explain.

On looking at the world, we see many properties – electric charge, for example. We have seen how atoms are made of protons, neutrons, and electrons, and how every proton has positive electric charge and every electron negative electric charge. There is clearly an enormous amount of electric charge in the world. But there is no difficulty creating electric charge. In the kind of experiments I used to do at CERN (Europe's main laboratory for particle physics) in Geneva with the big particle accelerator there, electrically charged particles are created all the time. The trick is not to try and produce the particles one at a time; instead several are produced together. That way the newly created positive electric charge on certain of the particles can be balanced by an equal amount of new negative electric charge on the others. Thus, there is no *net* increase in charge.

This being so, when we look at the Universe, the question we ought to be asking is not so much "How much charge is there in the Universe?" as "How much *net* charge is there?" It is then one discovers that the answer

– very, very precisely – is *zero*. There is no net charge in the Universe.

Take another property: momentum. This is a property possessed of moving objects and crudely speaking is a measure of the ability of the object to barge other things out of its way. As such, the momentum of the object depends upon the speed at which it is traveling, and how heavy it is. Again there is no difficulty in creating momentum. Get out of your chair and start walking, and you possess momentum that you did not have when seated. This was gained by pushing with your feet against the floor. This action sent the Earth recoiling in the opposite sense with an equal and opposite momentum (not that one notices this, of course; the Earth being so much heavier than you, it does not need to acquire much speed to match your momentum). Again there has been no *net* change in momentum.

When we look at the cosmos, clearly there is a great deal of momentum out there – planets orbiting their stars, the stars orbiting the center of their swirling galaxy, the motion of the galaxies within their clusters, and the recessional speeds of the clusters themselves. But note that there is as much movement in one direction as in the opposite sense, so the net amount is again zero.

The same argument holds regarding angular momentum – a property of rotating objects. One notices that there are as many stars and galaxies rotating in one sense as in the opposite sense. Again, this yields a nil result for the net total.

What this shows is that one can have as much as one likes of any property, but it will still add up to nothing if there is an equal amount of its opposite.

But, you might be thinking: "Surely it is not possible to get rid of *everything* that way. What about this book I am reading; where is the 'negative book' to cancel out this positive one?"

Here we must draw on an insight from Einstein's theory of relativity. Energy comes in different guises: heat, electrical energy, gravitational energy, chemical energy, and so on. What Einstein showed was that matter itself is a form of energy. An object with a certain mass, denoted by m, carries within it a corresponding amount of energy, E. All this is embodied in the famous equation $E = mc^2$ (c is the speed of light, and is included simply to allow us to write mass in the same units as energy). The energy contained in the book you are reading is equivalent to that of a nuclear bomb. Fortunately it remains securely locked up. Only under special circumstances, like those giving rise to nuclear synthesis in the stars and in nuclear bombs, does a tiny fraction of the energy locked up in matter get released. In the present context, it is sufficient for us to recognize that matter – like this book – is just a form of energy.

Now an interesting characteristic of energy is that, like the other properties we have been talking about, it comes in negative as well as positive forms. Whenever two bodies are bound together, it takes an input of energy (positive energy) to separate them – to tear them apart. That energy goes toward canceling out the negative energy associated with the binding.

So how much *net* energy is there in the Universe? Obviously there is much positive energy – all that locked up in the mass of the stars, to say nothing of that associated with their motions. But we must recall that everything is attracting everything else with gravity, and that introduces negative energy. In any case, there is a certain ambiguity as to how one defines the zero level of energy. To some extent one is free to define it in any way to suit the problem being addressed. So, a plausible case can be made for claiming that the net amount of energy in the Universe – like the other net quantities we have considered – can be taken to be zero.

Summing up this line of argument we can infer that there is no difficulty in getting a Universe for nothing. Why? Because the Universe amounts to nothing – albeit an ingenious rearrangement of nothing!

Which brings us to the second main problem encountered by those who believe the Universe spontaneously created itself.

(ii) *How to bring about the ingenious rearrangement of nothing.* This too, so it is argued, need not be an insuperable difficulty. We see this in the following way.

In the days of classical Newtonian physics, it was thought that everything that happens has to have a cause. Cause is followed by effect. The effect in turn becomes the cause of the next effect down the causal chain. Thus, for example, boy throws stone (cause) leads to window breaking (effect); window breaks (cause) leads to boy sent to bed early (effect); boy sent to bed early (cause) leads to boy growing up resenting parents (effect), and so on. In Newtonian mechanics everything is predictable – at least in principle. Repeatedly setting up the identical causal event always yields exactly the same effect.

But as was mentioned in Chapter 4, with the advent of quantum theory all that changed. Thanks to Heisenberg's uncertainty relation, we now know that from a given state of affairs, one can predict only the relative *probabilities* of a whole variety of possible later states: for example, a 60 percent chance of one, a 30 percent chance of another, and a 10 percent chance of yet another. Repeatedly setting up the identical initial state will lead to *different* end results. For instance, a neutron that is not bound tightly in a nucleus – a free neutron – is an unstable particle. It changes, or decays, into a proton and an electron (plus another particle called a neutrino). It has a 50 percent chance of decaying within twelve minutes of its creation; a 25 percent chance of decaying between twelve and twenty-four minutes; a 12.5 percent chance of decaying between twenty-four and thirty-six minutes, etc. But for any particular neutron there is absolutely no way of determining in advance when exactly it will decay; one just has to wait and see. All one can deal in are relative probabilities of various possible outcomes.

This element of uncertainty – unpredictability – affects everything happening in the world. The fact that it is not obvious in everyday life is because the effects only become noticeable on the small scale. This generally means one has to be examining the behavior of individual atoms, or of sub-atomic particles like neutrons. But the uncertainty is always there. For example, it is present every time a golfer strikes a golf ball. On the scale of golf balls, however, the uncertainty relation indicates a quantum uncertainty that is tiny compared to the other vagaries involved in trying to strike the ball – even when the club is being handled by a professional.

With quantum uncertainty being the rule, some physicists have been led to propose that we can invoke it to account for the way the Universe came into being. Starting from a state of nothing, it is proposed that there could be a small but finite chance that this will be succeeded by a state consisting of a Universe (the rearranged nothing).

One has therefore only to wait around for this quantum fluctuation to occur.

But, it might be objected, we have said that quantum effects become significant only on the small scale – that associated with atoms and sub-atomic particles. The Universe is the *biggest* thing we know. Well, it is certainly big today, but according to the Big Bang theory it was not always so; it started out as an infinitesimal point – the smallest possible scale. In that condition, one might expect it to have been subject to pronounced quantum fluctuations. Thus it is envisaged that the Universe began as a minute-sized quantum event, which then promptly underwent violent expansion to become the Universe we know today.

In summary, therefore, the proposal is that we could get a Universe for nothing, via a spontaneous quantum fluctuation, without the need to invoke the active involvement of any Creator God.

The suggestion, at first sight at least, appears quite plausible. But it is not without its difficulties. For example, it is all very well talking of a quantum fluctuation, but what exactly is fluctuating if there really is nothing there to begin with? Not only that, but quantum theory was devised to account for the behavior of the component parts of the Universe. It does not by any means follow that one is justified in applying it to the Universe as a whole. Besides, the theory is intended to provide a way for an observer to order his/her measurements on that component part of the Universe. So, who in the present context is supposed to be the "observer" – an observer external to that which is being observed? Is this not by implication God once more?

A further difficulty is that if there is a finite probability of this Universe popping into existence at some point in time, why not other universes at other points in time? Is one not led to the conclusion of there being universes without number? That seems a rather extravagant claim – a costly way of getting rid of a Creator God. It is one of the characteristics of scientific investigation that one goes for the simpler, the more economical, of two rival hypotheses.

A further problem with this suggestion will arise in a short while when we come to the subject of *time*, and whether one is justified in thinking of there being a "cause" of any kind for the Big Bang.

The source of the laws

But setting aside for the moment these various objections, suppose for the sake of argument we were to concede that the world had its beginning in a quantum fluctuation; would that in fact undermine the idea of a Creator God?

I think not. It is all very well putting the Big Bang down to a quantum fluctuation, but why a *quantum fluctuation*? Why was it quantum physics that was in charge of the process rather than some other type of physics? After all, we can all dream up imaginary worlds run according to laws of nature different from our own. Science-fiction writers do it all the time. Where is quantum physics supposed to have come from? Would it not have taken a God to have set up the laws of physics in the first place – a God who *chose* the laws for bringing this world (and perhaps others) into existence?

This would put God at one step removed from the origin of the Universe. Instead of initiating the world by direct intervention, he created the law – the natural outworking of that law then being the agency for bringing the world into existence. But note: ultimate responsibility for the existence of the world would remain invested in God – the creator of the law.

Such argumentation stems from the general observation that we live in a world that is law-like – it is intelligible. It presumably did not have to be that way. It is easy enough to imagine a world that was entirely chaotic in its operation. Indeed, certain ancient creation stories describe the initial condition as being one of chaos. The Babylonian story for example describes how the god of Babylon, Marduk, had to subdue the chaos, but there remained the fear that everything was liable to revert once again to its natural chaotic condition.

Indeed, the everyday world we live in is so complex and varied that it is easy to imagine that almost anything goes. We look around us at the bewildering variety of nature: hundreds of thousands of different chemicals; vast numbers of species of animals – no two animals being exactly alike; the many patterns of movement, ever-changing, ever-evolving. It looks confused – without rhyme or reason.

It is only under close examination that this is shown not to be so. Behind this richness there lies breathtaking simplicity. For example, most of matter is made up from just a few constituent particles – neutrons, protons, and electrons. The neutrons and protons are themselves made up of quarks. The fundamental quarks and electrons are believed to have no size at all, and hence no internal structure – they couldn't be simpler.

There are a few forces: gravity; the electrical force; the magnetic force; a nuclear force for binding the nucleus together; and a weak force that causes, for instance, the neutron to decay radioactively. And that's all; except that it is not even that many forces. In the nineteenth century, Clerk Maxwell demonstrated that the electrical and magnetic forces were simply different manifestations of a single force – the electromagnetic force. And in our own time it has been shown that the weak radioactive force, like the electromagnetic force, is just a manifestation of a single force, now called the electro-weak force. So, currently, we are down to just three forces. Who knows, perhaps the time will come when we are able to recognize that these three can be whittled down to a single force. That would be very exciting and aesthetically pleasing.

Based on those few particles, with the few forces operating between them, there are a few laws of nature: conservation of momentum, conservation of angular momentum, conservation of energy, etc. Could it be that one day we shall discover that these are simply different manifestations of the operation of a single law? That would give the physicist the ultimate satisfaction.

Whether this proves to be the case or not, no one at present can say for certain. But anticipating that this is how things might indeed turn out, this law has been given a name – the Theory of Everything. I have my reservations about the use of such extravagant language – a language that seems to imply that scientists are likely one day to be able to answer all questions. Questions regarding physical behavior maybe – but not *all* questions. Nevertheless, I do share my fellow physicists' hope that perhaps the time will come when I might be able to go into class with the new intake of undergraduate physics students, write a single equation on the board and declare, "Right, that's it. Any questions? If not, file out and collect your degree."

But even if that situation were never to materialize, one thing is already certain: despite appearances, the world is run on remarkably simple lines. In other words, the world is intelligible; it just takes a bit of intelligence to recognize it.

That being so, I find myself impelled to go a step farther and ask: "If it takes intelligence to work it out, might it not have taken an Intelligence to have put it in place to begin with?"

In summary, it may well be that one can have the Universe spontaneously come into existence by itself, from nothing, via a quantum fluctuation. But a question mark remains as to:

(i) how we should interpret the intelligibility of the laws that govern the Universe's operation. Does this not point to an intelligent source?

(ii) how we should account for the laws being these particular laws, rather than some other set. Did it not take a supreme Intelligence to decide? In other words, the plain fact that the Universe is run according to a particular set of intelligible laws can, in itself, be interpreted in the context of our God experiment as evidence in favor of the existence of God. It is evidence under our very noses – and hence easily overlooked.

The origins of space

I wish now to turn to what I regard as the most intriguing aspect of the Big Bang. So far we have been speculating on what might have caused the Big Bang – a quantum fluctuation or God. But what I want to talk about now throws doubt on whether there was a cause *at all*.

In describing the Big Bang I have probably given you the idea that it was an explosion much like any other explosion – bigger, yes, but essentially the same. By that I mean that it takes place at a particular location in space. In the case of a bomb, it might be located in the left-luggage office of Euston Station in London. Following the detonation, the pieces of the bomb come flying out so as to fill up the rest of the station. But this is not how it was with the Big Bang. Not only was all of matter concentrated initially at a point, but also all of space. There was no surrounding space outside the Big Bang.

Perhaps an analogy will help. Imagine a rubber balloon. On to its surface are glued some quarters. The coins represent the galaxies. Now we blow air into the balloon. It expands. Suppose a fly were to alight on one of the coins; what would it see? All the other coins moving away from it – the further the coin, the faster it recedes into the distance. A coin twice as far away as another recedes twice as fast.

But that, of course, is the observed behavior of the galaxies – they too are receding from us in exactly that manner. So far we have thought of the galaxies as speeding away from us as they move through space. But with the balloon analogy in mind, we now have an alternative way of interpreting that motion. It is not so much the case of the galaxy moving *through* space, as the space between us and it *expanding*. The galaxy is being carried away from us on a tide of expanding space, just as the quarters are moving apart on account of the rubber in between them expanding. And just as there is no empty stretch of rubber surface "outside" the region where the coins are to be found (a region into which the coins progressively spread out), so there is no empty three-dimensional space outside where we and the other galaxies are to be found.

Note that with the particular kind of expansion we are considering, where the speed of recession is proportional to distance, the situation is the same from all vantage points. In the case of the balloon, it would not matter which particular coin the fly happened to alight upon; all the other coins are receding from it in exactly the same manner. All points on the surface are on the same footing; there is no point *in the surface* that can rightly be called the "center" of that surface. (The balloon itself does, of course, possess a center, but that is situated outside the two-dimensional space under consideration.)

Bearing in mind that this two-dimensional rubbery space is the analogue of our normal three-dimensional space, we can conclude that Hubble's Law will hold regardless of which galaxy is chosen as the point from which to measure distances, i.e., there is no point out there in three-dimensional space that can be regarded as the center of that 3-D space, i.e., the center of the Universe. There is no privileged location out there where one would be justified in erecting a blue heritage plaque announcing "The Big Bang occurred here." In truth, the Big Bang happened everywhere.

It is this interpretation of the recession of the galaxies that leads us to conclude that at the instant of the Big Bang, all the space we observe today was squashed down to an infinitesimal point. Because of this, it becomes natural to suppose that the Big Bang not only marked the origins of the contents of the Universe, it also saw *the coming into existence of space*. Space began as nothing, and has continued to grow ever since.

The origins of time

That in itself is a remarkable thought. But an even more extraordinary conclusion is in store for us. Here we have to anticipate one of the results of a subject we shall be tackling in Chapter 13. There we shall take a look at Einstein's theory of relativity. We shall discover that space and time are more alike than one would guess from the very different ways we perceive and measure them. We measure spatial distances with rulers, and intervals of time with a watch or clock. Yet despite these different approaches, there is an exceedingly close link between the two, to the extent that we speak today of time as the fourth dimension. We are all familiar with the three spatial dimensions, i.e., we can designate them as up-down, backwards-forwards, and left-right. In a way that will become clearer later, time has now to be added as the fourth dimension. For the present, it is sufficient for us to accept that space and time are as indissolubly welded together as the three spatial dimensions are to themselves. *One cannot have space without time, nor time without space.*

The reason I am telling you this now (rather than waiting until we get to Chapter 13) is because of what I said a little earlier about space itself coming into existence at the instant of the Big Bang. In the light of what I have now asserted about the indissoluble link between space and time, we can immediately proceed to the conclusion that the instant of the Big Bang must also have marked *the coming into existence of time*. This in turn means that there was no time before the Big Bang. Indeed, the very phrase *"before the Big Bang"* has no meaning. The word "before" necessarily implies a pre-existent time – but where the Big Bang is concerned, there was none.

Now, for those who seek a *cause* of the Big Bang – whether a Creator

God or some impersonal agency – there is a problem here. We have already spoken of the causal chain: cause followed by effect. Note the word "followed": it refers to a sequence of events in time – first the cause, then the effect. But in the present context we are regarding the Big Bang as the effect. For there to have been a cause of the Big Bang, it would have had to have existed prior to the Big Bang. But this we now think of as an impossibility.

Stephen Hawking has come up with an interesting variation on this. According to the above ideas, time comes into being instantaneously at the moment of the Big Bang. There is a precise instant at which the cosmic clock begins ticking. But Hawking has suggested that this might not be so. He envisages the possibility that as we imagine going back in time toward the Big Bang, we do *not* come to a sudden start to time. Instead, time in a sense "melts away." The farther back we go, the more like the other dimensions it becomes. Ultimately it becomes a dimension much like the other three spatial dimensions and one never encounters time zero.

This idea is little more than a speculation, at least for the present. But on the assumption that there is something to it, we cannot but note that this would do away with any clearly definable time marking the origin of the Universe. It was this that prompted Hawking in his bestseller *A Brief History of Time* to remark: "What place then for a creator?" – a sentence that is probably the most often quoted in the entire book.

Actually it is beside the point whether or not Hawking is right about the nature of time changing as we imagine going back toward the Big Bang. In either case, the important thing is that there is no time before the Big Bang. This alone is sufficient to get rid of the kind of Creator God that most people probably have in mind: a God who at first exists alone (or in the case of the Christian God, a God consisting of the three Persons: Father, Son, and Holy Spirit). Then at some point in time – note *in* time – God decides to create a world. The blue touch-paper is lit, there is a Big Bang, and we are on our way. God becomes the cause of the Big Bang. But as we have seen, without time before the Big Bang, there could not have been a cause in the usual sense of that word.

It has to be said that exactly the same problem confronts the alternative idea we have been discussing whereby the cause of the Big Bang is thought to have been a quantum fluctuation. According to that scheme, an initial state consisting of nothing was (thanks to the quantum fluctuation) "followed" by a world that promptly underwent the Big Bang. In the absence of any prior time, there could no more have been that kind of "initial" state (one that could undergo a quantum fluctuation), than there could have been a God. Indeed, the only kind of quantum fluctuations we know of are those that occur *in* space as well as *in* time. Prior to the Big Bang, there was neither.

So, where have we got to? Have these considerations dispensed with a Creator God? Before jumping to that conclusion, let us consider the following quotation:

> It is idle to look for time before creation, as if time can be found before time. If there were no motion of either a spiritual or corporeal creature by which the future, moving through the present, would succeed the past, there would be no time at all. . . . We should therefore say that time began with creation, rather than that creation began with time.

If the archaic expression "either a spiritual or corporeal creature" had been replaced by a more up-to-date one – such as "a physical object" – one could well have thought that the quote came from Hawking or some other modern cosmologist. In fact, those are the words of St. Augustine. (Modern cosmologists find it hard to come to terms with the fact that, where the beginning of time is concerned, it was a theologian who got there before they did – 1,500 years before!)

How did he do it – bearing in mind that St. Augustine obviously knew nothing of the Big Bang? He argued somewhat along the following lines.

How do we know that there is such a thing as time? It is because things change. Physical objects (for instance, the hands of a clock) occupy certain positions at one point in time, and move to other positions at another. If nothing moves (or in the past had ever moved), we would not be able to distinguish one point in time from another. There would be no way of working out what the word "time" was supposed to refer to; it would be a meaningless concept. *A fortiori*, if there were no objects at all, moving or stationary (because they had not been created), clearly there could be no such thing as time.

In this way, Augustine cleverly deduced that time was as much a property of the created world as anything else. And being a feature of that world, it needed to be created along with everything else. Thus it makes no sense to think of a time that existed before time began. In particular it makes no sense to think of a God capable of pre-dating the world.

The distinction between origins and creation

Despite this, Augustine remained one of the greatest Christian teachers of all time. His realization of the lack of time before creation clearly had no adverse effect on his religious beliefs. To understand why this should be so, we have to draw a distinction between the words "origins" and "creation." Whereas in normal everyday conversation we might use these terms interchangeably, in theology they acquire their own distinctive meanings.

So, for example, if one has in mind a question along the lines: "How did the world get started?" that is a question of origins. As such, it is a matter for scientists to decide, their current ideas pointing to the Big Bang description.

The creation question, on the other hand, is different. It is not particularly concerned with what happened at the beginning. Rather it is to do with: "Why is there something rather than nothing?" It is as much concerned with the present instant of time as any other. "Why are *we* here? To whom or to what do we owe our existence? What is keeping us in existence?" It is an entirely different type of question, one not concerned with the mechanics of the origin of the cosmos, but with *the underlying ground of all being.*

It is for this reason one finds that whenever theologians talk about God the Creator, they usually couple it with the idea of God the Sustainer. His creativity is not especially invested in that first instant of time (if there was one); it is to be found distributed throughout all time. We exist not because of some instantaneous action of God that happened long ago – an action that set in train all the events that have happened subsequently – an inexorable sequence requiring no further attention by God. We do not deal with a God who lights the blue touch – and *retires*. He is involved at first hand in *everything* that goes on.

As an analogy, consider a pile of books stacked one upon another on a table top. The table is in contact with just one book – the bottom one. It is this book that is being supported directly by the table. This first book then acts as the support for the second book; the second book supports the third, and so on. In the analogy, the sequence of books represents whatever exists at successive points in time, the bottom book representing the state of the world at the instant of the Big Bang. With the table representing God, this is how many people see the supporting action of God: he is directly involved only in that first instant; this is his only point of contact. With this picture in mind, it is not surprising that Hawking's suggestion that there is no first instant of time (no bottom book) sounds worrying.

But the picture presented here is *not* that of a theologian. To gain insight as to what it means to be dealing with a God who is a Sustainer as well as a Creator, we have to pick up the pile of books and lay it down on its side. Now the table directly supports each book; they are all on an equal footing. If Hawking wishes to remove the book at one end of the line, so be it; it has no effect on the others.

An atheistic response to this discussion would be to dismiss the "creation question" as meaningless. Why not simply accept the existence of the world as a brute fact? What is to be gained by saying that God created the world – that only raises in its turn the question of who created God.

This is to misunderstand how we are using the word "God." God is not an existent object. One cannot say that God exists in the same way as we say an apple exists. If that were the case, then postulating one more existent thing – God – would not be any real advance in understanding. No, the point is that God is the *source* of all existence. "God" is the name we give to whatever is responsible for the existence of things – including you and me.

So, strictly speaking, the question posed by our God experiment ought not to be "Does God exist?" but rather "What, if anything, can we meaningfully say about God, the source of all existence?" In particular, can we think of that source as being in any way personal or conscious? Does it have an interest in us, or is it rather some mindless, inanimate "force" (for want of a better word)?

A reason why many believers resist the idea of there being no God before the Big Bang is that this seems to imply that God too must have come into being at that instant. How could God have made himself?

The trouble with this is that one's conception of God is again too small. Not only are we once more mixing up existent things with the source of existence, here we are compounding the mistake by regarding God as an object confined within the limits of space and time; it assumes that God can exist only *in* time. But again that is not the traditional belief about God. Certainly God is to be found in time; we are interacting with God in time whenever we pray. But he is also *beyond* time – God *transcends* time. What I mean by this will become a little clearer when later we acquire a whole new perspective on the nature of time in the light of Einstein's theory of relativity.

Genesis creation accounts

A further concern believers might have as a result of our discussions relates to the Genesis creation story. To put it bluntly, has modern cosmology caught out the Bible with its account of the creation taking place over a period of six days? Not only does the Bible not mention anything about a Big Bang, it seems to have got its chronology hopelessly wrong. Printed on the back cover of an old family Bible I once possessed was an article by Archbishop Ussher entitled "A Chronological Index of the Years and Times from Adam unto Christ, Proved by Scripture." The author industriously adds up the ages of Adam's descendants, at the time they begat the next one in succession. He ends triumphantly with the conclusion:

> Whereupon we reckon that from Adam unto Christ are three thousand, nine hundred and seventy four years, six months and ten days.

So, adding on the 2,000 years that have occurred since Christ (and neglecting the odd ten days) we would have to conclude that the world came into existence some 6,000 years ago – rather than the 12,000 *million* years ago indicated by the recession of the galaxies.

All of this assumes that the Genesis creation account was intended as a literalistic, scientific description of the origins of the world. But was it? This seems most unlikely.

For a start we note that there is no such thing as *the* Genesis account of creation. As we saw in Chapter 6, there are two of them. They are quite different from each other; indeed, as literal accounts they would contradict each other. This in itself should be sufficient to assure us that they were never meant to be read that way.

This view is confirmed when we note that people in those days were not particularly interested in scientific questions; our modern way of describing things with literal scientific accuracy had no place in their culture. Instead, as we noted earlier, much use was made of myths. Here we need to be careful. Words have a nasty habit of changing their meaning over time. Today if we call something a "myth" we are dismissing it as untrue. In terms of Biblical criticism, the same word acquires a strictly technical meaning. It refers to an ancient narration or story, the purpose of which was to convey to future generations some deep timeless truth or truths. As such, the incidents in the story might not have taken place in exactly the way described; everyone accepted that, and it did not matter. The story was merely the vehicle for conveying the truths.

We shall be saying a good deal more about this in the next chapter when we come to consider the Adam and Eve myth in the context of the scientific account of our human origins based on the theory of evolution by natural selection. For the present, all we need to know is that we do not look to the Genesis creation stories for a rival scientific cosmology.

Nor is this some modern insight. It is *not* the case that there has had to be a retrospective reappraisal of how to read the Bible, the earlier one having been discredited by modern scientific developments. There had always been two schools of thought regarding how one should read the Bible. The first, based in Antioch, adopted a literalistic interpretation. The second, and more influential one, based in Alexandria, treated the Bible in a more allegorical manner. It included noted thinkers such as

Origen, Basil, Clement, and Gregory of Nyssa. In the fourth century BC, Gregory for instance declared:

> What man of sense would believe that there could have been a
> first, and a second, and a third day of creation, each with a
> morning and an evening, before the Sun had been created?

(The Sun was supposedly created on the fourth day.)

What kind of truths are contained in the creation myths? In the first place, the world needed to be created. It has not always existed and it need not have existed. In other words, the world is contingent; its existence is not necessary. This in itself is an important notion. The ancient Greek philosophers reckoned that everything could be worked out by pure thought. They did not have to look at the world to discover what it was like. With sufficient intelligence they ought to be able to work it all out from first principles, or from common sense. The world was the way it was because that is how it *had* to be; there was no other way for it to be.

The Judaeo-Christian starting-point was quite different. The world existed because God decided to make it. It was up to God whether there should be a world, and if so, what kind it should be. This in turn means that anyone who wishes to find out what the world consists of and how it operates has to *look* at it – or in modern terminology, has to carry out experimental investigations on it to see which type of world God decided to make. This is a totally different mind-set to that of the Greeks and of other ancient civilizations. For this reason there seems some justification in the view, often expressed these days, that the Judaeo-Christian religious mind-set was the necessary forerunner for modern science to get started. In other words, the reason why science took off in the West (whereas it had not done so to anything like the same extent in other civilizations – civilizations that were in other respects as highly cultured and advanced) was that the religion of the West pointed the way to a mode of thinking firmly rooted in experiment. Far from science and religion being in conflict with each other, it was religion that helped give birth to science. Certainly when one considers the early scientists – for example, those who originally founded the Royal Society (the leading professional body of scientists in the UK) – one is struck by the number who were prominent church people and devout believers. They clearly had no difficulty reconciling their religious beliefs with their scientific activities. And, as you will be aware by now, one of the main reasons for my writing this book is to refocus attention on the way theology, in common with science, rests on an experimental underpinning.

A second feature of the Genesis creation stories is how the world is pictured as an ordered one. Remember how the Babylonian creation story told of a world of chaos. The Judaeo-Christian belief in an inherently intelligible world acted as an additional spur for later scientists to try and enunciate that intelligibility. Because of this intelligibility, the kind of world attested to in Genesis is one where the decisions we humans make lead to *foreseeable* outcomes. We are therefore to be held *responsible* for our actions in a way that would not be the case if the world were chaotic and nothing was predictable.

A third feature of the myth is that God is pictured as a personal deity. God knows what he is doing.

Fourthly, God sees that the world is good. The Genesis story is an optimistic, positive account of creation. Despite the many disasters that befall us humans – volcanic eruptions, hurricanes, floods, earthquakes, famine, etc. – in a deep sense the world is good; it is good to be alive.

Which brings us to one final feature: we ourselves owe our existence to God. Our lives are not given to us to live in whatever way we fancy. God gave us life for a purpose, and we should live it the way he wants.

These then are some of the enduring insights contained in the Genesis myths. It is for conveying these kinds of truth that they were first formulated, and why they remain as relevant for us today as they ever did. The myths of creation complement the scientific accounts of our origins.

10

Human Origins

So far we have concentrated on the Universe and how it had its origins in the Big Bang. But how is the Creator God supposed to have created ourselves – human beings?

Many would turn to the Bible for an answer – the Adam and Eve story. Adam, we are told, was formed by God out of the dust of the ground; Eve followed later, being fashioned from a rib taken from Adam's side. Recent polls held in the USA indicate that almost half those interviewed accept this as a literal account of our beginnings. One doubts that anything like that proportion would apply to the UK. Though it does have to be said that the part of the church that is growing fastest at the present time is that section where acceptance of the literal interpretation of Genesis figures prominently.

But the Genesis story, of course, bears little relation to the modern scientific account of our origins – that based on Darwin's theory of evolution by natural selection, as subsequently refined and developed by later workers.

The theory of evolution by natural selection

On a number of previous occasions, I have had cause to refer to this theory. Let us now examine it in closer detail.

It begins with the observation that offspring resemble their parents. The parental characteristics are encoded in the genes each parent contributes to the offspring at its conception. At the birth of a baby, the parents' relations debate endlessly whether the color of the baby's eyes or hair comes from their side of the family or the other – and which side should be blamed for the sticking-out ears. Later there will be arguments as to where the child's intelligence, musical ability, or temper have come from. To a large extent the child appears to be a mixture of the two parents' characteristics, plus others that appear to have more in common with those of the grandparents (we hear of characteristics that "skip a generation"), and yet others that are unique to the child. So, although offspring resemble their parents in various ways, there will also be differences between siblings.

We now have a good understanding as to how this comes about. Recapping from an earlier chapter, we note that the inherited characteristics are encoded in a molecule called the DNA molecule. It is in the form of a double helix – like two bedsprings enmeshed together. The long chain of this complex molecule is made up of an amalgamation of smaller molecules. It is the order in which these smaller molecules occur along the sequence that constitutes the code for determining the individual's physical characteristics. As the code has been copied from those of the parents, it is clear why there should be the similarities between parents and children. But in the copying process, mistakes sometimes occur; what is passed on to the child is not an exact replica of the parent's original. Thus new codes arise, and these in turn lead to novel physical characteristics. As we shall be seeing, these variants provide the all-important material on which the process of natural selection gets to work.

These considerations, of course, are not unique to humans. There are analogous similarities between parents and offspring throughout the animal kingdom. All animals have their characteristic DNA codes dictating the kind of animal they are to be. And as with humans, there will be mistakes in copying the DNA, leading to new physical characteristics.

In situations where food and shelter are in short supply, as is often the case, not all animals of a particular generation will be able to survive. Certain individuals will be fortunate in that their inherited characteristics confer upon them some survival advantage over their fellows. For example, a young cheetah that happens by chance to inherit a gene that endows it with an above-average ability to run fast, is the one more likely to catch and kill the scarce prey. Thus it has a better chance of surviving to an age where it can mate than some other cheetah that is less well endowed. In mating, the fortunate cheetah will pass on to its offspring the self-same advantageous "fast-running" gene that helped in its own survival. The less advantageous gene, on the other hand, tends to die out since the cheetah to whom it belonged has less chance of mating and passing it on. So we would expect the next generation of cheetahs to be somewhat faster runners on average than the previous one. And with each new generation, the process repeats itself once more, leading to yet faster-running cheetahs in each succeeding generation.

And what goes for fast running will hold for any characteristic that confers on its holder an edge in the competition to survive – sharp claws and teeth, strong jaws, powerful wings, a tough defensive skin or hard shell, greater intelligence, etc. In this way, over the course of time, we find that the cumulative changes become so great that, in effect, one type of animal has developed into another. In other words, one species of animals descends from another that was different from itself.

The fact that evolution has happened – to some extent – is indisputable. We know this because evolution is still taking place today all around us. An often quoted example is that of peppered moths (*Biston betularia*) living in industrial areas. Over the years their coloring has become darker. This is because the surfaces on which they habitually come to rest became progressively dirtier. Those moths that by chance had somewhat darker markings than the average had a greater chance of escaping the attention of predators; to some extent they were camouflaged. As a result, they had a good chance of surviving to the point where they could pass on the gene corresponding to that darker color to their offspring. The lighter-colored variety of moth, being more inclined to get killed before mating, had less chance of passing its gene on. Thus, over the years, the color of the species has progressively changed; it has evolved.

The evolution of humans

What about the evolution of humans? We descended from something like an ape. This ape-like creature in its turn had come from a small insectivorous mammal, that from a reptile, that from a fish, and so on, right back to a bacterium. Even that is not thought to be the beginning of the evolutionary trail. Most biologists today hold that evolution goes right back to inanimate matter – to chemicals or, if you like, to plain dirt or mud. They think of life emerging from some kind of primordial slime.

This suggestion as to our earliest origins receives some corroboration when one examines the composition of the gases and dust clouds to be found in the space between stars. They consist of many different kinds of molecule. Some of these are found to be exactly those that act as the basic building blocks of living creatures here on Earth. The raw materials for life are therefore spread throughout space. The scene appears to have been set from the earliest times for life to develop on planets like Earth.

Yet many people find it totally unbelievable that something as complicated as a human being could have evolved from inanimate primordial slime, without the intervention of an intelligent designer of some kind. The Argument from Design had long been held as an important way of arguing with skeptics that there has to be a God. After all, if one came across a watch lying on the beach, one could immediately infer that it must have been made by a watchmaker. Something as complicated and highly organized as that could not have arisen spontaneously. Thus, in similar vein, it was argued that everything about the bodies of humans, and of other animals, is so well suited to its function (with the possible exception of the appendix!) that it must have been deliberately designed by someone with that function in mind – and that someone must, of course, have been God. Hence one has to believe in God.

Even Darwin himself, in his book *The Origin of Species*, expressed a measure of concern as to how something as complicated as the eye could have evolved. And yet he was confident that it must have evolved somehow. It was not a matter of a fully formed eye suddenly appearing by chance. Rather, it had to be a case of a whole sequence of small changes being strung together, each small change conferring some incremental advantage. Over the course of time, the chain eventually added up to the eye as we know it today.

Even so, many still find it totally implausible that one could go all the way from slime to intelligent humans purely by chance occurrences. The answer to such objections is that although the mistakes in the copying of DNA do indeed take place purely at random, and these lead to random variations in physical characteristics, that is only half the story. One has also to take into account the selective manner in which the advantageous changes are preserved at the expense of the disadvantageous ones. This is not a random process; it is *systematic*.

Perhaps an analogy will help: In my garden I have a huge, 150-year-old oak tree. Normally I love the old thing. But in the autumn it is an absolute nuisance. It dumps a carpet of brown leaves over the entire garden. The leaves are spread out at random everywhere. It would of course be much more convenient for me if they came down in neat piles waiting for me to collect them up and put them on the compost. So what do I do? Do I immediately set to and rake over the whole area? No. There's no point in getting old if you don't get crafty with it. I leave them for a while. We are situated on the top of a hill. It can be very windy. The wind swirls in from all directions. Thus we have winds from random directions blowing leaves that have been dumped randomly. What happens? To a large extent they conveniently gather themselves into neat, organized piles ready for me to collect up! Order emerges out of chaos. How does this come about – without any help from an intelligent, purposive gardener? Simple: there are certain regions in my garden that are comparatively sheltered – odd corners next to the shed, or against the walls of the house – especially the angle between the studio extension and the living room. It is easy for a leaf to be blown into these areas but, once there, it is not subject to a wind that will blow it out again. Once it lands up there, that is where it will stay. One might say that, in a sense, that particular location for the leaf has "survival value." Thus, over time, more and more leaves accumulate in these preferred areas. Which is exactly what I want to happen – it makes life much easier for me.

So it is with evolution: it is no more likely that an advantageous gene will arise than a disadvantageous one (indeed, given the random nature of the process, it is much more likely that a change will have a deleterious effect – there generally being more ways of getting something wrong than there are of getting it right). But the process of natural selection operates in such a way that once an advantageous change does occur, it is likely to be perpetuated, whereas the disadvantageous ones, by their nature, have a tendency not to be retained. In this way it is wrong to object to evolution on the grounds that it is all down to chance. It is not.

The second factor to be taken into account when assessing the likelihood or otherwise of going from slime to humans is the enormous time-scale over which evolution has operated. From radioactive dating techniques it has been shown that the Earth, along with the rest of the Solar System, formed 4,600 million years ago (some 7,000 million years after the Big Bang). Exceedingly primitive life forms (bacteria) probably put in an appearance about 3,000 million years ago. Modern humans emerged from primitive ancestors only in the past 100,000 years.

To get that into perspective, we note that if the history of the Earth were in imagination reduced to one year, then our primitive ancestors came on the scene at about 10 p.m. on December 31, modern humans at 10 minutes to midnight, and you and I at half a second before midnight tolled the end of the year.

Compared to the evolution of humans, the changing of color of a moth is, of course, a very modest evolutionary change. But when it is realized that, on the reduced time-scale we have been considering, the moths achieved this transformation in no more than a fraction of a second, we begin to glimpse that unimaginably large changes could have occurred over the vast tracts of time that have been available to evolution.

Life from the non-living

But you might be asking, "How can life come from that which is not living?"

There are many who regard life as something so special that it is beyond the province of science to investigate at all. They would claim that scientists will never succeed in taking inanimate chemicals and converting them into something that is living – and this means it would be even less likely that this could have happened spontaneously in the past without intelligent intervention. Life, so it is held, is a special non-physical quality that is in the gift of God alone. But is it?

When it comes to drawing a distinction between living and non-living objects there is clearly no difficulty in classifying humans, cats, dogs, fish, and oak trees as living, and water, rocks, trains, and buildings as non-living. It is when we come to much simpler objects that problems can arise. Yeast, for instance, can be bought in shops as a powder in a packet, and yet it is alive. Viruses, such as a flu virus, can be made into inert crystalline preparations much like sugar or salt. But they also reproduce (after a fashion), this making it difficult for biologists to know quite how they should be classified.

There is in fact no single criterion for deciding what is living. Living objects usually have more than one characteristic in common. These distinguishing characteristics include *nutrition* (the ability of the body to take in substances from the environment and use them to promote growth and to provide energy for the body's activities); *growth,* with changes in shape as well as in size; *respiration* (the process of taking in substances, like oxygen, and using them as sources of energy); *excretion* (the ability to get rid of waste products); *responsiveness* (the characteristic of reacting to stimuli coming from the environment); and *reproduction,* whether that involves sex or otherwise.

Inanimate objects can exhibit one or more of these characteristics. A piece of iron, for instance, will react to a damp atmosphere by becoming rusty; ice crystals will grow by freezing the surrounding liquid water; a computer virus will reproduce itself on gaining access to another computer system. As I said, there is no single watertight criterion by which one can judge whether something is living or not. Rather it becomes a matter of looking for a cluster of criteria to be satisfied. Biologists cannot even agree on what exactly the set of criteria should be. The list given above is just one attempt to do this. Thus, it can become a genuine problem as to how to categorize something as simple as a virus. Strictly speaking, a virus cannot reproduce *itself*; what it has to do is infect an animal and get the animal to manufacture the virus material on its behalf. In this way it becomes a moot point whether the virus really has satisfied the relevant condition to do with reproduction.

Thus, there exist today uncertain gray areas, bridging the gap separating the clearly identifiable living from the clearly identifiable non-living. This surely makes it all the more reasonable to suppose that in the far-off evolutionary past, the world imperceptibly developed from an exclusively non-living environment, through a transitional phase containing something as simple as our current viruses (but *not* our actual modern viruses), to a state where the first clearly living plants and animals were present. Thus, the living evolved out of the non-living.

Evidence from the fossil record and from DNA sequencing

The clinching evidence for our evolutionary past could of course come only from a complete fossil record charting all the minute changes that have marked the development of the human species through its antecedent species, and back to the primordial slime. But the record has many gaps in it. Although the gaps are continually being narrowed with the making of ever more finds, it is unlikely ever to be complete. For instance, not all past primitive species are expected to have left fossils; and some of those that were left have subsequently been irrevocably destroyed. In this regard we have to bear in mind that the surface of the Earth is continually shifting and reforming itself. The surface of the Earth is made up of crustal "plates" floating on top of molten rock (rather like the skin on custard). The plates move about and collide with each other. Sometimes they buckle to form mountain ranges. Sometimes they get caught up with each other where their boundaries come into contact; the sudden release of the built-up tension is what causes earthquakes. In some locations, one plate is pushed under its neighbor, carrying everything on and near its surface – including any fossils – underground and into the molten rock beneath. For this reason we have to expect that some vital links in the fossil record will have been lost for ever.

An alternative approach is offered by the study of DNA sequencing. To some extent we can determine how close we are to other species by comparing our respective DNA. Thus, for example, quite independently of the fossil record allowing us to trace our ancestry back to primitive ancestors we have in common with chimpanzees and gorillas, we can note that 99 percent of our human DNA is identical to that of chimpanzees and gorillas. That alone is a measure of how closely related we are to them. And the fact that certain DNA sequences are common to *all* living animals and plants appears to be a clear sign that we all have a common ancestry in primitive life forms if we go back far enough.

Problems remaining

Having said this, I do not mean to gloss over the difficulties remaining.

It is hard to understand how, at various points along the evolutionary path leading up to humans, certain crucial steps were negotiated – for example, the formation of the first cell. There can also be disagreements about the way progress is made in evolution. For example, whether it is a matter of smooth, continual, steady change, or whether the changes occur in fairly rapid bursts, interspersed by rather lengthy periods of time when not much change is happening – the so-called "punctuated equilibrium" scenario. If it is the latter, then this will make it even more difficult to find the fossils relating to the brief transitional stages marking the change from one clearly defined species to its successor. This might be a contributory cause as to why there are so many crucial gaps in the record.

And yet, despite these reservations, I join with the vast majority of scientists in fully accepting that we humans, and the other species we have today, are the products of evolution by natural selection.

Biblical interpretation

But of course not everyone is happy to accept evolution. I mentioned at the outset the large number of people who continue to adhere to a literal understanding of the Adam and Eve account. So it is now time to address this issue. How ought we in fact to interpret what we read in the Bible? I have already said a little about this, but now it is time to go into it in more depth.

The first thing one has to recognize about the Bible is that it is not a book, but a whole library of different types of writings: history, biography, songs, statements of law, poetry, theological reflection, collections of sayings and proverbs, and so on. Just as it would be foolish to enter a public library today, take books down from the shelves at random, and read them all in exactly the same frame of mind, regardless of whether one was reading a work of fiction, a history textbook, poetry, a science book, etc., so one should not expect to be able to open the Bible at random and just start reading without first considering what the intention of the author might have been. Finding that out is often no easy matter. We need to be guided by Biblical scholars who have made a lifelong study of the culture and practices of people living long ago.

Only when one has steeped oneself in the mind-set of those who lived 2,000 to 4,000 years ago, can one begin to appreciate what they were really trying to get across in their writings.

Does that mean, for example, if one has identified a piece of writing as setting out an episode in the history of the Jewish people, that one can immediately go ahead and read it, and judge it, as one would a piece of modern historical writing? No. The writers' approach to history was radically different from ours. Whereas we put great store on trying to get the facts right – what people actually did and said, where they did it and on what date – ancient writers would have been inclined to dismiss such an approach as irrelevant – a pointless exercise. What possible use could such a cold recitation of facts have? How boring. For them history was intended to be uplifting and inspiring. Great heroes of the past – such as Moses and David – were held up as examples to the young. If a little elaboration would make the account more effective in bringing about desirable attitudes in the readers, such as emulating worthy role models and having pride in one's nation, then why not? This process of enhancing figures of the past was so prevalent that it is nowadays wondered whether some of these people even existed – whether their supposed deeds and victories in battle were just an amalgam of various people's achievements. Such practices might strike our modern mind as exceedingly dubious, if not fraudulent. But surely it is not if everyone is aware of what is going on; if everyone knows what the underlying intention is.

Another aspect of Jewish historical writings we gleaned from Chapter 6 was that they were primarily concerned with the developing relationship between the Jewish people and their God. Historical fact and theological interpretation were inextricably intertwined in a way that would be most unusual in an historical account written today. Thus, even the identification of a piece of writing as being largely historical in character still leads to difficulties of interpretation for those unaware of the hidden agendas that make ancient historical writings so different from our own.

The role of story

So it is we come to the Adam and Eve account of our human origins. What kind of writing is that meant to be?

One kind it *cannot* be is a scientific treatise. Ancient civilizations simply did not think or reason in accordance with modern scientific practice. No, the Adam and Eve account is an example of myth. Earlier we discussed the subject of myth in connection with the two accounts of the creation of the world in the first two chapters in Genesis. There we used the word "myth" in its original, technical sense to refer to an ancient story that acted as a vehicle for conveying deep, timeless truths. Although myths described events that might not have actually happened as such – not in the literal manner described – that did not matter because a literal account had never been the intention behind them.

You might have been prompted to wonder why the ancients should have adopted such a procedure. Why not simply write down what they had to say in plain language which everyone could read and understand – without the need to *interpret* it? Why run the risk of causing confusion over readers mistaking the dividing line between the fictional story-line on the one hand, and the inner spiritual content on the other?

Here we have to recognize that for much of the time that these stories were in circulation, they were not written down, as the majority of people could neither read nor write. Whatever wisdom one wished to pass on from one generation to the next had to be done orally – by word of mouth.

But we all know how difficult it is to remember oral messages. Recall the game of "telephone" where a chain of children have progressively to pass on a certain message by whispering it into a neighbor's ear. A comparison is then made between the final version and the original, often with hilarious results (even in the absence of someone mischievously distorting the message on purpose).

We must not imagine that ancient people were as bad as we are today at remembering what we have been told. They made a point of training people in learning things by rote. We on the other hand, in accordance with modern educational thinking, tend to downplay such training. Nevertheless, despite their greater skills at rote learning, the ancients still had a problem transmitting information down through the ages without progressive distortions taking place.

In this respect they noted that there was one kind of narration the human mind was especially good at remembering – a *story*. There is something about a story-line that is particularly memorable – the way thinking about one event prompts the recollection of what happens next, which in turn prompts the recollection of the next incident, and so on. So there grew up the custom of passing on truths in story form – stories that translated abstract theological ideas into concrete analogies, using vivid imagery.

It was a custom that was to be perpetuated. We see this in the teachings of Jesus. There we don't refer to the stories as "myths" but as "parables." The tradition is continued in our own days. We have only to think of George Orwell's *Animal Farm* or William Golding's *Lord of the Flies*. In neither case does it matter whether the events described actually happened as such. (Animals talking!?) That was not their point. Both stories have powerful messages to convey about human nature.

The truths behind the Adam and Eve myth

What then are the timeless spiritual truths conveyed in the Genesis myth of Adam and Eve?

In the first place we note that the name Adam is no ordinary name – not like John or Paul, say. It means "man." So straight away we have the clue that what we are reading applies not to an individual but to humankind in general.

Adam is placed in the garden of Eden. He is not there to sit around having an easy time of it; he is there to tend it, to look after it. Perhaps one can see in this something of the modern Green message – a vision of stewardship we urgently need to recapture in our own times where, through the power that has come from scientific and technological advance, we now have the ability to transform for good or ill the garden we call planet Earth.

Eve is described as being made from a rib taken from Adam's side. This is pointing us to the nature of marriage – the idea that man is not complete without woman, nor woman complete without man. Again, as we see the institution of marriage – the idea of making a binding commitment to a partner – coming under increasing threat, this is another message as relevant for our own times as it was in the past.

Then we have the strange story of the taking of the forbidden fruit. The couple were expressly told not to eat of that particular tree. They had no need of it; they were amply provided with alternative food. And yet they rebelled against this injunction. Rather than do what God wanted of them, they decided they would please themselves regardless. They had no right to the fruit – it did not belong to them – and yet they greedily, selfishly took it. In the words of the song for which Frank Sinatra was most famous: "I did it *my* way."

What this is telling us is that humans are basically selfish and self-centered. No matter how perfect the surroundings in which we find ourselves, there is a mean streak in us that is bound to spoil that paradise. We read how Adam and Eve were banished from the garden of Eden, never to return. The same was to apply to their descendants – you and me. From that time, humankind was to be under a kind of curse. We are condemned never to be able to regain paradise on Earth. From the moment of conception we have built into us the seeds of selfishness; we are born self-centered rather than God-centered.

This idea is formulated in the religious notion of "original sin." While we might be inclined to assume that all babies are born perfect, and when they eventually fail to live up to that standard, the blame can be put down wholly to a bad environment or upbringing, Genesis says no. Even if it were possible for children to live a cocooned existence, protected from all undesirable external influences, they would still turn out to be sinful and self-centered. That is their basic make-up – their intrinsic nature from the moment of conception.

Original sin in the light of evolution

The doctrine of original sin has never been popular – for obvious reasons. But, with the insights that come from the modern understanding of our evolutionary origins, we can begin to appreciate how that doctrine does in fact make a lot of sense.

So far, we have seen how our physical make-up is determined by the codes to be found in our DNA molecule. But that is only part of the picture. In the evolutionary struggle it is no good for a cat to have sharp claws if it does not know what to do with them. A cat that has in addition a natural, unthinking, automatic tendency to hunt and use those claws to kill suitable prey has a clear advantage over another that has to reason everything out from the beginning each time it is faced with the opportunity of a meal. Accordingly, besides there being survival value in having certain inherited physical characteristics, there would also be survival value were certain inherent behavior traits to be passed on. And as we noted earlier, that is in fact what happens. Certain of the codes in the DNA are to do with behavior that is conducive to survival. In fact, it appears that a great deal of animal behavior is genetically influenced; it is behavior the individual did not have to learn from its own limited experience of life. As part of its inherited survival kit, the animal comes to some extent "pre-programmed." It instinctively operates in ways that assist it to survive to the point where it, in its turn, can pass that same genetically influenced behavior trait on to its own offspring.

Genetically influenced behavior helps us to understand much of what is going on in the animal kingdom. In Chapter 5, when we first introduced the subject, we noted the hunting behavior of today's domesticated cat, and the manner in which the baby kangaroo, on being born, instinctively heads up its mother's fur to the pouch awaiting it. These and many other behavior traits in animals were vital to the survival of their ancestors. Because the ancestors had these traits, today's animal also has them – even though, in the case of the domesticated cat, the hunting instinct is now no longer needed.

Once one accepts that we humans are also a form of animal – a product of the same evolutionary process – we can begin to learn things about ourselves by studying the behavior of other animals. If we find that their behavior is to some extent influenced by their genes, then we must expect the same to be true of ourselves. Genetically influenced behavior is something we earlier recognized to be connected to the Jungian idea of a collective unconscious. Given the nature of the evolutionary struggle, if there is survival value in selfishly grabbing limited food supplies for oneself, and for one's close kin, regardless of the consequences to others, that is a behavior trait that is likely to be preserved and passed on.

So, what we find is that the theory of evolution, far from discrediting the Adam and Eve story, actually backs up one of its important spiritual truths about ourselves: namely, that we must expect to find a measure of self-centeredness in us – from the moment of conception. Before the theory came along one just had to accept, as a matter of observation, that that was the way humans behaved. Now, thanks to evolutionary theory, we can understand the mechanism.

Competing interpretations of Genesis

Earlier, in connection with the creation myths, we saw how this non-literal way of interpreting the early Genesis writings was not new. Recall how St. Augustine had already worked out that there could have been no time before the world had been created. We noted that he must have had a quite sophisticated appreciation of what it meant to regard God as creator (God not being a pre-existent "cause").

St. Augustine also had a presentiment that Adam's arriving on the scene fully formed did not seem right. Indeed, he advocated that in the beginning there were only the germs or causes of the forms of life which were afterward to be developed in gradual course. It was an evolutionary theory – of a sort! Naturally, this should not be taken to imply that St. Augustine got there before Darwin. What he had in mind bore no relation to an evolutionary theory incorporating the mechanism of natural selection. But Augustine's views on the subject confirm what we noted in the last chapter, namely that one does need to exercise care over the interpretation of Genesis. One cannot simply take it at face value and read it with our modern scientifically conditioned mind-set; one must do a little probing to get back to the authors' original intentions.

This is the view of the majority of Biblical scholars. Yet it is a view not universally held. There remains today a strong literalistic school of thought. Repeated attempts continue to be made to have the teaching of evolution in US schools, if not banned, then downplayed, with the theory presented as no more than a speculative hypothesis. Coupled with this is the attempt to accord equal time to the teaching of so-called "creation science" – with the Adam and Eve story put across as a rival scientific account of our origins.

The advocates of this view are obviously well-intentioned; they act out of a deep sense of reverence for the Bible; and they sincerely believe they are defending the original interpretation of the Bible. What they do not seem to recognize is that the strictly literalistic interpretation of Genesis rose to prominence only as late as the sixteenth century – the time of the Reformation. How did this come about?

Disillusioned by the way power was being wielded in Rome, the Protestants, under the leadership of people like Martin Luther, broke away from the rule of the Pope. Their authority for taking such a step? The Bible. From now on, the ultimate authority rested with Holy Scripture, not with the Pope. Those remaining loyal to Rome, not to be outdone, reaffirmed that their respect for the Pope in no way diminished their acceptance of the authority of the Bible. One side vied with the other as to who most truly reverenced the Bible. In the process, it became more and more difficult to question any feature of the Bible: one's standing as a Christian depended on how much of the Bible one could accept unquestioningly. In the 1540s, the Roman Catholic church set up the Council of Trent primarily with the aim of clarifying its position on aspects of belief challenged by the Protestants. From this council a statement was issued to the effect that God was to be regarded as "the author" of the Bible – both the Old and New Testaments. The writings had been produced "at the dictation of the Holy Spirit." In other words writers such as Matthew, Mark, Luke, and John had simply acted as secretaries taking down dictation.

It is hard to understand how such an attitude toward Scripture could have come about. After all, when one gospel is compared to another, it is not difficult to find manifest contradictions – the type of discrepancies one would expect in comparing the recollections of different people some thirty or more years after the event (which is when the gospels were written). For example, did the disciples have to go to Galilee in order to meet Jesus after his Resurrection, as Matthew and Mark say, or did he appear to them in Jerusalem, as Luke and John would have us believe? A small point admittedly, but one we might expect God to have got right – if indeed the words had come directly from him. Not only are there these discrepancies, there are changes of writing style, and even examples, so I am told, of bad grammar.

It was this hard, uncompromising line the church had taken toward the Bible that did much to bring about the Galileo affair. In our earlier discussion of that episode we examined some of the background that had led to the notorious trial. It is relevant to add that the trial took place not long (some seventy years) after this shift in attitude toward the Bible. Martin Luther had already denounced the Copernican theory (that it was the Earth that went round the Sun rather than the reverse) by appealing to the Bible:

> This fool wishes to reverse the entire science of astronomy; but Sacred Scripture tells us that Joshua commanded the Sun to stand still, and not the Earth.

Given the prevailing climate of the time, where no one wished to be thought of as taking a casual attitude toward the Bible, one can appreciate that the situation needed especially careful handling – a sensitivity beyond the capability of the forthright Galileo.

Fortunately the Roman Church's attitude has been modified since those times. In 1965, at the Second Vatican Council, it was stressed that it was not the words themselves that had come directly from God, but rather it was a case of the writers of the words having been *inspired* by the Holy Spirit – they had written under the influence of God:

> . . . the interpreter of sacred Scripture, in order to see clearly what God wanted to communicate to us, should carefully investigate what meaning the sacred writers really intended, and what God wanted to manifest by means of their words.

Thus, we can see that when modern-day fundamentalists defend a literalistic interpretation of Genesis, it is not that they are getting back to the original understanding of Scripture, but one that gained the ascendancy in the Reformation – one more likely to be a *mis*interpretation.

To some extent one can appreciate the attraction of the literalistic interpretation. I know many fundamentalists; they live deeply religious lives and have a genuine relationship with God. Indeed, I sometimes find myself envying them their buoyant, joyful type of faith. (I myself probably agonize too much over my beliefs!) They show great love and respect for the Bible – which is only to be applauded. But I suspect that many of them fear that once they start to question some aspect of the

Bible – once they approach it in a *critical* sense, allowing for the possibility that some of it might not be true in the literal sense – then they are on a slippery slope. Where is one to draw the line? Is there not a danger the baby goes out with the bath water?

It is an understandable concern. Where interpretation is concerned there are bound to be differences of opinion. But a blanket literal approach to the Bible is itself an interpretation. The line *has* to be drawn somewhere, and I believe that the one place it cannot be drawn is where the literalists draw it.

Now you might respond to this by asking, "Does it matter what they think? If, as you say, they enjoy a genuine, joyful, loving relationship with God – if they are effective in attracting growing numbers of people into the church and into loving relationships with God with their simple, straightforward, uncomplicated beliefs – where's the harm?"

I think it is all very well pointing to those who are attracted by this approach to religious belief, but what of those who are *repelled* by it? I know that the attitudes toward religion of several of my academic colleagues in the biological sciences are significantly colored by their need to be constantly defending the integrity of their work from attacks by religious fundamentalists. If I as a physicist had been faced with attempts to pass a law that compelled me to downplay the convincing nature of the evidence for the Big Bang, and even worse, afford the six-day creation story as much time in the physics curriculum as is at present devoted to the Big Bang theory, it would have done nothing toward helping me to take religion seriously.

In summary, what I am saying is that there is absolutely no need to see religion and science on a collision course over the subject of human origins. To my mind the only course of action a religious believer can take – with intellectual integrity – is to accept that, with all its possible faults and deficiencies, evolution by natural selection is currently our best scientific description of our origins. We can regard it as God's way of bringing us into existence. It is then up to us to use that knowledge to discover more about ourselves and about God's ways of working.

Further Insights from Evolution

The Biblical Fall

We have already noted a correspondence between, on the one hand, self-centered genetically influenced behavior, and on the other, the religious notion of original sin contained in the Adam and Eve story. But what of the Fall? The Fall is the idea, contained in the same Biblical account, that initially all was well – Adam and Eve living a happy life in paradise. Only later did they spoil this sinless state when they ate the forbidden fruit. How does this ideal first state fit in with the theory of evolution?

In a nutshell, I don't think there ever was such a state. That certainly would not be part of the evolutionary scenario as we know it. But that is not to say that the Bible was wholly wrong on that count. There *was* a crucial stage of development that clearly delineated our present state from another that preceded it. I refer to the emergence of self-consciousness – that stage in our evolutionary history when for the first time a creature acquired a brain sufficiently complex for it to become consciously aware of itself.

How this came about we do not know. As we have had cause to note previously, the nature of the relationship between the physical brain and the mind remains a mystery. The activities of the brain are described in terms of electrical currents and chemical changes; those of the mind consist of thoughts and feelings. But whatever the nature of that relationship, we do know there must have been a point in the evolutionary past where there was some kind of crossing over from unthinking matter to mental beings.

Although one cannot be sure, it probably began with a mental awareness of feelings such as pain, fear, hunger, cold, satisfaction, etc. These were possessed by what we might regard as the first primitive animals. In time the thoughts became progressively more sophisticated and complex. No longer confined to simple automatic mental reactions to stimuli, they began to include powers of reasoning. In particular there would, at some stage or other, have developed an awareness of oneself as an entity in one's own right – as distinct from the environment. There would be the recognition that the environment was partly made up of creatures similar to oneself, but distinct from oneself. This was the acquisition of self-awareness.

Somewhere along the line would come the ability to make decisions – conscious decisions. Although the tendency to behave in certain pre-programmed ways according to the dictates of the genes would still be there, for the first time there would have arisen the ability consciously to decide to act differently from the dictates of one's inherited traits. Whereas the behavior of more primitive animals might be spoken of as genetically *determined*, now it was no longer the case. Genetically *influenced*, certainly; but no longer determined.

This coming into existence of an ability to act otherwise than in conformity with one's inborn instincts marked an important transition – one that I suggest can be seen as evolution's equivalent of the Biblical Fall. Up to this point, the world had indeed been *sinless*, as the Bible would have us believe. But this was not because everything had been perfect. It was because prior to this transition stage it would have been a misuse of the word to describe any action as "sinful." One can hardly speak of "sin" in the absence of any alternative choice of action. Exactly the same kind of situation would arise today were one to describe a domestic cat as "evil and wicked" when it kills innocent birds. How could it really be held culpable if it knew no other way of behaving?

The point in evolutionary development where it truly became possible for a creature consciously to decide to act in a moral manner, marked a watershed. From here on, "sin" became a *meaningful* concept. Sin entered the world, not as a dramatic change from a previous state of peace and harmony to the one we find ourselves in today, but when primitive humans were able for the first time to be held *accountable for their actions*.

The image of God

But that in turn raises another question: why should we in any case *wish* to act differently from what our genes would have us do?

This is where another Biblical insight comes to the fore: that not only were we fashioned out of the dust of the ground (in itself literally true if we think of "the dust" as being "the primordial slime"), but we are also spoken of as being made "in the image of God" – we have within us the potential to be God-like. One must stress the word *potential*, because being God-like does not happen as a matter of course. As the Christian rite of baptism affirms, we have to "repent and turn to Christ." We noted earlier that the word "repent" means more than simply feeling sorry for what one has done; it has much more to do with changing one's mind; having a change of heart; resolving to act differently in the future. Like the prodigal son, one has consciously to decide to "come home"; one has to *decide* to become God-centered rather than remain self-centered.

The idea of being made in the image of God implies that ultimately we cannot be *truly* fulfilled until we are at one with God. You will remember we talked of this in Chapter 5 in connection with Jungian psychology. Given the nature of that God – the good God who is the father of us all – that means not only being at one with God, but also with all our brothers and sisters. Hence the two great commandments: loving God and loving one's neighbor as oneself.

It is when we try to respond to the demand to live up to that second commandment – treating everyone equally as our brothers and sisters, sacrificing our own interests on their behalf if need be – that is when we are likely to have to make decisions as to whether or not to act differently from the promptings of our genes. And that is where decisions of a moral nature come in, and where it becomes meaningful to speak of sin and virtue.

Genetically based altruism?

One of the concerns you might have about what I have said so far is that we seem to have equated genetically influenced behavior *exclusively* with selfishness – an absorption with the self which readily leads us humans into morally reprehensible behavior. But what about other behavior traits – altruism, for example? Could there not be survival value for a species if there were to develop a genetic code that led to cooperation between members of the species? Could we not hold to a much more positive assessment of our likely genetic characteristics – one where everyone had a natural inborn tendency to look after each other's interests? That way one would not have to invoke a God as the source of our higher, more laudable motivations. This is an intriguing question with various ramifications.

For a start we noted earlier that mothers have a natural tendency to care for their young. They might have to put themselves to great inconvenience, all for the sake of their offspring. Indeed, one knows of situations where a mother bird, on seeing a predator, will leave the nest and make a great display, thereby attracting the predator's attention toward herself and away from the contents of the nest. She is prepared to sacrifice herself if necessary for her young. Such behavior is quite the opposite of what we would expect if a selfish concern for one's own interests were the whole story. Such self-sacrificing behavior in a human would be accounted most commendable.

But such instances have a simple explanation in terms of evolutionary theory. Instead of thinking primarily in terms of the survival of the *individual*, we perhaps ought to be concentrating our attention more on the selection and survival of the *gene*. In this context, the self-sacrificing, "altruistic" behavior of the mother bird makes perfect sense. The mother and her young share the same genes. If it becomes a case of either the mother or the young getting killed, the genes are more likely to be preserved for posterity if it is the young that survive. The mother bird, having done her job of passing the genes on to the next generation is now, in a sense, expendable. A gene that in effect says: "When you are a mother, be prepared to sacrifice yourself if necessary for your young" is more likely to get passed on and survive than one that says: "Under all circumstances put your own interest first." In this way the self-interest is a feature of the gene rather than of the individual – hence the commonly used term "the selfish gene." So it is we can expect a certain measure of altruistic behavior to be encoded in our genes as well as the selfish behavior we spoke of before.

But one should note that this type of self-sacrificing behavior would be expected only on behalf of close kin – those (like one's young) who in large measure share the same genetic material – including the "self-sacrificing" type of gene.

Altruism beyond close kin?

Having established the survival value (for the gene) of parents being altruistic toward their young and possibly other close family members, we must next ask whether there could be survival value for a gene that promoted altruism on behalf of the wider community.

For a time it was thought that there was a known example of this at work. It concerned the behavior of blackbirds. It was noted that on the approach of a hawk, a blackbird would immediately issue a cry to warn the rest of the flock of the approach of the predator. In so doing, it betrayed its own position to the hawk, placing itself in imminent danger for the good of others – many of whom would not be related particularly closely to the individual giving the warning. Laudable altruistic behavior on behalf of the community of blackbirds as a whole. Or was it?

Later workers noted that the warning cry emitted by the blackbird was pitched high. It is a characteristic of high-pitched sounds that their source is hard to locate. So, in truth, the bird had *not* given away its own position. And what was the consequence of issuing that cry? The rest of the flock had taken to the wing in alarm. But only one bird knew in which direction the hawk lay. So, on average, half the flock would be flying in the wrong direction toward the source of danger. In other words, the bird's act of so-called altruism had been nothing of the sort; its cry had successfully sent up into the air a flock of decoys that would effectively cover its own – selfish – escape! This example demonstrates just how careful one has to be when drawing conclusions about the motives at work in the animal kingdom.

In fact, there is a good theoretical reason why a gene concerned with the general welfare of the community might find it hard to get established. Such a gene would be of the general kind: "I'll scratch your back, if you scratch mine." As far as it goes there seems to be plenty of survival value in such a strategy, as much more can be achieved cooperatively rather than having everyone trying always to go it alone. The trouble is that the success of such a gene is likely to be undermined by the development of a further type of gene – one that in effect says: "I'll scratch your back, if you scratch mine (except that when it comes to my turn to do you the favor – I won't)." This is referred to as a "cheater" gene. The trouble is that the survival value of the cheater gene is likely to be greater than that of the non-cheating type. After all, it can only benefit from the arrangement, never having to put itself at risk. In the end there would only be the cheater genes left – in other words there would be no generalized altruism.

There is one caveat to make about this. This line of argument holds for communities where one does not know who the cheaters are. But in small closed communities where everyone gets to know everyone else rather well, it presumably could become known that certain individuals, having reaped the benefits of the reciprocal arrangement, never in fact put themselves out for others when it is their turn. They could then be excluded in future from the arrangement, and be at a survival disadvantage relative to the non-cheating types. That being so the cheater gene would not be able to gain the ascendancy.

So, in conclusion, has the case been made that, to some extent at least, there could be a genetic tendency toward altruism? As far as close kin are concerned, yes. The selfish gene concept allows for altruism between those sharing the self-same gene. In addition, within tightly knit closed communities one might expect altruism of the sort "you scratch my back, and I'll scratch yours." The mutual grooming of monkeys would be a (literal) example of that.

Altruism in humans

In the above discussion, we have to recognize that we have been using the word "altruism" in a rather specialized *biological* sense. It has to be said that a philosophy of "you scratch my back, and I'll scratch yours" falls far short of what *morally* we would regard as true altruism in humans. In fact, what we have been describing could perhaps more accurately be regarded as enlightened self-interest than altruism. True altruism – the type that figures in religious discussions – is one where one sacrifices oneself for another *without any thought of getting repaid*. Moreover, this is done for those beyond the circle of close kin. That is a type of altruism that does not seem to figure at all in the context of the selection of genes.

And yet such altruism does exist among humans, and in existing, raises the question of its source. According to the Bible, this is all bound up with the idea that, beyond the purely physical side of ourselves, in some sense we are made in the image of God.

A genetic basis for religion?

In our earlier discussion of Jungian psychology, we noted just how deeply embedded in the psyche is the sense of the religious. A tendency toward religious observance seems to be part and parcel of what it is to be human.

This raises the question whether it might have been genetically encoded in the same way as our species came to acquire other behavior traits. What we have in mind is that long ago there might have been a random change to the genes such that the resulting code corresponded to the individual acquiring a belief in a god – an imaginary god. Though the belief was wholly spurious and unfounded, if it conferred some survival advantage over those who did not have this code, then it could have been selected.

To some extent we have already examined this possibility. In Chapter 5, in our discussion of the origin of the religious archetype, we noted that such a belief might have encouraged those possessing the gene to act cooperatively. Working together, rather than as individuals, has undoubted advantages, as witness wolves hunting in packs, or ants living in a colony. But in that previous discussion we drew attention to the fact that it was hard to see how loyalty to an imaginary, invisible god would be effective when there were clearly much more tangible alternatives that might act as the focus for the shared loyalty.

However, a more severe weakness in this attempt to dismiss belief in God as a mere artifice thrown up by an evolutionary accident, comes from considering the *type* of God that is worshiped. As already noted, the most prominent characteristic that comes to mind in thinking about God is that of love. And this is not just love for people we like. Followers of the Christian God are to love their *enemies*. They must forgive to the point where, having been attacked, they are to turn the other cheek. This being so, one has to ask where the survival advantage in a strategy like that might lie. One suspects that a predator confronted by such a cooperative prey would simply think its luck was in. No, anyone acquiring a genetic code giving rise to such behavior would have been rapidly eliminated.

Thus, evolutionary theory seems unlikely to come up with any satisfactory explanation of the origins of the innate religious sense, and its accompanying characteristic of truly moral, self-sacrificing altruism. We must look elsewhere for its source. Many would claim that source to be self-evident; it is to be found in the God hypothesis. The innate moral sense certainly must be included in the data to be assessed in our God experiment.

The evolutionary tree and survival

In talking of evolution, it is common to have in mind a tree. The trunk represents our earliest common ancestors, emerging out of the ground – the primordial slime. Out of this common trunk grow various branches; these in their turn split up into side shoots; and these into individual twigs. The twigs represent all the different species of animal alive today. Being a tree, it has to have a topmost branch, and of course, it is natural for us to think of ourselves as being at the very top.

But this prompts us to ask: "Top, in what sense?" If what we have in mind is the ability to survive, then that distinction is hardly ours. Modern humans have been around for only about 100,000 years. How much longer does our species have? Given the ever-present threat of a nuclear bomb capability getting into the hands of an irresponsible world leader, or a nuclear holocaust being triggered accidentally, one might be hard-pressed to think that humans will be around for another 100,000 years. Even an optimist can surely not imagine that we shall be able to match the dinosaurs, who thrived for a thousand times longer than that. When it comes to surviving, humans have become too clever for their own good. *Tyrannosaurus rex* survived longer than we are likely to, not because it was better behaved, or more sensible than we are, but because it did not have as much potentially destructive power as our superior intelligence has given us.

The dinosaurs did, of course, eventually depart the scene. This, it is thought, was due to tremendous climatic changes brought about by the impact of a meteorite. This might also be the fate of the human race – if we have not already blown ourselves up in the meantime. Certainly destructive objects are still hurtling about space – witness the recent collision between a comet and Jupiter. No way could we, or other advanced forms of life, survive an impact of such magnitude were one to involve the Earth. The only types of life to stand any chance would be very small simple forms like bacteria. In fact, where survival is concerned, bacteria are the most successful. They were one of the first forms of life to appear, and they are still with us today. Indeed, there are more types of bacteria around today than at any previous time.

So, with regard to survival, humans don't rank at all.

The survival advantage of the human brain

If we are to regard ourselves as top of the evolutionary tree, we must specify which particular characteristic we have in mind when we make that claim. Humans have a number of particular advantages: they walk upright and this frees their front paws to operate as hands. These hands have developed great mobility, with a thumb that is set in opposition to the four fingers, so giving greater manipulative capability. We have developed good hand-to-eye coordination.

But our most important distinguishing asset is, of course, our brain. It is not that our brain is bigger than that of all other animals. Part of the brain is devoted to keeping the body functioning, and the bigger an animal's body, the larger the brain it needs simply to keep itself going. As far as intelligence is concerned, the crucial thing is not so much brain size, as how big the brain is in proportion to body size; in other words, how much brain capacity is left over for doing intelligent thinking after the ongoing needs of the body have been attended to. It is in this respect that humans have the advantage over other animals. But there is a price to be paid. Fortunately for us men, it is women who pay that price – at childbirth. They have to give birth to a baby whose brain size is relatively large compared to the size of the body of the mother giving birth to it; that is to say, the baby's head is large compared to the size of the hole it must pass through. Humans partially overcome this difficulty by seeing to it that, in a sense, their babies are all born prematurely – while the head is still small enough to get through. That is why human babies are so much less mature than the offspring of other animals. A newborn calf or foal, for example, is up and about, walking, in no time at all; a human baby on the other hand has to wait until he/she is older.

Somewhere along the line, the complexity of the brain would have become such as to make possible the use of speech. This was a great leap forward. Now it was no longer the case that one's understanding of the world had to be confined to whatever one had learned from one's own direct experience of life (plus the inherited information genetically encoded). Through speech one could learn from other people's experiences. One generation could build on the knowledge accumulated by former generations. This pooling of knowledge led to a vast explosion of understanding as to how the world operated. This in turn led to the ability to manipulate the environment for one's own ends. What need had humans for sharp claws, protective shells, powerful legs, etc., when the equivalents of all these could be had at will through sheer ingenuity?

The origins of the human spirit

In the evolutionary past a point was reached where the brain capacity became such as to permit the individual to think of more than just how to get shelter, the next meal, sex, etc. The first thoughts would have formed as to whether there might be something beyond what one could see and touch. This is where there opened up for the first time the possibility of entering into a conscious relationship with God. Here we have the birth of the first primitive spirit.

There would also have been a sharing and comparison of religious experiences. With the development of speech there would come the ability to articulate and further develop one's appreciation of God – opening up the possibility of a fuller, more enriching relationship with God. Indeed, where spirituality is concerned the first conscious thinking about God might not have happened before the development of speech.

The evolution of the spirit might strike some people as an odd idea, especially if they have been brought up to think that humans have a spirit and go to Heaven, while animals do not. In the light of evolutionary theory, it is hard to see how such a clear-cut distinction can be made. But why should it have to be all or nothing? To the extent that a dog or a dolphin today – or a primitive ancestor of our own in the distant past – has any capacity to think about why it might be here, and what the purpose of life might be, I don't see why they should not be accorded a rudimentary spirit. By this is meant the ability whereby they can experience to some small, superficial extent a relationship of sorts with God, and have a glimmer of appreciation of a life beyond death. But then again, perhaps this animal appreciation is so utterly rudimentary, it remains valid to reserve the word "spirit" to refer to something that, to all intents and purposes, is a distinctive characteristic of humans alone.

So, in summary I would say that when it comes to thinking of ourselves as being at the top of the evolutionary tree, this is specifically in regard to intelligence and spirituality.

The future evolution of the human species

So much for the evolutionary development that has taken place in the past. What of the future? Where might further evolution be taking the human race?

If evolution were to continue as it has done, then we might expect humans to develop into a super-intelligent species. But this is unlikely. The reason is that we have now entered a stage where the evolution of humans is being frustrated. Describing evolution by natural selection (very crudely) as "the survival of the fittest," we have only to look at the practice of modern medicine to realize that this is not happening any more. We are taking the most extraordinary measures to ensure that those who suffer from disabilities and ailments of all kinds should be preserved. Even with the comatose brain-dead, there is great reluctance to switch off the life-support system. Not only that, but people are living longer – well past the age where they have served their evolutionary usefulness in passing on their genes to the next generation. In evolutionary terms, once the young are able to stand on their own feet, the sooner the older generation dies and stops using up space and food the better. To some extent it can be argued that on average the more intelligent people are inclined to get the better-paid jobs (not always of course), and the higher the standard of living the *fewer* children they are inclined to have. In contrast, those in lower-paid jobs have somewhat bigger families. This is not conducive to raising the average IQ. In any case it is hard to see how, in today's society, the more intelligent have a better chance of surviving to the age where they have children. And without that, there will be no further selection in favor of greater intelligence.

All this makes it sound as though the human species is on a downward slide. And in terms of being a successful evolving animal, that is probably true. But I doubt that there would be many who would wish to withhold the benefits of modern medicine from those who need it, and exchange our present society for one that does not look after its weaker members – even though this might be storing up trouble for the future.

The Human Genome Project

So far in our discussion of where the human species might be heading, one factor has not been mentioned: the Human Genome Project, or as it is sometimes called, the Human Genome Initiative. It might completely turn the above argument on its head.

In speaking of our genes, we refer of course to our DNA. Looking at its structure in more detail, we note that DNA (short for *deoxyribonucleic acid*) contains two chains of smaller molecules (nucleotides) twisted around each other into a double helix. There is a link between each small molecule on one of these chains to a complementary molecule on the other strand. These linked pairs of molecules are called *base pairs*. There are some 3,000 million of them in the typical DNA molecule. It is the order in which the base pairs occur along the chains that constitutes the genetic code. One might regard the base pairs as the letters, and the genes as the meaningful sentences made up from those sequences of letters. Altogether in human DNA there are about 100,000 genes or coded messages. These govern our physical characteristics and also our genetically influenced behavior.

The aim of the Human Genome Project (HGP) has been to sequence all the base pairs. In 1987, the US government agreed to fund it at the rate of $200 million per year. This work was completed in 2000. The task of identifying which sequences make up which genes, and how the genes function continues. The purpose, as far as the scientists are concerned, is simply that of finding out what is there. But there are potentially great pay-offs. For example, it is thought that 4,000 human diseases are caused one way or another by genes. These include Huntington's chorea, cystic fibrosis, Alzheimer's, etc. There are hopes of locating a gene responsible for most forms of breast cancer. If this is achieved, then it opens up the possibility that, through genetic engineering, the harmful gene might be eliminated, leaving future generations free of this kind of disease. This would be a contribution to the overall aim of genetically engineering a healthier human species.

In the same way one might find a genetic link with intelligence. If so, not only could we produce a healthier species, but a more intelligent one. Indeed, what of other characteristics such as strength and longevity? And if that is thought desirable, how about a taste for blue eyes and blond hair? Could we be on the way to producing the perfect child?

At this point, one is likely to experience a vague unease. All this smacks of *Brave New World* and past attempts to breed super-races. Where is the line to be drawn as to what is thought desirable and what not? Are imperfect humans ever likely to be able to manufacture humans that are perfect? What about all the people who are unable to afford the expensive, customized genetic engineering of their offspring?

These concerns apart, one thing is certain: in a few years we shall have the ability, should we so wish, to give a helping hand to evolution. We shall be able to direct it down paths of our own choosing. No longer shall we need to wait for changes in the coding to happen at random – changes caused by mistakes in the process whereby the parents DNA is copied to provide that of the offspring. From here on we shall, in principle, be able deliberately to direct the course that evolution shall take.

I say "in principle" because this presupposes that one is able to anticipate all the side-effects and consequences of "playing God" in this manner. Perhaps there are some unforeseen and unpleasant surprises in store for the unwary.

What I find particularly worrying is that there seems little or no control over the process. Who is to make the decisions as to which manipulations should be made to the DNA. According to what criteria are these decisions to be made, and in whose interest? It looks at the moment as though there is no responsible overall supervision in place, and that decisions are being made on an ad hoc basis, with only the commercial interests of mainly pharmaceutical companies at stake.

There are further ramifications. If a person is revealed to have a defective gene that increases the chance of later developing some illness or disability, should an insurance company have the right to demand access to such information before agreeing to issue a policy?

The genes and human responsibility

The implications of the HGP go deeper still. There have been reports of the identification of genes to do with behavior traits that can lead, for example, to a certain type of alcoholism, to a certain kind of homosexuality, and to aggression. Does this mean that someone with an innate aggressive streak can claim that they were not really responsible for having carried out an act of, say, grievous bodily harm? ("It wasn't me, m'lud; it was me genes wot dun it!") Is it not unfair to expect the same standard of behavior from someone who has a genetic tendency making it more difficult for them?

It is an interesting question, but not one I think that introduces any fundamentally new challenge. It has always been recognized that we are all "born different." We know for instance that some men have much stronger sex drives than others; that presumably makes them more liable to succumb to the temptation to commit rape. Some exhibit violent tempers; they are the ones more likely to commit crimes of violence. All the genetic information is doing is helping us to localize the source of these traits.

The fact that life is not fair also manifests itself, of course, on the "nurture" side of the argument as well as the "nature" side. If one is brought up in a bad home, or in a bad neighborhood where one cannot avoid unsavory company and influences, then again one's chances of running foul of the law are greater than if one has had a comparatively sheltered upbringing.

In both cases, whether one is thinking of unfortunate genes or unfortunate environment, the important thing is that we are not blind victims of our fate – we have the power of choice and are expected to exercise that choice and shoulder responsibility for our actions. Recall how we are genetically *influenced* rather than genetically *determined*. At least where humans are concerned, there is the ability (our free will) deliberately and consciously to go against one's natural inclinations where necessary. And that is what society, and religion, require of us. We are expected to take responsibility for our actions.

But you might be thinking, in a world where one seeks justice – and God is supposed to be a God of Justice – is it not unfair that some people begin life with the cards stacked against them? From the moment they acquire their genes they find it harder than others to live up to the standards of acceptable behavior.

It would be unfair only if God expected the same standards of behavior from everyone regardless of individual circumstances. The fact that this is unlikely to be the case is manifestly demonstrated by the Biblical warnings that we ourselves should refrain from judging others – "Judge not, that ye be not judged." This implies that true judgment is not a matter of simply comparing one person's behavior with that of another. If that had been the case we would all be in a position to judge. No, we are to refrain from judging because we are not in possession of all the relevant facts.

The role of death

One further interesting question that will be thrown into sharp relief by the HGP is the role of death. The prospect is held before us that we might soon understand a great deal about the genetics of ageing and the onset of death. To what extent is longevity to be prized?

Whether it is a good thing or not is likely to depend in large measure on one's state of health. If one is constantly fighting for breath, or in pain, or crippled with arthritis, or one's mind has gone, then there seems little point in prolonging that state indefinitely. But suppose it were possible to alter the genes in such a way as to slow down the ageing process. Suppose one could live to 150 or 200 years of age with the body of a 40-year-old; what then?

This raises a serious question: Are we to regard ageing as a natural process that ought not to be interfered with, or as a disease which like other diseases ought to be attended to once this becomes possible? What would be the effects on society if people lived twice or three times longer than they do now? Many ambitious young people already feel frustrated at not being promoted as fast as they would like because the senior positions are still occupied by older staff. Can we psychologically adjust ourselves to a working life extending to 100 or 150 years before we become eligible for a pension? Do we really have to try and sustain the excitement of sex in our marriage over *that* span of time? Or in our leisure time, how many *Monday Night Football* games can we bear watching before it finally palls? In short, is our psychological make-up capable of coping with a significantly extended life span?

This brings us to the subject of death. It is important for us to accept that in evolutionary theory, death has an important part to play. Evolutionary change can only come about if each generation at some point gets out of the way, thereby making room for the next. This applies not only to those individuals with disadvantageous characteristics (the ones that need to be weeded out before they mate), but also to those with the advantageous characteristics – once they have successfully mated and passed the advantageous gene on to the next generation. Death is such an integral feature of the successful species that it might well be that there is a specific gene in our DNA responsible for seeing to it that we do not hang around too long. The "eventual-death-of-the-individual" gene would then have to be regarded, somewhat paradoxically, as an integral part of the survival kit of the species as a whole. That being so, should we be tampering with it?

Such a discussion quickly highlights the need to adopt a constructive attitude toward death. Too easily it comes to be regarded as an evil to be resisted in almost all circumstances. Only in extreme old age, and in the throes of unremitting pain and disability, might it be spoken of as "a merciful release." But why? For those of us with a belief in a life beyond death, might not death be a merciful release in *all* cases? Perhaps from the vantage point of Heaven it will be those who live to a ripe old age who will be aggrieved because they were left down here so long while those who died young had longer to enjoy Heaven.

The HGP undoubtedly raises a host of questions, promises, and problems. It is good to note that, from the outset, 5 percent of all its funds have been set aside for the study of the ethical, legal, and social implications of the project.

The human species and the Son of God

Let us return to the prospect of further evolution of the human species. If this were to happen in the natural course of events (despite the apparent frustration of the process of natural selection at present), or if it were to happen as a result of directed evolution through the controlled manipulation of our genes, a religious question arises for Christians. It comes about in the following way: Christians hold that the eternal Son of God took on human form as Jesus. But if we present-day humans are merely a staging post on the way to some superhuman species, that later species will doubtless look back at us and regard us as primitive – in much the same way as we regard our ape-like ancestors as primitive. Thus the question arises as to why the Son of God took on the "primitive" form of a human, rather than waiting for the superhuman species to come on to the scene.

By way of an answer, one might begin by saying that by the term "superhuman" one presumably has in mind a species that has greater intelligence. But intelligence does not necessarily equate with spirituality. A highly intelligent person might have no conscious relationship with God, whereas someone with a low IQ might enjoy a deep and sincere love of God, and have a keen sense of the presence of God. Inasmuch as we take the term "spirit" to refer to the immortal spirit that is in active communion with God, the first person might be a spiritual little person, the latter a giant.

The heart of the spiritual life is the depth of one's love for God. The measure of love is the extent to which the lover is prepared to sacrifice his or her own interests in favor of those of the beloved. The supreme loving sacrifice is that one be prepared to lay down one's life for the other. Jesus did precisely that on the cross, and since that time there have been countless martyrs who have also voluntarily given everything they had in order to be true to their faith in God. It is in fact impossible to imagine greater acts of self-sacrifice than those that have been offered out of love of God. While it might be possible for some future superhuman species to have deeper spiritual insights and knowledge, and more intense religious experiences than we, in *practical* terms they would be incapable of demonstrating greater loyalty to God than many humans have already done, and others would be prepared to do if faced with similar circumstances. That being so, it does indeed make sense that the Son of God should come in human form, even though those endowed with superior intelligence might still be to come. The point is that no one can be *spiritually* more mature and advanced than we are.

Evolution elsewhere in the Universe

One final point before we close this discussion of evolution. What of evolution elsewhere in the Universe?

Whether life has evolved on any other planets in the cosmos, we do not yet know. Given the vast number of stars (each one a sun like our own Sun), and the knowledge that a significant proportion of them have planets going round them, and many of those will be at the right kind of distance from their star to have a temperate climate, it strikes me as highly unlikely that the Earth is the unique home of life in the cosmos. There are some who would be inclined to the opposite view. They hold that the evolutionary path from slime to intelligent life is so beset with difficult steps that it might well have happened only the once. But suppose my guess is right and life has evolved elsewhere, what are the implications for religious belief?

If I were to meet aliens from outer space, I suppose one of my first questions would be to find out whether they believed in God, and if so what their ideas were on the subject. I would suspect that they would indeed have a religion. I would also suspect that if they have evolved in the same kind of way as we have, through evolution by natural selection, their behavior will be to some extent genetically influenced, and like us they will be inclined to self-centeredness – they would be subject to original sin. Like us they will be in need of a savior.

So how does the Son of God fit in here? Are we to regard the Jesus who lived here on Earth as the unique saviour of all intelligent forms of life throughout the cosmos? I personally shouldn't have thought so. Any belief that implies that we humans are uniquely privileged is liable to run the risk of being arrogant. I see no problem with the idea that the Son of God should visit each planet. He would not do so in human form, of course, but in whatever form was appropriate to the life to be found there.

We have spoken of the possibility of humans developing into a species of super-intelligent beings. Might this not already have happened on other planets in the cosmos? Because of the relatively short time over which we ourselves have evolved from markedly more primitive ancestors (100,000 years compared to the 12,000-million-year history of the Universe) a civilization would have to be only fractionally out-of-step with us for there to be a marked difference in intelligence between us and them. Thus one might expect there to be many alien civilizations ahead of our own.

But this leaves out of account one important factor. In the development of intelligence there comes the stage where language emerges. From then on, there is an explosion of knowledge arising out of the sharing and accumulation of experiences. This leads to the knowledge, among other things, of nuclear power. Just as the basically sinful nature of humans is liable to bring about their destruction here on Earth in a relatively short time (speaking in terms of evolutionary epochs), so it might well be that the pattern repeats itself endlessly throughout the cosmos. Each advanced civilization reaches the point where it has the intellectual capacity to engage in science, and through religion establish contact with God, but then soon afterward – because old, genetically encoded habits die hard – destroys itself.

A sober thought perhaps. But even if that scenario were roughly correct (and of course it might well be wide of the mark for some hitherto unknown reason), there is a crumb of comfort I can offer. It would mean that not only were humans the most intelligent creatures here on Earth, but our intelligence would be on a par with the best there is in the entire Universe!

In summary, I would say that evolutionary theory has many insights to offer concerning the nature and status of human beings – where we have come from, why we are the way we are, and where we might be heading. At no stage does it come up with any evidence that is contrary to the findings of our religious investigation. Indeed it can offer fascinating glimpses into the method God has adopted for working out his creative purposes. We understand now, for example, how it incorporates an element of chance. This leaves the world free to do its own thing – a very subtle form of freedom, embodying as it does a systematic selection procedure ensuring that, one way or another, creatures consciously able to relate to God will somehow emerge, thus fulfilling the overall Divine intention.

12

A Case of Over-design?

Toward the end of Steven Weinberg's popular introduction to Big Bang cosmology, *The First Three Minutes*, the author concludes: "The more the Universe seems comprehensible, the more it also seems pointless." A little earlier, he dismisses human life as "a more-or-less farcical outcome of a chain of accidents."

It is not difficult to understand how Weinberg arrives at such gloomy assessments. Take, for example, the size of the Universe. Are we really expected to believe that God designed it as a home for humans? It appears somewhat excessive – a case of over-design, perhaps.

Here we come across seemingly powerful evidence against the fundamental religious notion that we humans are important to God. If God's prime purpose in creating the world was to bring into existence creatures that could respond to him in a loving relationship, then we would expect the world to look as though it had been designed with that end in mind. Weinberg clearly thinks it does not. This is not something our God experiment can ignore.

In Chapter 8 we made a start on this question by recognizing that size was not everything – one must also take into account the role of consciousness (Pascal's thinking reed). We also noted that we did not have to regard the Universe as solely a home for humans here on Earth; there could be additional forms of life elsewhere in the Universe just as precious to God. But we are still led to ask: is the type of Universe revealed to us by modern cosmology and astronomy one that can be regarded as an *appropriate* home for life? Or rather is the character of the world such that life – *any* kind of life – could only be regarded as an accidental by-product?

A world hostile to life?

Most places in the Universe are hostile to life. The depths of space are incredibly cold; that is why most planets are freezing. To be warm a planet needs to be close to a star. But get too close – like Mercury and Venus – and they become too hot. And of course the most prominent objects in the sky, the Sun and the other stars, are in themselves balls of fire and hence not suitable places to find life. Planets tend to be without atmospheres, or if they do have one, it is unlikely to be the right sort for sustaining life.

For much of the past history of the Universe there was no intelligent life. Looking to the future, we expect after a further 5,000 million years our Sun will swell up to become a star of a type known as a *red giant*. Though it is unlikely that its fiery surface will reach out far enough to engulf the Earth, our planet will become unbearably hot – to the extent that all life will be burned up. Indeed, life might already have been eliminated long before then through the violent impact of a meteorite.

And what of the long-term future of the Universe and of life elsewhere? We have spoken much about the *origins* of the Universe in the Big Bang, but what of its *end*?

We have seen how the Universe is expanding. The distant galaxies of stars are still receding in the aftermath of the Big Bang. But as they rush off into the distance, they are slowing down. This is due to gravity, each galaxy exerting an attraction on every other one. Keep this up, and eventually the galaxies will be brought to a halt. Except that we have to remember that the force of gravity reduces with increasing distance. It goes down as the inverse square of the distance. Galaxies that are twice as far away exert only a quarter of the force on each other; three times further away, 1/9 the force; 10 times further away, 1/100 the force. . . . So, with the galaxies receding to ever greater distances from each other, the slowing down force is steadily reducing with time.

The big question then is whether gravity in the Universe is strong enough to stop the galaxies before it has essentially vanished to nothing, or alternatively the speeds of the galaxies are sufficiently great for them to succeed in escaping the pull of gravity. We are thus presented with two alternatives:

(i) *Big Crunch scenario.* If gravity is strong enough, then the galaxies will one day come to a halt. From then on they will be drawn back toward each other. All their separations will reduce until eventually everything comes piling back in at the same instant of time. This prospect is called the *Big Crunch.*

What would happen after that is anybody's guess. As with the Big Bang itself, one has here an instant in time where all the contents of the Universe are contained within a volume having no size, i.e., the density is infinite. Our understanding of physics is unable to handle that. It could be that this marks the end of everything; the Universe goes out of existence. On the other hand, it might rebound – a *Big Bounce.* The expansion of the Universe would then happen all over again. Perhaps this is how it has always been: a constant repetition of expansions and contractions – what we call an *oscillating Universe.* According to this scenario, what we have been calling the Big Bang would merely have been the most recent of the Big Bounces. It would mean that the Big Bang did *not* mark the origin of the Universe. It would mean that all that discussion in Chapter 9 about the Big Bang marking the beginning of time would also be wrong; there *was* time before the Big Bang – the time needed to accommodate the previous oscillations. It could be that we are dealing with a Universe that has *no* beginning, nor any end.

By way of an aside: would *that* get rid of the Creator God? Previously we were discussing this question in connection with the assumption that there was no time before the Big Bang – and hence no time to accommodate a God lighting the blue touch-paper. A Universe that had no origins *at all* would – superficially – be an alternative way of getting rid of him. Except that it is not. You will recall how earlier we made a distinction between the word "origins" and the word "creation." Whether the world had a beginning or not – an origin – we are still left with the creation question as to why there is something rather than nothing – a question to which the religious answer is God.

So that, then, is one possible scenario: the clusters of galaxies will one day come to a halt and thereafter come back together in a Big

Crunch. Were that to be the case, there would clearly be an end to life not only here on Earth but everywhere throughout the cosmos.

(ii) *Unending expansion scenario.* The alternative is that gravity is too weak to stop the galaxies, and they will continue flying apart for ever. What would be the significance of that for life in the cosmos?

Each star has only a limited amount of fuel. Eventually its fire must go out. For a medium-sized star like the Sun that would take about 10,000 million years. More massive stars have greater supplies of fuel, but they achieve higher temperatures and burn their fuel faster – so much faster they might live for only one million years. What happens to the star as it runs out of fuel depends critically on how massive it is. The Sun, having swollen up to become a tenuous red giant, will shed some of its outer layers before sinking back to become a compact *white dwarf* star. This in turn will continue to radiate away its heat until it becomes a cold, black cinder.

What of more massive stars? In order for a star to remain a stable size, it relies on all the vigorous jiggling motion of its atomic particles to counteract the inward pull of its own gravity. But as the fuel runs out and the star begins to cool, the movements become less vigorous and the outer parts of the star no longer experience the same resistance to being pulled in closer to the center. The star shrinks. The more closely packed, the stronger becomes the mutual gravity between its component parts, and hence the greater the tendency to become even more tightly packed. For a star several times heavier than the Sun, the situation suddenly becomes unstable. In no more than a second, the massive star undergoes catastrophic collapse. In the process, some of the material is blasted out. The star goes out with a bang – literally; it is called a *supernova.* This is one of the most spectacular occurrences in the cosmos. For a few days, a supernova will shine as brightly as a whole galaxy – as brightly as 100,000 million stars. As for the rest of the star's material – the bulk of it – it collapses down to a super-dense ball, a few miles across, called a *neutron star.* It has a density equivalent to that of an atomic nucleus; one teaspoon of the stuff would weigh as much as 10,000 melted down aircraft carriers!

Even something as rigid as an atomic nucleus, however, might not be sufficient to withstand the intense gravity force for an even heavier star. In fact, given enough mass, nothing at all can withstand the force of gravity, so the heaviest stars collapse down to a point – what we call a *black hole*. In the immediate vicinity of this point – within a distance called "the event horizon" – the gravity is so strong there is no escape; even light itself is unable to drag itself away – hence the adjective "black." A black hole emits no light of its own, nor does it reflect any light that falls on it. If we can't see it, how do we know it is there? From the way it continues to drag in any other material that passes too close to it, and from the way it might leave companion bodies still orbiting it at a safe distance.

But whether a star ends up as a cooled down white dwarf, a neutron star, or a black hole, the end result is the same – it becomes cold and no longer able to keep companion planets warm enough to sustain life.

As one generation of stars dies out in this manner, so new stars continue to form. A star is created when the hydrogen and helium gases that were emitted originally from the Big Bang collect together under the influence of their mutual gravity. The gas squashes down, heating up as it does so (in the same way as air squashed down in a bicycle pump gets hot). If enough gas is collected, the temperature rise becomes sufficient at the center to ignite nuclear fusion. In a very hot gas, the atomic nuclei are moving about so fast they can fuse together to form heavier nuclei. These heavier nuclei are so efficiently packed together that they are able to release unwanted energy – the energy of nuclear fusion. (The modest heat of the squashed-down gas acts merely as a trigger to get the much more energetic nuclear fusion reactions going. This is similar to the way we light a domestic coal fire by first setting light to some rolled-up paper and sticks of wood – the small output of heat from this being the trigger to get the coal burning.)

Not all the gas from the Big Bang was used up in producing the first generation of stars. Our own Sun was one of those formed at a later stage. Still more stars are to be seen today in the very earliest phases of getting underway. But it is clear that this is not something that can go on indefinitely. At some stage, *all* the hydrogen and helium gas will have been drawn together to form stars, or will have been dispersed so thinly as never to be incorporated into a star. From then on the last stars live out their active lives, and die. Everything cools down, and we are left with the *Heat Death* of the Universe.

So what we find is that if we are dealing with a Universe where the expansion goes on for ever, there will come a point when there can be no further life. One is then left with an ever-dispersing, lifeless Universe for an infinity of time.

So, Big Crunch or Heat Death – either way, the future for life is bleak. Yes, it is easy to see how Weinberg was led to the conclusion that the Universe seems pointless, and life but an accidental by-product of no significance.

The Anthropic Principle

But are we being too hasty? Let us change tack and introduce some reflections on the cosmos of a very different nature. These have surfaced only recently – in the past couple of decades. They go under the general heading: *The Anthropic Principle*.

To see what it is about, I want you to imagine that you have the responsibility of designing a universe. You have freedom to choose the laws of nature and the conditions under which this imaginary universe is to operate. The aim is to produce a universe tailor-made for the development of life – the kind of universe God presumably *ought* to have created if it really were intended primarily as a home for life. There are various decisions you have to make:

(i) *The violence of the Big Bang.* Assuming that you will start off your universe with a Big Bang, how violent will you make it? You might feel, for example, that the actual Big Bang was somewhat excessive if the aim was simply to produce some life forms.

It turns out that if you make the violence of your Big Bang somewhat less – only a little less – then the mutual gravity operating between the galaxies will get such a secure grip that the galaxies will slow down to a halt; they will thereafter be brought together in a Big Crunch. That in itself need not be a problem. The difficulty is in ensuring that the crunch does not happen too quickly – in a time shorter than the 12,000 million years needed for evolution to produce us. Turn the Big Bang wick down too much, and there is insufficient time for intelligent life to develop.

This danger might prompt you to err on the other side: you turn the wick up a little, i.e., make your Big Bang just a little *more* violent than the actual one. What happens now is that the gases come out of the Big Bang so fast that they do not have time to collect together to form embryo stars before they are dispersed into the depths of space. There being no stars, there is no life.

In fact it turns out that as far as the Big Bang violence is concerned, the window of opportunity is exceedingly narrow. If you are to get life in your universe, the thrust must be just right – as it happens to be with our actual Universe.

(ii) *The strength of gravity.* The next point to consider is the force of gravity. We have already seen that the force between two objects varies inversely as the square of the distance between them. But that just determines the *relative* values of the force for different separations. What of the intrinsic strength of the force? This depends on one of the physical constants of nature – one represented by the symbol G in the relevant equations. How big will you make G in your imaginary universe? If you make it a little less than it actually is, the strength of all gravity forces in your universe will be correspondingly less. You now run the risk of a universe that has no stars. Although the gas from the Big Bang collects together to form dense clouds, the mutual gravity force is not strong enough to collect the amount needed to produce a temperature rise sufficient to light the nuclear fires. Out there in space are objects called *brown dwarf stars.* It's a misnomer because they are not proper stars. They are collections of gas that become warm at their centers as the gas is squashed together, but they do not heat up sufficiently to trigger the nuclear fusions. Without access to the main source of energy, they just peter out after a while. In our own Solar System, the planet Jupiter is, or was, a brown dwarf. It is a globe of hydrogen and helium gases which is warm at its center. If it had originally collected about seventy times as much gas as it actually did, it would have caught fire properly and become a companion star to our Sun. So, if you decide on a gravity a little weaker than it really is, you will have a universe that has only brown dwarfs – and that means no life.

On the other hand, you must be careful not to have your gravity too strong. That way you would get only the very massive types of star. Recall how massive stars burn themselves out quickly – perhaps in only one million years. For evolution to take place you must have a steady source of energy for 5,000 million years – you need a medium-sized star like the Sun.

Indeed when you come to think of it, the Sun is a remarkable phenomenon. After all, what is a star? It is a nuclear bomb going off SLOWLY. In practice this is very difficult to achieve. I recall soon after the Second World War hearing a talk extolling the virtues of unlimited cheap supplies of nuclear power to be obtained from the fusion of the heavy hydrogen found in abundance in the oceans. How long would it take for this to be a commercial proposition? Fifty years, we were told. Since then, at regular intervals, I have heard talks updating us on progress in harnessing the power of hydrogen fusion. Always someone in the audience asks the question: "How long will it take for this to become a commercial proposition?" And the answer is always the same: "Fifty years." The past decades of research, costing countless millions of dollars, must surely have brought us somewhat closer to the goal – but sometimes it does not seem so. Not surprising really. It is incredibly difficult to contain fuel at temperatures reckoned in millions of degrees, and to persuade this bomb to go off in a controlled manner. Yet the amazing thing is that the Sun does all this – for nothing! The secret is the way the force of gravity in the Sun conspires to feed the new fuel into the nuclear furnace at just the right rate for the nuclear fires (governed by the nuclear force – an entirely different force from that of gravity) to consume it at a steady rate extending over a period of 10,000 million years.

Thus, in order for there to be life, the gravitational constant, G, must lie within a very narrow range of possible values. The gravity of the actual Universe does just that.

(iii) *Raw materials for making the bodies of living creatures.* Next you must turn your attention to the materials from which you wish to build the bodies of living creatures. This is no small matter. All that is emitted from the Big Bang are the two lightest gases – hydrogen and helium – and precious little besides. And it *has* to be that way. Remember you need a violent Big Bang to stop your Universe from collapsing back in on itself prematurely. And because of that violence, only the lightest atomic nuclei could survive the collisions occurring at that time – anything bigger getting smashed up again soon after its formation. But one can't make interesting objects like living bodies out of just hydrogen and helium. So the extra nuclei – those that go to make up the ninety-two different elements (i.e., types of atom) found on Earth – must be manufactured somehow *after* the Big Bang.

That's where the stars have another important role to play. Not only do they provide a steady source of warmth to energize the processes of evolution, they first serve as furnaces for taking light nuclei and fusing them into the heavy ones that will later be needed for producing the bodies of the evolving creatures. Again, it is a case of no stars – no life.

(iv) *The special problem of carbon synthesis.* But we are not home and dry yet. Perhaps the most important element for the making of life is carbon. In a sense it has an especially "sticky" kind of atom – good at cementing together the large molecules of biological interest. But forming a nucleus of carbon is by no means easy. Essentially it requires the fusion of three helium nuclei. Whereas it is relatively easy to get two billiard balls to collide with each other (a two-particle collision), to get three colliding all at the same instant (a three-particle collision) is an entirely different matter. The same goes for the three helium nuclei. Common sense would say that this simply is not going to happen in stars. Yet somehow it does – obviously (otherwise we wouldn't be here). But how? In the first place, when two helium nuclei collide they momentarily stick together to form a beryllium nucleus. That would make it easier for the third nucleus to collide a little later – it does not have to collide with the other two helium nuclei at *exactly* the same instant as they do. First the two helium nuclei collide to form beryllium, and then in a separate (two-particle collision) the third helium nucleus joins them. Unfortunately the first two stick together so briefly, this is but a small improvement – not enough to make any substantial difference.

This is where the most extraordinary coincidence emerges. To understand how it comes about, you must first know that a collision between nuclei is not the same as that between billiard balls. How big one nucleus looks to another depends on how fast they approach each other. This is obviously not true of macroscopic objects like billiard balls, but it is true of sub-atomic particles. Now, it just so happens that at certain special approach speeds, one nucleus can look absolutely enormous to the other – they can hardly avoid banging into each other. We call it a *nuclear resonance*. And that is what happens inside stars. By a most extraordinary chance, at the speeds characteristic of the nuclei moving about in stars, the beryllium nucleus (made of the first two helium nuclei briefly attached to each other) looks absolutely enormous to the approaching third helium nucleus. They hit each other, fuse together, and produce the desired carbon.

It is hard for a lay person to appreciate the sheer unlikeliness of this. It was the physicist Fred Hoyle who first made this seemingly outrageous suggestion. He knew that carbon had somehow to be made in the stars and was led to make this brilliant deduction that it must be due to a resonance. His suggestion was at first greeted with skepticism. But in response to his persistence, a laboratory experiment was mounted to reproduce the conditions in a star. The resonance was found just where Hoyle had predicted it would be. It was a great triumph for him.

In his younger days, Hoyle had been a noted and militant atheist. I well recall the outrage he caused in the 1950s when he used one of his Reith Lectures on BBC radio to attack religious belief in a Creator God. Some time after his unraveling of the mystery of carbon synthesis, I was to hear him deliver a talk about this resonance. In the course of it, he spoke of "He who fixed it." In a private conversation I had with him afterward, it was clear that his discovery had had a profound effect on him. While still disavowing any association with "organized religion," Hoyle nevertheless felt the "coincidence" was so way out, it could not have been due to mere chance.

So you have your precious carbon. Collisions between some of these carbon nuclei and further helium nuclei yield oxygen – another vital ingredient for life – and so on. Thus you must be sure in your imaginary universe to incorporate that fortuitous nuclear resonance!

(v) *Escape from a star.* Does this mean that the stage is now set for evolution to take over, converting these raw materials into human beings?

Not so. You have your materials, but they are in the center of a star at a temperature of about 10 million degrees – hardly an environment conducive to life. The materials have to be got out. But how, in your imaginary universe, are you going to arrange for that? After all, we know how difficult it is to lift something off the surface of the Earth and out into space; a rocket is needed. Your stars have no rockets, and the gravity forces at the surface of stars are in any case stronger.

What happens in this actual Universe is that a proportion of the newly synthesized material is ejected by supernova explosions. As we noted above, these occur when a massive old star collapses in on itself. But that raises a new problem. How can an *implosion* produce an *explosion*? This was a conundrum that exercised the minds of astrophysicists for many years. In the event the mechanism turned out to be the strangest imaginable. The material is blasted out by *neutrinos*. Like the quarks that make up the neutrons and protons of nuclei, and the electrons that attach themselves to nuclei to form atoms, neutrinos are one of the fundamental particles of nature. They are produced, for example, when the protons of a star absorb electrons to convert into neutrons as they collapse down to form the neutron star remnant. Perhaps the best-known feature of neutrinos is that, unlike the other fundamental particles, they hardly interact with anything. As you sit reading this book, millions upon millions of neutrinos coming from the Sun are passing through you every second and yet you are unaware of this. Indeed, one could pass a neutrino through the center of the Earth to Australia 100,000 million times before it had a 50:50 chance of hitting anything. They are incredibly slippery. And yet it is the neutrinos coming from the region of the newly forming neutron core at the center of the collapsing star that blasts out the precious stardust. So, in your imaginary universe, make your neutrinos slippery if you wish, but be sure not to overdo it – otherwise you will not get life.

(vi) *Last-second synthesis.* A further provision you need to allow for is that not all the nuclear materials for forming living bodies are produced in the steady nuclear synthesis taking place in stars prior to catastrophic collapse. Those heavier than iron don't exist up to that point. So, where do *they* come from? They are manufactured in the extraordinarily short-lived conditions of the supernova explosion itself. It is as though someone has had an afterthought and said, "Whoops. No bromine, cobalt, copper, iodine, or zinc; they'll be needing those as trace elements. I'd better make some double-quick." They are made in the few seconds of the explosion itself (making use of the exceptionally high density of neutrons flying about at that time).

(vii) *Further requirements?* The material is now out among the interstellar gases. In time, this collects together to form a dense cloud, which squashes down to form a new star. Outside the star there can be secondary eddies that settle down to form planets. It is now possible for some of these planets to be of the rocky kind, like Earth, Mercury, Venus, and Mars. For the first generation of stars this had not been so; at that stage there had only been hydrogen and helium around. Given a rocky planet at a reasonable distance from the star for a temperate climate to prevail, one has now at last a chance of life evolving from the primordial slime.

How likely this is to happen is not known. If one is a physicist like myself, one tends to be impressed by the vast number of planets there must be out there – in other words how many attempts there have been to produce intelligent life. On this assessment, there is almost certainly life out there. If, on the other hand, one is a biologist, one might be more impressed by the size of the hurdles that have still to be negotiated on the way to intelligent life – like for example the formation of the first cell. This might require yet more "coincidences" – biological ones this time rather than the physical ones we have been considering.

Inferences to be drawn from the Anthropic Principle

It is impossible to put a hard figure on the likelihood of getting life from simply throwing together a bunch of physical laws at random – laws incorporating arbitrary values for the various physical constants. In talking, for example, about the strength of gravity having to lie within a narrow range, it is impossible to be more quantitative unless there is some way of specifying a permissible range of values that the strength could conceivably take on. If it could be *any value whatsoever*, then the finite range compatible with the production of life would be divided by infinity – and the chances would be virtually zero. Whatever the true odds are, it is probably fair to say that to have a universe that, purely by chance, satisfies all the requirements appropriate to the development of life is less likely than winning first prize in the State Lottery.

All of this goes under the name of the Anthropic Principle. It calls for an explanation of some sort – though to hear some people talk one might think it doesn't. What they say is this: "Of course, the world has to be suitable for the development of life – otherwise we wouldn't be here asking these questions." There is a certain element of truth in this. Given that we are here, we *must* find ourselves in such a universe. But that still doesn't address the question of *why* we should be here in the first place. Richard Swinburne puts it nicely when he describes a prisoner facing a firing squad. There are ten marksmen; they have never been known to miss. But on this occasion all ten miss the target. The prisoner, when interviewed afterward about his miraculous deliverance, is quite unimpressed. "There's no mystery," he declares. "Of course they missed, otherwise I wouldn't be here talking to you about it."

No, we have to face the fact that we are presented with a Universe that, although at first sight appeared somewhat hostile to life, on closer examination is found to be exceptionally fine-tuned for the development of life. Thus, for instance, we began thinking that the immensity of the Universe was far in excess of requirements, but now we recognize that if the galaxies are to continue receding at high speed for the 12,000 million years of evolutionary history, a life-bearing Universe cannot be any smaller.

Such then are the experimental data before us. Now comes the interpretation. What might be the explanation of the mysterious appropriateness of the Universe? There are essentially three alternatives:

(i) *Science will one day come up with an answer.* The first is to pin one's faith on science, and assert that in the end a natural explanation of it all will be forthcoming. From that vantage point we shall be able to realize that there was no mystery – no need to invoke coincidences.

To a limited extent, this explaining away of the coincidences appears to have begun already – at least in respect of getting the thrust of the Big Bang right. Recall that there are two broad scenarios: a Big Crunch or expansion for ever. Which one do we think it will actually be? As indicated before, that depends upon whether gravity is strong enough one day to halt the expansion. And that in turn depends upon how much matter there is in the Universe acting as the source of the gravity. If one imagines all the matter bound up in galaxies to be uniformly spread throughout space, that would give us an average density of the Universe. The greater this average density, the greater will be the slowing down effect of the gravity. Indeed, there will be a certain value for the density that marks the borderline between the two scenarios; this is called the *critical density*. If the density is a little greater than critical then we get a Big Crunch; a little less and we get expansion for ever.

So, what is it to be? If we count up all the matter we can see – that bound up in stars, planets, and interstellar gas clouds, then it adds up to no more than 0.3 percent of the critical value. That would indicate expansion for ever. But we must not be hasty. The stars are gathered into rotating galaxies. They are held there by their gravitational attraction for each other. Except that the galaxies rotate so fast, no way can the gravity between stars hold them together; they ought to come flying out like a child on a fast-rotating roundabout who does not hold on tightly enough. The conclusion is that there must be more matter in the galaxy than we can see. It is called *dark matter*, and it is the added gravity coming from the dark matter that holds the galaxy together. How much dark matter is needed? At least ten times as much as the matter we can see.

Nor is that the end. The galaxies are gathered together into clusters of galaxies. They move about within their cluster, but are held by their mutual gravity so as not to move too far from each other. Except that again there does not seem to be enough matter around to stop this random motion from tearing the cluster apart. The dynamics are such that one must postulate that not only is there dark matter within each galaxy, there must be yet more dark matter in between the galaxies belonging to a cluster. And who knows, there might be yet more on the scale of superclusters. Currently it is thought that the density of matter is within a factor of 2 of the critical value.

What the dark matter consists of is the subject of much conjecture. At present there is no consensus – which is rather embarrassing, because it means we are completely in the dark about 99 percent of the Universe's contents!

Of all the conceivable values the density could presumably have taken on, it appears most odd that it should come out to be so close to critical. This is especially so as it can be shown that any slight deviation from criticality in the early stages of the Big Bang would have become enormously magnified by now. To get this close to critical today, the initial density must have departed from critical by no more than one part in a million billion billion billion billion billion billion. (It is rather like standing a pencil on its point. Only if it starts out *absolutely* vertical can it maintain its upright position. The slightest initial deviation from the vertical rapidly becomes magnified as it falls flat.) The only way the density of the Universe could be close to critical today is if it started out spot-on the critical density initially.

This is where a new theory called *inflation theory* comes into the reckoning. It is all to do with what happened a tiny fraction of a second after the instant of the Big Bang when the dropping temperature passed through a particularly crucial value. At this temperature the behavior of the particles underwent a radical change. It is called a phase change. A phase change we are all familiar with in everyday life is the freezing of water as the temperature drops below 0°C. Suddenly the liquid crystallizes out as solid ice. In doing so, it expands a little (which is why ice is less dense than water and floats, and why water pipes burst). According to the inflation idea, the most spectacular effect of the phase change that occurred in the early history of the cosmos was that it gave rise to a special period of superfast expansion. It took place 10^{-34} second after the instant of the Big Bang – that is to say:

$$\frac{1}{10,000,000,000,000,000,000,000,000,000,000,000} \text{ second}$$

and it lasted 10^{-32} second. Although it was all over so quickly, what happened during that brief interval of time sealed the subsequent fate of the Universe. This was because the very nature of the inflation mechanism drives the density toward the critical value. No matter what the density might have been before the onset of inflation, it assumes the critical value by the end. After the inflation period, the Universe then undergoes the familiar Hubble-type expansion, with the density remaining critical.

How inflation comes about is a complicated matter. For our purposes it is sufficient to know that cosmologists have come up with this plausible mechanism for explaining why the density should be critical. That being so, we can predict that the long-term future of the Universe is one in which the expansion will continue for ever, slowing down to the point where the recession velocities of the galaxies approach zero – but only in the infinite future.

This affects our discussion of the Anthropic Principle in that inflation ensures that the Universe will never undergo a Big Crunch. It therefore becomes impossible to turn the violence of the Big Bang down to a level where the Universe comes to an end before there has been time for evolution to have given rise to intelligent life. So that is half the problem of the Big Bang thrust solved. Of course, we could now start to worry about what a coincidence it was that the Universe had such a mechanism built into it to prevent collapse. Who ordered *that*?! We also still have the problem as to how the violence was not too great to prevent the dispersal of the gases before it could collect together prior to the formation of stars. But it is perhaps not surprising that inflation theory has been a source of encouragement to those who hold to the belief that one day science will come up with naturalistic explanations of all the so-called coincidences. For what it is worth, I am personally very dubious that this will prove to be the case.

(ii) *The possibility of our Universe being one of many.* The second way of addressing the puzzle posed by the Anthropic Principle is to assert that our Universe is not alone. There are a great many universes – perhaps an infinite number of them – and they are all run on different lines with their own laws of nature. The vast majority of them have no life in them because one or other of the conditions was not met. In a few – perhaps in only this one – all the conditions happen by chance to be satisfied and there life is able to get a hold. The probability of a universe being of this type is exceedingly small, but with there being so many attempts, it is no longer surprising that it should have happened. As a form of life ourselves, we must, of course, find ourselves in one of these freak universes.

This is a suggestion that has been put forward by some scientists, but that does not make it a scientific explanation. For one thing, the other universes are not part of our Universe and so by definition cannot be contacted. There is therefore no way to prove or disprove their existence. Not only that but the suggestion goes against the conventional way scientific development has tended to go. As pointed out previously (in Chapter 9), scientists are in the business of trying to explain things as economically as possible. Describing the enormous variety of materials in the world in terms of just a few quarks and electrons, or the collapsing down of the various forces of nature into ever fewer types of force is all part of this process of going for ever-simpler explanations. This being so, to postulate the existence of an infinite number of universes all run according to their own laws of nature is to go as far in the opposite direction as is imaginable. Which is not in itself to say that the idea of an infinite number of universes is necessarily wrong – merely that it does not count as science.

In fact this idea of many universes has gained a measure of support from the inflation theory we were dealing with just now. You recall how I described the phase change in the early history of the Universe as somewhat analogous to the phase change of water becoming ice. Well, the analogy can be taken further. A crystal of ice has certain well-defined axes. The directions in which they set are purely a matter of chance, the original liquid water having no preference for any particular direction. If ice starts to form at different positions, there is no reason why the separate crystals should have their axes aligned. Each crystal will grow until it comes up against the boundary of some other crystal.

In the same way, it is believed that the phase change in the early history of the Universe started out from various independent locations. One of the effects of inflation is that, not only should there be a period of superfast expansion, and not only should it produce critical density, but this is the point in the history of the cosmos when the various physical constants (those appearing in the laws of nature – such as the magnitude of the electric charge on the electron) took on the values we find them to have today. The values they assumed were to some extent arbitrary. That being the case, there was no reason why the same values should have materialized in the various independent domains. What this means is that we should end up today with a Universe divided up into domains where the laws of physics are somewhat different from each other. What we know as "the Universe" – or more strictly speaking "our observable Universe" is but one tiny section of one of these domains. Hence the laws seem to us to be the same everywhere. But according to inflation theory, there might well be other domains of the overall Universe that are very different from ours. These other domains are not exactly "different universes," but their laws of nature will be somewhat different. This idea therefore makes more plausible the suggestion that there might have been many attempts at getting the conditions right for the development of life, so it is not surprising that our part of the overall Universe is the way it is.

This is getting us part of the way toward a scientific explanation of the Anthropic Principle, in that it is an inference drawn from what we know about our world and how those laws might plausibly be extended into other realms. However, we are never likely to get experimental evidence one way or another about the existence of those other domains. This is because they are believed to be so incredibly larger than our known observable Universe that it is unlikely we shall ever be able to observe the boundary between our domain and its neighbor. This in turn denies us confirmation of the existence of those other domains.

So, an infinite number of universes, or other domains of the one Universe, is the second way of accounting for the Anthropic Principle.

(iii) *A Universe designed for life.* The third alternative is simply to accept that the Universe is a put-up job; it was designed for life, and the designer is God.

When it comes to arguments about God based on Design, we need to be cautious. We saw in Chapter 10 how the original Argument from Design held that everything about our bodies, and those of other animals, is so beautifully fitted to fulfill its function that it must have been designed that way – the designer being God – and therefore you must believe in God. The rug was pulled from under that argument by Darwin's theory of evolution by natural selection – at least in terms of it being a knock-down proof of God's existence – one aimed at convincing the skeptic.

Bearing that in mind, I would advise religious believers today against making too much of this new Argument from Design – one based this time on physics and cosmology rather than biology. God can neither be proved nor disproved on the basis of such reasoning. Someone inclined to reject the idea of God can do so in the expectation that science will one day show how the coincidences are not really coincidences, or on the basis of there being many attempts at different universes, or domains of this Universe.

On the other hand, for religious believers, the simplest explanation is in terms of a Designer God. The Anthropic Principle therefore plays an important part in building up the cumulative case for the God hypothesis. It is further persuasive evidence to be taken on board by the God experiment.

The cosmos as a reflection of God's nature

Accepting God as the Creator of the world opens up the possibility of learning more about him from the study of that world. After all, if we look at human creations – for instance, a disturbing painting by Francis Bacon of a screaming Pope with his face horribly distorted, and compare that with the serenity of a saint painted by Fra Angelico – one can hardly escape the conclusion that the painting reveals something of the artist as well as the subject. Or, to use another analogy – one that takes note of the feminine attributes of God – one might think of the world as being born from the womb of God. Again, one would be looking for similarities between the originator and that which is produced. Thus we come to expect that the cosmos ought to hold clues as to God's own nature.

For instance, take the size of the cosmos. Though one's first reaction was to think of one's own insignificance in the face of such vastness, perhaps it would be more appropriate to think of it as reflecting the unimaginable glory and the sheer power of God. In which case, with such a powerful God taking a personal interest in each and every one of us, that can only *enhance* our own sense of significance.

Then there are the vast aeons of time over which God has worked, through evolution, to bring us into being. Surely this bears testimony to long-sightedness and patience. It puts a different perspective on our own petty annoyances at things not being sorted out immediately to our liking. One of the difficulties of life is always that of keeping things in perspective – God's perspective.

We see in nature the way God is prepared to employ an element of randomness. We have already noted how God allows the chance processes of evolution by natural selection to give rise to intelligent life forms. Before that he might have used inflation theory to throw up many differing domains of the overall Universe, allowing chance to give rise to those that were to be capable of sustaining life. There is an openness to creation; God is the kind of god who allows the Universe to be itself, knowing that in broad terms at least, his will for the world will be accomplished.

There is an orderliness to the way the world runs – it is not chaotic. It is beautiful; there is a lovely use of symmetry; there is breathtaking simplicity and economy in the basic building blocks of matter and the interactions between them – and yet these are able in ingenious ways to give rise to unlimited richness and variety. Is this not saying something about the way the mind of God works?

One final thought about the cosmos

In discussing the Anthropic Principle we have focused attention on the nature of the cosmos as seen in relation to the life it contains. In this context it is to be seen as "a vale of soul-making." In the cut and thrust of day-to-day living, our spiritual selves take form. According to Christian belief, these then live on in some other embodiment when this present physical body is discarded at death. Eventually, the cosmos, having acted as the mold from which this store of spiritual beings has been shaped, is then itself to be discarded as having outlived its usefulness.

But, as has been mentioned before, there is no reason to think of the cosmos as having but the one function – a receptacle for transitory life. After all, in most regions of space there is no life. For much of the Universe's past history there was no intelligent life anywhere within it. An infinity of time lies ahead after the Heat Death when again there will be no life. If inflation theory is correct, the vast majority of the domains of the overall Universe will *never* house life. Are we to regard this as a waste? Not necessarily. God's interest might not be narrowly confined to life. That is why I suggest that God might take delight in the physical world for its *own* sake. Who knows, perhaps the making of the physical cosmos was God's primary intention. Perhaps God took so much pleasure from what he had made that he wanted others to share some of it – and that is at least part of the reason why we are here!

13

God and Time

God in relation to time

The God experiment not only examines evidence relating to whether God exists or not, but aims also to find out something of the nature of the supposed God. Chapter 6 was devoted to tracing out the development of ideas as regards God's personal qualities – culminating in the all-powerful God of love, justice, and mercy. How about the way God is thought to relate to time and space?

It has long been recognized that God's relation to time could be different from our own. Although we interact with God *in* time – for example, when we engage in prayer, perhaps asking for some future favor – it is also believed that God is, in a sense, *beyond* time – transcendent, unchanging. But this raises a difficulty: if God never changes, our request will not change his mind, so what is the point of asking for anything?

And that is not the only problem over God and time. It is held by Christians that God has foreknowledge. But how is this possible? How can God know the future before we ourselves, for instance, have made up our own minds as to what we shall do? Surely God could only have such knowledge if humans were nothing more than totally predictable automatons. What then of our supposed free will? It is understandable that many people – including those theologians called "process" theologians – reject this claim. They regard it as a logical impossibility for there to be knowledge of a future that does not yet exist. And as we noted before, even God cannot be expected to do things that are logically impossible.

And yet, God's foreknowledge is part and parcel of orthodox Christian belief. It is what gives believers added confidence in the assurances from God that all in the end will be well for those who love him. It is not a case of God having a better judgment as to what the future *might* contain; he actually *knows* the future – so it is claimed.

This is not the first encounter we have had with the subject of time. We noted earlier how time appeared to have had its origin at the instant of the Big Bang. This led us to reconsider what exactly was meant by the term "God the Creator." If we are now somehow to accommodate these strange ideas about God's foreknowledge, then our common-sense notions about time need to be shaken. That, as I hope to show, is what modern physics does.

Common-sense notions of time and space

Time is divided into past, present, and future. The past consists of all those events that have happened. These happenings might well have left memories and other lasting effects, but the past events themselves no longer exist. As for the future, by that we mean all those events that will one day happen, but as yet do not exist. The present is that instant in time we label "now." It divides the past from the future. We live in the present. All that exists is what belongs to the present – what is happening right *now*.

Time moves on. We are being swept toward the future. What lies in the future becomes the present, and is then left behind in the past. What will be becomes an actuality, before passing once more out of existence in the past. We call this the "flow of time," or the "passing of time." We might disagree about how fast time flows (it seems to speed up with old age), but we are all agreed that time does indeed pass.

The future is open, uncertain. Through what we do now, we can affect the future. The past on the other hand is fixed. We might not agree on what happened then; memories can play tricks, or we might put different interpretations on past events. But whatever it was that happened, we have no power to change it now.

The future differs from the past in another sense. This is summed up in the Second Law of Thermodynamics – a topic briefly mentioned in Chapter 2. The First Law is to do with conservation of energy; the Second draws attention to the way disorder tends to increase with time.

For example, one might have a glass of water with an ice-cube in it. This is an ordered situation in that all the "cold" water molecules are together in one location (vibrating gently in the ice-cube), while the warmer molecules are on the outside (moving about in the liquid water). But after a while the heat is randomized, leading to the ice melting and the water cooling. Now the slow- and the fast-moving molecules are all jumbled up together.

Another example of the Second Law at work is to consider a tall chimney. Put a stick of dynamite to its base and it collapses into a heap of bricks. If, in contrast, one starts with a heap of bricks lying on the ground, one is unlikely to find the rubble spontaneously coming together to form an intact chimney (with a stick of unused dynamite at its base). This means if one were to be shown a photograph of a chimney, and another of the same chimney felled, it would not be difficult to decide which came first in time. The same with photos of the ice-cube in the glass of water, and of the same glass but with the ice melted. This shows that the time axis is not symmetric; there is more disorder toward the end labeled "future" than there is toward the end labeled "past."

We exist in time; we also exist in space. But space and time are very different from each other. We measure distances in space using a ruler; we measure intervals of time on a watch. There is just the one three-dimensional space, and the one one-dimensional time, and both are common to us all. Thus we can all agree as to the order in which events occur – whether one occurs before the other, or they happen simultaneously.

These then are some of our commonly shared ideas about time. In fact, as we shall be seeing, most of them are *wrong*.

Undermining the arrow of time

We begin with the idea that one can tell the direction of time from the increase in disorder. Suppose you are shown a film of rubble lying on the ground. Suddenly, all the pieces of brick come together to form an upright chimney. Immediately you would know something was wrong. Play the film the other way round – chimney collapses – that's fine. You conclude that, at the first showing, the film was being played backward. In other words, you can distinguish the correct direction in time.

But in fact, there is something odd going on here. The scene we have been considering was made up of atoms and their movements. One type of atomic movement is a vibration. But if you saw a film of an atom vibrating, you would not be able to tell whether the film was being shown the right way or the reverse; either way looks normal – in the same way as a film of the swing of the pendulum of a grandfather clock would look the same whether it was played backward or forward. Another type of movement consists of atoms moving through space and colliding with each other. Again, a film of that event would look equally plausible whichever way it was shown – in the same way as a film shot from above a billiard table showing a ball coming in from the east and another from the west, colliding and going out north and south respectively, would look just as likely as balls coming in north and south and going out east and west.

These examples show that with a film dealing with individual atoms, or individual collisions between atoms, it is *impossible* to tell the direction of time. And yet with the film of the chimney and the rubble, one *could* tell that one way of showing the film was "wrong" – despite the fact that the scene was exclusively made up of atoms vibrating and colliding! How can one put together a whole lot of movements, none of which carries the slightest clue as to the direction of time, and yet one ends up knowing the right direction of time?

The answer to this conundrum comes from studying the way the individual events are *related* to each other. We have already established that a collision – a *single* collision – between billiard balls says nothing about the direction of time. But what if you saw a film in which *many* pairs of balls collide? Suppose you observed them coming in from random directions, but always going out after the collision in exactly the east and west directions. That would appear distinctly odd. What a coincidence, you might think. It is almost as though there was something sucking the balls out in the east-west directions. That doesn't happen in practice. Next, you are shown the same film, but running the sequence in the opposite sense. All the balls now enter from the east and west, and leave in random directions. Is that any better? Obviously, yes. You conclude there must be two players, situated just out of shot, one to the east, the other to the west. They each have a pile of balls which they propel toward each other, allowing them to bounce off in random directions. This second sequence is wholly plausible and easy to set up; it requires no wild coincidences.

Thus, it is the *relationships* between collisions (how the directions of the balls in one collision relate to those of the others) that provide the information on the direction of time. But note – and this is important – although one way of showing that film is more probable than the other, the reverse sense is not impossible. It *cannot* be impossible because each of the individual collisions could occur equally well either way round.

Now, you might be wondering what this might have to do with the film sequence of the chimney and the rubble. Simply this: the whole sequence of events was made up of vibrating and colliding atoms. None of these atomic events, in themselves individually, carries any information about the direction of time. Physicists call this *time-reversal invariance*. But put a lot of atomic events together and you *can* tell the direction of time – from the way the individual events relate to each other. The "chimney collapse" version of the sequence is much more likely than the "spontaneous chimney-making" version of the sequence. But, as with the balls on the pool table, although the reverse sequence is less probable (overwhelmingly so), it is *not* impossible – it cannot be impossible because each of the individual atomic events making up the sequence *could* have occurred either way.

But you might be wondering how. How, for instance, could the bricks leap off the ground into the air?! I refer you back to our previous discussion (in Chapter 2) of the cup that spontaneously leapt up from the kitchen floor: The heat vibrations of the atoms making up the ground generally occur in random directions. However, it is conceivable – just conceivable – to imagine them all by chance momentarily moving in the same direction – the upward direction. It would require an incredible coincidence, of course, but if it were to happen, a brick, or cup, or any other object that happened to be lying on the ground, would be flung up into the air.

And this does not just apply to cups and bricks falling to the ground or leaping up off the ground; everything happening around us could conceivably happen in precisely the opposite sense. And that does mean *everything*: Cars, for example, could end their journey with more gas in the tank than they had when they started out; people could rise out of their graves and live a life where they gradually got younger –

the "tomb-to-womb scenario." These occurrences of course do not happen – in practice. But this is not because they are impossible; it is simply that they are less likely.

What this means is that the firm distinction between past and future appears not to be as surely based as one might have thought.

Einstein's theory of relativity

This undermining of the distinction between past and future is taken a stage further by Einstein's theory of relativity. But first a word of reassurance: it is *not* my intention to put you through a crash course on relativity theory! It is sufficient for our purposes merely to point out some of the theory's more startling consequences – consequences which I hasten to assure you have been fully vindicated by experiment.

Let us imagine an astronaut in a high-speed spacecraft, and a mission controller at Houston. The astronaut leaves Earth at a speed of nine-tenths the speed of light. (The speed of light is 300,000 kilometers per second, so such a rocket engine is clearly not a practical possibility. However, it is more striking to illustrate the effects with somewhat exaggerated examples!) Relativity theory is able to show that the astronaut and mission controller, being in relative motion, do not agree on the distance the craft has to travel to reach a distant planet. At the particular speed we have chosen, the astronaut calculates the journey distance to be about half that estimated by the mission controller.

Nor is this the only effect of their relative speed. The two not only disagree over their estimates of distance, but also of the time the journey takes. According to the controller, time for the astronaut is passing at about half the rate it does for himself. Thus, everything happening in the spacecraft – the ticking of the clocks, the astronaut's breathing rate, her heartbeats, her ageing processes – everything has slowed down by a factor of a half. Not that the astronaut will be aware of this; a slow clock looked at by a brain in which the thinking processes have been slowed down by the same factor appears perfectly normal.

Which of the two observers is right in their assessments of distance and time? It is impossible to say. But why? Won't the astronaut realize that something must be wrong with her observations when, because of her slowed-down clock, she arrives at her destination in half the time she should have taken? No. Remember, she thinks the journey distance is only half that which the controller claims it to be. Both the astronaut and the mission controller have sets of measurements that are entirely self-consistent.

But, it might be argued, the mission controller is stationary, whereas the astronaut is traveling at high speed; perhaps the speed of the astronaut is making her measurements unreliable in some way – and so one should place greater weight on those of the stationary observer. This is to lose sight of the fact that the mission controller is *not* stationary – he is on the Earth's surface, and the Earth is spinning; the Earth goes in orbit around the Sun; the Sun goes in orbit around the center of the Galaxy; the Galaxy is moving in its cluster of galaxies.... How does one define a "stationary observer"? All uniform motion is relative; the two observers are in relative motion, and that is all we can say – hence the name "relativity theory." There are no grounds for according preference to the measurements of one observer over those of the other.

Confusing? It certainly appears that way when one comes across the ideas of relativity theory for the first time. We are so accustomed to thinking in terms of us all inhabiting the one space and the one time, that it requires a severe mental wrench to conceive of something radically different: namely, that we each inhabit our own space and our own time, and these will differ from each other if we are in relative motion. The reason most people go through life unaware of this is that for most everyday purposes, the differences between our various estimates of distance and of time are so small as to make no practical difference. For example, those who decide to drive express trains all their working lives, age less quickly than those who opt instead for sedentary office jobs. The effect of the train's motion is to increase the driver's life expectancy by one millionth of a second – hardly a factor worth taking into account when deciding careers. (The effect is that small because even the speed of an express train is negligible compared to that of light.)

Four-dimensional space-time

How are we to understand these differing spatial and temporal measurements? Let me give you an analogy:

A lecturer holds up a pen. What do the students see? They all see something slightly different – some a long shape, others a short one. Confusing? No. We think nothing of such differing observations. We realize that what each student sees is merely a two-dimensional projection of what in reality extends in three dimensions. The two-dimensional projection is at right angles to the line of sight, and this line of sight will vary depending on where the student observer is seated relative to the pencil. We are unperturbed by the different observations because we know that when each observer makes due allowance for how the pencil extends along his or her line of sight, they come up with identical results for the true length of the pencil. Thus, for example, someone who sees a short-looking pencil (the projected length is small) compensates by having a large value for the length along the line of sight. On the other hand, someone who sees a big-looking pencil has only a small contribution coming from the direction along the line of sight.

The situation just described can be used as an analogy for the case of the astronaut and the mission controller. Just as the students in the lecture theater had differing perceptions as to the length of the lecturer's pen, so the astronaut and the mission controller have differing perceptions of the distance to be traveled to the distant planet, and also of the time the journey takes. The solution is to regard both the spatial distance covered by the journey, and the time taken for the journey, as mere *projections*. We are *not* dealing with a three-dimensional space and a separate one-dimensional time – two separate realities. Instead, we are dealing with a combined *four-dimensional reality* in which three dimensions of space and one dimension closely related to time are inextricably mixed together. We call this combination *space-time*. The astronaut and mission controller are observing the contents of this 4-D reality from differing viewpoints. And that is why they are confronted with different appearances. Each is dealing with an alternative set of projections.

What kind of "object" do we find in this 4-D space-time? Firstly, it must be characterized by a value for each of the three spatial dimensions, i.e., it must have a location in 3-D space; secondly, it must be characterized by a value along the time axis, i.e., it must occur at a point in time. This means we are dealing with *events*. An example of an event might be the launch of the spacecraft from Earth (which defines its spatial location) at noon on January 3 (which is its location in time). Another would be the arrival of the spacecraft at a distant planet at some later time.

What does it mean to observe this 4-D reality from "different viewpoints"? Because of the way space-time mixes up space and time, a "different viewpoint" means more than just being at a different position in space (like those students in the lecture theater). One has to be at different positions in space at different points in time – in other words one observer has to be moving relative to the other observer. Two observers in relative motion (like our astronaut and mission controller) have differing perspectives on space-time by virtue of that motion.

If we are to regard the direct measurements made by the astronaut and controller as mere 3-D spatial projections and 1-D temporal projections of the "space-time distance" between the events marking the beginning and end of the spacecraft's journey, then it does not matter in the least that both their spatial distances and their time intervals are different. The important thing is that when they each plug into the relevant equation their *own* measurements for the spatial and the temporal projections, they obtain identically the *same* value for the 4-D space-time separation. Thus, for instance, the astronaut regarded the distance covered by the journey as being shorter than that determined by the controller. But she also regarded the time of the journey as being shorter. Combining the two projections in the appropriate mathematical way, it turns out the two effects cancel out, and she ends up with the same overall result for the 4-D separation as the controller. And what goes for the astronaut and mission controller holds for anyone else observing that interplanetary journey. The four-dimensional separation is the one thing they can all agree upon. It is for this reason one is led to the conclusion that what really counts is not the individual estimates of spatial distance or temporal interval but the four-dimensional space-time separation. Einstein himself once declared that henceforth we must deal with "a four-dimensional existence instead of, hitherto, the evolution of a three-dimensional existence."

It is an extraordinary conception. There is little point in trying to visualize four dimensions – one just gets a headache. The best one can do is to stretch out the thumb and three of the fingers on one hand. (Hold them out such that each is as far from the other three as you can make it.) The thumb represents the time axis; the three fingers the three spatial axes. Reality is more like that than having three fingers up on one hand (representing 3-D space), and one finger up on the other hand (representing time as a separate reality). But even then it is an inadequate analogy for space-time. Strictly speaking the thumb and three fingers ought all to be mutually at right angles. That is a physical impossibility to demonstrate (and it always hurts to try and do impossible contortions – so don't try). But if one does not pay too much attention to the wrong angles, this is the best one can do by way of visualizing the situation.

Actually, the preferred course of action among professional physicists is to ignore such visual aids, and just allow oneself to be guided by the mathematics. Mathematically speaking one can handle any number of dimensions.

But there is no doubt that the thumb-and-three-fingers approach does have its merits. For example, it reinforces the idea that the time dimension is welded on to the spatial ones; they are inseparable. We have already come across a consequence of this. Recall how when dealing with the Big Bang, I stated that the expansion of space, carrying the galaxies apart, was an indication that space itself started out from a point – from nothing; space was created at the instant of the Big Bang. I then went on to assert that if space was created then, so also must time have been created in that event; the Big Bang was the instant at which the great cosmic clock began ticking. With the thumb-and-three-fingers analogy in mind, you are now in a better position to understand how one arrives at that conclusion. There can be no space without time, nor time without space.

The block universe idea

We have already noted how one must stop thinking of events in three-dimensional space evolving in a separate time reality. One must additionally not get lured into thinking of events in four-dimensional space-time evolving in a separate time reality. Time is *already* incorporated into the 4-D reality as the fourth dimension. What that means is that four-dimensional space-time does not change. Something can only change *in time*. But space-time is not in time; on the contrary, time is in space-time. In our analogy, the instant at which you picked up this book to start reading it can be represented by one point along the thumb denoting time, the present instant can be represented by another, and the instant at which you will eventually lay the book aside (and reach for the aspirin bottle) by a third point along the thumb. It is all there along the thumb: *past, present, and future.* Space-time is static. We call it a *block universe.*

We are accustomed to think that all of space exists at each point of time. So, for example, at this instant in time there exists not only the location where you happen to be, but also New York, Hong Kong, planet Jupiter, and distant galaxies. We have no difficulty getting our mind around the idea that all of space exists at each point in time. What the block universe idea is saying is that likewise *all of time exists at each point in space.* That means, for instance, at this point of space here – where you are seated – all of time exists: the instant you started reading the book, this present instant, the instant you lay the book aside, the day the building you are sitting in gets demolished and replaced by something else, the day the site gets burned up when the Sun becomes a red giant, and the endless aeons of the eventual Heat Death of the Universe. In some sense, it all *exists.*

What exactly do I mean when I say "in some sense"? I don't know; I cannot say more. It is a sense that defies the imagination. All I can say is that the thumb (or if one prefers, the mathematics) implies that this is so. We must simply allow the analogy, or the mathematics, to be our guide.

According to this viewpoint, there is nothing special about the particular instant we choose to label "now." All points in time are on an *equal* footing. The future in itself is *not* uncertain. We might not *know* what the future holds. But that is only because the sum total of the information to which we have access (at this point in time) is too limited to permit such a deduction of what lies ahead. This is in contrast to the type of information we have at the present instant concerning past events. This is often of a kind that does indeed allow us to be reasonably sure of what exists in the past. But regardless of the inadequate nature of our knowledge of future events, our modern understanding of time would seem to indicate that whatever the future holds, in some sense it is there, fixed, waiting for us to come upon it.

This is so counterintuitive that many people – including several noted and highly respected physicists – find it quite impossible to accept. But as far as I am concerned, I think the conclusion is forced upon us for the following reason.

The loss of simultaneity

So far, I have indicated that our astronaut and mission controller do not agree about the time the interplanetary journey took. That is not their only disagreement about time. Relativity theory has a further surprise for us. It concerns the simultaneity of events. There is no problem about events occurring at the same location. For instance, if a stone is hurled at a window, everyone can agree that the event known as "ball arrives at window" is simultaneous with the event known as "window breaks." But what if we are talking about events occurring at *different* locations? Relativity theory shows that two observers in relative motion do *not* agree about the simultaneity of events that occur at a distance from each other.

For instance, at Houston it is 12 noon exactly. The controller is wondering what the astronaut is doing at this precise moment in time far out in space. He cannot know immediately; it takes time for information to travel at the speed of light from the spacecraft to the base. (It is another consequence of the theory of relativity that nothing can travel faster than light. This is a speed limit that requires no speed cameras for enforcement.) Eventually the controller receives the requisite signals from the spacecraft. Knowing the distance of the craft from Houston at any time, and making allowance for the time taken for each of the signals to travel from the craft, he is able to work out which event must have occurred in the craft at 12 noon Houston time. These calculations reveal that the astronaut had just started to do a series of exercises on her bicycle machine. Thus, according to the controller, he now knows that the astronaut started her exercises at the instant the Houston clock had indicated noon. So much for what the controller concludes.

The astronaut has likewise been thinking. She longingly wonders what has been happening back at Houston. She receives signals from home, and carries out analogous calculations to those that were done by the controller. She concludes that at the instant she had begun her exercises, the clock at Houston had been reading 12:10. There is a disagreement. Whereas the controller concluded that the event marking the start of the astronaut's exercises was simultaneous with the Houston clock showing 12 noon; the astronaut is equally convinced that the start of her exercises was simultaneous with the Houston clock showing 12:10.

The fact that they disagree is perhaps not all that surprising. Their conclusions can be arrived at only after calculation, and as we have already seen, they do not agree about the values of the distances and times to be put into the calculation.

The loss of agreement over simultaneity for events separated by a distance has serious repercussions for those anxious to retain the idea that only the events that occur *now* can truly be thought to exist (prior events no longer existing, and future ones not yet existing). In speaking of such contemporary events, one presumably needs to include those events occurring "now" in locations other than where one happens to be oneself. But in the example just given, there is no agreement as to which event in the control room at Houston existed at the same time – the "now" – as that which marked the astronaut commencing her exercises on the craft – the clock reading 12:00 or the clock reading 12:10. Indeed, there is no need to confine the possibilities to these two. Depending on one's speed relative to Houston, there can be any number of possibilities. There is no way to decide between them. In relativity theory, no one takes precedence.

For many of us physicists, it seems that the natural way of understanding this (perhaps the *only* way) is to regard each observer as taking a different slice through four-dimensional space-time – through the all-existent block universe. Accordingly, along with the bicycle-mounting event happening in the craft, *all* events in Houston exist – the clock saying 12:00, the clock saying 12:10; the clock saying 11:50; the clock saying anything at all. The disagreement is not over which event *exists* in

Houston, but merely over which event happens to share the same time coordinate (the same "now") as the event in the craft.

It is the fact that there is no agreement over what happens "now" that forces us to abandon the notion that existence is something *exclusively confined* to events that occur "now."

Mental time as distinct from physical time

But, you might be wondering, if physics does not pick out any special instant in time to be called "now," where does the concept of "now" come from? And if nothing is changing (the block universe idea), what about the flow of time – where does that come in? Not only that, if the future already exists, where do we get the notion of the future being uncertain and open to being affected by what we do now? What does this do for our free will? Are we not reduced to the level of automata?

Here we touch on one of the truly great mysteries: the fact that we have *two entirely different approaches to the concept of "time."* So far I have spoken of time exclusively in the way the concept is addressed in physics. We must now examine how this same word "time" is used in a different context – the description of what it is to be a thinking human being – a *mental* being.

On examining the contents of the conscious mind, we find mental experiences – sensory experiences, feelings, decisions, etc. These occur in sequence. What separates one experience from the next? We call it "time." We are able to estimate and compare these separations or intervals of time. This might be done through noting the extent to which the memory of a past experience has faded – the greater the separation in time, the greater the degree of fading. (Here we take it that one is not constantly recalling that experience and keeping it vivid, for then one is more likely now to be recalling the most recent earlier recall rather than the memory of the original experience itself.) So the fading of the memory is one way of estimating how long ago that experience was.

In addition there might be an indication of the time interval based on the number of other notable experiences we have had subsequent to the one in question. If this is the case, then it might give us a clue as to why time seems to speed up as we get older. When one is young and inexperienced, everything is new and catches the attention – one is laying down memories at a furious rate. As one gets older and more worldly-wise – or dare one say, jaded – most experiences are so familiar they are liable to pass us by without being recorded as faithfully as in the past. So, if one is using a time estimate based on the number of notable experiences one has had since the one in question, it will seem that not much has happened since that event, and hence, presumably, not much time has elapsed – a conclusion contradicted by the calendar.

The precise mechanism by which we subjectively assess time intervals is not at all well understood. The most we can say is that we do appear to have our own internal, mental way of doing it – semi-quantitatively at least.

For each mental experience there are other experiences on either side of it along the sequence, with one exception – the experience that marks the end of that sequence. This end point of the sequence we designate "now." It is only in consciousness that the "now" acquires its special status.

Although we use the word "time" to describe the separation between our mental experiences, it does not follow that this is the same "time" as is used in the description of what is going on in the physical world. For one thing, mental states occur in time but not in space. (It would be absurd to ask how much space a big decision like getting married takes up, compared to a small decision such as which tie to wear today.) And yet we know how indissoluble is the link between physical time and physical space.

Only through the recognition that we use the word "time" in two distinct ways can it make sense to say that all of time, including the future, exists now. What this means is that all of *physical* time exists at the instant of *mental* time called "now" – and indeed at every other instant of mental time.

It is perhaps unfortunate that the same word "time" is used in two such dissimilar contexts. The reason it is, of course, has to do with the fact that, despite the distinctiveness of physical and mental time, there is a close correspondence between them. A sensory experience which is part of the mental sequence (e.g., the hearing of a shot now) is correlated to a feature of space-time (the firing of a gun at a particular point in space-time). The "now" of mental time is correlated to a particular instant of physical time. Although, as I have said, *all* of physical time exists now, consciousness (not physics) singles out one particular instant as having special significance for the "now" of mental time.

A short while later (according to mental time, that is) the "now" correlates to a different physical time. The difference between the two physical times, judged on a clock, when compared with the perceived lapse in mental time, gives rise to a "flow" of time. Note that unless there were two types of time, there could be no flow. A flow is a change of something in a given time. The flow of water from a hose-pipe, for instance, is the amount of water emitted in a given time. But what possible meaning could be given to the phrase "a flow of time"? The amount of time passing in a given time? That means nothing – not unless we are talking of *two* different times. When the bored reader of this book complains that time is passing slowly, she means that, based on her subjective mental assessment of how much time separates her from the beginning of her reading, the physical time, registered by the hands of her watch, is not what she reckons it ought to be. There is too little physical time corresponding to the perceived span of mental time.

Earlier we noted that, in dealing with a physical time that was seamlessly welded to the three spatial dimensions to form a four-dimensional existence, one should not fall into the trap of thinking of this four-dimensional world as evolving in time – as though time were still somehow separate. That is true as far as *physical* time is concerned. Four-dimensional reality never changes. And yet, as far as we conscious human beings are concerned, there *is* change. Physical time might be integrally part of that four-dimensional existence, but mental time does appear to stand outside it. It focuses conscious attention and mental experience on one particular instant of physical time, and temporarily correlates it with the mental "now." That conscious focus then appears to move steadily along the time axis in the direction labeled "future." But it is important to understand that this so-called movement is not out there in the physical world itself; *it is a feature only of our conscious experience of that physical world.*

In passing, I should perhaps mention that some people find the idea of the non-changing physical world puzzling in the light of the Second

Law of Thermodynamics. This is often stated in the form that disorder increases with time. So, does that not imply the dynamic passage of time? No. All the Second Law tells us is that there is more disorder toward one end of the time axis (that labeled "later," and having, by convention, the higher values of the time coordinates), than there is toward the other end (the one labeled "earlier," and having the lower values). But that in itself does not say that we mentally experience events sequentially in the direction toward the end labeled "later," rather than the reverse. The Second Law is solely concerned with describing the physics of the situation, not how a conscious being might perceive it.

God's foreknowledge and transcendence

Why have we gone into this lengthy discussion of time? Partly because it is a fascinating subject in its own right. But it also has an impact on religious belief. Once it is accepted that in some mysterious sense, it is possible to assert that the future "exists" – on the same footing as the present – this must surely go some way toward adding plausibility to the idea that God might have knowledge of it. According to the block universe idea, it is all out there; it is fixed. All God has to do is find a way of looking at it. I would not have thought that would be too difficult for a god! We saw with the analogy of the outstretched thumb and three fingers representing four-dimensional reality, we ourselves could look at it from outside. In a similar way, one suspects that God has the ability somehow to take in the whole of four-dimensional reality from some "external point" of view lying beyond the confines of that four-dimensional world. This is what we mean when we speak of God as being *transcendent*. That is not to imply that God is to be found located in yet more physical dimensions – a fifth, sixth, etc. But he is "in some sense" (to use an overworked phrase) *beyond* space-time.

God in time as well as beyond

But there is another aspect to this. Religious believers accept that God is a *personal* god. We might have difficulty over the lack of a suitable inclusive pronoun, and are not sure whether to refer to God as a "he" or a "she," but one thing God is not; God is not an "it." In thinking of God we have in mind attributes such as love, justice, and mercy; we think of God as having a purpose. None of this makes sense except in personal terms.

So, in the same way as we interact with other persons, we expect to be able to interact personally with God. We expect to be able to speak with God. Partly this is in order to ask him for things as a child would ask a parent – in anticipation that we shall receive an answer. We expect on occasion to find that our asking has had an influence on what later transpires. Such interpersonal actions take place *in* time. Thus, God has to be *in* time as well as *beyond* it.

But you might be wondering: how can my asking God for anything in time affect the outcome when the future, in physical terms, is fixed – set in concrete? As I see it, there is no difficulty in that future outcome already having built into it the effects of one's prayer to God at an earlier time. Indeed, I and certain others of my acquaintance, think nothing of praying for events that have already happened, but about which we do not as yet know the outcome. (It might have been through some oversight that we did not pray about it beforehand, or we might not have had prior knowledge of the situation as being one requiring prayer.) We offer up these after-the-event prayers confident that an all-knowing God will be aware that we will be doing this, and will be able to take our prayers into account in determining the outcome. As you see, thoughts stemming out of the idea of a block universe really transform one's thinking about what can and cannot be done!

A compromised free will?

One concern you might have about all this is the extent to which one's free will might be compromised. How can one be truly free if the future is already known – not known to us, but known to God?

Perhaps another analogy will help: Without your knowing, you have been caught on videotape. A security guard has been following your movements. He has monitored you walking down the street, entering the building, going to the lifts, deciding which one to take. On entering your chosen lift, another camera took over and recorded the button you pressed. It also caught you in the act of picking your nose when you thought no one could see you. Yet more cameras tracked your movements along the corridors of the upper floor, until you reached the door of the office you were seeking. The security guard has seen the tapes. In fact, he has now seen them so often he knows them by heart. Show him any incident, and he knows exactly what happens next. There is nothing you do on those videotapes that he doesn't know about. There is no element of surprise for him. So, what does that mean? Does it mean the guard is looking at a recording of an automaton – a predetermined robot that has no free will? Obviously, no. The tapes are a record of the actions of a free person making free-will decisions. The fact that when the guard plays the tape, he knows ahead of time the outcome of each of your decisions, does not in any way detract from them being your freely made decisions.

In that analogy, the guard, of course, is playing the role of God – the transcendent God. Just as he is outside the confines of the videotape and is able to view any part of it at will, so God lies beyond this four-dimensional world, etched as it is with the record of our lives.

But the analogy is closer. That videotape shows not only you, but also the guard himself. He is the man who greeted you as you entered the building; he is the one who answered your question as to which floor you needed. The tape incorporates a record of the guard interacting with you. He doesn't just watch these tapes at the end of the working day; he also takes part in them at first hand. So it is with God; when he surveys the four-dimensional world with its record of our lives, he sees in it himself relating to and interacting with us. If you like, the world is not a video he has rented from the video store; it is God's own home video.

So ends our discussion of the fascinating – but difficult – topic of time. If you feel you haven't quite grasped it all, be assured that that is exactly how it *should* be! *Nobody* truly understands time. Ultimately, it is a mystery. Here, as on previous occasions, we use the word "mystery" not to mean a puzzle – something that future scientists and thinkers are likely to get sorted out eventually. We mean something which, by its very nature, lies beyond the full grasp of the human mind, and will always remain that way. All we can ever hope to do is skirt around its edges, grateful for the occasional flicker of insight.

What I hope to have shown is that our modern understanding of the subject goes some way toward adding plausibility to the ideas of God's transcendence and foreknowledge. It helps confirm the insights of early religious thinkers.

14

The Ultimate Nature of God

The God behind the relationships

Throughout this book we have talked much about God, but always in terms of *relationships*. First, we examined how God relates to the physical world:

+ His role as Creator/Sustainer; he is the source of all existence.

+ The Divine Intelligence is the source of the intelligibility of the laws of nature.

+ God is the reason why, seemingly against all the odds, that set of laws provides just the right conditions for nurturing life.

+ Just as we ourselves, operating within that law-like structure, nevertheless affect the world through our free-will decisions, so God too exercises a continuing influence on the world in conformity to those laws.

+ But they are *his* laws; he need not always abide by them, should he choose to act otherwise. Nor do such occurrences have to be regarded as "violations" of the laws; such miraculous interventions might be seen as having a natural place within a hierarchy of laws, of which the physical laws are but a sub-set.

+ We have seen how God relates to the world both within space and time, and transcendentally from beyond it.

Secondly, there are God's relationships with us at the personal level:

+ There is the meeting of minds when we engage in the various forms of prayer that are open to us. In prayer we are confronted by a presence – the sense of the numinous. Unexpected thoughts come into the mind which appear to have come from outside ourselves –

thoughts that seem to be the guidance one has been seeking.

+ There are those who have experience of answers to prayers for the sick – the kind of response that the prayer experiment is trying to illuminate.

+ We have the voice of conscience – the moral law within.

+ There is the experience of trying to put the teachings of the great spiritual teachers into practice – giving rather than receiving, loving your enemies rather than taking revenge, turning the other cheek – very strange teachings that seem to fly in the face of common sense and the dictates of our own genetically influenced behavior traits. Inasmuch as they do appear to lead to deep inner contentment and fulfillment in a way that nothing else does, one has to ask who or what the source of this strange wisdom might be.

+ God meets us in our contemplation of the beauty of nature and of the splendor of the heavens.

+ He is to be found in the working out of history and in the way our own personal lives develop a purposeful pattern once they have been surrendered to him.

+ He relates to us through the lives of the saints – those of the past as set down in Scripture, and those we meet today.

+ Above all, for the Christian, God makes himself known to us through his Son, Jesus.

Those, therefore, are some of the ways in which God impacts upon the world and upon ourselves. They are the data of our God experiment.

But note that this is all we have ever talked about – God's interactions with the physical world, or with ourselves. At no time have we said anything about who or what God is *in himself*. Before we conclude, we are bound to address this one last issue.

The Bible informs us:

God is spirit, and those who worship him must worship in spirit and in truth.

(*John* 4:24)

But what exactly is meant by the word "spirit'? We all have direct experience of what is meant when something is spoken of as "physical" or "mental" – but what is the word "spiritual" supposed to convey?

It is here some people see a crucial difference between our religious quest – the God experiment – and *true* science, or *real* experimentation. In science we are dealing with something tangible; we all understand the intrinsic nature of what is under investigation. When it comes to spiritual matters, however, as soon as attention becomes focused on the supposed intrinsic nature of this spiritual world, the discussion becomes vague, obscure, and unsatisfactory.

This is taken by some to be an indication that there is, in fact, no such thing as an objective spiritual realm. God in himself does not exist. Religion is purely a subjective matter. "God is what man does religiously," as Don Cupitt once put it. The inference to be drawn from this presumably being that if no one is acting in a religious manner, the word "God" refers to nothing. It also implies that there has been no God during most of the time the Universe has been in existence – because intelligent life had not yet evolved. Nor will there be a God once the stars have exhausted their fuel and become cold cinders, and the so-called Heat Death of the Universe expunges all life.

But for most of us, God is more than just our subjective religious experiences. God has a reality independent of ourselves. He was there before we existed; he will be there long after we have ceased to exist. It is God who gives *us* existence, not we who give *God* existence.

All of which raises the question of how we *know* he is there as an independent reality. In short, how are we to reach beyond our various types of religious experience and get at the true nature of the objective God who allegedly lies behind them?

The quantum world

Before tackling that question I'd like us to look at what would appear to be a less contentious issue: knowledge of the physical world. What do we know of the physical world in itself?

In case you are thinking this must surely be a very straightforward question, allow me to point out that many physicists would say that the answer to that question is – nothing! We know absolutely nothing at all about the physical world – a world existing independently of our interactions with it. If they are right, then that does not augur well for what we might be able to say about God – a God existing independently of our relationship with him. Perhaps the demand to be more specific about what we mean by "the spiritual world" can be shown to be wholly unreasonable. So it is we ask: how *do* these physicists arrive at such a seemingly outrageous conclusion about the physical world?

It has long been recognized that in order to describe the world, one has to observe it. As we noted earlier, science began in earnest in the West with the rise of experimental observation. The world is contingent – it did not *have* to exist. The job of the scientist is that of describing whatever world we happen to have been presented with. And to do that, one has to look at it – one has to interact with it.

But what exactly do we mean by "interact with it"? To answer that, we must turn to the insights afforded by quantum physics. Again, let me hasten to say that, just as in the case of relativity theory in the last chapter, it is not my intention to give a crash course on quantum physics. I need simply to draw your attention to some of its implications.

We begin by noting that at this present moment you are physically interacting with this book. As far as you are concerned, it is part of the physical world you are observing. How are you doing it? Light from the page enters your eye and hits the retina – the surface at the back of the eye. What is it like for the retina to be hit by light? If we were to examine this in great detail we would find point-like exchanges of energy and momentum. Point-like: You are not viewing the page continuously. The situation is rather similar to being in a cinema. There one has the illusion of seeing the scene in uninterrupted fashion. But, of course, it is an illusion. What one actually sees is a series of individual pictures. If each of these pictures is slightly different from its predecessor, then one gets the further illusion of movement – continuous movement. Thus when you look at this page, or at any other scene, at the back of your eye there is a series of isolated, intermittent events – what we call "quantum interactions." I repeat: you are *not* presented with a continuous image.

In addition to seeing the physical world, you can also hear it. When you do so, your eardrum is being bombarded by vibrations in the air.

As we know, air is made up of molecules; molecules are made of atoms; atoms are made of electrons and nuclei; nuclei are made of neutrons and protons; neutrons and protons are made of quarks. So, ultimately air – and all matter – is made up of electrons and quarks. How do these interact? Again, in point-like fashion. If we were to examine very closely how the energy of the sound was being transferred to your eardrum, it would be seen to be taking place as a series of pinpricks. Yet the impression we get is that of continuous sound.

This point-like behavior is universal. Even when we have a macroscopic situation like, for example, you sitting in this chair, although it appears that your body is being subjected to a steady upward push (resisting the steady downward pull of gravity), in truth it is not. As far as quantum physics is concerned, we are again talking about point-like interactions – billions upon billions of them. Averaged out over time they give the illusion of a steady push.

Bearing in mind this point-like behavior, we now ask, "What is light?" or "What is an electron, or a quark?" The answers seem obvious: they are particles; tiny, localized particles. The light striking your retina hits it like a hail of gunfire. Indeed we are able to measure the energy contained in each bullet-like packet of energy: it is proportional to the frequency of the light. A packet of blue light, for example, has roughly twice the energy of a packet of lower-frequency red light.

But that is only half the story. There is more to this than meets the eye – literally. So far we have asked how light interacts and gives up its energy on striking a surface. But suppose we were now to ask a different question: "*Where* will this interaction take place?" In order to answer that, we note that before the light reaches the retina at the back of the eye, it has first to pass through the opening at the front – the pupil. How does light pass through an opening – through a hole?

If it were truly made up of a stream of tiny particles, we would expect it to produce a sharp shadow of the hole when it falls on a distant screen. It would be like the sharp shadow one gets on the wall when one sprays paint on it through a hole cut in a sheet of cardboard – the paint being made up of tiny droplets (or particles). But that is *not* how light behaves. The shadow is not sharp. The light beam, on emerging through the hole spreads out; it encroaches upon the geometrical shadow. This spreading-out effect is called *diffraction*. It is a characteristic of waves. Waves – not particles. Diffraction occurs every time a wave passes through a hole in a screen, or a gap in a barrier. It becomes especially noticeable when the dimensions of the gap are small enough to be comparable to the wavelength of the light – the characteristic distance between successive humps or troughs in the wave. When this is so, the smaller the hole, the more pronounced the spreading-out effect becomes.

In this way we get a marked contrast between the behavior expected of a beam of particles and that expected of waves. In the first case, a reduction in the size of the hole should always lead to a diminution of the size of the beam on the far side of the hole; in the second case, once the dimensions of the hole are comparable to the wavelength of the wave, further reduction in the size of the hole will lead to an *increase* in the size of the transmitted beam. And, as I have said, light behaves in this second manner – the manner expected of waves.

This is not the only indication of the wave-like behavior of light. There is refraction. This refers to the way a light beam can alter direction as it passes from one medium to another (from air to glass, or from water to air, say). When taking a bath, you have probably noticed that when your leg is partly in, and partly out, of the water, it appears to develop a kink at the surface of the water. This is because of the way the light from the submerged part of your leg gets bent, or refracted, on emerging out of the water – giving the impression it has come from some other direction. This bending of light is a characteristic of lenses, such as the lens in the eye. Refraction can be explained in terms of light behaving as a wave.

As yet further evidence of wave behavior, we have Polaroid sunglasses. Light normally vibrates in all directions at right angles to the direction in which it is moving. Polaroid glasses have the characteristic of cutting out all vibrations except those in a given direction. They would not function in the absence of vibrations – in other words, if light were not behaving as a vibrating, undulating wave.

Now this, of course, is very puzzling. Earlier we had clear-cut evidence for the particle-like behavior of light – the manner in which light interacts with a surface. The particles were tiny; indeed, they appeared to have no size at all – no extension. But now we have equally convincing evidence that light behaves like a wave. And waves, by the very fact that they are characterized by a wavelength, must have size; they must extend over a distance at least comparable to that of the wavelength. So, we are faced with a dilemma: how can something have no size, and yet it *does* have size?

It is a paradox – an apparent contradiction. Moreover, it is a paradox not confined to light. The same schizophrenic behavior afflicts electrons too. Electrons, when they interact, behave like point particles – as I indicated earlier. The picture one sees on a TV screen is made up of scintillations given out as individual electrons bombard the screen – as a hail of gunfire – clear evidence of particle-like behavior. But just as in the case of light, once one switches attention from the question of *how* electrons interact, to that of *where* they will interact, one has to treat them as a beam of waves. For example, a beam of electrons passing through an aperture will be diffracted. The beam will be characterized by a well-defined wavelength. The degree of spreading out into the geometric shadow will be governed by the ratio of that wavelength to the dimensions of the aperture – just as for light.

The connection between the particle nature and the wave nature of electrons is that the wavelength of the wave is inversely proportional to the momentum of the particle. The greater the momentum, the smaller the wavelength. And the smaller the wavelength, the more difficult it becomes to see the diffraction of the beam as it passes through the hole. With a very tiny wavelength, there is little deviation – little encroachment of the beam into the geometric shadow of the hole; the beam behaves like the paint spray, casting a sharp shadow.

Wave/particle duality affects not just light and electrons, but *absolutely everything* – including droplets of paint. The only reason we do not notice droplets of paint behaving like waves is that they are so much heavier than electrons; their momentum is always so much greater than that characteristic of electrons, and hence their wavelength is microscopic compared to the dimensions of any hole they are likely to pass through. The droplets do encroach somewhat into the geometric shadow on account of diffraction, but the extent of the overlap is too small to notice.

Even large objects – like you and I – have a wave nature. When, for example, you eventually stop reading and get up and leave the room, on passing through the doorway you will get diffracted; ever so slightly you will be deflected sideways. How much will depend on how fast you amble through, and how heavy you are (the two factors governing your momentum and hence your wavelength). I hasten to say it is a small effect – a *very* small effect. Having gone through the door, if you were then to continue in a straight line, by the time you reached the end of the observable Universe you would find that you were likely to have been deflected to a point about one millimeter from where you would otherwise have ended up. As I said, not a big effect – but nevertheless it's interesting to know that it is there.

In summary, therefore, quantum theory leads to the conclusion that everything has a wave and a particle character. And that in turn raises a big, big question: How can something be, at one and the same time, both a point-like particle of no extension, and also a wave spread throughout space?

As far as *interactions* are concerned, there is no problem. If we are asking: "*How* will it interact?" the answer is in terms of particles – point-like exchanges of energy. If, on the other hand, we are asking: "*Where* will it interact?" the answer is in terms of waves. The diffraction pattern one gets on a screen the other side of a hole gives the relative intensity of the beam falling on different areas of the screen, and hence the number of point-like interactions one will get in different regions. So, as far as interactions are concerned, we are either asking *how* it will interact (particle), or *where* it will interact (wave). We cannot be asking both questions at the same time, so we never need to use both the particle and the wave aspects at the same time. In terms of interactions, the two concepts are kept separate.

The trouble comes when we try to go *beyond* the interaction and talk about the electron, or the light, or whatever, *as it is in itself* – as it is divorced from the context of an interaction.

Let us suppose there is an electron out there in space – on its own. No one is looking at it. It is not hitting into anything. It is just sitting there. We are not asking how it interacts, or where it interacts; it is not interacting at all. Under *those* circumstances – what is it? Is it to be described as a particle, or as a wave?

This is a problem that was posed in the early 1930s. It exercised the minds of the world's greatest physicists of the time: Einstein, Bohr, Heisenberg, de Broglie, Schrödinger, Born, and others. There was no agreement then; there is no agreement today. All possibilities were tried. Some held that the electron was really a particle; it simply had a wave associated with it to guide it around. Others said no; the electron was really a wave; it just appeared to be a bit gritty at times. Really a particle; really a wave. Each had its advocates.

Then there were those who felt that this was the wrong approach altogether; it was not a case of either/or. This wave/particle duality, as it was called, was highlighting the need for a more thorough-going change in thinking. This revolution in thought went something along the following lines: all along we have been supposing that the task of science was to describe and understand the physical world. To do that one had to interact with it; observe it, experiment on it. But having performed those observational acts, what one wrote down in the physics books was a description of the way the world was and how it operated, regardless of whether it was still being observed.

Of course, in writing down that description one had to take account of any disturbance one's act of observation might itself have had. For example, we are all familiar with the idea that if we take the temperature of a beaker of liquid, the fact that the thermometer has to take up some of the heat to adjust itself to the temperature of the liquid will affect the temperature it is trying to measure. But this effect can, in principle, be allowed for and a correction made to arrive at what the temperature would have been without the disturbance caused by the measurement.

In the same way it was recognized that *all* observation affects that which is observed – even when the only thing we do is *look* at something. The act of looking seems harmless enough, except of course, it does involve shining a light on the object. According to quantum physics, that means the object is being hit by a hail of tiny bullets conveying energy and momentum. If what one is looking at is very small – say, an electron – it will recoil away under the impact of the quantum, or particle, of light hitting it. At first one might think that it should be a straightforward matter to make due allowance for the impact; to work out what the electron was doing before it was hit – before it was observed. But this proves extraordinarily difficult – in fact, it proves to be impossible. In order to be able to make the correction to the behavior of the electron, one would need precise information on both the momentum and the position of the light quantum hitting it. Unfortunately, the wave/particle duality of the illuminating light prevents one from gaining such information. It is denied to us by Heisenberg's Uncertainty Relation – something we briefly alluded to in Chapter 4.

Thus we find that we are denied complete knowledge of what is happening out there in the physical world in itself. Indeed, each time we try to talk about what is going on there we get enmeshed in impenetrable paradoxes – such as how something can be confined to one point in space, and at the same time be spread out over space.

Some physicists pin their hopes on this being but a temporary restriction. They claim quantum theory to be but a staging-post on the way to a fuller, more complete understanding of the world. Although admittedly at the present time our descriptions are on a firm footing only when it comes to accounting for the where and the how of our interactions with the world, one day, so they claim, we shall achieve what we always regarded as being the goal of science: namely, a description of the world as it is in itself, divorced from whether anyone happens to be observing and interacting with it. Such an optimistic stance was in fact the one adopted by Einstein himself. It might be correct. But one does have to say that it is now over sixty years since discussions on these matters were initiated, and we seem no closer to getting such a theory of the world in itself – a theory free of paradox. And as each year goes by, and still there is no complete theory of what might be going on out there, attention becomes more and more concentrated on a further possibility.

It was one advocated by Niels Bohr and his supporters in the great debates of the 1930s. Bohr proposed that the job of science is *not* to describe the world in itself – a world isolated from the observer. Such a description is impossible – *intrinsically* impossible. We were wrong ever to suppose that what we had written down in our physics textbooks was a description of the world we had observed. Instead it is *a description of ourselves observing the world* – and that is all we shall ever get. The observer, and that which is observed, are inextricably welded together.

Accordingly, none of the concepts we use in physical description applies to the world in itself. It is wrong to think (as we did earlier) of an electron sitting out there with a well-defined position and velocity, and that it is just our clumsy measuring techniques that deny us completely precise estimates as to what that position and velocity are (the operation of the uncertainty relation). Bohr claimed that terms such as "position," "velocity," "momentum," and "energy" were coined specifically to help us explain the results of our measurements of, or our interactions with, the world. As such they apply *solely* to the act of observation. It is *a misuse of language* to apply those concepts to what is supposedly happening in between the interactions. Recall how our interactions are discontinuous and point-like, these discrete observations being punctuated by periods where the world is not being observed. The concepts we use have relevance only to the discrete acts of observation – not to the gaps in between.

If this is the first time you have come across this sort of argument, I can well appreciate your reaction. It demands an enormous shift in thinking to recognize that all we ever talk about is *behavior* (how something interacts, or where something interacts); we never, never talk about what something *is* (what it is in itself). It is a difficult idea to swallow because in our ordinary, everyday language we appear to be talking about what things *are* all the time.

For example, I might hold up an object and say, "This object is blue." In doing so, I appear to have said something about what the object *is*. But have I? Suppose I were to hold it up under a yellow street light, would it appear blue? No. It would appear black. So, why not say, "This object is black"? Because we assume that one is not doing anything so silly as holding it up to a yellow light; it ought to be looked at in white light – light that contains some blue light that can be reflected.

All right, suppose I now heat up the object so that it is red hot. Why not say, "This object is red"? The answer is that it is tacitly assumed that one is not heating the object to ridiculous temperatures.

What this reveals is that, when I say, "This object is blue," what I *actually* mean to say is: "When I expose this object to white light, at normal room temperature, it will absorb all the colors of the white light except blue, which it reflects." In other words, it is a statement of behavior – how the object will interact, under a given set of circumstances. But, of course, that is such a long-winded statement that it is not surprising we come up with a shorthand way of putting it: "This object is blue." But we must not allow ourselves to be misled. The fact that we use the word "is" in that shorthand statement does not mean we have said anything about what the object is in itself; the statement merely describes how something interacts under a given set of circumstances.

And what is true of that statement is true of *all* statements that appear at first sight to be specifying what something is. When one takes the trouble to unpack what the statement actually means, it will come down to a statement about interactions.

If you are having difficulty with this (and who doesn't?), I don't think I can do better than quote a passage from a favorite book of mine. It has nothing to do with quantum physics, but it nevertheless accurately portrays the "feel" of what I am trying to get across. I refer to John Hull's book *On Sight and Insight*. It describes his experiences as he comes to terms with having gone completely blind.

> I heard the footsteps of passers-by, many different kinds of footsteps. . . . From the next bench, there was the rustle of a newspaper and the murmur of conversation. Further out, to the right behind me, there was the car park. Cars were stopping and starting, arriving and departing, doors were being slammed. Far over to the left, there was the main road. I heard the steady deep roar of the through traffic, the buses and the trucks. In front of me was the lake. It was full of wild fowl. The ducks were quacking, the geese honking. . . . There was the splash of paddle boats, the cries of children, and the bump as two boats collided. . . . Over this whole scene was the wind. The trees behind me were murmuring, the shrubs and bushes along the side of the paths rustled, leaves and scraps of paper were blown along the path. I leant back and drank it all in. . . .
>
> The strange thing about it, however, is that it was a world of nothing but action. Every sound was a point of activity. Where nothing was happening, there was silence. That little part of the

world had died, disappeared. The ducks were silent. Had they gone or was something holding their rapt attention? The boat came to rest. Were people leaning on the oars, or had they tied it to the edge and gone away? Nobody was walking past me just now. This meant that the footpath itself had disappeared. . . . Even the traffic on the main road had paused. Were the lights red? When there is rest, everything else passes out of existence. To rest is not to be. To do is to be. Mine is not a world of being; it is a world of becoming. The world of being, the silent, still world where things simply are, that does not exist. . . . The acoustic world is one in which things pass in and out of existence.*

What is true of the acoustic world of the blind is true of each of us. We all live in a world of action – interaction and observation. And that is all our science deals with.

John Hull in that passage talks about things going in and out of existence. He is talking in a rather poetic vein there, of course. But there are some physicists who regard that as *literally* true of the physical world. In between our intermittent observations of it, the world goes out of existence. The only physical reality is the reality of observations. Such a position reminds us of the philosopher Berkeley posing the question of whether or not the tree in the college quadrangle went out of existence whenever it was not being observed by anyone.

That seems to me to be an extreme position, and one that is hardly tenable. But what is not to be denied is that, if there is a real physical world in itself, in between our intermittent observations of it, then there are great difficulties in saying anything sensible about it. Heisenberg came to the view that it was, in fact, quite meaningless to try and talk about it.

The mental world

From knowledge of physical reality, let us now turn – very briefly – to knowledge of mental reality.

As was the case with physical reality, the mental domain is one where, at first, there appears to be no difficulty knowing exactly what we are talking about. We can be pardoned for thinking that there surely can be nothing more transparently straightforward than the contents of our own minds. Yet it is not so. An exactly similar revolution has occurred in the philosophy of mind as that which has occurred in physics.

Suppose I were to ask: "What exists in your mind at the present instant?" An unconsidered reply might list such things as a mental picture of this page you are reading; the sounds of traffic or birdsong coming into the room from outside; a memory (hazy or otherwise) of what you have read earlier in the book; and so on.

But there is a problem: if there is a visual picture of this page in your mind, with what are you looking at it? The mind's eye? What does that mean? Where is this inner eye? As for the sounds in your mind, with what are you listening to them? A mental kind of ear? And what of the memories of the earlier part of this book? Are they still in the form of mental pictures of the words you have read? Are they too being looked at by the supposed inner eye?

When one stops to think about it, none of this makes sense. Since the time Gilbert Ryle wrote *The Concept of Mind*, philosophers of the mind have come to recognize that when one searches the mind's contents, one does not find pictures and sounds and memories sitting there. Instead, one finds *experiences*. That is all; dynamic experiences – experiences involving the ego (the center of consciousness): an experience of seeing the page; an experience of hearing the sounds; an experience of recollecting what you have previously read. One is aware of conscious mental experiences – that and nothing else.

Perhaps you found that stuff on quantum physics just now rather heavy-going. You might have dozed off for a while. Did you dream? Dreams are believed to stem from the mind's unconscious. But all we find in the mind is the conscious experience of dreaming. The idea that this is the work of an unconscious part of the mind – a part of the mind lying beyond the mental domain of conscious experience – must be an hypothesis. We cannot consciously and directly note the contents of the unconscious, for they would then, by definition, become an aspect of the conscious part of the mind.

So we find that, on turning from the physical to the mental domain, we encounter the same kind of two-level knowledge structure. First comes the dynamic experience or interaction – whether we are thinking of physical observation and experiment, or mental experience. At this level we have good solid knowledge. Beyond that we have the cause of the experience – whatever it is we are interacting with – whether that be a paradoxical physical world-in-itself, or an unconscious part of the mind-in-itself consisting of unconscious processes, repressed past experiences to which no conscious attention is currently being paid, and other memories. Here we are on less certain ground.

The spiritual world

What has this to do with God – knowledge of God? Simply this: Faced with such difficulties over saying anything meaningful about a physical world-in-itself lying beyond our physical experiences, to say nothing of the difficulties attendant on accounting for the nature of the mind-in-itself lying beyond our mental experiences, is it reasonable to expect a clear unambiguous account of the nature of a spiritual realm lying beyond our religious experiences? If nobody can provide a satisfactory answer to the question: "What is an electron – in itself?" can one really expect an answer to the question: "What is God – in himself?" In the same way, if nobody can explain what the unconscious mind is through some "direct" route into it that bypasses subjective conscious mental experience, can one really expect to get a direct route into knowledge of God that somehow bypasses our experience of him?

As with the physical and the mental domains, when we enter the spiritual domain of knowledge we must pay heed to its two-level structure. First there is the level of interaction and observation – our experience of God. I listed some of these at the start of this chapter. These – the data of our God experiment – are the equivalent of the scientists' observations and experiments on nature. But, of course, some will argue that none of this amounts to *proof* of the independent existence of God – the supposed second level of knowledge lying beyond the first; all we have to go on are the so-called "interactions with God." True. But that is also how it is with the physical realm. As we have noted, some physicists think that the domain of physical interactions, or observations, is the *only* physical reality and that the independent world is an unsubstantiated hypothesis – a convenient fiction. Others say that there might or might not be a world in itself, but we shall never be able to say anything meaningful about it, so why worry our heads over it. Yet others believe that those interactions possess an "otherness" about them – an "otherness" indicative of an existence lying *beyond* the interaction.

What do I mean by "otherness"? I mean this: to some extent the scientist controls the observation to be made. The decision might be to ask how the quantum interacts. The fact that that is the kind of question chosen dictates that the answer will be in terms of particle-type behavior. On the other hand, if the decision is to ask where the interactions are likely to take place, then the answer will be of the wave-type. To that extent the scientist controls the situation. But it is not absolute control. The decision to ask where the interaction will be does not in itself dictate the actual location subsequently found. That is an input into the interaction that the scientist does not supply. It comes from some other source. What source? A plausible answer appears to be that it is some feature of a physical domain – a domain lying over against, and distinct from, the scientist.

In a similar way, a person can decide to go to sleep – a decision entailing the possibility of having a dream. But that does not mean the sleeper can consciously decide what to dream about. The subject matter of the dream (if there is to be a dream at all) comes unexpectedly; it is unanticipated. It is this "otherness" of the dream that points to some other source – an unconscious aspect of the mind.

So it is with the spiritual domain. With all the religious experiences I listed, there can be an otherness to them too. And it is that which leads to the inference that there is a spiritual being beyond those interactions – something or someone other than oneself that is inputting that unexpected quality of otherness.

If one accepts that there is indeed such an objective God lying behind the religious experience, what can be said about him? Not a lot. Indeed with the Christian conception of God, when one does try to talk about the nature of the Divine, one quickly becomes enmeshed in paradox. Here of course I refer to the doctrine of the Trinity. Part of that doctrine is the idea of there being one God. As we saw in our outline of the historical development of the idea of God, the insight into monotheism was hard-won, and it is firmly incorporated into the Christian conception. But we cannot just leave it at that. Christians believe that Jesus was so special that to encounter him is to encounter God. He is fully divine. Not only that, but God dwells inside us in the form of the Holy Spirit. Thus, we have three main ways of encountering God: God the Father (God over us); God the Son (God with us); and God the Holy Spirit (God within us). As far as the interactions are concerned, no problem; there are three ways of interacting with, or relating to, God. The problem comes when we try to go beyond those interactions and talk of who or what God *is* – in himself. Three in one; one in three. What does that mean? It is hard to say. It is a paradox.

And it is not the only paradox to be found in Christianity. Who was Jesus? We have said that he was the Son of God – fully divine. But it is also held that he was fully human. He was not a God merely pretending to be human. Nor was he a human with aspirations to be God-like. He was fully both. But how is that possible? A human is limited in understanding and in power; God is not. A human is localized to one point in space and time; God is everywhere all the time. It begins to sound a little like the wave/particle duality that required the electron to be both a localized point-like particle, and a spread-out wave.

The similarity is not surprising because we are doing the same kind of thing in both cases. We have gone beyond the interaction-with-God and are trying to say something about who or what God is, or who or what Jesus is – in himself. This is exactly analogous to how earlier we tried to go beyond our observations of the electron to state what an electron is – in itself. We encountered paradox in the physical realm; we encounter it again here in the spiritual realm.

Personally, I find this fascinating. The same kind of thinking involved in trying to understand the created world is to be used in trying to understand the Creator of that world.

And note the precedence. It was not a case of theologians hastily having to readjust their thinking about God in order to make it conform with the new quantum type of thinking. They were thinking in these terms around the fourth century – when they were putting together the Christian creeds. Indeed, if anything, the cross-fertilization between science and religion has been in the opposite direction. It is known that Niels Bohr, one of the great architects of the new quantum approach, was an avid reader of the Danish philosopher Søren Kierkegaard. Kierkegaard wrote extensively about the Trinity, maintaining that when the truth viewed objectively appeared to be a paradox, then this was an indication that subjectivity was the truth – meaning that the truth had to involve one's own active participation. This theological insight might indeed have been the trigger for Bohr to concentrate his attention on the observer's involvement, and backing off from the problematic paradoxes that arose whenever one tried to speak of the physical world in an objective, detached way – independent of the act of observation.

The fact that one must expect difficulties in trying to speak of God in himself goes back even further than Christian times. Philo, the Jewish philosopher (*c.* 20 BC–45 AD), drew a distinction between the "essence" of God, which is absolutely unknowable, and his activities in the world, his "energies." We could comprehend the energies because that was God revealing himself to us, but not his essence – what we have been calling God-in-himself. Augustine took up the same theme in the fourth century when he said that we could not expect to know the name of the substance of God. And Gregory Palamas, the fourteenth-century Archbishop of Thessalonica, who had a strong influence on the development of thought in the Eastern Orthodox Church, expressed similar views, as did Martin Luther later still.

Concluding thoughts

The recognition of the need to take into account our own involvement in whatever it is we are trying to understand – whether it be God or the physical world – is not the first time theologians have beaten scientists to the punch. In Chapter 9, we saw how Augustine arrived at the conclusion that there could have been no time before the world was created, long before modern cosmologists got there on the basis of their understanding of the nature of the Big Bang. These instances serve to illustrate how the two-way relationship between the religious and scientific enterprises sometimes gives precedence to the one, sometimes to the other. Here it was a case of theology leading the way; earlier we came across instances where science highlighted a need to refine and adjust one's understanding of God and of our relationship to him.

For example, the vast scale of the Universe revealed by modern astronomy and cosmology, with the possibility of teeming life forms out there, cannot help but force a reassessment of the sheer scale on which God works, and our own relatively humble position in the overall scheme of things. In similar vein, our modern understanding of the law-like nature of the world makes us much more cautious these days when it comes to accepting claims for miracles; it encourages us to work out what alternative ways God might adopt in order to have an effect on the world. It is only right and proper that the God experiment should embrace these, and whatever other new data come to hand through science, in order to promote progress in theology toward an ever-improved understanding of God and his ways.

On yet other occasions, it is more a case of science coming up with evidence that serves to confirm long-standing theological insights. Here we think of the role of genetically influenced behavior in connection with the doctrine of original sin, or the interpretation of relativistic theory that holds that the future in some sense exists – thus making more plausible the idea that God could indeed have foreknowledge, as has long been thought to be the case.

I would not myself go so far as to claim theology to be a science just like the physical sciences. Nevertheless, it has to be said that the two-way mutual interchange between theology and science could only take place if the approaches adopted in these two enterprises had much in common. By this I mean they are both based ultimately on the outcomes of practical experience, and both are open to modifying their assumptions in the light of that experience. In this regard, one should not be taken in either by dogmatic religious people, or by triumphal scientists when they claim to have once-and-for-all absolute knowledge and truth. The majority of theologians and scientists are content to accept that their respective theories are fallible and always open to improvement in the light of new evidence. Certainly, the developmental histories of theology and science provide ample confirmation that both are willing to change. Hence I do not feel it inappropriate to have called this investigation into the evidence for God the "God experiment."

And the conclusion to be drawn from that experiment? The types of evidence considered were listed at the start of this chapter. None on its own was adequate to provide clinching proof of God's existence. But as became clear early on, from our analysis of possible outcomes of that carefully controlled prayer experiment, this was not to be expected. It is unreasonable to demand such proof. The question is rather whether the *totality* of the various types of evidence surveyed in this book makes better coherent sense under the assumption that there is a God, or whether such an assumption is unhelpful. As far as I am concerned at least, the case has been made.

Note
*John M. Hull *On Sight and Insight: A Journey into the World of Blindness*, Oxford, Oneworld, 1997, p. 72.

Afterword

To end with, you might like to know that the thoughts presented in this book were based on the two series of Gifford Lectures I delivered at Aberdeen University in Scotland during 1997 and 1998.

On receiving the invitation to give those talks, I believed I knew what was expected of me. Judging from books based on previous Gifford Lecture series, I assumed they were to be given at an advanced level, to an audience of knowledgeable academics. But I thought I had better check. So I consulted the terms of Lord Gifford's will. I was in for a surprise. The will makes clear that the lectures were originally intended for the *public*; they were to be directed to "the whole population." It states: "The lectures shall be public and popular, that is, open not only to students of the universities, but to the whole community without matriculation."

How had that early vision become obscured? According to Stanley Jaki's book *A Hundred Years of Gifford Lectures*, the trouble can be traced to the size of the bequest. Each lecturer was to deliver two series of lectures, the fee for each series being equivalent to a professor's salary for two years! As Otto Pfleiderer, the third Gifford Lecturer at Edinburgh, was to remark: "The honour is not great, but the honorarium is colossal." With such generous resources at their disposal, the appointment committees set up by the four participating universities, Edinburgh, Glasgow, St. Andrew's, and Aberdeen, were able to attract the leading academic figures. Over the years they vied with each other as to how eminent a figure they could appoint – regardless of whether the speaker had any ability at communicating with the public. Thus, the needs of the public came to be discounted. The distinguished list of lecturers grew; the honor of being selected as a Gifford Lecturer increased accordingly. By the late 1960s, as Sir Malcolm Knox commented, it had become a widely expressed view that the honor of being selected as a Gifford Lecturer came second only to winning the Nobel Prize. (Meanwhile, I hasten to add, a hundred years of inflation had reduced the "colossal honorarium" to a much more modest figure!)

Having discovered this, I decided that for my two series of lectures, I would break with what had become established custom; I would return to Lord Gifford's original intention. My target audience would be the general public. And it is to that same general public that this book, based on those lectures, has been addressed.

In order to cover a wide spectrum of topics, and provide sufficient explanation of the many difficult underlying ideas, something had to be omitted. That was the historical background. Not that this was meant in any way to downplay the importance and interest of studies into the historical development of ideas. Several scholars in that field have given distinguished Gifford Lecture series in the past. The historical approach is one way of addressing the subject; my concern, however, was more with the contemporary situation, and how that might be made accessible to a general audience. Whether I succeeded is, of course, for you to decide!

Index

The Iron Façade

The Iron Façade

CATHERINE MARCHANT

William Morrow and Company, Inc.
New York   *1980*

Originally published in the United States of America in 1965 by
Lancer Books under the title *Evil At Roger's Cross*

Revised edition first published in Great Britain in 1976 by William
Heinemann Ltd. under the title *The Iron Façade*

Library of Congress Cataloging in Publication Data

Cookson, Catherine.
  The iron façade.

  Originally published under title: Evil at
Roger's Cross.
   I. Title.
PZ4.C7735Ir 1980 [PR6053.O525]   823'.914   79-27604
ISBN 0-688-03624-4

Printed in the United States of America

First Revised U. S. Edition

1 2 3 4 5 6 7 8 9 10

The Iron Façade

I

∼✤∼

'I'm going to be sick again.'

'Oh, Aunt Maggie!'

'I—I can't help it. I—don't like it any better than you —Stop the car!'

'I didn't mean it like that. Hang on, I must find a place to park off the road.'

When I saw my aunt put her hand swiftly to her mouth, I didn't wait to find a suitable place on the grass verge but pulled the car abruptly to a stop and, getting out, ran round the bonnet and was only in time to hold her head as she retched for a second time into the ditch.

Straightening up and wiping her mouth, she muttered weakly, 'I'm sorry.'

'Oh, Aunt Maggie, there's nothing to be sorry for. Come on.' I turned her about and led her towards the car again.

'There is to me. I'm supposed to be looking after you.'

'It'll do me good to think of somebody else for a time.'

'It might at that, but I don't want to be sick to give you that opportunity.' Although she was leaning weakly against a fender, my aunt glanced at me with a shadow of the twinkle that was nearly always present in her eyes. She then said, 'If only I had a drink of soda water I'd be all right. Unless I've lost my bearings altogether,

I

there's a village somewhere near here. We've crossed the River Eden, passed Appleby, Colby, and Strickland. Now before we get to Brampton, there's this little place I remember called Borne Coote.'

'You should have let us stop in Appleby and have a meal as I suggested.'

My aunt turned her eyes to mine again, then lowered her head and leaned heavily against the side of the car. I turned and walked a few steps along the grass verge and looked down over rolling green hills, down, down to a valley, where the faint froth of water was discernible. Beyond, the hills rose again to fall, I knew, on the other side to more burns and rivulets and cascading water. This was Cumberland, a county new to me, and although beautiful in some of the areas through which I had come, it was wild and desolate in others. But that was how I wanted it—desolate—lonely. That was why I had suggested that we stop for a meal in Appleby. Aunt Maggie, thoughtful as ever, had said she wasn't hungry; all she wanted was to reach our destination.

We had started from Eastbourne shortly after five o'clock that morning. Just before we left, after she had been round the house to give a last check-up to windows and doors, Aunt stopped for a moment in the hall and touching me gently on the cheek had said, 'You'll sleep tonight, Pru, without pills, I promise you.' Then, with her ability to bring laughter out of nothing she exclaimed, 'Pru, pills and promise. You wouldn't like to partake of a little repast before we depart would you?' If laughter had not been dead in me, I would have laughed. I only smiled at her and we had left.

'It's a grand sight, isn't it?'

I hadn't been aware that she had joined me. I turned to her. 'Are you feeling better?'

'Yes, yes,' she nodded. Then she added: 'Until the next time. So much for palliative pills.'

2

'It's this heat,' I said. 'It's so unexpected.'

Aunt Maggie was gently shaking the neck of her blouse back and forth as she answered. 'It must be ninety—and at the end of August. There's one good thing about it—it won't last. I can't stand the heat, not this kind at any rate. But look, isn't it bonny?'

My aunt moved her hand in a wide half-circle, and my eyes followed its course and saw that the scene was indeed bonny. It should stir me as lovely scenery had always stirred me; my breath should be catching with the effect of all this rolling beauty; my heart should be singing with the knowledge that I was to live in it for three months; but there was no emotional response in me, nothing but an icy numbness which melted only to make room for fear—fear that made me walk with my head down and my eyes fixed on the ground.

'Remember,' Aunt Maggie had chided me, 'when you used to be afraid of getting a double chin?—Come on, lift that head up.'

Could I be the same person who had once had a horror of a double chin, the person who had been careful to sit upright in a chair and never to cross her legs in case her hips spread? It had been said, and not so very long before, that Prudence Dudley, besides being clever, had a lovely figure, and a remarkable face—not beautiful, but remarkable. Yet there was someone who had said that the face went beyond beauty. He had said that there was plainness and prettiness, then beauty, and, after beauty, exquisiteness. That exquisiteness had nothing to do with beauty or prettiness, it was something on its own—yes, that had once been said to me. . . .

'Now stop it, you're tired. Come along, stop it.'

My Aunt Maggie's hands were covering mine, pulling them from the lapels of my suit, easing the fingers away one after the other. Her voice, stern now, was saying, 'Pru, you're tired. That's all. Stop contemplating.

3

Remember, you've had bad patches before—they come and they pass. Remember that—they pass.'

I was in the car now sitting at the wheel. My body had stopped trembling, but the perspiration was running down my face, and it was only faintly that I heard my voice saying, 'I'd better take a couple of pills.'

'But there's no water.'

'I'll swallow them dry.'

'No. No, don't do that, my dear. I seem to remember this road. Go along there and turn off left. I'm almost certain you'll come to Borne Coote. There'll be a café, or some such place in it. Perhaps we'll each get a drink. If not soda water, a cup of tea.'

My hands began to shake again as I started the car but I kept repeating Aunt Maggie's formula, 'It will pass'.

A few minutes later, there was the road Aunt had remembered, and a half mile further along it, we ran into the village and saw immediately, and to my consternation, that there was something on. Most of the villages we had passed through had been sleepy, almost deserted, places. Whether this was natural to them or due to the unexpected heat, I didn't know. But now, at a quarter to two in the afternoon during the hottest part of the day, the village was abuzz. There were at least a dozen cars, none of them very smart, lined up along one side of a low granite block wall which bordered a cemetery as bright with flowers as any park. And sitting among the flowers, on the grass and gravestones were groups of people, all laughing, joyous people. Similar groups were repeated at intervals all along the main street.

Neither of us spoke. My Aunt Maggie didn't make the comment that would have been natural, 'It's a wedding.' But, when we had reached the end of the street and had come to a little square with a stone cross in its centre, she said, 'Over there, look, where it says "Ices", we'll get a drink of some sort.'

The shop, I saw at once, sold everything, including

4

paraffin oil, but there was no one in it. Aunt Maggie knocked on the counter, and when she did so for the third time, she accompanied it with a sharp command: 'Hello, there!' Receiving no answer to her call, she did not, even now, make the obvious statement, 'I bet they've gone to the wedding,' but, taking a basketful of groceries from off an upturned lemonade box, she placed it on the floor, then sat down on the box and, pointing to what looked like a butter cask, said, 'Sit yourself down on that and we'll wait. It's cool in here, anyway.'

I didn't want to sit down; I wanted to stand, or rather walk. At this moment I wanted to walk quickly away from everything, especially from this village and all its laughing people. I knew the signs, I knew what this feeling would lead to. My heart would begin to jerk, then race. Then my limbs would tremble, and this would be followed by that dreadful feeling that I was about to die. But wasn't that what I wanted—to die? Yes, but not in that fear-ridden way. They—they being the doctors—said I could conquer the feeling. They all said it was up to me now. . . .

'Well, Aa never! Aa never knew there was anybody in. It's the weddin' you know. Aa was out back lookin' over the top wall. You can see the side path into the church from there. Well, now.'

The little thin wisp of a woman with the painfully straight hair and bright bead eyes looked from one to the other of us. Then, her gaze settling on me, she said in rapid sympathetic tones, 'It's a drink you'd be wantin'. I should say you do. You look as white as a strip of lint. It's this heat. Did you ever know anythin' like it? And us steppin' into September. Just like the weather, isn't it—contrary? But could you have it better for a weddin'?'

'Do you happen to have any soda water?'

'Soda water?' The little woman confronted Aunt Maggie. 'That's a thing we haven't got. Practically

5

everything on God's earth we've got in this place—' she spread out her short arms '—but no soda water. "Syphons," I said. That's what I said to Talbot. "We want syphons." "Who's going to pay four bob or more for a syphon?" Talbot asked. "But, as I said, "that's only at the beginning, you'd get them refilled for next to nothing." But he wouldn't hear of it. 'No, we haven't got any soda water, but the next best thing's ice-cream soda—look!' She pointed to a row of coloured bottles. 'How about that?'

'Yes, I'll try that—anything.' Aunt Maggie was moving her head slowly in assent.

'And you, miss?' the bead eyes were turned on me now. 'Are you going to share, or would you like one to yourself?'

'Is it possible to have a cup of tea?'

'Oh-h!' As if the eyes were being moved by a switch, they now did a series of jerks between my aunt and myself. And with this action, the little woman made it evident to us that tea was going to be a bit of a bother at this moment, so I put in quickly, 'Oh, it's all right; I'll have a bottle of lemonade.'

'Well, now, not that Aa wouldn't make it for you, an', if Talbot had been in, Aa would have done it like a shot. Aa would do it if you'd hang on, but oh, Aa'd like to see the weddin' and Aa daren't leave the shop, you see, not for long like. But, if you like, Aa could put the kettle on and come back in a few minutes.'

'It's all right, I'll just have the lemonade.'

'You sure now?' She bent towards me as if trying to persuade me out of my choice.

At this point, the shop door opened abruptly to the sound of heavy breathing and the sight of a hand thrust in towards where Aunt Maggie was sitting on the lemonade box brought our eyes towards the round, red, slightly indignant face of the newcomer.

'Oh, it's on the floor at t'other side.' The little woman darted forward, picked up the basket and pushed it into

6

the outstretched hand. 'The lady wanted to sit down. . . .
Is she coming yet?'

There were a couple of wheezy breaths before the
woman answered, 'No, not due for five minutes yet.
I've run all the way.'

The basket and the round face disappeared, and the
little woman, addressing Aunt Maggie, said, 'That's
Alice Merely. She used to work up at McVeighs' for
years, and her mother and father afore her. The weddin's
for McVeighs', but it's not one of the McVeighs. Miss
Doris is a Slater. Her and little Janie were old McVeigh's
young sister's children, if you see what I mean. They've
lived with the McVeighs since their mother died. It's
Miss Doris who's being married this day.' The little
woman suddenly stopped and patting her lips with a
childlike gesture at her forgetfulness exclaimed, 'Oh!
you want glasses.'

As she dived into the back room, Aunt Maggie
signalled to me with raised eyebrows.

'There you are. Mind, it's fizzy, and it might go all
over your frock. . . . You're not from hereabouts?'
The shopwoman was holding the bottle over the glass
as she put the question.

'No. No, I'm not.'

'Aa thought you weren't. But Aa thought you might
be.' She was now looking over her shoulder with a
cunning expression on her face towards Aunt Maggie.
'Somethin' in your voice, like ours sort of.'

'Well, it should be,' said Aunt Maggie. 'I was born not
so far from here—in Evenwood near Bishop Auckland.'

'Well, Aa never! Do you know the McVeighs then?
Have you come for the weddin'?'

The froth was spilling onto the shirt of my grey
wool suit, and gently I guided the woman's hand aside
and took the glass from her.

'No. No, I don't know the McVeighs. Bishop
Auckland isn't exactly on the doorstep,' my aunt
informed her.

7

'No, it isn't that, I grant you, an' I'm well aware of it.' The little figure was inclined to bristle now. 'But the McVeighs are known far and wide. If you ever lived in the county, you couldn't help but hear of the mad McVeighs. Of course, it was the old man an' his father afore him that made the name. The two that are left now aren't very hectic, although Mr Davie is mad enough in his own way. Yet everybody in the county knows the McVeighs.'

'It must be more than thirty years since I was in these parts, you must forgive me.' There was a small note of sarcasm in my aunt's voice. It was a danger signal that brought me from my low seat to my feet. My lovable kind aunt had a tongue like a rapier at times. Although we owed nothing in courtesy to this woman, for she had not put herself out very much on our account, I still did not want her to be hurt. I did not want anybody to be hurt. Some part of me was always wishing for a miracle that would make mankind immune to hurts and the results thereof.

'How much do I owe you?'

'Well, you're not taking the bottles.' The eyes were darting now between the two bottles. 'That'll be elevenpence each. You haven't drunk half of it but that's not my fault, is it? One and tenpence, please.'

We were just going out of the door when the little woman, almost on my heels, addressed me pointedly, practically turning her back on Aunt Maggie as she asked, 'Are you stayin' hereabouts or are you just passin' through?'

As my mouth opened to answer, Aunt Maggie's sharp voice came over her shoulder, 'We're just passing through.'

While I started the car once again, Aunt Maggie, looking straight ahead and speaking under her breath, exclaimed, 'Nosy Parker! These out-of-the-way villages seem to breed them.'

'I should have asked the way.'

8

'Yes, I suppose you should. She'd have known every step of the road, I bet. Look, there's a car drawing up in front. It looks like some form of taxi. I'll ask him.'

I drew out car once more to a halt, and Aunt Maggie, leaning out of the window and looking along the curb to where a man was alighting from a dignified pre-war Bentley called, 'Can you please tell us the way to Lowtherbeck at Roger's Cross?'

The man came to the car and bent down towards my aunt. He was tall, thin, with a grey moustache and a solemn face, the only solemn face I had seen in the whole village. His voice sounded serious as he asked, 'Are you for the weddin'?'

Although I could only see the back of my Aunt Maggie's head, I knew that she had closed her eyes. Her voice told me so.

'We are not going to the wedding,' she answered him. 'We would just like to know the way to Lowtherbeck, if you don't mind.'

'No—I—don't—mind.' The man's voice was slow and held the same note of controlled patience as did Aunt Maggie's. I could remember the time when I would have laughed at the implication in their tones. 'Go round the stone cross there and out of the village that way until you come to the three roads. If you want to get there quickly, take the gully sharp left. It's steep and it's narrow, but it will bring you to the very door and it will save you a couple of miles or more. But if you want to do it in leisurely fashion, take the middle road. There's no shelter from the sun that way, you'll be dead on top of the fells, but it's a good road and five miles long to the very inch—now, is there anything more I can do for you?'

My Aunt Maggie drew her head back inside the car. Her eyes were turned sideways up at him. 'No, thank you,' she said. 'You have been very explicit.'

'The—pleasure—is—mine—madam.'

Oh, if only I hadn't forgotten the way to laugh! I set

9

the car moving slowly forward, and, as we rounded the cross, I glanced to the right. The tall man was standing beside the little woman storekeeper outside the shop watching our departure.

'That,' said Aunt Maggie slowing, 'is Talbot, I bet me bottom dollar.' And then she burst out laughing.

'Oh, Aunt Maggie,' I said.

'Oh, lass,' she said, mimicking my tone. Then she added, 'Oh, well, we know where we're bound for, five miles to the inch or down the narrow gully straight to the front door. Which is to be it? I leave it to you.'

I took the narrow gully.

And you could almost say it *was* a gully. It was a track between two high banks beyond which towered tall trees, a great part of their trunks covered by an undergrowth, the whole making a deep shade over the roadway which was most welcome after the glare of the sun.

'Ah, this is nice.'

As Aunt Maggie spoke, I turned the wheel sharply to follow a bend in the lane, the bend was followed by another and yet another very much on the hairpin style. My foot was already on the brake as the road itself was steep, but, on turning the third bend, I instinctively pressed it down hard, for there, tearing up the incline towards me at a pace that should never have been attempted on such a gradient, was a big black car. My mind registered it as an old Rover.

My hand brake was tight on, and, although I had shut off my engine, I still held my foot on the brake as I stared from my elevated position down through two windscreens into a large face that was screwed up in a sort of amazed perplexity—and something else.

The cars were almost bonnet to bonnet. I did not move from my position at the wheel. Only with my eyes did I follow the other driver's movements. He wrenched his car door open; he took the few steps which brought him to my open window; now his face was thrust through it at me.

His appearance was strange, to say the least. At first I thought I had been looking down at an old man, a white-haired old man—this man could not have been more than thirty-five—his hair was so fair as to look almost bleached. This was emphasized by the colour of his skin which had that ruddy brownness produced by sun, rain, and wind. But it was much later in the day before I realized I had taken any note of his appearance, for at this moment he was awakening in me a feeling that had been dormant for many months. It was anger.

'What the hell are you doing on this road?'

My answer was so trite that, again, it was only later when going over the incident in my mind that I censured myself for it; it was the kind of double cliché that I was careful to keep out of my own writing, and criticized when I found it in the writing of others.

'Who do you think you're talking to?' I demanded. 'It's a free country. At least, so I understood.'

Under the chemical reaction of the man's anger, the irises in his dark blue eyes were widening, and he held his breath before bringing out, with a slowness that was in itself a calculated insult, 'Would you care to take a look into that car?' He thrust his arm out. 'You will notice, unless your eyesight is as much affected as your road sense, that there's a bride sitting in it. And, naturally, she's on her way to her wedding—at least, she was. . . . What is more, she happens to be late already.'

I did not do as he commanded and look at the bride. I hadn't noticed there was a bride in the car although I had taken in a silvery mass behind the dark blur of the driver. I was about to say, 'Well, you'll just have to go back because I cannot reverse up this steep hill,' when Aunt Maggie spoke my thoughts and in a much cooler manner than I could have achieved. Yet there was a cutting edge in her voice. Bending across me, she peered up at his supercilious face as she said, 'If you're in such a hurry, I shouldn't stand there wasting time.

You back down the hill until we can pass you, because we cannot reverse backwards round these bends.'

Again the man held his breath, but not for so long this time, and his tone when he answered was rapid, 'Madam, there are two more cars at this moment setting away from the bottom of the bank, if they are not already halfway up it.'

'Well, then!' Aunt Maggie laid particular stress on these two words with which she usually preceded any admonitory sentence. 'Well then! They'll have to back, too, and the quicker you get started the more likelihood you have of getting to the church, if not on time, then sometime today.'

'Davie.'

The man turned his head sharply toward a hand which was waving out of the car window. Evidently the bride was not going to risk damaging her head-dress by getting out. I was looking at her now through the intervening windscreens and an awful feeling of resentment flooded my body. The longer I could keep her waiting, the better I would like it.

'No, no! Don't be like that.' The voice was loud in my head. I looked at the man and said, 'I can't attempt this winding road in reverse; it's too rough. How far before I can pass you downhill?'

I wasn't looking at the man's eyes but at his mouth—it was very thin for such a large face. It was a cruel mouth, I thought. All men were cruel—I hated men, all of them—all of them—all of them! My mind was beginning to race again. 'It's not true.' The voice in my mind was speaking again. 'You only hate one.'

'No—two,' I almost answered the inner voice vocally because, at this moment, I was hating this big face, and these dark blue eyes, and this head covered with odd bleached fair hair.

My gaze, lifting to the man's now, was undoubtedly expressing my feelings and, as his eyes held mine, I shouldn't have been surprised if his hand had come up and struck me. But almost in one leap, he was back at the wheel of his car and talking rapidly to the girl behind him. I could not hear what he was saying for the noise of the engine—doubtless, the substance was vitriolic.

With a driving dexterity that deserved credit, he backed the big car down the incline, and, as I followed, Aunt Maggie's voice came to me, cautiously saying, 'Now, go steady. Don't be silly, go steady.'

Did she know that I had a strong desire to drive my bonnet forward and crash that arrogant bully off the road?

For a moment, the black car disappeared round yet another bend and when it came into view again it had stopped. From my superior position I saw, at two points of the road lower down, two more stationary cars. The man was out of the Rover now and running down towards them. The sound of his voice shouting orders came to me, but now I wasn't paying much attention to it—I was looking once again through the windscreens straight at the bride, and was looking at me. She was leaning forward over the front seat staring at us.

I willed my Aunt Maggie not to say, 'My! she's bonny. Isn't it a pity—all this mix-up?'

I gave another extra tug to the hand brake before I started to get out of the car.

Now Aunt Maggie put her hand on my arm and her voice had an underlying note of anxiety as she said, 'Now, Pru.' Then, again, as I shook off her hold and stepped into the road, she repeated, louder this time, 'Now, Pru!'

I walked the few steps to the window of the Rover, and there was the girl's face staring at me. I have no idea what I first intended to say, nor what impulse brought me to this action, but I surprised myself I know when I did speak.

'I'm sorry for all this,' I said.

13

'Oh, don't worry.' The happy smile on the girl's face pained me. The kindness in her words pained me. I would have felt much better if, like the man, she had raged. The bride-to-be spoke now as if I knew all about her. 'Jimmy'll wait for years. Don't worry. Anyway, it isn't your fault, no matter how Davie goes on. I've always said there should be a notice at the top of the lane.'

'This way was recommended to us.'

'It was?' There was surprise in the girl's voice. 'Who told you that?'

'A man in the village.'

'Now I wonder who that could have been?'

I found that I was amazed at the girl's attitude. She was going to her wedding and her pleasant pretty face was twisted slightly with enquiry as she wondered who my informant had been. All her concern at this moment seemed to be taken up with this wondering.

From the corner of my eye, I saw the man running back up the bank, and, after saying once again, 'I'm sorry,' I retreated hastily towards my car. But before I was settled in the seat, the face was hanging above me again, the voice snapping out orders.

'About half a mile down the bank there's a grass verge—sort of. It's on a slope. See what you can do about it.'

The Rover was moving backward again, but more slowly now for the driver had adjusted its speed to that of the cars behind. It seemed a long time before we came to the grass verge. Even then I wouldn't have recognized it as such but for the gesticulating of the man at the wheel in front.

Aunt Maggie objected, 'You can't get on there; that's a bank.'

I stopped the car. Yes, it was a bank—not much of a bank as banks go, but nevertheless a bank. My car was a modern one and had little weight. Likely the old Rover in front of me could have taken this slope and held it, but I could see myself doing a back somersault into the road again.

My head was out of the car and I was shouting, 'It's too steep.'

Now the big face was facing me at an angle. 'You can take it. Look, stay where you are a minute an' I'll show you.'

I watched the Rover mount the bank and hang there at a dangerous angle.

'You'll never be able to do that. Don't you attempt it,' Aunt Maggie protested.

'I'm not going to let that big head get the better of me.' I answered Aunt Maggie without looking at her. Then, as the Rover backed once again onto the road, I went into first gear and slowly, very slowly, mounted the incline.

'Oh, my God, we'll be over! I tell you we'll be over!'

'Be quiet, Aunt Maggie.'

To my surprise, Aunt Maggie was silent. When she grabbed at the handle to balance herself, for she was now leaning heavily against the car, I said tersely, 'Don't move.'

Her answer, a deep intake of breath, was smothered under the noise of the cars as, one after the other with throttles open, they sped past us. The other two cars were packed to capacity and I was aware of a number of bobbing heads and eyes turned in our direction. Then they were gone and we were alone.

For the first time, I realized that the road was no longer shaded with trees but was open to the glare of the sun. Gently I reversed and cautiously edged the car back down the bank onto the road once more.

'Thank God!'

Although Aunt Maggie uses the expression 'Thank God!' a number of times a day, it is not in an irreverent way. Not at all. When you hear my aunt use the words 'Thank God', you know they mean just exactly that, and, at this moment, I was endorsing them.

'You did that very well, lass. I would have said nobody could have stuck on that slope without overturning. Well, that was an experience. They say that all experience is grist for the mill, but I can do without that kind, what do you say?'

'I would like to tell that big lout what I think of him!'

I had been thinking along those lines, but with no intention of voicing my thoughts. But that was the way of things. Although I had no conscious wish to hurt anyone either by word or deed, I seemed to have little control in mastering my emotions. That was one of the reasons I wanted to get away from people. I knew as yet I wasn't ready for civilized society, in which you do not say immediately what you think, in which your thoughts, before they leave the channels of your mind, must be sorted out lest they embarrass or hurt the hearer. No, I knew I wasn't ready for an ordered civilized community, for when I spoke I wanted to speak nothing but the truth, plain fact and truth—and life can be very uncomfortable with unadorned fact and truth.

This phase, the doctors had told me, was a natural reaction to having suffered due to lies. All my life I had suffered the one way or another because of lies. I had been brought up on lies. I can still hear my mother saying to me, 'Tell Daddy I've gone over to Kay's.' I was eight before I knew that Kay was a man. I was twelve when I knew that father did not go to the continent for business alone but for pleasure as well, a special kind of pleasure. And yet for years they had both lived together, been polite to each other, talked to each other, and acted as if nothing unusual were happening.

I cannot believe now that I was just fourteen when the farce of the three of us living as if we were a normal family ended, for I seemed to have been playing at their game for a great number of years. I say when the 'farce ended', for it ended only to break up into two separate

16

farces, shameful and humiliating farces, at least to me. But not to my mother, or my father either.

My mother said, 'You will love it, darling; Joey is such fun. He's young and gay and has such a lovely boat. Oh, you will love it.'

I didn't love it, and I hated Joey.

When I had attended boarding school afterwards, I had spent half the holidays with each parent and I could never decide which I hated most, Joey's hands searching my waist or my father's bachelor apartment, which could be in France, Spain, or Italy—or wherever the fancy took him. Each apartment was presided over by a different housekeeper who did no work; but all of the housekeepers had one thing in common—they all had big busts—and they all disliked me as much as I did them.

I was seventeen when my mother divorced Joey and said that I must leave school and come and live with her—we 'had only each other'. Those were her words and I believed her. I didn't mind giving up the idea of going to the university. I had only been working half-heartedly for it anyway. I knew what I wanted to be, I wanted to be a writer, and I couldn't see that I was going to be helped very much more by another three to four years of mental slogging.

Mother and I 'had only each other' for six weeks— then Ralph came on the scene. Ralph was four years younger than mother, which made him thirty-one. Quite suddenly I was packed off to my father.

I was put in the first-class Pullman with chocolates, magazines, a travelling rug—like an old lady, and a last-minute present was thrust into my hand—it was a three-strand pearl necklace. Then Mummy was waving frantically from the platform, with Ralph by her side. Her eyes were full of tears—I swear she had a glycerine phial in her handkerchief. And so she was rid of me once again.

But that was one journey I did not complete. I got off

at the next station, put my new yellow hide cases in the 'Left Luggage' office, and went to the coach station. A little over an hour later, I was sitting in the kitchen of my Aunt Maggie's house in Eastbourne. Her arms were around me and her tears, real tears, were mingling with mine as she pressed me to her, murmuring over and over again, 'Don't worry, my love. There now, there now. You'll stay with me. Just let them try to get you— just let them.'

They did try, but not overhard. My mother descended on the little house and accused her elder half-sister of being an interfering, frustrated old maid.

'Was I coming back home?'

No, I was not.

She would write to my father—something would be done about it.

Nothing was done about it. That was the humiliating thing. The knowledge that they were glad to be rid of me was more devastating than the game of tug-of-war they had played with me for years. And all the love and kindness Aunt Maggie showered on me couldn't make up for the feeling of being rejected, of being thrown aside, put out of the way.

I was eighteen when I first took ill, and neither of them came to see me. My father was in Australia by then. He sent me money to buy an expensive present and said he had been in touch with the doctor and I must get out and enjoy myself. My mother was in France on an extended honeymoon. She, too, had been in touch with the doctor and her advice was similar to my father's—I must get out and enjoy myself. When she returned she would get Ralph to introduce me to some nice boys. With my looks I could pick and choose. But, in the meantime, I must get about and amuse myself. There was no better cure for—*nerves*!

Neither the doctor nor Aunt Maggie had called my illness 'nerves'. The doctor had said it was a form of exhaustion. I was so weak I couldn't lift hand or foot. I lay in bed day after day looking out the window at the trees across the road through which I could glimpse the chimneys of the big empty house beyond. It was thinking about this house that brought vitality back into my body. I found I was filling the empty rooms with people and making up stories about them.

I made up several stories about the house and, always, the occupants were a close-knit family, a happy family. Then, one day, my dreams turned into reality. A family came to live in the house. It seemed to me at the time that I had conjured them up out of fantasy. It was a happy family; I became connected with it, and the connection ruined my life.

It says somewhere in the Bible: 'And their second state was worse than their first.' This was true for me, too. . . .

'Well I never!' These words must have escaped Aunt Maggie's guarded lips, for her lips were always guarded on any subject that might bring me added hurt.

The man in the village had said the road would take us to the very door. And that is what it had done. The path had widened out into a kind of drive, and the drive encircled a large round of lawn, and, beyond it, stood the house—a replica of the house I had been thinking about only a moment ago. There were the steps leading to the front door, four in this case, the other house had six. And, on each side of the steps, there were two large bow windows. Above them were six long windows which spanned the front of the house. The windows in the other house had been footed with iron balconies. There were no balconies here, but the side of the house was almost covered along its ground-floor level and halfway up its height with a conservatory, an exact replica of that other conservatory.

'Well, we're here.' Aunt Maggie's voice was low. 'We'd better make ourselves known. Everything seems very quiet—no!'

It was at this point we turned and looked at each other, the same thought speaking from our eyes. We were at the bottom of a valley. It seemed a dead end and there was no other house to be seen. The wedding party must have come from here.

My Aunt Maggie was biting her lip and she pulled on it hard before saying, 'But this can't be Lowtherbeck! That woman said the name was McVeigh—I mean those concerned with the wedding.'

'No, "Slater", I think. She said the name was "Slater".'

'Well, Slater or McVeigh, that's got nothing to do with Cleverly, has it? Miss Flora Cleverly, that's the name on the letter.' Aunt Maggie rapidly opened her bag and, producing the last letter of correspondence that had passed between her and the owner of the cottage we had taken, she tapped the signature, saying, 'Flora Cleverly!'

'Well, there's bound to be someone about. We'd better enquire—we can't just keep going on.'

Simultaneously we got out of the car and together we walked up the steps to the front door. It was wide open, showing a half-panelled hall with stairs leading off at the end. On a polished table to the left side of the door stood two twisted candlesticks with a bowl of roses between. The hall floor was bare except for one rug in its centre, and, although the boards showed the dusty marks of many feet, I could see from the surroundings it had been highly polished. I have always had an observant eye, seeming to take in everything at a glance. I suppose it is a natural part of a writer's stock in trade, and, from the first glimpse of the interior of this house, I sensed that there was little money about—at least not enough to keep up with the ordinary wear and tear of such an establishment—for, although I could only see two steps of the stairs I noted that the stair carpet was worn, so worn it was torn in the middle of the treads.

After I had rung the bell for the third time, Aunt Maggie said, 'Let's walk around.'

So we went down the steps again and along the front of the house, but before we reached the second bow window we had both stopped again, our glances drawn to a length of whiteness stretching from the window to the other side of the room—a table laden with the wedding feast.

My Aunt Maggie's crisp tones brought my gaze from the window. 'Well, I just can't understand this. There's only one thing I know: this can't be the place we're looking for.'

We were now on the side of the house opposite to the conservatory. This side was open to a courtyard—but an unusual type of courtyard, for it was bordered on one side with a hill of stark solid rock. On our journey over the fells, we had passed great outcrops of rock—the fells themselves were composed of such, as were sections of the hills and mountains—but it seemed odd to find the rock so near to the house when all around there was evidence of a green valley which was wooded in parts. The rock looked out of place, as if the house had been there first.

'Hello, there!' Aunt Maggie was calling now, her voice loud. 'Hello, there!' When there was no answer, she turned towards me and lifted her shoulders significantly. 'Surely there must be someone about—they couldn't leave the place to God and good neighbours and all the doors open and everything.'

My aunt was moving now towards the middle of the rock wall in which, oddly enough, there was a door— and the door stood open. I had turned and was looking towards the side of the house, which I realized was the kitchen side.

Aunt Maggie said, 'Here, a minute!'

Her tone was urgent, and when I walked towards the rock I thought how odd it was to see an ordinary door-way in that massive stone. The doorway spoke of a

21

hollowness inside which belied the impression of the rock itself. Then I was standing by Aunt Maggie's side and she was pointing into the dim depths. As I peered I saw what had caused her exclamation.

'They grow mushrooms—look at the boxes. That must be a cave in there. But the smell! Still, it's fascinating.'

'Yes, yes, but let's try to find someone.' I wasn't interested in the mushrooms or the cave. Of a sudden, I was feeling very tired, physically tired; I had been at the wheel of the car for hours. What was more, I hadn't had a solid meal since six o'clock last night.

As we turned away, I almost tripped over a piece of wood at the foot of a small lean-to which covered an old rusty coke stove. I kicked it aside and said to Aunt Maggie, as she was going to some pains to close the door, 'I wouldn't shut it; it was likely left open for a purpose.'

I was to remember these words of mine some time later.

'This is fantastic,' said Aunt Maggie, dusting her hands. 'If this is Lowtherbeck, where are the Cleverlys in all this? Evidently, the bride is from here, and if she is, then so are those McVeighs.'

'Well, if that's the case—'

'Ssh! Look there.'

Stemming my rising indignation, I turned in the direction of Aunt Maggie's gaze. Standing at the corner of the house watching us from underneath lowered lids, I saw a young girl. The sun was full in my eyes and, from that distance, I guessed she could have been any age from fourteen to eighteen.

'Hello!' called Aunt Maggie. She moved forward and I followed her, and now we were standing close to the girl.

As I looked at this being, I felt a tremor pass through me. It wasn't a tremor of revulsion, but a feeling that always prepared me inwardly when I was confronted

22

with something odd in nature. I have experienced it on a bus occasionally, and on board ships when sitting next to someone who looked quite ordinary, but proved to be slightly deranged.

However, it did not require any gift of insight or deep probing to know that standing before us was an unusual person. I was more puzzled than ever now about her age, but what intrigued me more was the beauty of the creature—immediately on looking at this girl, I had termed her in my mind a 'creature', a delicate, rather unearthly, creature. Her head was still inclined forward, but her eyes were wide open now and it was for all the world as if we were looking into the eyes of a young antelope. Her skin was cream-coloured—one could almost imagine that it would feel pleasantly warm to one's touch. Her mouth was full and beautifully shaped. But it was not the face that gave the impression of strangeness so much as the girl's body, for it seemed to droop; rather, it was relaxed like that of a very young child.

'Hello, my dear.' Aunt Maggie's voice was soft and low as if speaking to a child whom she did not want to startle. 'I think we are lost. We are looking for a house called Lowtherbeck at Roger's Cross. Can you help us?'

For answer, the girl turned slowly and pointed towards the house, and, as she did so, there slipped from her hand a book. As it fell to the ground, I saw that it was a Beatrix Potter book. There was nothing strange in that—this was Beatrix Potter's country—yet, was there not something extraordinary in a girl of this age reading such a baby book? Well, why not? I was still reading, at intervals, A. A. Milne's *Winnie-the-Pooh*. But there was a difference here, for this book seemed to be part of the girl. As if she were reclaiming part of herself, she stooped quickly, grabbed up the book, and held it to her chest with both hands.

'This is Lowtherbeck then?'

The lips parted, the head nodded and she said, 'Yes.'

Her voice would indicate her age as six or seven years old.

Speaking for the first time and, also, keeping my voice low I asked, 'Does anyone called Cleverly live here?'

The had bowed again. 'Yes.'

Her answer surprised me. If the Cleverlys lived here, what were the McVeighs and Slaters doing in the same house?—all living together, apparently. If that were the case, that settled that. I was certainly not going to live within sight or speaking distance of the gentleman with the odd-coloured hair—cottage, or no cottage. We would have to find someplace else, even taking into account that already we had paid quite a substantial amount to reserve the place.

'My name is Fuller, and this is my niece Miss Dudley. We have rented a cottage near here, it belongs to—'

'The cottage—yes.'

The girl was smiling quite brightly now and nodding her head. Then, with a darting movement she ran past us onto the drive to the car and, opening the back door she turned and glanced towards us before getting in.

Neither of us had moved, but Aunt Maggie exclaimed, 'Well, I never!'

With no more words, we went forward and took our places in the front seat.

Because of the luggage stacked on the back seat, the girl was sitting forward on the edge of it, and Aunt Maggie's face was close to the girl's as she asked, 'Will you show us the way?'

'Yes—round the side.'

'Which side, my dear?'

'Side of the house, 'course.' She laughed—the sound was slightly eerie.

'You'd better try it.' Aunt Maggie spoke under her breath.

I set the car in motion and edged it slowly down the path by the side of the house. It was just wide enough

for us to pass. Then we came to what should have been
the back of the house, but had more the appearance of a
front façade because it was bordered by a wide terrace,
which was now studded with deck chairs and odd tables.
Two French windows leading into the house were wide
open.

I spoke over my shoulder, asking, 'Are you sure this
is the way?'

'Yes.'

We passed the terrace, then a rose shrubbery and a
vegetable garden.

'You're all right. There's been cars along here before.'
Aunt Maggie pointed through the window. Then, turning round again, she asked of the girl, 'How far away
is it?'

'By the Lil Water.'

The 'Lil' I knew to mean 'Little'.

Aunt Maggie's rejoinder was not, 'That doesn't help
much,' as it might have been to anyone else—she only
smiled at the girl and nodded her head before she turned
towards the front again.

'Oh, look at that! Isn't it beautiful?'

The path had come abruptly into the open—it actually
ran on the rim of a hill and the scene below was, indeed,
beautiful. There again was the sparkle of water—not a
rivulet this time, but a lake.

Aunt Maggie had twisted to the back seat once more.
'Is that the water?' She was pointing behind my back.

'No, that's the Big Water.'

'Oh!' Aunt Maggie, looking ahead, was muttering
now. 'Little Water; Big Water, sounds as if we had
struck an American Indian reservation.'

I was driving very carefully for there were only a
couple of feet between the edge of the road and the
steep sloping hillside.

'I wouldn't like to come along here on a dark night,'
Aunt Maggie commented.

I endorsed this mentally and was beginning to censure

myself for bringing the car along the path. We should
have walked to the cottage first, yet it seemed as if it
were a goodish way from the house or the girl wouldn't
have got into the car. The path now took a deep curve
and began to descend steeply. Leaving the sunlight, the
trail entered the coolness of a small copse, but only for a
few minutes; then we were in the sunlight again and I
pulled the car slowly to a halt.

I knew, as I stared at the scene before me, that if
nature alone could cure a troubled mind that I would
soon be better. There to the right of us lay a small lake,
bordered on one side by the continuation of the copse
we had just passed through. On the opposite side, rose a
hill covered with great patches of heather. Slowly I
brought my gaze from the right and looked to the left.

Aunt Maggie was also looking in this direction. She
turned her wonder-filled eyes towards me and breathed,
'My, isn't it bonny!'

'Bonny' was not the correct word to describe the
cottage. It was two-storied and built of blocks of granite
which in the late afternoon light, had a warm pink hue.
Profuse clematis covered one corner and lent an added
beauty to the stone. Before the door and the two windows were wide flagstones intersected with heather.
There was nothing between the flagstones and the grass
bank that sloped very gently towards the lake. A railing,
a garden ornament, even a chair would have marred the
whole at this moment. The lake and the cottage were
one and I was to live here for three months.

For the moment I had forgotten about the man with
the odd-coloured hair.

'Well, well!' Aunt Maggie was slowly moving towards
the cottage now with the girl walking slightly in front
of her, her face half turned towards my aunt as if she
were leading her. And Aunt Maggie might have been
speaking to herself, for I was still in the driving seat, but
I caught her words as she said: 'She didn't exaggerate—
"a haven of peace" she called it.'

And yes, that's what the letter had said, 'a haven of peace'. And the writer had added, 'I'm sure your niece will benefit from her stay, it's worked little miracles with a number of convalescents.' Recalling these words, I felt a quick stab of resentment, resentment that anyone else should have lived in this cottage, should have come here before me. I was aware that the feeling was ridiculous and unreasonable.

I got out of the car and watched my aunt and the girl walk out of the sunlight into the dark shadow of the doorway, but I made no haste to follow them for I was experiencing another odd feeling. I was resenting the fact that Aunt Maggie was with me. I had the strangest desire that I should be alone in this place, along with the cottage and the lake. I turned my eyes to the water. A strip of it, near the right bank where the trees were, lay in shadow. The rest of the water was a magnet for the sun, and, as if being caressed with jewelled rain, the surface sparkled and shimmered. So bright was the reflection that I closed my eyes against its brilliance.

'Pru!'

I turned towards the cottage. There was Aunt Maggie beckoning me from the window. I walked slowly towards the door; when I reached the threshold I stopped. Nothing that I saw surprised me; I seemed to know exactly how the place would be furnished. No wheel-back cottagey chairs, no chintz, no gay assortment of coloured cushions. There was no femininity at all about the long low room into which I walked straight from the open door.

I looked first to the left of me where Aunt Maggie now stood near an open fireplace which was just a large inlet in the wall and was made of the same rough stone as the outer walls of the cottage. There was a fire basket flanked by a pair of iron dogs in the aperture. Opposite the fireplace was a long deep brown leather couch holding cushions of the same hue. Behind this, running lengthwise with the room, was a rough refectory table, definitely handmade, and well made at that. Even my cursory glance took in this fact. The wall opposite to me had been boarded halfway along its length, and this was topped by a shelf on which stood, at intervals, three wooden animals: a horse, a fox, and a dog. The dog was a perfect replica of a Labrador. Aware that my Aunt Maggie was watching me intensely, as was the girl, I turned and looked towards my right. In the middle of a wall which was entirely stark stone, there was another door which led into, I could see beyond, a kitchen. To each side of me, and flanking the front door, were two windows. They were square and rather high, and the sills were the same thickness as the stone.

'Like it?'

Aunt Maggie's question startled me for a moment and I repeated her words 'Like it?' Then I answered, 'I think it's amazing—out—' I had been about to say 'out of this world' but I checked myself in time. It would have been a trite summing up, an easy summing up. I often become annoyed at myself for lazy expression, for not translating my thoughts into meaningful words, and this cottage—this house—this setting deserved meaningful words.

'Where are the stairs?' My Aunt Maggie was bending down slightly towards the girl now.

With a skipping movement that had about it the jerky abandoned style of a child at play, the girl went towards the other doorway, and we followed.

The kitchen I saw was for use as a kitchen and nothing else. It held a Calor gas stove and a shallow stone sink above which there was a Calor water heater. On one side of the sink was a draining board, on the other, a small table. Beyond this, there was a door which doubtless opened into a pantry. On the wall opposite the stove and the sink was another door, which evidently led outside. And next to this, sprouting almost vertically out of the room, were the stairs.

The sight of their steepness had almost silenced Aunt

Maggie. Except for a noise that was a cross between an 'Oh!' and a groan she made no verbal comment, and bringing her eyes from the dim tunnel of the staircase she looked at me. Then, being Aunt Maggie, she smiled, although somewhat wryly.

'Shall we try it?' she asked.

My lips at least were smiling as I said, 'I'll go first,' but before I had finished speaking the girl was in front of me and she ascended by the simple method of using both her hands and feet.

I disdained to follow her example, at least for the first four stairs, but before I had reached the twelfth and final stair, I had resorted to her sensible means of going up this particular stairway. There was no landing, and, as I stepped out of the well of the stairs straight into a room, I did not look about me but turned swiftly and, bending forward, held out my hand to assist Aunt Maggie.

But my help was disdainfully thrust aside, not by my aunt's hands, she was using those as I had done, but by her voice, saying, 'Don't fluster me else I'll be over.'

I had never looked upon my Aunt Maggie as old— she was an ageless creature. Some days she appeared thirty or younger, at least in her outlook, and, physically, never over fifty. But, as she pulled herself up into the room and I put out my hand to steady her, I thought— this is going to try her—and I remembered that Aunt Maggie was sixty-five. Yet, when she straightened up, her breathing was even and she seemed undisturbed.

We moved away from the unprotected well of the staircase as if afraid of becoming overbalanced, then we looked around the room. It was the lowness of the ceiling that I noticed first; it was not more than six feet high. A tall person would have had to stoop. I am five feet seven and I felt that my hair was almost scraping it. There was one window in this room, small and square like those downstairs. Under it was a single wooden bed covered with a thick plaid travelling rug. There was a chest of drawers against the wall at the foot of the bed, and on the top of them was a small swing mirror. On the wall opposite was a long oak plain wardrobe like a detached cupboard; and, between the two walls, a door led into another room.

The girl again went first. When we followed I found that the same pattern was repeated here; a single bed, a chest of drawers, a mirror and a wardrobe; no facilities for washing. The question did cross my mind at that moment. Not—is there a bathroom? I hadn't expected that. But—was there an indoor lavatory? And where did we wash and bathe? These questions were to be answered when we returned downstairs, but my attention was drawn now to yet another staircase, or, to be more explicit, a ladder placed straight against the wall and leading to a hatch in the low ceiling. When I looked up towards it, then down again, it was to find the girl's eyes fastened on mine. I could see she wanted to speak, so I waited.

What she said was straight to the point. 'That's mine.' She pointed upwards.

'Yours?' I inclined my head towards her. 'You sleep here?'

She shook her head from side to side vigorously. 'Just play—my toys up there—I sleep with Grannie.'

'Oh!' I glanced swiftly at Aunt Maggie. She wasn't looking at me, but at the girl, and, when the girl turned towards her, they smiled at each other.

The girl leading the way again, we descended to the ground floor. I think it was more awkward getting down the stairs than going up. I went face forward but Aunt Maggie, being more sensible, returned the way she had come, using her hands and her feet.

In the kitchen once more, dusting her palms against each other, Aunt Maggie remarked, 'There's going to be some washing of hands around here if nothing else. Which reminds me—' She looked from me to the girl and asked on a little laugh, 'Is there a bathroom of sorts?'

The girl answered Aunt Maggie's laugh with one of her own which was again of a high squeaking quality exactly like that of an excited child, and, opening the back door, she pointed to the wall. There, hanging on a nail, was a long zinc bathtub.

The girl was already running down a roughly paved path to some bushes, amongst which stood a sentry-like structure.

The twinkle was deep in Aunt Maggie's eyes as she turned to me and said, 'It's been known to freeze up around here in November!'

'We needn't stay that long.' I was thinking with nostalgia, but only for a moment, of the beautiful sanitary arrangements in our house in Eastbourne, but as Aunt Maggie said airily, 'Aw, well, sufficient unto the day. . . .' I thought, yes, sufficient unto the day. What did sanitary arrangements matter anyway? So close had I become entwined in my surroundings within a matter of not more than fifteen minutes, that had Aunt Maggie said anything detrimental about the amenities of the cottage I would have resented it as a personal affront.

I turned and went into the kitchen and opened the pantry door. It was dim and very cool. It went quite a way back with shelves all around it; opposite to me was a marble slab on which stood a large brown loaf, two bottles of milk, and a round of butter with an acorn pattern on the top. There was some tinned food on one of the shelves and a number of empty screw-top jars.

Aunt Maggie, coming to the door and looking past me towards the bread and butter, exclaimed, 'Well, that'll give us a start.' She narrowed her eyes as she spoke. Then she exclaimed, 'I've not seen butter done like that for years. Well, now we can get settled in.'

Aunt Maggie turned away and I was about to do the same when the girl almost overbalanced us both as she pushed past us into the larder and, reaching to the far corner of the marble slab, she grabbed up two china mugs. They looked like Coronation mugs, but I couldn't see what was written on them because, like the book, she held them tightly pressed to her chest. Then, looking at me said, 'Mine 'n' Davie's.'

I had a picture of the bride's hand waving out of the car window calling 'Davie' and the name put my teeth on edge—I had already associated the name Davie with the surname McVeigh. It didn't need much stretching of the imagination to know where the designation 'Mad' came in. But what had this Davie—this Davie McVeigh—to do with the cottage? A little tentative quizzing might enlighten me and I was about to proceed with it when the girl, now standing by the kitchen table and still holding the mugs, jerked her head upright and appeared to listen. So definite was her attitude that both Aunt Maggie and I listened with her. We could hear nothing, but the girl now moved swiftly to the kitchen door and stood on the stone slab outside, her head still cocked to one side. Then we heard what she had heard, the sound which made her turn and run like a deer, past us again, through the kitchen, through the living room and out onto the path that led through the copse. I had just reached the door when I saw the pink flash of her dress among the trees.

'That was a whistle.'

I turned to Aunt Maggie. 'Yes, but from quite a distance away.'

'You don't think it was from the house?'

'No.' I shook my head.

The whistle had been thin and high, like notes from a reed pipe. I turned my gaze from my aunt and looked down the gentle slope to the lake as I said, 'I once saw a shepherd in Spain playing on a pipe that sounded like that.'

I had said I had 'seen' the shepherd; but I had never seen him; he had been miles away in the hills. I went out and walked towards the car, amazement filling me. I had spoken of Spain, I had spoken about the shepherd. I hadn't mentioned the name of the man who had told me that the pipe I was then hearing was being played miles away in the hills, but he had been in my consciousness and he had remained there for some seconds without causing me panic. I stopped and looked back at the stone cottage. Already it seemed to be working, already its calm strength was oozing into me.

I began to unpack the car rapidly, carrying the heaviest cases into the house, making two journeys to each one of Aunt Maggie's, aware all the time that she was covertly watching me. It didn't matter. Aunt Maggie was always watching me. Well, she could watch me now getting better. I couldn't wait to get settled in.

2

It was seven o'clock and Aunt Maggie and I were sitting in two rather decrepit deck-chairs outside the cottage. We had sat in silence for at least fifteen minutes before Aunt Maggie commented for the second time in the past hour, 'You know, I've a good mind to take a dander over.'

'I wouldn't. They're bound to know we're here; the girl would have told them. Anyway, as this is the only place the road leads to, they will know it was us coming down.'

'Yes, that's the funny thing. As you say, they were bound to know it was us. Then why hasn't somebody been across? Poor manners, I should say.'

'At a wedding—' There I had said the word, and I went on boldly, 'There is always so much to do, everybody getting in everybody else's way. You know how it is.' I was looking at the darkening water, but I knew that my Aunt Maggie's eyes were full on me.

It was some minutes before she spoke and then she remarked, 'It was odd that bed being used, wasn't it? You would have thought they would have stripped it after the last tenant. And, then, it being made up with a sleeping-bag—funny.'

Yes, I myself had thought it was funny. Underneath the plaid travelling rug, there hadn't been the usual bedclothes but a home-made sleeping bag, comprised simply of an old eider-down sewn together to form the bag. This was covered inside and out with two sheets which had also been sewn to form bags. Doubtless it was a very easy way to deal with bedding but I couldn't see myself climbing into a sleeping-bag each night. In the far room, which was to be Aunt Maggie's, there were three blankets and two pillows under another travelling rug, but no sheets. The lack of sheets she said wouldn't worry her for that night—she was so tired she could sleep on the grass.

We had come prepared with a lot of tinned food as Miss Cleverly's letter had indicated we were off the beaten track, so, together with the bread and butter from the larder and a tin of tongue and some salad stuff we had bought on the way, we made quite a satisfying meal. Later, as we washed up, Aunt Maggie was so funny about the zinc bath, going to the length of giving a demonstration of how she would get in and out of it, which included slipping on the soap, that I laughed outright.

A quaint silence had followed my unusual burst of merriment, then Aunt Maggie put her arm about me and pressing me to her said, 'I'm going to enjoy myself here.'

What she really meant was—she was going to be happy here because she thought that in this charming oasis I would regain health of both mind and body—and, perhaps, enough self-confidence to enable me to live with my fellow creatures.

Because of my parents, I had lived with distrust from my earliest memories, and this did not engender faith in others. Yet I had lived in faith for one glorious year. But the shattering of my faith for the second time was more destructive than anything my parents had dome to me, or maybe I had felt it more keenly because of the quicksand foundation they had laid—I didn't know. At this moment, I didn't want to think. Let the past creep back gradually.

I looked over the lake, and saw a swallow darting in and out of the last rays of the sun as it flickered on the water. He was after his evening meal, and, as he darted and bobbed and twisted, I realized I was setting his motions to the distant sound of music.

'They'll likely be having a dance on the lawn,' said Aunt Maggie. 'Well, if they go on till midnight they won't keep me awake. Once I get my head down I'll be gone.'

'It'll soon be dark,' I said. 'I'd better try lighting that lamp.'

'That's not a bad idea.'

Aunt Maggie hoisted herself out of the chair and, folding it up, carried it and laid it against the wall of the cottage. I did the same with mine, and then we went indoors.

The lamp stood on a side table. It was an old-fashioned one with a pink bowl but it had been converted to take Calor gas. This conversion had been ingeniously achieved by a tube which ran from the bowl down to a junction near the floor boards. There it joined a metal pipe and, so, went to the main tank in the kitchen which reposed in a cupboard under the sink and fed both the water heater and the stove as well. Being so fixed, the lamp was not movable and I had noted that, unless one had very good eyesight, it would be difficult to read sitting comfortably before the fire for the table was some distance from the couch. I probably could manage, but I doubted whether Aunt Maggie would be able to read unless she was sitting directly under the lamp. But, as she had said, all she wanted to do tonight was to get her head down on the pillow.

I had the match lit in my hand and was bending over, my face close to the globe, and was about to cautiously turn on the tap when I was so startled by the door being thrust open that I swung round and almost upset the whole contraption.

'What the blazes!'

Opposite to me stood the man with the odd-coloured hair. He had appeared a big, bulky individual on the road, but now his size seemed to have doubled. He looked enormous, ungainly, crude; there was about him some quality of the rugged stone of which the cottage was built. But the stone of the cottage gave out a warmness; this man did not. His face was not contorted with anger as I had seen it earlier, but now was wide with surprise and what I could only think of as blank amazement tinged with annoyance.

'You two!'

The words were certainly not complimentary in their implication.

'Yes. We two!' My back was stiff and my chin thrust out. I had said 'We two,' but Aunt Maggie was in the kitchen.

'What are you doing here?'

The man took two slow steps towards me and, as he approached, I was overwhelmed with the fear that we had settled in the wrong cottage.

My voice had a weak note as I asked, 'This place is Lowtherbeck, isn't it?'

'Yes, it's Lowtherbeck.'

'Roger's Cross?'

'Roger's Cross—right again.'

'There isn't another cottage about?'

'No. There isn't another cottage, not hereabouts.'

'Well, we've taken this cottage for three months.'

'You?' He screwed up his face. 'We were expecting a Miss Fuller and—and, I understand, her young niece—but not until Monday.'

'I'm Miss Fuller.' Aunt Maggie came slowly from the kitchen. 'I sent Miss Cleverly a wire saying that we were coming today instead of Monday. She had told me previously that the cottage was ready for us at any time.'

The man had not moved his body, but had turned his head and was looking down at Aunt Maggie.

37

'We didn't get your wire, unless—' He paused. '—unless it got mixed up with the wedding ones.'

'Well, be that as it may, I sent the wire and here we are.'

'Yes, I can see that, and it's damned awkward. My brother was sleeping here tonight; the house is full.'

'Then you'll just have to let him share your room, won't you?' Aunt Maggie's voice was deceptively civil.

'That again, is going to be slightly awkward, madam.'

'Miss.'

'Miss.'

He turned his big head gravely towards her. 'You see, I sleep here most of the year. When it isn't let, I could say I live here.'

'Miss Cleverly should have explained this in her letter.'

'There was no need. I'm always out before the tenants arrive.'

I watched Aunt Maggie and the man survey each other, weighing up the form as if before combat. And now Aunt Maggie, dropping into old-fashioned prim courtesy as she was at times wont to do, said, 'I don't know whom I have the honour of addressing.'

As the man laughed, I could have lifted my hand and struck him across the mouth so strong was my anger against him.

'You have the honour, Miss—' he stressed the miss —of addressing David Bernard Michael McVeigh.'

'Thank you.' Aunt Maggie seemed to be losing ground. She swallowed, then indicating me with a motion of her hand, she said, 'This is my niece, Mrs Lac—'

I closed my eyes for a second as Aunt Maggie, retracting quickly, changed my name to 'Miss Prudence Dudley.'

When I opened my eyes, the man was looking at me full in the face. I did not expect him to say anything so trivial as 'How do you do' or 'Pleased to meet you', and he didn't.

He said instead, 'Why the devil did you come down the lane?'

Here we went again! My chin moved twice before I replied; then, and not too quietly, I said, 'We were directed to come that way.'

Before McVeigh could make any comment on this, Aunt Maggie put in, 'Why are you pretending you are surprised to see us here? You must have known who we were this afternoon. That road leads nowhere else but to the house up yonder.' She thrust a sharp finger towards the large house.

'There, you are mistaken. There's a turning that branches off to the right about a quarter of a mile before you reach our place. It connects with the fell road. If you had taken the fell road, you would have come in by that way.'

'Well, we didn't, and we're here, and that's all about it. And I don't think we're answerable to anyone but Miss Cleverly.'

'Really?' There was question in the word.

'Yes, really! I made arrangements to take the cottage through a Miss Cleverly and I will continue to do business with her—perhaps, you'll enlighten me—' Aunt Maggie was back on the pedantic line again. 'Where do you come in on all this?'

'Me?' He was pointing to his chest where I could see the muscles bulging under a starkly white shirt. 'Oh, me. I only happen to be the owner of the set-up.'

I swallowed dryly. Aunt Maggie swallowed. I clasped and unclasped my hands as my mind repeated again and again: oh, no, no.

It seemed a long time before I heard Aunt Maggie ask in a slightly subdued tone, 'Who, then, is Miss Cleverly?'

'That will take a lot of explaining, Miss Fuller.' There was a trace of sardonic laughter in his voice now. 'Miss Cleverly is a lady who runs my house. She fills the position of housekeeper and adviser, and—and performs lots of other functions.'

I felt my face turning scarlet. Again, I wanted to take my hand and strike out at the mouth from which the deep cool-sounding words had come. There flashed into my mind the picture of my father's last apartment, and his last mistress—the last one, that is, that I had seen. I was glaring at the man's back now for he had turned round.

As he walked towards the kitchen door, he said over his shoulder, 'I'll collect my bed if you don't mind.'

Aunt Maggie moved across the dim room and stood near me. Under her breath she muttered, 'Don't let him get you down. We'll not see much of him—there'll be no need to. Anyway, if you can't stick him, we'll find some other place.'

Yes, we would certainly have to find someplace else, for I couldn't tolerate that individual. I couldn't put up with David Bernard Michael McVeigh for long without bursting asunder. The man did something to me; he made me want to hit out. It was a terrifying feeling for I had only hit out once in my life before, and then I had been driven to it, and was half-mad.

'There is always a fly in the ointment, lass. That's life.' Aunt Maggie's voice was sad now and this broke my thoughts away from myself; I was now filled with concern for her. She had put up with the long hot journey, even car sickness. She had put a good face on everything, and, not only today, but for years past, she had done everything to smooth the granite edges of life that would from time to time dig at me. Now she sounded tired, and not a little sad. Making an effort, I put out my hand and touched hers and whispered a saying to her she had often extolled in my childhood: 'Big balloons make the loudest bang.'

The balloon appeared at the kitchen door.

'Two mugs that were in the pantry?' the balloon asked.

'The girl took them,' I said.

'The girl?' McVeigh was moving into the room now. Under his arm was the rolled-up sleeping-bag. 'You mean Frannie?'

'I don't know what her name is, but she took them.'

'Oh, well.'

He was standing with his back to the front door, and, through narrowed lids, he looked first at Aunt Maggie and then at me—his gaze taking in, not only my face, but the whole of me.

His voice slightly mocking, he said, 'Well I suppose it'll sort itself out. Sleep well. I put a clean set—' he hitched at the bedding under his arm '—on. You'll find plenty of linen and such in the loft if you require it. Good-night.'

Neither of us answered. And, not until I watched through the window the dark bulk of him disappear in the copse, did I turn to Aunt Maggie.

She was seated now and was silent—her silence disturbed me.

'Let's go to bed,' I suggested. I put my hand on her shoulder.

She turned her head, looked up at me, and remarked, 'So Miss Cleverly is the housekeeper. Well! Well! From her letter, I would have said she was around the same age as myself. Funny, the impressions one gets—the wrong impressions.'

'I don't think you could have got a wrong impression about that individual—shall I light the lamp?'

'No, don't bother. If we have a good sleep, we'll see things differently tomorrow, be able to laugh at life again, eh?' My aunt patted my hand where it still rested on her shoulder. Then, with an endearing movement, she lowered her cheek towards it.

These were the moments in my life when I knew that deep feeling was not dead in me. When I could respond to affection. In this moment I knew I loved my Aunt Maggie very deeply.

The bed was placed in such a position that, when you were sitting propped up, you could see the lake out the window and, because of the added height, over the hill bordering the left side of the water as well to a range of higher hills beyond. I could pick out small details quite clearly because there was moonlight, strong white moonlight, that made the scene almost as clear as it had been in the sunlight.

It was nearing eleven o'clock and I had been in bed for almost two hours but I had not yet been able to approach sleep. In fact, I was much wider awake than I had been when driving in the heat of the day. My mind seemed alert and my thinking was devoid of the slightest trace of panic, which was strange to me, especially as my thoughts were delving into the past. It was the moonlight that had done it.

When I had first come to bed, I had been thinking of our visitor. It was odd, but I hated to think of him as the owner of the cottage, yet I found, as I continued to gaze down into the lake where the moon was buried fathoms deep, and watched its light softly dimming now and again as a cloud raced across its surface, that I was forgetting the man. At least, my anger against him had subsided. He was, in this moment, washed of all importance; his rudeness had not the power to anger me any more, and it seemed that it would never again have such influence—he just didn't matter. Yet it was because of the feeling he had aroused in me, the feeling of retaliation, that my mind had slowly sunk back into the past, the not so very distant past, until it reached the point where, for the first time in my life, I had lifted my hands with the intent to hurt another; I had been incensed to the point where I was struggling madly with a man—with my husband.

There was a contraction of the nerves of my stomach now. My mind skirted round the thought of violence and moved quickly away—further back—to the time when I had lain in the bedroom of my Aunt Maggie's house and peopled the empty house opposite with characters. That was until the day when the real characters took over.

A family, as I've said before, came to live in the house. The daughter was at college. When she came home and heard there was a sick girl lying in the room that she could see from her bedroom window, she came to visit me. With that visit began my friendship with Alice Hornbrook.

Alice was twenty-three. She was what could be called an intellectual. She had just received her degree in English and had secured her first teaching post in Eastbourne. When she learned that I wrote stories, she asked to see them, merely I think out of politeness or to give some comfort to a sick person, but her praise of my work, which I knew to be genuine, acted like an injection of elixir on me.

'You must write, write seriously. Go on with this.' Alice's high, clear voice seemed to come across the lake now. A night bird was calling; it was saying, 'You must go on with this; you must go on with this.'

I did go on with it. I wrote a sixty-thousand-word story which, when Alice read it, she criticized.

'I would rewrite this again,' she told me. 'Make it eighty-thousand, and you'd do well to cut out the chunks of homespun philosophy and bitter passages. There's enough acid in your cynicism to make it a winner.'

I did as she advised, and the day I received a letter from a publisher stating that he would take pleasure in publishing my work and asking if I would come up to town to have a talk, my nervous complaint was cured and I got out of bed.

From this distance, I think my early success was on a par with that of Françoise Sagan. The critics hailed me for my youth while praising me for my knowledge of life, for the cynicism of a professional, for the competence with which I had handled the eternal triangle. But, didn't I know a lot about the eternal triangle? Hadn't I been brought up with it, fed on it from my earliest days? The characters in my books were only thinly disguised replicas of my mother and father, together with the second and third husbands on the one hand, and the numerous mistresses on the other.

I wrote three books in just under two years and I was there—I had arrived. I was selling so well, especially in America, that I need not worry about money ever. And I did not worry about money. That was one thing that had never caused me any anxiety. It seems to me strange at times that people should worry so much about money. If I had not a penny tomorrow, I know it wouldn't worry me; truthfully, it wouldn't.

Alice Hornbrook and I were friends for five years. She, too, called Aunt Maggie, 'Aunt Maggie'. And I called her mother and father 'Aunt Ann' and 'Uncle Dick'. Ours was that kind of close relationship. Then Alice's uncle came to stay with them. He was young, as he was her mother's youngest brother. His name was Ian Lacey, and from the moment I first looked at him my life was changed. Not that I fell in love with him straightway; no, I would say that he gradually charmed me into loving him. But, right from the first moment, I was fascinated by him—for, besides his charm, he was amusing, and he was helpless, so helpless that he needed me—at least part of me.

And we had something in common, a strong bond— we were both writers, the only difference being that I had been published and he hadn't. When I say that Ian was helpless, I mean he was helpless with regard to money. He was helpless as a writer. He wanted someone to lean on, to guide him, and, although he was nine years older than I, I felt the elder. I also thought that I was the only one who understood him—had ever understood him, or could ever understand him. Ian indoctrinated me well.

For the first year of our acquaintance, Ian only stayed for short periods with his sister Mrs Hornbrook. But, on these visits, he spent most of the time with me in Aunt Maggie's house, and during this time my own work suffered—if I may use that word to imply neglect. For I would spend days reading and revising his work, or advising him about some story he was concerned with at the moment.

Before Ian took up his abode permanently with his sister in the house across the way, I was aware that it was impossible for him to follow my advice. Put a pen in his hand and a ream of paper on the table and his words flowed. Showy, flowery, verbose words—words resulting in long sentences with obscure meanings. He would spend hours with a dictionary and *Roget*'s *Thesaurus* looking for a glorious ornamental adjective. But his prolixity did not cause me to withdraw my help, or lessen the love I then had for him.

On the night that Alice came to tell me that she was going to marry a schoolmaster (this came as something of a shock, for I wasn't even aware that she was interested in a man; she didn't seem the mating type, and never discussed the male)—it was on that night that Alice asked me, 'You're not getting serious about Ian, are you?'

For answer, I said, 'Is there any reason why I shouldn't?'

And to this she shook her head as she replied, 'No. Only that he's unstable; he's never been able to hold down a job in his life. Ian was the youngest, and my grandmother spoiled him. When she died, she passed on the task to her four daughters, and now it'll be up to a wife to complete the course. You want to think seriously about it. And, by the way,' Alice had nodded sagely, 'don't waste your good time on his stuff—he'll never be able to write in a month of Sundays. And Ian's kind can become as jealous as hell of another's success.'

I had said somewhat bitterly, 'You seem to love your uncle.'

Alice answered, 'I'm very fond of you and would hate to see you hurt.'

'Is that all you have got against Ian?'

She had considered for a moment, and then had said rather doubtfully, 'Yes. Yes, that's all.'

Many months later, when I recalled this conversation, I knew that Alice had spoken the truth when she said that was all she knew.

But at that time, when Aunt Maggie spoke along lines similar to Alice's, I began to think, and I knew I must get away and sort things out in my own mind. I did not want my marriage to repeat my mother and father's life all over again. I felt that if my marriage went on the rocks it would surely kill me—I had enough experience of marriages going wrong. So I went away and thought things out, and I came to the conclusion that my parents' marriage had broken up because neither of them needed the other sufficiently. Ian needed me. He might be weak, but was that a great fault? My father wasn't weak, he was strong, and look what he had done to himself and to others. My decision was—if Ian wanted me to, I would marry him. . . .

I waited and waited, but Ian didn't mention marriage. Then, one night, the situation, which was becoming emotionally unbearable for me, was brought to a head. It was the night I told Ian that I was going on a tour with Aunt Maggie and might be away for two months or more. At that moment, he seemed to become hysterical—I wasn't to leave him, he needed me. How was he to exist without me?

I had never felt so happy in my life. I consoled him, saying I would never leave him—we would be married and go touring ourselves. Aunt Maggie would understand.

It was one of the awful blows to my pride when later he reminded me that he had never mentioned marriage to me, it was I who had done the proposing. And, dear God, how true that had been!

Ian and I were married in the autumn and we spent our honeymoon in Spain. It was then that I had heard the thin whistle of the pipe which was like the sound that had made Frannie run to answer the call today.

46

When we returned to England, we stayed, at her request, with Aunt Maggie. She said she would be lonely without us. That I am sure was a lie for my benefit—Aunt Maggie sensed disaster.

And disaster came early in the year, in the form of a letter from Wales. In an old magazine, a woman had seen the picture of a man boarding a plane with the authoress Prudence Dudley. The caption stated that the man was Prudence Dudley's husband. She wanted to know if there was some mistake because the man, she felt sure, was her own husband, and the father of their two children, one aged three and the other seven. He had deserted her three years ago.

My mind had now reached a point again where I was fighting with a man, with Ian, going for him like a savage wild creature as if with intent to kill. And I think that had been my purpose, for when, in his easygoing, charming fashion, he admitted the contents of this woman's letter to be true, I did go mad for a time.

The Hornbrooks were devastated by the turn of events. Our association naturally was broken. I could not bear Alice's sympathy for her eyes seemed to say 'I told you so.' Although she had not known the facts of her uncle's life, from her estimation of his character, she had made a pretty shrewd guess.

When the case was brought to court, the newspapers did not hesitate to make top-line news of it. I had felt very ill during all that time, ill and dazed, and, if it hadn't been for Aunt Maggie, I think I would have ended my life. But it was nearly ended in a natural way by the premature birth of my baby.

From the moment I knew that I wasn't Ian's legal wife, there had arisen in me a horrible distaste for the child I was carrying, and when, three months ago, it was prematurely stillborn I knew a measure of relief. But the relief was very short-lived, for in its place came a deep sense of guilt—I felt I had killed the child—I had wished it out of existence.

After the disastrous birth of the baby, I lay in a dark, muddled kind of numbness for weeks. I was back in the state of 'nerves' that had hit me once before. Once more, I was retreating from myself, or, more true to say, I was dragging myself from contact with life—unbearable life.

Again, it was Aunt Maggie, and only she, who pulled me back to the surface of living. Now, here I was, my head just breaking water. I was looking about me realizing that I was a free agent. I could do what I liked, go where I liked—stay put where I liked, and write, write again. The thought of writing again brought back the thought of Ian. Ian's last words to me had been, 'No matter what you think, I love you—above all I need you.'

I didn't know so much about the love, Ian's kind of love was worthless anyway, but I did know quite a lot about the need. Ian had needed me all right, he had needed me to support his ego, for he was a writer who couldn't write, at least, except for his own enjoyment, to satisfy his taste for words, elaborate words. Well, he had plenty of time to ponder over words now. He would have enough food for thought in prison.

Prison! I looked out onto the moonlight-swept scene before me—the wide, wild, free scene, and, for the first time since the sentence of six months' imprisonment had been passed on him, I realized the awfulness of his punishment; after all, his crime had been weakness, breaking the law through weakness. At this moment, he was encased in a cell, perhaps lying there thinking as I was. I was amazed at the voice in my head which said, 'Poor Ian.' Yet I knew at the same time that, if I lived to be a hundred, I did not want to set eyes again on the man who had played husband to me.

I told myself I must stop thinking, I must go to sleep. But I didn't go to sleep; I lay looking out of the window across the water, the Little Water. It was really a charming name for the lakes—the Lil Water and the Big Water, the girl had said. Did the Big Water lie within the grounds too? This thought directed my mind to the house along the hill path. The music and the noise had died down some time ago. Perhaps the guests were indoors now continuing the jollification, as Aunt Maggie would have termed it.

As if in denial of their presence indoors, there came to me now the sound of laughter, the mingled laughter of men and women. It rose and fell as if being carried by the wind, or it may have been the laughter of people running. I sat up straighter in the bed and turned my head round so that my eyes could take in the black blur that was the thicket. The moon was shining on the top of it, but the side of it was casting a deep shadow and, under my widening gaze, there came running out of the shadow a number of people—six or eight—I didn't know how many at first. They were laughing and talking. One figure that had been carrying a basket of some kind ran to the edge of the lake and, after dropping the basket onto the ground, he began leaping madly about.

Someone shouted, 'Look at Alec!'

The leaping figure now stopped and caught hold of a girl and waltzed her madly over the grass. When he stopped, the girl fell over and lay laughing loudly. The man called Alec shouted, 'Give us a jig, Peter.'

A member of the party who stood by the lakeside swaying gently as if rocked by the breeze brought his hands upwards and began to play what looked like a small concertina. The air became filled with the strains of a Highland reel accompanied by shouts and whoops from the rest of the party.

'Here we go—upsy-daisy!'

'Yipp-ee!'

'Oh! me boys; Oh! me boys of Barrow-in-Furness!'

The laughter was loud now, wild-sounding.

I was kneeling on the bed gazing downwards. I

49

flicked my eyes around as I heard Aunt Maggie shuffling into the room.

'Well, this is too much—it's beyond a joke.'

'Were you asleep?'

'I was dead to the world. The sound frightened the life out of me for a moment. They're all mad drunk.'

'They're certainly not sober.'

'I wish I could see that McVeigh, I'd give him the length of my tongue. Look! look!' Aunt Maggie was kneeling on the bed beside me now. 'It's like a witches' Sabbath. There's two of them dancing in the water. Well, they can dance where they like, but they're not doing it here at this time of night—we've rented this place.'

She had pulled open the window before I could stop her but with the sharp command of 'No! Aunt Maggie,' I prevented her from calling out. 'Let them alone. In their present mood, you don't know what they'd do. They might come in here or—'

My voice trailed off and my eyes turned in the direction of the copse, for there, coming to a halt on the edge of the moonlight, I saw the tall thin figure of a young man. His hair looked black and his face very white and he was biting on his lip as he smiled. Then, apparently hearing a noise that was not distinguishable to us because of the music, singing, and shouting, he cast a glance over his shoulder. As if the man had been conjured out of the shadow itself, there stood Mr David Bernard Michael McVeigh! I found that, ironically, I was giving him his full title when I thought of him. I saw him grab at the dark man's arm and point; then I watched the young man pull himself away, apparently giving an angry retort.

I kept well back from the window, indicating to Aunt Maggie to do the same. The two men were now standing near the corner of the cottage and some of their words were audible.

I recognized McVeigh's voice saying, 'I told you to keep them clear of here.'

The dark man's immediate answer was lost to me, but I noted that his tone sounded angry; and, then his voice rose and I heard the words: 'You try telling Alec anything when he's on the bottle.'

'That crowd should never have been asked in the first place. I was against it—I told you.'

'You're always against some damn thing—your life is made up of being against things.'

'Look!' McVeigh's voice was deep and low, and I found myself bending forward to catch the words. 'I don't want any trouble with you tonight, Roy. Let the wedding day end in peace.'

'Huh! You're the one to talk about peace!'

'Now, look.' The voice was brittle. 'If you want to take up where we left off, it's all the same to me, but first I'll get this lot away from here.'

McVeigh's head looked as silver as the moonlight as I watched it move towards the man with the concertina. The music stopped abruptly, but the dancers, still laughing and yelling, continued their capers for some seconds before their laughter petered out in spluttering and coughing.

The night returned to its serenity for a second before the ringleader Alec shouted, 'Aw, Davie, man, why d'ya stop it? Come on, come on and fling it! Hoots! Toots! an' a drop o' the hard!'

'Be quiet, Alec.'

'Aw, man, it's a weddin' night. Come on, let your hair down.'

'I've told you—'

The rest of the words were lost, but I knew that McVeigh was telling them that the cottage was occupied for I saw a number of faces turn in our direction.

Then Alec's voice rose again, not so loud this time, but quite recognizable: 'Well, you said yourself they were stinkers, didn't you? "Prudence by name and prudence by nature"—that's what you said—so why worry? I don't give a damn, Davie man.' The words were slower now. 'It's a weddin' night and nobody should go to bed 'cept those concerned.'

There was a great shout of laughter at this quip. And my hand was moving forward to close the window when the man's next words caught and held my attention.

'Why are you doin' the considerate landlord stunt now, when earlier on you said they were a fossilised pair—the old 'un talkin' like Queen Victoria herself?' he shouted.

'Be quiet, I tell you.'

'Now, Davie, don't tell me what t'do—you know it won't work, not with me it won't.' The voice was menacing one moment, then gay the next. The man now cried: 'Come on, let's have a singsong . . . the one about Pru. How did it go?

> Oh, Prudence, dear one, take this ring,
> And wear it near your heart—'

As the man's voice rang out high over the lake, I saw the silver-headed figure spring forward, only to be stopped by a number of arms. I saw the man retreating towards the water singing tauntingly as he went:

> 'And give me but one word of hope
> Ere I this night depart.'

Aunt Maggie and I exchanged glances, mine indignant, hers surprised. Then we were looking down towards the edge of the lake again. There seemed to be a number of people sprawled about, but McVeigh was standing, and so was the man who had sung the rhyme. I put my hand over my eyes as the fist shot out, yet I seemed to see Alec's feet fly from the ground. I certainly heard the splash as his body hit the water. I kept my eyes covered for two or three minutes, and, when I next raised my head and looked downward, I thought I must have dreamed the whole scene—but for the fact that Aunt Maggie was sitting close to me and was trembling slightly. For the greensward was empty of people, that is, with the exception of two shadows which supported another shadow, and moved into the darkness of the copse. And if I hadn't known that the shadows were two men assisting the drunken brawler whom McVeigh had hit, I might have taken the movement for the swaying of the trees.

'Well, I've seen some things in my time!' Aunt Maggie was shaking her head. 'It didn't seem real, did it?'

When I didn't answer, she patted my arm and said, 'Take no notice of the rhyming; it strikes me the whole lot of them are blind drunk. . . . And this—' she spread wide the palms of her hands '—and this is the haven of peace. Wait till I see that Miss Cleverly.'

'When you do see her, you can tell her that we are going.'

'Yes. Yes, I will, indeed. There'll be plenty more places to get. It's the end of the season anyway—people will only be too glad to rent cottages or such. There was never a good but there's a better. Well, now—' she stood up '—do you think we'll get to sleep after this?'

'We'd better,' I said, 'or we'll be dead beat tomorrow when there'll likely be another long car journey before us.'

'Good-night, lass.'

'Good-night, Aunt Maggie.'

The strangest thing about that strange day was that almost as soon as I lay down again I found myself dropping into sleep, and, as I lost consciousness, I imagined that the scene that had taken place before the lake was part of a dream, and, as sometimes happens in dreams, I desired to continue dreaming, but I didn't.

I must have slept soundly until the next morning, when I was awakened, not only by the smell of frying bacon, but by Aunt Maggie standing over me shaking me gently, saying, 'There's somebody moving about downstairs—and can you smell that?'

Slowly I pulled myself upwards in the bed and blinked the sleep from my eyes—then I sniffed. Following this, I looked up at Aunt Maggie.

'Peace offering from the lord of the clan, I suppose,' Aunt Maggie was whispering down at me.

'You mean *he* is cooking the breakfast?' I was whispering back.

'Who else? And we hadn't any bacon with us. It's going to be awkward giving someone the length of your tongue when they are handing you a plateful of bacon and eggs, isn't it?' Aunt Maggie's eyebrows were now straining towards her hairline.

I swung my legs out of the bed, slipped my feet into slippers, and grabbed up a dressing gown. As I zipped it up to the neck, I said flatly, 'I never eat breakfast.'

Tricky as it was I descended the staircase face forward; I was not going to give Mr McVeigh food for laughter by presenting him with a view of my rear.

When I stepped into the kitchen, the frying pan was on the stove. There was steam from hot water in the sink, and on the side table were two trays set most tastefully for breakfast.

My back stiff again, my chin up, I moved into the sitting room, and there the wind was completely taken out of my sails, for I was not confronted by McVeigh holding out the velvet glove, but by a stranger. She was a woman well into her sixties—as old, I should say, as Aunt Maggie. She was extremely thin, of medium height, and had abundant brown hair without a streak of grey in it. But the face that I saw in profile, first one side then the other, as she darted about the far end of the room was extremely lined.

I knew that she was aware of my presence for some time before she gave the false start, saying, 'Oh! Oh, my! Well, you're up now.'

She came towards me, her step almost on the point

of a run, and, when she was standing opposite me, she looked up into my face and smiled, saying, 'I let you lie, you had had a long journey yesterday. And, oh, I am sorry about the place not being ready. You see, I didn't get your wire—it got among the wedding ones, and half of them weren't read, what with one thing and another, you know?'

The woman had almond-shaped eyes—they had been very beautiful eyes at one time—and these had widened at me as she had asked, 'You know?'

Then she went on, 'And not a flower in the place, and it like a pigsty. Davie—you know Davie?—he sleeps here at times, and you know what men are. You know?' Again the eyes widened with the question. 'And you see I never knew a thing about it—I mean that you were here or anything till they brought Alec Bradley in and then it all came out. They said they hadn't told me because it would fuss me—fuss me, indeed! As if I couldn't cope—oh, good-morning.'

She was now holding her head on one side and looking beyond me to Aunt Maggie. Like a gramophone that was wound up and wouldn't stop until it ran down naturally, she went on. 'You're Miss Fuller? Yes, I can see you're Miss Fuller, and this is your neice. I've been telling her everything. I'm so sorry, but things will be quiet and peaceful after this, dead as a doornail you might say. Nothing much happens here. But it was the wedding. You know?'

I moved aside to let Miss Cleverly get into the kitchen and I was now abreast of Aunt Maggie. As we looked at each other, I knew we were both thinking the same thing: that no matter what capacity Miss Flora Cleverly served David Bernard Michael McVeigh in, it certainly was not that of his mistress.

'Now, your breakfasts are ready. You could have them out on the lawn. It's warm enough and nobody will disturb you.' She turned and wagged her finger at us. 'I promise you that. There's bacon and egg and fried bread and mushrooms. I've brought a couple of bottles of milk over; we have our own milk. We run seven cows, sheep and chickens, and a few pigs, but we go in for mushrooms, you know.'

'It's very kind of you—' my Aunt Maggie had moved forward '—but you shouldn't have done this.'

'No trouble. No trouble at all. All in a day's work.' She was moving quickly here and there as she spoke, mashing the tea, turning the toast. She worked with the sure precision of a robot and seemed to be drawing on a store of energy that would never go dry. That was really the thing that struck me immediately about Flora Cleverly—her outstanding energy.

'We are—' Aunt Maggie hesitated. 'I'm slightly at sea with regards to who's who about here. I understand that Mr McVeigh owns the place.'

'Yes, yes, that's right. The one you met—Davie. He's the eldest—he owns Lowtherbeck and what's left of the land, not fifty acres now. It used to run into thousands—would you believe that? Yes—' she nodded her head at me '—it was a wonderful estate at one time. Still, we're thankful for what we've got—we must be thankful.'

'Are there other McVeighs?' Aunt Maggie's head was inclined to one side with gentle inquiry.

'There's Roy—he's three years younger than Davie. A nice boy, Roy. That's all that's left of the McVeighs. But we have young Janie with us. It was her sister, Doris, who was married yesterday. They're cousins of the McVeighs.'

'Are you a relative, too?'

For the first time Flora Cleverly's hands ceased their moving and she looked down at them for a moment before she answered Aunt Maggie.

Then, on a laugh she said, 'No. It's funny I'm not, but I've been connected with them all my life. I brought up the two boys after their mother died, and I've always run the house and seen to everything. When Davie was away I ran the whole place, and everything went on just the same. I've run it now on my own—that is, I mean the house—for thirty-two years. But I ran it even before that, because Mrs McVeigh was never very healthy—I mean strong. There, I mustn't talk any more, you must have your breakfast. I've brought you over a piece of lamb and some vegetables for your dinner.' She thumbed in the direction of the pantry. 'And if you will, we'd be pleased to see you at tea—there's so much to be eaten up,' she added. 'And after that you can settle down and only see us when you want to. But, if you're short, you've just got to ask—I'm nearly always sure to have what you want; I've always kept a good larder. There, now.'

With an oven cloth she whisked the hot plates one after the other out of the oven onto the trays and we lifted them up and followed her into the living-room.

'Would you like to have breakfast on the porch?' I asked Aunt Maggie.

'Yes, that would be nice.'

Even as I spoke, Miss Cleverly had lifted the table into position and brought forward a couple of chairs.

'There now, you're all set. Don't forget what I told you—anything you want.'

She was standing on the threshold of the door when I asked, 'Who is the little girl we saw here yesterday?'

'Oh, you mean Frannie? She's from across the hill. She lives with her grannie on the road to Brookfield. But she's always about here, has been from when she was a child. We couldn't get rid of her if we wanted to. The boys have sort of adopted her, you know. Quite daft over the boys she was.'

'How old is she?' asked Aunt Maggie.

'Coming up sixteen. It's a pity, isn't it?'

'Has she always been like that?' I asked softly.

'Oh, no, no. It happened one day on the Big Water. That's the other lake, you know.'

It seemed that whenever Miss Cleverly used the words

57

'you know' in either the form of a statement or a question she accompanied them by a widening of her almond-shaped eyes. It was an odd co-ordination.

'They were all out in a boat,' she continued, 'her father and mother and her. They were always quarrelling, the pair of them, and he must have gone to hit her—he was a jealous man—and the boat capsized. And that must have been that. Their bodies were never recovered—the Big Water's very deep in the middle—but the child was found lying, late that night, floating face up in the reeds. They thought she was dead at first, but she was just unconscious, must have been like that from the time she hit the water, and that saved her. Anyway, whatever it was, when she pulled round, well, she was like she is now. She's never developed. It's a pity, isn't it?'

Both my Aunt Maggie and I nodded slowly in assent. Yes, indeed, it was a pity.

'Now eat your breakfasts. I'll be seeing you at tea.'

With that, Miss Cleverly left us abruptly.

There had been a matron at my boarding school who used to speak in the same manner. Eat your breakfast, do your nails, tidy your room. I felt like a child again.

Aunt Maggie cut into her bacon, but before she conveyed the piece to her mouth she leaned across to me and said quietly, 'Variety is the spice of life.' Then, with an effort, she smothered her laughter.

3

The day should have passed peaceably enough. The sun was hot again, but not so fierce as the day before, just comfortable enough to lie in, and that's what I was doing. I was lying on the green slope near the lake while Aunt Maggie lay in a deck-chair higher up in the shade. Earlier in the day, I had sampled the water but, to my disappointment, I found I could not stay in it very long for the temperature was almost freezing.

Together, Aunt Maggie and I had made lunch, eaten it, and washed up. Now, to all appearances, we were relaxed. Aunt Maggie might be, but I certainly wasn't. I was all keyed up inside waiting for Aunt Maggie to say, 'Well, isn't it time to make a move?' If there had been anyone to send with a message, I would have certainly sent a note with our excuses, for I didn't want to listen to apologies about last night—the rhyme was still running in my head. Thinking along these lines, I found I was wishing that the girl Frannie would make her appearance, but no one disturbed us.

And then Aunt Maggie's voice came at me saying, 'Psst!'

I rolled over on my face, my hands under my chin, and looked at her. Aunt Maggie was sitting straight up now and pointing towards the copse. She wagged her finger while she mouthed silently: 'Someone coming.' I swung round and sat up, supporting myself with my hands, and waited, my gaze directed towards the hill rising from the far shore of the lake.

'I hope I'm not disturbing you?'

The pleasant voice brought me from my studied pose, and I saw, standing a few yards from Aunt Maggie's chair, the young man whom I had seen last night in the moonlight, the one who had argued with McVeigh.

'No, no, not in the least,' said Aunt Maggie.

'I'm—I'm Roy McVeigh and I've come to fetch you over.'

The man was looking across towards me now and, as I rose slowly to my feet, I saw that his eyes, like those of his brother last night, were taking me all in. But there was no covert insolence in this face—interest, perhaps, and, if I had felt inclined to search for compliments, I might have said, some admiration. The fabric of the sun-suit I was wearing had an orange-and-yellow pattern on a white background and was an attractive thing in itself.

'This is my niece, Miss Dudley,' said Aunt Maggie.

'How do you do?'

We each inclined our heads slightly to the other. Then I said, 'I won't be a moment.'

'That's all right. There's no hurry.' Roy smiled, a wide easy smile. I did not return it, but moved away and went indoors where I changed the sun-suit for a white linen dress that was deceptively simple. I brushed my hair, noting, as I always did when I looked in the mirror now, that there were single grey hairs among the dark brown ones. I applied a lipstick. That was all. I suppose I was fortunate in having a skin that didn't require much make-up.

When I appeared on the lawn, the young man's eyes again moved over me. After a space, during which Aunt Maggie heaved herself up out of the chair with his assistance, Roy looked at me and said, 'It's nice having people in the cottage again.'

'Do you have many here?' Aunt Maggie was straightening her skirt.

'No, not often; not for long leases.' He smiled. 'Perhaps two or three lots a year, for a week or so. It isn't everybody's cup of tea you know, stuck out in the wilds.'

'It suits us.' Aunt Maggie now turned to me and added, 'will I go and change?'

'That looks quite all right,' I said.

'Oh, please, don't dress up for us. Wait until you see our set-up. It's rough and ready, I can assure you.'

'All well and good then. That suits me.'

Aunt Maggie moved towards the copse; Roy waited until I was abreast of her, then he walked by my side and I found he did not disturb me one way or another. He made no mention of last night, leaving that to his brother I supposed.

The 'set-up', as Roy McVeigh had called it, was homely and comfortable, yet, over-all, there was a shabbiness that spoke of hard wear. Like the treads in the carpet on the stairs the curtains, chair covers and cushions looked as if they hadn't been renewed for several years. Although the curtains on the windows were thick and lined, their colour, except where the big old-fashioned curtain rings caught them, was drab beige, but the material near the rings indicated that they may at one time have been blue or green. Yet the room we were sitting in was definitely a drawing-room. There were a number of small tables, two of which I noticed were Louis Quinze and probably authentic antiques. Then there was a china cabinet holding odd pieces of Wedgwood and Spode; and, lastly, a large deep old-fashioned suite of furniture in faded red moquette.

Flora Cleverly was presiding at the tea table, her hands darting over a two-handled Sheffield silver tray holding an ornamental tea service of the same design, all brightly polished. To her side were two cake stands and a small table laden with eatables. Besides Miss

Cleverly, Roy McVeigh, and ourselves, the only other person in the room was Janie Slater.

Janie was ten and her face had a similar expression to that of her sister when she had looked at me from the back window of the car the day before. But, as yet, Janie didn't get much chance to talk. *'Hand Miss Dudley the sandwiches, Janie. Pass the sugar to Miss Fuller.'* Do this. Do that. See to this. See to that. I could almost see Miss Cleverly's brain at work, organizing, docketing, thinking, thinking ahead to tomorrow when it would organize, reorganize and docket again. Miss Cleverly also did the talking. Her conversation took the form of questions which were mostly addressed to Aunt Maggie, but, as I sat trying to think of something to say to the shy child beside me, Miss Cleverly addressed me pointedly for the first time.

'And what are you? I mean, in what line of business?'

My head had turned sharply towards her and, whatever answer I might have given, I certainly wouldn't have told her the truth, for I knew what disclosure could mean—even in out-of-the-way places. Dead manuscripts pressed on you to be read. *'When you have a minute, you know.'* But I hadn't a chance to say anything— Aunt Maggie was there before me.

'My niece is the writer Prudence Dudley.'

She didn't say, *'a writer'*, but, *'the writer'*. I knew my face had gone a deep pink; I was also aware that Flora Cleverly had never heard of the writer Prudence Dudley, but that Roy McVeigh had.

So it was he who spoke first, exclaiming, 'Good gracious! Yes, yes, of course, I remember seeing your photograph.' He stopped, embarrassed when it came to him just where he had seen my photograph.

'Davie makes up rhymes. He makes up funny ones.'

Janie, speaking for the first time, was silenced almost immediately. 'Be quiet, Janie! Here, hand Miss Dudley the cake. Well now, to think you're a writer.'

Miss Cleverly did not look at me, all her attention

was directed towards the tea tray, but she went on talking to me. 'We're honoured. We've never had a writer stay before, a painter, yes—two painters, and a singer. We certainly knew we had the singer—he practised morning, noon, and night. He even had the piano carted over. Oh, yes, we knew all about having a singer, but we've never had a writer—well, now!'

It was at this moment that the door opened and Davie McVeigh came in. Automatically, I sat up straighter on the couch, thinking, Yes, Davie makes up rhymes all right. He was wearing a white shirt and riding breeches. It was evident he had left his top boots outside for on his feet were a pair of old red slippers. His shirt was buttoned at the neck and wrists. I remember noticing this because Roy's shirt was open at the neck and his sleeves were short. One of the men looked free, and the other encased. Now Roy spoke to his brother as if there had never been any harsh words between them.

'What do you think, Davie? This is Miss Prudence Dudley the writer.'

'Yes, I know.' The voice was calm. The big head was turned in my direction; the man was looking down at me, his eyes smiling quite pleasantly. His face had no aggressiveness in it at this moment.

'You know? How do you know? You couldn't have known.' This was Miss Cleverly, her hands still now as she stared towards Davie McVeigh.

'I know because I happen to read now and again. It may be surprising to you, Flora—' the sarcasm was back in the voice so the man was more recognizable '—but I do read at times. The cottage is made for reading. I think Miss Dudley—' he glanced at me '—will discover that.' After some seconds of silence, he turned and, facing me, said, 'By the way, I never managed to read your second book but I read the first and the third. I liked the third best. Less harsh, more compassionate, if you'll allow me to say so.'

People, I noticed, always added, 'if you'll allow me to

say so' after making some cutting criticism. Yet I knew that what he had said was true. I had softened a lot by the time I had written my third book. I also knew that I was pleased, and surprised, that this objectionable man had read my books.

'I don't believe you could have known anything about it.' We were all looking at Flora Cleverly again. 'If you had known she was—*the* Miss Dudley, why didn't you say?'

The atmosphere in the room had changed. The fact that I was a writer of some importance was now of little or no consequence. All that was of consequence was the fact that Davie McVeigh had withheld something from Flora Cleverly.

'And have you turn the place upside down in preparation for a celebrity? I'm sure Miss Dudley would not have wished that. Am I right?'

He was gazing down at me once more, and in my embarrassment at the situation that I had unwittingly brought about I stammered, 'Yes—well, I mean, everything is quite all right as it is. The cottage is lovely—'

'There! Does that satisfy you?' Davie was looking once more towards Miss Cleverly. She had poured him out, I noticed, a cup of tea, but had not handed it to him. He now went behind the couch and took it from the side table; then he filled his plate with sandwiches before taking a seat in a chair to the right of Aunt Maggie near the empty fireplace from which, when he raised his eyes, he could look straight at me.

Roy McVeigh came and sat on the couch beside me. His opening remark did not alter my opinion that he was a nice young man, but it confirmed my suspicion that he was an ordinary one. 'I always wanted to write a book,' he said.

As he spoke, I heard my Aunt Maggie remark to Davie McVeigh in her conversational way, 'I see you go in for mushrooms.'

And the answer she received was, 'Oh, my God!'

64

But the older brother was not speaking to her. He was looking at his brother, and Roy, his face almost livid, was returning his scathing stare. But the incident was all over in a second.

Davie McVeigh had turned to Aunt Maggie and was saying, 'Yes, we go in for mushrooms, there's money in them; at least, there should be.' He paused before asking, 'Did you by any chance look into the cave yesterday when you came into the yard, Miss Fuller?' His tone was mildly inquisitive and quite civil, yet there was something behind it.

Aunt Maggie cast a quick glance in my direction before saying, 'Yes, yes, we did. We thought there might be someone inside who could guide us.'

'And you forgot to close the door?' David was smiling now.

It was I who answered him, and stiffly: 'No, we didn't forget to close the door. We purposely left it open because we found it open.'

His eyes were looking straight into mine. Then he said, 'Don't worry, I believe you.'

'Thank you!'

'You and that cave door—you dream about it half the time.' Miss Cleverly poured some water into the silver teapot.

'Oh, no, I don't, Flora. I'm not given to dreaming; there's no time. I only know that before I got into the car yesterday I saw to it that the door was closed, well closed, and, when I came back, it was open. I had let the stove go out. He turned his head and addressed himself pointedly to Aunt Maggie now, looking sharply into her slightly perplexed countenance. 'If the weather had suddenly changed, say it had rained—if it had, it could have meant a drop in temperature. The matter of a few degrees applied often enough can ruin six months' work—not only that, it could ruin me.'

He gave a laugh—it was not a pleasant sound—before adding, 'Never go in for mushrooms, Miss Fuller, unless you are very wealthy and can play at it as a hobby on a losing basis.'

I enquired of Roy McVeigh: 'Have you ever done any writing?' My motives for asking were mixed. I had resented Davie McVeigh's outrageous reaction to his brother's natural statement—natural, because writing a book is the desire of many people, and also I felt I must bring his attention from his brother at whom he was still staring. When I achieved this, he turned on me what could have been a glance of dislike, then drawing his lower lip in between his teeth he shook his head.

'No. No, I haven't,' he said, his voice sounding like that of a youth, a petulant youth.

'Don't you worry, Roy—if you want to write a book, you'll write a book. You can do anything you put your mind to.'

I looked over the back of the couch to Miss Cleverly, who was looking towards Roy McVeigh. Then she shifted her glance to me and added, 'Isn't that so, Miss Dudley?'

'Yes, yes. If you want to do a thing strongly enough, I am sure you can do it.'

I wasn't sure. I was just answering the woman the way she wanted to be answered. There was something here I couldn't understand. The tea party had turned into a battleground, but perhaps the battle had been raging before we had come into the house. I had the feeling that this was so—that it was a battle of long standing. Quite suddenly I found myself thinking, this woman loves one man and hates the other. And, from the little I had seen of the two men, I certainly couldn't blame her.

Even with stretching politeness to its limit, you could hardly say the tea was a pleasant interlude. I found it embarrassing, even unnerving, for the atmosphere from the moment Davie McVeigh had entered the room had been pervaded with bitterness.

A signal passed between Aunt Maggie and me which

66

was achieved with our eyebrows, and I was about to rise to my feet when there came a tap on the open French window and all the occupants of the room turned towards it. The girl, Frannie, was standing there.

With an odd sort of stiff agility, I watched Davie McVeigh swing his heavy body up out of the low chair, but, before he was squarely on his feet, Miss Cleverly was at the window.

'Run along, Frannie, and play. That's a good girl.'

She was standing in front of the girl to prevent her entering the room.

'Leave her alone,' McVeigh's voice was quiet.

He did not thrust Flora Cleverly aside, but, in the position he took up, she was forced to step back into the room. He was now bending down towards the girl, talking softly in a different tone than any I had heard him use.

'Where have you been?' he asked. 'We haven't seen you for days. . . . What's that?'

I could see him now holding up her arm and examining it. Then he looked at the other arm.

'Who did this?'

He was now touching Frannie's brow.

'Leave her alone. Her grannie's likely had to chastise her.' Flora Cleverly was seated once more, sipping at her tea now, and, addressing Aunt Maggie, she went on in a low tone. 'The girl gets out of hand—becomes very destructive. Her grannie has got to use the cane; it's the only way she can manage her.'

I prevented myself from saying, 'I don't believe it.' I wanted to rise and go towards the girl; however, I couldn't make myself do it when McVeigh was there. But now, although she was very reluctant to enter, he was drawing her into the room.

'I'll give that old girl a taste of her own medicine one of these days.' He was speaking as he pressed Frannie down on to the wooden seat near the fireplace.

'Not Grannie.'

'What!' He looked down at her bent head. 'Who then?'

The girl shook her head and turned it away until she was staring into the empty fireplace.

'She'll get herself into trouble one of these days.'

So quickly did McVeigh swing round that I started nervously. He was glaring at Flora Cleverly and there was undisguised hate in his eyes but he did not speak.

In a way I admired the man for championing this poor undeveloped girl, but my condemnation of him was much greater than any approval I felt for his kindly attitude. For, no matter what he thought about his housekeeper, he had no right to treat her as he was doing in public. On the other hand, she had certainly goaded him more than a little.

When Frannie suddenly began to cry—and her crying had a heart-rending sound—it had differing effects on us all. It brought a pitying look from Aunt Maggie. It brought Janie to kneel in front of her saying, 'Ah, Frannie, don't cry. Don't cry like that.' It made Flora Cleverly move quickly between the tables, pushing at the plates, arranging and rearranging their depleted contents. It brought Roy McVeigh's head drooping and his teeth pulling at his lips. The latter gesture I noted seemed to be characteristic of the young man. It drove Davie McVeigh onto the terrace outside the French windows. From there he called sharply, 'Frannie! Frannie, come here!'

The girl rose obediently, her head hanging, the tears dropping off her chin, and when she reached Davie McVeigh he held out his hand and she placed hers in it. I watched them walk over the lawn towards the road that rounded the hill and led to our cottage.

I was about to rise to my feet when Roy McVeigh spoke: 'Will you excuse me?' Getting up, he nodded towards Aunt Maggie before going hastily from the room, not through the French window, but out into the hall.

Flora Cleverly now came and took up her position on the home-made wool rug flanking the wide fireplace. She had her hands clasped loosely in front of her and her jaws moved back and forwards causing the wrinkles of her face to flow into each other before she spoke.

'I'm not going to apologize,' Flora said. 'You can't be expected to live on top of a family and not know all the ins and outs about them. We're no better or no worse than the next.'

'Oh, please don't apologize to us.' Aunt Maggie was standing now, smoothing down the front of her dress.

'I'm not. I said I wasn't, and I'm not. I just made a statement. But you'll be able to pick out the gold from the dross for yourselves. It would be a very unusual family if it had all saints and no sinners, wouldn't it?' Flora was smiling at me as she put this question. But it was Aunt Maggie who answered her, saying, 'Very . . . very.'

'I made a pie this morning. I thought you would like it. If you'll just wait, I'll fetch it.'

If we had made any protest she would not have heard us, for in her lightning fashion she was out of the room so quickly it was impossible to realize she hadn't run or flown. And now we were left looking at each other, and Janie was looking at us, first at Aunt Maggie and then at me.

It was to me that Janie finally spoke, and what she said was, 'Davie's all right.'

Her tone was aggressive; it was as if she felt we were putting the blame for the whole scene on Davie McVeigh.

'He gets the backwash, always has.'

It was an odd, old expression to come from a child of ten, and it brought a twisted smile to Aunt Maggie's lips.

I was too embarrassed to answer and was relieved when Aunt Maggie asked, 'You are very fond of Mr McVeigh?'

'Yes, I am. And so was Doris.'

With this last statement, Janie cast a quick glance towards the hall door, then, with one more direct look shared between Aunt Maggie and myself, she turned and ran out of the French window. A moment later, Flora Cleverly came in with the pie which she handed to Aunt Maggie. I was glad, for I myself had a great desire to refuse her gift. . . .

Aunt Maggie and I were walking back along the hill path towards the cottage but, so that she wouldn't be overheard, it wasn't until we were well past all the shrubbery and in the open that she began to talk.

'It would appear,' she said, 'that the lord of the manor has the loyalty of the young'uns at least.'

'And he would need it,' I said, 'for Flora Cleverly hates him.'

'They hate each other I would say. You know—' Aunt Maggie turned her face towards me '—it's a very queer set-up. If I were in your shoes I'd be saying to myself, here's the nucleus for a very good story.'

I smiled, then looked ahead. Perhaps my aunt was right, I thought. There was everything here for a story, certainly a background, one could even call it a 'romantic' background. I felt no pain at this moment as the word presented itself to me. The people in the house called Lowtherbeck were certainly heading for one big flare-up, and, unless I was very mistaken there was a deep underlying reason for it. But I couldn't compose a story without a love element of some sort, and there was no love element in that house so far as I could gather.

But wasn't I a writer? Couldn't I concoct such an element? If I did, it would be to bring it to an unhappy conclusion. And who would I make the hero, the one who fell in love, to be, in the end, frustrated? David McVeigh?—oh, no, not David McVeigh—And yet, why not? He had all the ingredients needed to make a lover, a strong, passionate, headstrong lover. I stopped dead on the hillside and looked down.

70

Aunt Maggie asked me, 'What is it?'

I just shook my head slowly before moving on again. In the shaking of my head, I was rejecting, clamping down heavily on the idea of the elder McVeigh as a hero of any story I would write. Roy, yes, perhaps, but David Bernard Michael McVeigh—never!

And no one had said a word of apology about last night—no one.

4

～✻～

When you have done something that surprises you, you search the past to see what elements precipitated your action. What surprised me was that I had now begun my novel and its hero was Davie McVeigh. This change of mind had come about through a series of incidents during the previous three weeks, but I think it really began on the hillside that Sunday afternoon. And it bore fruit one early dawn when I discovered what Davie McVeigh was hiding, but that was later.

On the Monday following that first Sunday at the cottage my aunt and I drove into the village of Borne Coote to replenish our supplies, or rather, to stock up with tinned stuff and other necessities. And, as Borne Coote had only one actual shop, we were confronted for the second time with the little woman, Mrs Talbot, and, not only with Mrs Talbot, but Talbot himself. They were both behind the counter and they gave us the full benefit of their combined stares on our entrance. Then, with the embarrassing straightforwardness which seemed to be prevalent in this part of the country, the little woman, pointing at me, spoke.

'I thought you didn't know the McVeighs?'

'Nor did we when were last here.' My reply was stiff.

'But you were going to the cottage—you were going to stay?'

'I made the arrangements through a Miss Cleverly. Does that explain things?' Aunt Maggie's head was cocked to one side.

'I told you so; I said it would be her that did all the arranging.'

Talbot was looking down at his wife. Then, turning his gaze towards Aunt Maggie, and seeming to pick up the tone of their last conversation, he said slowly, 'The misunderstanding is pardonable, madam. Now, what can I do for you ladies?'

Here was the businessman speaking.

We had written out an order and I handed it to him. The length of it seemed to please him, for he turned, and looking down on his wife, said, 'You leave this to me; get about your business.'

And Mrs Talbot got about her business. Talbot saw to us himself, going as far as to pack the goods in boxes and to place them in the boot of the car, assuring us as he did so that he would be pleased to be of service to us —any kind of service.

He explained, 'The shop's only me sideline, you see, ma'am.' (The 'ma'am was divided between us now, it had taken the place of madam and miss.) 'I do a bit of taxiing, although there's not much in that line, except for a wedding and a late dance or such over in Penrith. An' I turn me hand to a bit of plumbing and decoratin'. Besides which, I'm the gravedigger for the three villages hereabouts. And in me spare time I go up and help Davie, big Davie. Now, there's a man for you.'

Talbot was pulling down the boot of the car, and he swivelled his long face towards me as he demanded, 'What do you think of big Davie?'

I case I might go so far as to forget myself and say what I did think of—big Davie, Aunt Maggie put in quickly, 'What do you do up there—at the house— Mr McVeigh's?'

'Oh, there's plenty to do up there. He'd have me full time if he could manage it. He thought he would be able to last year, but then he had to buy the horses.' He bent over Aunt Maggie and shook his long face in front of her as he stated: 'You can't grow mushrooms without manure, an' the cheapest way to have manure is to have horses, isn't it? Three he's got now, two old shires. The heavy ones are the best. Like old times to see horses on a farm, an' he uses them all, doesn't keep them just for—' He stopped, coughed, and added the information: 'Well, it's always better from working horses—they eat more, see? It's natural.'

I had got myself into the car. As on Saturday when these two had met, the desire to laugh rose in me. I dared not look at Aunt Maggie as she sat down beside me, but now Talbot's face was close to mine at the open window of the car.

'What do you think of Flora Cleverly?' This was asked in a loud whisper.

'What?'

'I asked, what do you think of her?'

'Well—er.' I glanced at Aunt Maggie, but Aunt Maggie was looking straight ahead. 'I should say she's a very capable housekeeper.'

'A very good featherer of nests if you ask me,' Talbot's nose was almost touching mine, and I couldn't get my head any further away from his long sombre face.

'You know her an' me nearly become related?'

'You did?'

'Aye, she was after me brother. He was gardener up there to the old people in the days when they had land to have gardens, if you know what I mean. But he upped an' skedaddled off to America.'

I shook my head.

'He died just three years gone. An' you know what?' He went on. 'Left her what he made.'

'Really?' I commented.

'Was it much?' This came from Aunt Maggie.

'Two thousand, seven hundred and fifty pounds. I

contested it rightly but I lost 'cause we were only half-brothers really, and he had always fended for himself since he was a lad. Aye, Flora got the lot. But do you think she'll spend a penny on the place, or help Davie? No, not a brass farthin'. But she gives young Roy backhanders. Oh, aye, he's her bright boy is Roy, and the biggest cadger from here to—'

Talbot just managed to replace the destination with the name 'Cockermouth'. Then he continued. 'You be on guard, ma'am, if he comes askin for a sub. You won't be the first one that Davie's had to refund money to afore they left.'

Again, I could only say, 'Really?'

'Aye, really.' The big nose was moving up and down now.

'Do you believe in jinxes?' Talbot asked now.

'Jinxes?—well, I don't know.'

'That means you don't believe in them, but there are such things. Davie's got a jinx on him; it's been put on him.'

Now Talbot withdrew his head a little from the window and his expression changed, even took on a semblance of hauteur. He said, 'I hope you ladies don't think I'm shootin' me mouth, but, as you're goin' to be up there for God knows how long, I thought it best to put you wise to a few things. Ladies are apt to get the wrong impressions at times—bit gullible like.'

And now he leaned forward again and almost across me, and addressed himself pointedly to Aunt Maggie this time. 'I'd like you to understand, ma'am, that I don't talk so glibly to everybody, but I'm concerned with them up at Lowtherbeck.'

'Yes, yes, of course,' said Aunt Maggie.

Now that he thought Aunt Maggie understood the situation and the reason for his verbosity, Talbot withdrew himself, straightened up to his limit and inclined his head slowly downwards. And we took this as a signal that we now had his permission to depart.

We drove off and when we got into a quiet lane, we laughed—I laughed as I hadn't done for many months. Yet, in spite of our making kindly fun of him, I knew we had gathered more than groceries from Talbot's shop, and that we had met a man who could be a very good friend—to those he took to.

We did not return straight to the cottage, but did a round of sight-seeing going as far as—Talbot's Cockermouth—then on to Maryport, returning around Derwentwater and Keswick, past Ullswater, and on home. I thought of the cottage as home now.

It had been a long drive and, for the most part, a beautiful drive. When we arrived at the cottage about five o'clock, we were both rather tired; consequently, I did not mount the stairs to put our things away until sometime after six. And it was as I opened the doors of the big cupboard that the sound came to me distinctly and brought my eyes upwards towards the ceiling. It was the sound of smothered weeping and I recognized it immediately.

Within a moment, I had mounted the ladder and pushed open the trap-door. There, on the floor, almost on eye level with me, lay Frannie. She lifted her head when I entered and I was quick to note the look of disappointment coming into her eyes. Without getting from my hands and knees, I crawled the short distance to her, asking, 'What is it, my dear?'

On this, the girl turned her head from me and buried it once again in her arms.

'Don't cry like that, you'll make yourself ill. Come, sit up.' I put my hand on her shoulder, but, with the peevish attitude of a child, Frannie tried to shake it off.

'Come along.' I was coaxing her gently. 'Would you like a drink?'

There was no response.

'Come, don't cry like that—don't.'

The sound was hurting me. I wanted to take her in my arms and comfort her, and the next minute that's what happened—she was in my arms—brought there by the suggestion that I should take her over to the house.

'Come along, get up and I'll take you to the house,' I had said. On this, Frannie turned and flung herself on me, pressing her head between my breasts and gripping me with her arms as a frightened child clings to its mother.

'There now, there now. Don't—don't cry any more. What is it? Can't you tell me?'

It was at this point that Aunt Maggie's voice called up the stairs to me and I called back, 'Can you come up a minute?'

When I heard her come into the room down below my voice drew her to the foot of the ladder, and, twisting round on the floor, the girl still in my arms, I leant over the hole and said, 'It's Frannie; she's up here and upset about something. You'd better go and fetch one of them.'

At this, the girl's grip tightened about me and I looked down into Aunt Maggie's perplexed face and said quietly, 'Better try and find—him.'

Whether the girl knew to whom I referred I don't know, but she made no protesting movement.

I heard the creak of the stairs under Aunt Maggie's weight; then there was no sound except the girl's lessening sobs. She was lying now, her full weight on me, her head still pressed into my breasts, her arms gripping me, her legs entwined around mine, her whole attitude that of a child in distress. Stroking her hair, I looked around as I waited.

As McVeigh had said, there was plenty of bedding up here. Half of the small floor space seemed to be taken up with it. The rest of the floor, except where we were sitting, was covered with a conglomeration of books and soft stuffed animals, among them a panda and a teddy bear with long flopping ears. There were no dolls, I noticed. The only light came in through a minute skylight.

77

How long it was before I heard the quick scraping of footsteps on the stairs I don't know, but I had been aware for some time that one of my legs had gone to sleep and was now becoming very painful.

Davie McVeigh's head did not shoot into the attic, but rose slowly into the room, and he, too, did not rise to his feet but crawled forward.

Davie did not touch Frannie but asked gently, 'What is it?'

I had expected her to turn from me and fling herself on him, but she remained still.

'Frannie—Frannie, look at me.' Davie was bending down close to her now and his face was not more than inches from my own. His eyes were downcast and I noticed that the lids were heavy and fringed with short, thick, dark lashes. I felt embarrassed, slightly disturbed, and very uncomfortable as well. Trying to move my leg, I gave vent to a stifled groan. The lashes lifted and the eyes were looking into mine.

'I—I've got cramp.'

He bent forward to relieve me of Frannie and as his hand cupped her head his fingers touched the flesh of my neck near the breast. Instinctively, I recoiled. In a flash, his eyes were holding mine again.

His voice was low and cutting as he said, 'The action was involuntary.'

I wanted to say, 'I'm sorry.' But how could one explain a thing like that. What I did now was to try to loosen the girl's arms from around me, and, in doing this, I almost lost my balance and had to put my hands behind me to save us both from falling sideways. Then, with a movement that could only be called rough, Davie pulled Frannie from me and, gripping her by the shoulders, brought her round to face him.

Frannie did not protest. She was no longer crying but her head was hanging and she would not look at him.

'What is it? Tell me. Your grannie been at you?'

'No, Davie.'

78

'Someone said something to you?'

She shook her head.

'Have you been breaking things again?'

'No, Davie.'

He raised his eyes and looked at me. Then turning his gaze once more on Frannie, he smiled. It was a movement of his features I hadn't seen before. There was no sarcasm lifting the lips, no malice in the eye; his whole face looked gentle.

He said now, as he put his finger under the girl's chin, 'Come on, come on, you've got the hump. What do we say when we've got the hump?' He jerked her chin further up. 'Come on, what do we say?' He waited. Then he prompted slowly, 'Buck up and be a rabbit. Come on, say it.'

Frannie was looking at him now, her face unsmiling, but she repeated after him slowly: 'Buck up and be a rabbit.'

'Where's that book?' He was scrambling around the floor like a romping bear now. He pushed me aside slightly as he reached out and pulled towards him a large red-backed book. Then sitting down beside Frannie again, he said, 'Come on we'll read some poetry —right out loud.' He pointed the words out with his finger and began:

Slowly Frannie repeated, 'Promise to look at a leaf on a tree.'

Then she went on in a halting fashion:

> 'Promise to look at a leaf on a tree,
> Promise me, promise me;
> Promise to stand and look at the sea—'

Then breaking off, she turned her eyes up to his and tears were in them once more as she whimpered, 'I can't, Davie, I can't.'

Gently Davie laid the book down by his side—which was almost against my knee—and cupping Frannie's face with his thick square hands he asked in a perplexed fashion, 'What is it, Frannie? You can tell me. Someone has frightened you. Tell me—who?'

I watched her look at him for a moment, then lower her head, and, after she lowered it, she shook it from side to side.

'You'd better tell me—' his voice was softly insistent '—because I'll find out anyway. I find out everything, don't I?'

At this, like a slowly overbalancing sack, Frannie drooped forward and lay against him, her head buried in his open coat.

Over the top of her head, he looked at me and asked, 'How long has she been here?'

'I don't know. We've been out all day.'

'Come on. We're going home.'

He made a movement to rise to his feet, but, as he did so, the girl pressed herself tighter to him.

He said sharply, 'Now, Frannie! no more of it. I'm taking you home.'

Then, very much with the reaction of a father who had stood enough from a petulant child, he put his arm around her middle and drew her towards the ladder. Holding her like a bundle of bedding, he descended into the bedroom and placed her on her feet.

He turned and, looking up at me, asked brusquely, 'You coming down?'

'I'll manage, thank you.'

'Good enough.'

I sat on the floor where he had left me, the red-backed book in my hand. Frannie was an odd creature, but so, indeed, was he. 'Promise to look at a leaf on a tree'. I looked down at the book. It was a loose-paged book comprised of thick handmade paper, and on each page, in spiderly italic writing, was a verse of some kind—I would not have called it poetry. The book had a frontispiece which bore the date, January 24th, 1919, which was followed by the strange inscription: 'Came home today with the desire to live.'

Further down the first page, standing alone, were the words: Buck up and be a rabbit. On the opposite page were two verses—the words which Davie McVeigh had tried to get the child to repeat. I read them slowly:

Promise to look at a leaf on a tree,
    Promise me, promise me.
Promise to stand and look out to sea,
    Promise me, promise me.
And at noon on the day look up to the sky,
And make it a habit. Try, Try.

But if you haven't a tree, or the sea, or sight,
    What will you promise me?
To reach inside and find the spark
That started the tree, gave sight, and the sea, and
so say with me:
Buck up and be a rabbit.

The sentiment was simple, but charming. I turned over the pages. The book was full of such pieces, simple rhymed philosophy. I wondered who had written it. There was no name on the book, but the date was 1919. Likely, McVeigh's father—very likely.

Besides the litter of books on the floor, I saw, tucked neatly in the corner, a pile of books dealing principally with art, bearing such titles as *Perspective* and *The Art of Etching* by Rex Vicat Cole. There were books on woodwork and large flat books that spoke of art plates. But what drew my attention at once was a piece of paper hung between two stacks of books on which was written simply: 'Don't touch.'

The command I felt was meant for Frannie and not for the tenants of the cottage. It gave me a strange insight into the relationship between these two people. Davie McVeigh had placed that order there knowing that, although the girl would be alone in the attic, she would obey it.

My Aunt Maggie called again from the kitchen, and I descended into the bedroom and then to the ground floor, to be greeted by Aunt Maggie not with: 'What was she upset about?' but with: 'I don't like that woman!'

'Miss Cleverly?'

'The same.'

Aunt Maggie turned and marched into the sitting-room, and I followed her. And sitting down there, she looked up at me and said, 'I nearly broke my neck getting there. It was her I saw first; she was in a conflab with the younger one, Roy. Those two are as thick as thieves. I must have surprised her when I called through the kitchen window, for she turned on me. You wouldn't believe it but her face was really contorted with fury. The young fellow was sitting at the kitchen table and she had her arm around his shoulders. When I had called, they had both been startled—and she actually yelled at me. 'What are you doing there?' she asked. And, when I told her—she was at the door by now and slightly calmer—she said, 'Oh, that girl is becoming a proper nuisance. I'll have to tell her grannie to keep her home. You'd better go and see what's up with her, Roy.'' After a pause: 'You know something, Pru?'

I shook my head negatively.

'There's something between those two. He calls her "Aunt Flora." "I can't do that, Aunt Flora," he said. "I'm due back—I'm taking over for Fenwick. I told you." Did you know that the young one was only a garage hand?'

'No, I didn't know what he was.'

'Well, the way she put it was, he was in the car business and they were very busy at the present moment. But, by the look of his overalls, he had been under a number of cars. It's odd, don't you think, that he hasn't been put to something different from a car mechanic?'

'There's money in cars today, Aunt Maggie.'

'Yes, there might be in the big garages, but I shouldn't imagine there's much in that line in the garages around these quarters.'

'It may be a garage on the main road.'

'Perhaps. Anyway, she told me to go to the shed—that's what she called that cave—she pointed across to it. She said I would find McVeigh in there and to tell him. And do you know something else?'

Again I shook my head.

'When I walked in, he nearly hit the roof. He was laying pipes or such from that coke stove, and when I pushed the door open I must have moved them out of line. Anyway, he calmed down when he saw it was me and not you.' Aunt Maggie grinned at me. 'And he was off like a shot when I told him about the girl.'

Now Aunt Maggie screwed her eyes up, and nodding her head at me, she ended: 'You know, Pru, I don't like this set-up at all, and, the less we have to do with the folks in that house, the more comfortable will be our stay. At least, that's how I see it. How do you feel?'

'I don't really know,' I said. 'I'm only sure of one thing—and that is that David McVeigh is more objectionable than any of the others.'

Later that night, the weather broke with a really terrifying storm. There was a thunderclap that drove Aunt Maggie and me to cling together. We had been watching the lightning streaking over the hill beyond the lake, and one flash seemed to stab the lake right in its centre. Following that, the thunderclouds burst above us.

We went to bed early, voting it the best place to be as we were cold. I would have lit a fire if there had been anything with which to light one. I guessed that the main fuel used was wood, and, although there was evidence of logs having been stacked against the back wall, at present there were not even any chips there with which to make a flame.

So it was early the next morning, while it was still

raining, that I made my way over to the house to see about some form of heating. I made the trip reluctantly, I fear, and would gladly have left it to Aunt Maggie. Surprisingly, she had expressed a preference to stay in bed that morning, as she felt as if she had a slight cold coming on. I knew this was a sensible decision, for the room downstairs, although attractive in the sunlight, was fireless and, lacking any form of heating, it had lost something of its charm. So, as I said, I went to the house.

Thinking I would encounter someone in the courtyard, I went straight there, but there was no one to be seen. So I crossed over towards the kitchen, but at the sound of Miss Cleverly's voice, I stopped before I reached the door or the kitchen window.

Miss Cleverly was saying, 'How do I know why he's decided to sell the land? You should have been here instead of in your bolt hole.'

There came a pause. Then I actually heard a deep intake of breath before the deep, guttural voice of Davie McVeigh ground out his answer.

'Flora Cleverly,' Davie was saying, 'you'll try me too far one of these days and I'll throw you out on your neck. I warn you, mind, I'll do it, because you've stripped me of all sentiment concerning you or anything you've done in the past.'

'Oh, be quiet! Don't act the big fellow with me. You'd be finished flat if I left here, and you know it. Who'd work like I have done for years for nothing? And supplied the food for many a mouth at that? You can't do without me, and you know it. Everything you touch dies on you.'

'Yes, because you've willed it. Don't think I don't know who left that shed door open. That's the third time it's happened since I spawned the beds.'

'I've told you I didn't touch the shed door; it was them two up at the cottage nosing about.'

'I'd believe them before I'd believe you, Flora. But that's beside the point. What I want to know is, what made Alec Bradley decide to sell that bit of land and the cottage? The old woman has lived there since she was a child. What's going to happen to her and to Frannie?'

'Don't ask me. I don't know. If you make them your concern, that's up to you—and while I'm on about it, whose concern is it? It's puzzled me a bit why you should trouble yourself so much about the pair of them. It wouldn't have been you who was after her mother, would it? Funny, if I'm hitting the nail on the head.'

There came a long silence, during which I found myself backing cautiously away. It wasn't until I had reached the beginning of the courtyard again that I heard McVeigh's voice and the end of his reply as he came busting out of the door.

He was shouting: 'It's a wonder you weren't hit on the head a long time ago.'

I almost ran round to the front of the house and I was about to mount the steps to ring the bell when I heard the clink of heavy boots coming in my direction on the stones of the courtyard. So, as if having just made my appearance, I walked back towards the end of the house, and there came up with Davie McVeigh.

I have said earlier that the man's complexion was a ruddy brown, but I now saw that it was grey. His cheeks seemed to have been pulled in and he looked much older at this moment than I had yet seen him. Although he looked straight at me, I am positively sure he did not see me. When I spoke, as I did rapidly out of embarrassment, he jerked his head a little to the side before bringing his eyes back to focus on my face.

'—and my aunt's in bed with a slight cold and we would like a fire—if that is possible,' I finished.

'A fire? Yes. Oh, yes. Of course.'

Again, he shook his head. Then, to my astonishment, he began to apologize. 'I'm sorry about this. Of course, you need a fire. I generally see to a load of wood being dumped before anyone goes in—summer or winter. It's always cool in the evening.' He, too, was talking rapidly now. 'I'll get Talbot to saw some up—he should be along shortly. But in—' he turned from me '—in the meantime, you'd better have an oil heater.'

So unexpectedly civil had he been, so unlike himself, that I answered, 'I'm sorry that I have put you to all this trouble.'

I was following him back across the yard in the direction of the cave wall now, and, as he looked at me over his shoulder, I fully expected some remark, such as, 'And so am I.'

But what Davie said was: 'We've slipped up a lot where you and your aunt are concerned—the place wasn't ready and it should have been. But I suppose you can lay that down to the wedding.' As he pushed open the door and stood aside to allow me to enter, he added, 'They don't happen every day, do they?'

My back was stiffening again. Was he probing? If he had known who I was he had likely got his information from the splash the papers made about the court case and the break-up of my marriage.

We were in the cave now, all the way in, and, for a moment, my mind was diverted from him by what I saw. Stretching away into the far distance was what looked like an allotment, and covering the surface was a network of grey stuff, like solidified mist.

'The—the beginning of the mushrooms?' I pointed.

'Yes. This is the spawn. It's doing fine. It's all ready for the casing now—that is, the soil that goes on top.'

'It's very interesting. Can you make a living out of them—a reasonable living?'

I wasn't really interested in the mushrooms, nor yet in whether McVeigh would be able to make a living from them, not at this moment—for I was almost overcome with the oppressive atmosphere of the place.

'Yes. Yes, I can make a living, if I get the chance.'

On his last words, his head went down and he turned away and walked along the path bordering the beds. I could do nothing but follow him. There had been some light given off by a weak electric bulb, but now, walking away from it, I could barely make out his back in front of me, until he came to a stop in front of the cave wall. There, in the Open-Sesame manner, he pushed at what must have been a door, and we passed into another cave, which was cooler and much lighter. After a moment, I saw that this cave got its light and air from two sources —from an open door in the far distance and from a sort of funnel in the rock that opened up just above my head.

I was looking upwards, trying not to gulp openly at the refreshing air, when Davie said, 'I'm going to do something with that when I can get round to it. The wind whistling down there in the winter would cut you in two, and that's no use for mushrooms. That's why one's got to be so careful about doors.'

Our glances crossed for a brief second on this last remark but I did not take it up. Instead, I said, 'It's an amazing size. You'd never dream from outside that there was so much space in here.'

'It's wasted.' Davie flung his hand out with an impatient movement. 'I use it as a storeroom, but one day—' He nodded his head—he seemed to have made a promise to himself.

We were moving towards the far doorway now. Again addressing his back, I asked, 'How does one start a business like this?' For the moment I had forgotten that I didn't like the man; I suppose it was my writer's instinct at work gathering data.

'You go to school and learn.'

'School?' The word was high in my head.

He had stopped and was looking at me. 'Well, sort of. When you want to get mushrooms beyond a back-yard and a seed-box business, you've got to learn many things. There's much more in it than people think. But, whichever way you do it, there's the secret.' He had stepped through the doorway and was pointing across a wide farmyard to an open barn beyond, within which was a great mound of steaming manure. 'Preparation of that,' he said. 'But it's become so damned scientific, I sometimes wonder how the mushrooms managed before the lads started on them. That's the worst part. You turn that stuff until you hate the sight of it.'

'Have you been growing them long?'

'Three years. But I was nearly finished last year—the crop went dead on me. There can be two a year, you know—if you're lucky. But, when a thing like that happens, it can knock you back somewhat.'

'Yes, yes.'

Our glances had crossed again, and I looked away from him at the farmyard. I saw that it was bordered on one side by stables, on another by byres. In a field beyond the open barn, were a number of small black hutches which I knew to be chicken runs.

I turned to him, and, my voice showing my genuine amazement, I said, 'You would never dream that this lay behind the caves—I mean the hill—not from the other side—the courtyard side.'

'No. It is rather surprising.'

I looked up at the wall of the stone-cased hill. 'It's like a basin,' I said. 'It looks much bigger inside than it does out.'

'It is. This hill gives no indication whatever of the size of the caves inside. They go for miles. I haven't even been in some myself—too big to get through the passages.'

'Really?' I was finding my interest deepening. 'How were they discovered?'

'Discovered? Oh, they've always been there, as far as I understand. My great-grandfather used to hide whisky in the far ones when they used to distill the stuff in the hills around here and were on the run from the Excise. They used to search the caves, but more often than not they got lost themselves and had to be brought out—now, there's material for a story.'

He was actually smiling at me in a kindly fashion. He

didn't seem the same person whom I'd heard talking to Flora Cleverly not more than minutes ago. He not only looked agreeable, he sounded agreeable. I had the fanciful thought that passing through the caves had cleansed him of his roughness, brusqueness, and boorish manner.

David McVeigh stood now rubbing his hand over the head of a collie dog which was pressed close to his knee. Near a gate at the far end of the yard, with their heads well over it, stood two heavy feathery-footed horses—Talbot's shires.

It had stopped raining. There was no sun, yet this place seemed lit up in a fashion I couldn't describe. I sensed it. And I felt accurately that it was in this part of Lowtherbeck, and only in this part, that this man could feel at ease. I could see him, as it were, cut off from the rest of the household, working here and sleeping at the cottage. He need hardly come in touch with anyone at the house unless he wanted to—I cut off my thinking about him abruptly. I did not want to have to change my opinion of him.

I asked now, 'Do you have help?'

'Only occasionally. Talbot, you know, from the village, when he can give me a few hours. But Janie is a grand help; she's got a marvellous way with the animals. But from today, she's back at school. Her sister Doris—that's the one who was married on Saturday—she was very handy, too. And there's Roy; he helps when he can. We get by.' He squared his shoulders. 'It all gets done in the end.' Again, it seemed as if he was assuring himself instead of making a statement.

I knew absolutely nothing about farming and the work it entailed, yet I would have had to be a very stupid person if I hadn't realized that there was a great deal too much work here for one man with occasional help to get through.

As if reading my thoughts, Davie said, 'There's a bit overmuch for one, yet not enough for two.'

'Your brother works away?'

'Yes, he's in the car business. And that's what he likes—he can't stick this.' He moved his arm to indicate the yard. Then, as if he had been betrayed into saying too much, he added abruptly, 'I'll get you a stove and oil.'

When he came out of a shed carrying a stove and a can of oil, I said, 'I can manage these. I'll make two journeys.'

'No. It won't take me but a few minutes to go there and back. Come this way.'

I could see he would brook no argument and I did not protest, but again followed him. Once more I experienced surprise for, as he said, it was only a matter of minutes before I saw the cottage—but the back of it this time. He had brought me through a narrow overgrown path that I guessed had been used before only by himself. It came out in the thicket behind the sentry-box lavatory. Another minute, and we were in the sitting-room. He did not simply deposit the things, but he filled the stove and lit it.

'There,' he said as he looked at the stove after it had given a final *plop plop,*, and settled down to glow. 'That should be all right now. And I'll see you have the wood this afternoon. By the way—'

He had turned from me and was walking towards the kitchen as he spoke. His walk was slow, his head was bent downwards, and his words seemed muffled as he said, 'I wonder if you would mind Frannie coming to the attic occasionally? It's the only place she can feel—well—' I thought he was going to say 'safe', and I'm sure he was, but he changed it to: '—at home. She's played up there since she was a small girl. She gets fits of moodiness and likes to be by herself.'

I hesitated in my reply because my mind had jumped back to the conversation I had heard from the courtyard concerning the child and her grandmother.

Davie turned to me and said, 'I'm sorry. I shouldn't have asked.

I stammered, 'Oh really, please, it's perfectly all right. Yes, tell her to come when she likes. She won't be in our way.'

'You are sure?'

'Yes, perfectly.'

I wasn't perfectly sure. If I had stopped to think and told myself the truth, I didn't want anyone coming in and out of the cottage, least of all this lost soul of a girl, for I found she disturbed me emotionally, and I myself was staying here to calm my own emotions.

'Thanks.'

David McVeigh was standing outside the back door and, before turning abruptly and striding away, he said—in a tone that was an echo of what I had come to look upon as his natural disgruntled voice—'If you want anything just tell me.'

As he did not wait for my reply, I did not offer any, but returned to the room, thinking of the words of Flora Cleverly: 'If you make them your concern, that's up to you—and while I'm on about it, whose concern is it? It's puzzled me a bit why you should trouble yourself so much about the pair of them. It wouldn't have been you who was after her mother, would it? Funny, if I'm hitting the nail on the head.'

5

✤

We had been in the cottage, as I have said, for over three weeks now, and I was feeling much better. I had had no bout of nerves, no trembling, no retching, and no fear. That indescribable panicky fear and inability to describe what I was afraid of had not returned.

And during this time, I had, in a way, come to know quite a lot about the occupants of Lowtherbeck. I learned, for instance, that Flora Cleverly had actually been born in the cottage. Her father had been a sort of working manager of the estate. She had been brought up side by side with Davie McVeigh's father, John McVeigh, and she had helped in the big house long before John McVeigh had married.

I further learned, from short conversations I had had with Roy, that, compared to his brother, he was of rather low if not exactly dim intellect, and the rude exclamation that Davie McVeigh had made when Roy had said he had always wanted to write a book was now understandable to me, although I still thought the remark had been unnecessary. As for Janie, I found her a nice child, but I saw little of her. Likely, she spent all her time helping with the animals as McVeigh had said.

Then McVeigh himself. Had he kept up his pleasant manner towards me? Yes—yes—strangely enough, yes.

I had been amazed at his change of front, yet I had had
further proof that under this thin skin of civility still lay
the demanding, dogmatic master of all he surveyed. This
was proved one morning when I came upon him and
the man Alec Bradley in the farmyard behind the hill.
It was almost a week from the time that he had brought
me through the caves and shown me the short cut to the
cottage. From then on, I had used that way when going
for the milk. I was just about to come out of the
overgrown pathway one morning when I heard Davie
McVeigh's voice raised high in anger.

Davie was saying, 'The hell you will! Not if I can
stop you. There's something behind this.'

'There's nothing behind this except that I want to
plough my own land.'

I would not have recognized Alec Bradley's voice
from my memory of it on the night of the mad dance
near the lake, but, from where I stood, I could see his
profile with his chin thrust out. It was the same man
who had shouted out the rhyme.

'You can't plough within twenty yards of the cottage
—it's solid rock underneath. If you want to plough,
plough round it and leave a path to the road.'

'I'm pulling it down.'

'By God! I'll see you don't!'

'Try and stop me.'

'Aye, I'll stop you. You take my word for it, Bradley.
I'll stop you. I've still got some say around here.'

'Pooh! Don't try to bluff me. Everything you've
touched has dropped to pieces under your hand for
years. You're nothing but a byword. An' I'm warning
you, I'm not drunk this time, so don't try anything
with your fists. But you won't, will you, because
Cissie's in the car above on the road watching us. You
wouldn't like Cissie to see you hit out first, would you?
You've never been the same since you lost Cissie to me
—and then to go and lose young Doris to Jimmy. It
was another bad blow, wasn't it?'

'Get out!'

'I'm goin', but I just stepped in to warn you. Keep your nose out of affairs that don't concern you. Even Meg Amble herself doesn't want you interfering. She's all set to go down to her brother in Dorset, an' the girl with her.'

'You're a liar!'

'Go and ask her?'

'Get out!'

I waited a while until I heard the car on the road beyond start up. Then I still waited—for Davie McVeigh had not moved from the spot on which he had stood while talking to Alec Bradley, and something in the look on his face warned me not to make my presence known, yet for some unexplainable reason I wanted to go to him. I was just about to turn round and go back to the cottage when I saw him stride over to what was presumably a chopping block and there, lifting up the axe high, he swung it down and buried its head in the scarred wood.

The action was so ferocious, so terrifying, that I found my breath checked by my own hand pressed tightly across my mouth. The next thing, I had turned without taking heed to be quiet and was running along the narrow path to the cottage; and I didn't stop running until I was actually in the sitting-room.

Aunt Maggie, who had been sitting before the fire, turned startled eyes on me. And then, rising quickly, she asked anxiously, 'What is it? What's happened?'

'Nothing. Nothing.' I shook my head. Then going towards the burning logs, I held my hands out to the blaze.

'You're shivering.' Her hand was on my arm. 'What is it? Something's happened.'

'Not to me. Don't worry. It was—' I sat down on the couch, then told her of the scene I had just witnessed, and ended, 'It was the fury with which he wielded that axe, as if he were hitting out at the man, this Alec

Bradley. And not only him.' I shook my head and closed my eyes tightly. 'I just don't know; I've never seen anyone so angry before.' For a fleeting moment, I remembered my own anger against the man who had deceived me, but it was not comparable with the anger of Davie McVeigh. His anger seemed to be against the whole world—except, perhaps, the girl Frannie, and young Janie.

Aunt Maggie was looking straight into the fire now. She had her hands joined on top of her knees and her body was rocking gently back and forth. This movement indicated that she was troubled.

I said quickly to her, 'Don't worry; *I'm* not upset. It's odd, but—I was frightened, and yet I wasn't—I can't explain. I had to run away—because, if I hadn't, I would have run forward to him, and I felt I mustn't.' My voice trailed off.

Aunt Maggie had turned her head and was looking at me. She said quietly, 'Look, lass, things are not turning out the way I thought. What about us making a move, eh? We can even pay them the full amount. They seem hard up, the lot of them. What about it, eh?'

I considered for a moment. Yes, we could easily pay them the remainder of the three-months rent and pack and leave this moment—we had nothing but clothes with us. But, wherever we stayed this night, I knew that I would be thinking back to this cottage and what was happening to Davie McVeigh and those concerned with him.

It was I who was looking into the fire now, and I spoke slowly as if reading my own thoughts: 'The doctors said I had to fight this thing—didn't they?—this thing that has urged me for years to give up and let life walk past me. This thing that won't even let me finish with life. They said that, if I wanted to win the battle, I had to do exactly the opposite. I had to take an interest in things outside myself—pretend an interest, even if I didn't feel it, and, eventually, the shadow life would take on some form of reality. Well, Aunt Maggie, as you know, I've been trying hard for many months with little result, yet here in this out-of-the-way place I think the shadow is turning into reality because I've become interested in the people in that house in an odd way.' I looked at her now. 'I can't explain it except to say that I suppose it's the writer in me coming alive again. But I want to keep going there and finding out things. I'm not being nosy, you know that.'

Aunt Maggie's hand was patting mine now and she smiled as she said, 'That's good news anyway, and if the place and that lot are having such a heartening effect on you we'll take it on a three year lease—'

Between that morning and the time I want to describe now, I only met with Davie McVeigh three times. I had seen him in the distance, but, even at the distance of a few yards, he took no notice of me, seeming unaware of my presence. But at the other times when he did speak to me, his manner and tone were back to what I thought of as the 'real' David Bernard Michael McVeigh. And then came the morning of the soft dawn, the morning when I knew I had a story, when I knew I had a story of the house, of Lowtherbeck and the people therein.

I had been restless all evening and took my restlessness to bed with me. This was often the case when a story was brewing in my mind. I dropped into fitful sleep and woke as the light was just breaking over the lake, revealing the mist as a grey net that was being dragged gently across the water. I opened the window further and leant out. The air was cool but not cold. It was going to be a lovely day, a rare September day.

Previously, when I had woken up at this time of the morning and had not had this view to look upon, my mind had turned inwardly to my own troubles and coated them further with resentment, but, since I had

96

slept on this narrow bed with my head on a level with this window, my thoughts had been drawn outwards, as my whole being was being drawn outwards at this moment. I wanted to walk near the lake.

I strained my eyes towards the travelling clock. It said half-past five. If I were to get up now, I would likely disturb Aunt Maggie. But the urge to get outside conquered consideration for my aunt. I was wearing a short nightie, but did not take it off; I just pulled a skirt and twin-set sweater over it. Then, donning my slippers, I crept quietly towards and down the ladder. In the kitchen, I changed my footwear, and, going from the room, I opened the door.

The daylight was creeping higher into the sky now. It seemed to be drawing night shrouds from the trees, trailing them like stencilled veils over the dewy, weeping grass. Slowly, like one entranced, I walked down to the lake. But here the picture had changed. I couldn't see the edge of the water—I couldn't see my feet either. I was now walking in a swirl of mist. It was a slightly eerie, yet wonderful, feeling. The hill beyond the lake was showing a pale mauve tint; it looked high and far away like a mountain and of a sudden I had the desire to climb it. I had walked round the foot of it a number of times. The hill rose from a valley bottom which was a field with a boundary wire running down its middle. I had never been to the top, and now I was going to climb it.

As I walked in the mist-covered grass, I experienced a feeling that was not joy. I knew what joy felt like— this was not joy. Was it contentment? No. No. There was nothing static about it. In fact, one of its ingredients was a desire to run, to skip like a child over the carpeted ground.

At one period I lifted my feet high in a dancing step almost, then admonished myself, 'Don't be silly!' Nerves didn't always show themselves in despondency; they often took the form of high laughter, and silly antics—

one must be aware. I found myself shaking my head to throw off my own admonition. I was always too careful, always watching myself. Suddenly, I heard the voice in my head saying, 'Run if you want to; go on,' and I obeyed. I ran through the mist until I reached the foot of the hill, and then I began to climb, and, as I climbed the sun climbed with me. When, panting and laughing to myself, I reached the top, I stood in its light and it warmed me through to my heart.

I had not felt like this for years; truthfully, I had never felt like this in my life before. I knew in this moment I was beginning to live and was experiencing life as I had never done. I knew also that, whatever happened to me in the future, I myself would be in the forefront of its creation. The misfortunes which had happened to me in the past had come through my mother and father—and through Ian. I felt now, and with deep conviction, that not one of the three could touch me again. . . .

Why don't such moments last? Perhaps they are just given to us to use as a memory of strength with which to combat our fear when it descends on us yet again. Perhaps this moment I was experiencing was what is meant by drawing strength from nature. Anyway, I had the urge to throw my arms wide, so forceful was this feeling of new life within me, but warned myself that I was on a high elevation and could be seen. Yet, who would be about at this time of the morning? Who, except myself? I had the world to myself. It was as I gazed over this world that I caught a glimpse of the Big Water.

I had never been near the Big Water and when I blinked the sun from my eyes and shaded my vision, I could see part of it quite clearly. Away across an open stretch of land, which headed the top of the Lil Water —which I could just make out from my bedroom window—was a deep belt of trees. This was the border of the Big Water.

I was going towards the border now. I was going to see the Big Water. I was running down the hill. There was no mist here; that is, until I reached the valley, when once again it swirled round my ankles.

Before I could cross the open land, I had a barrier to surmount. It was a dry-stone wall; many of then intersected the fields in these parts. But this one was about four feet high and two feet thick and its top was rough and hurt my hands and knees. Although I was now in the valley, the land was still on a slope, and, as I gripped the top of the stonework to heave myself over, I had a momentary impression of men struggling with these great boulders, carrying them up the incline, lifting them into place—all without the help of machinery. These were the men from the stock who had fought to defend this country against the Scots. No wonder they gloried in being tough.

I was not thinking so much of Davie McVeigh at this moment as of Talbot, and was remembering the day he brought the wood to the cottage. He had taken up a great pile of logs in his arms and brought them into the sitting-room; I had remarked about their being too heavy to carry at one go. Talbot had turned on me a look that was almost scornful. Then, over a cup of coffee in the kitchen, he had regaled me with stories of the glories of Cumberland and the achievements of her men. It was only when he started to relate the passionate romances of some of the ladies of the county that I withdrew. There were still certain subjects I could not listen to, and one of them was the romantic loves of others.

But this memory fled, wiped away by the floating mist. I was over the wall now. I found I had to tread carefully, because twice I almost stumbled, for the field was undoubtedly studded with small outcrops of rock.

Then, as if it had been pushed aside by a giant hand, the mist drifted away as I entered the trees. When I emerged on the other side, there was nothing before me but a large stretch of water—at least four times the size of the cottage lake.

I was disappointed in the setting. It did not have the attractiveness of the Lil Water. Although it was bordered for quite some way by trees and had the advantage of what looked, from this distance, like a miniature beach, there was something forbidding about the entire scene. There was a rowboat lying on its side away to the right. It was old and unused and I wondered if it were the same boat that had capsized and drowned Frannie's parents.

Although the morning sun was touching the water, it did not seem to add any warmth to it. I was reluctant to go farther. I said to myself: 'Don't be silly. Walk around it; it's only a lake.' But, instead of doing so, I sat down on a low flat-topped boulder near the fringe of trees. It was as if the excitement of the morning were seeping out of me. I felt rather tired and I recognized, with a feeling of dread, that a depression was descending upon me. I looked around. I was very susceptible to atmosphere—I had found this out long ago. Perhaps I was experiencing this feeling because two people had died in this water. And not only two— there could have been many victims down the generations who had started to cross this lake and never reached the other side. Yet why should it affect me so adversely? I didn't know.

I was about to make the effort to rise and retrace my steps when there came a movement in the trees away to my right. It brought my head round and then my mouth open as I saw—walking down to the miniature beach—Davie McVeigh. I saw him drop something from his hand—it could have been a coat. I realized that he was naked, but what brought my hand up to my face was the fact that my eyes were conveying to my senses a horror because I was not looking at naked flesh, but at limbs that were covered in patches with a sickly looking light pink skin, and in between the patches were patterns formed by scarred flesh—in some places, it was drawn together in a series of weals. The weals moved as his muscles worked; they rippled like dissected snakes with each step he took. I found myself repeating Aunt Maggie's reverent phrase: 'My God!' I said to myself. Then I added, 'Oh, dear God!'

This, then, was why Davie always wore his shirt buttoned up to the neck and the cuffs of his sleeves fastened. But when his body was scarred like this, how had his face escaped? I had noticed a broad scar leading from his collar to the back of his ear and thought it might have been the result of a war wound. A great many men carried these badges of war on them, but he was surely too young to be carrying such a badge. Nevertheless, this man was carrying more than a badge, he was carrying a burnt body around with him. I found myself standing on my feet, my head shaking slowly. I was thinking: what does one know of another? I detested this man—at least, I had detested him. I looked upon him as a sneering, arrogant individual, yet all the time he was carrying, behind the façade of the big he-man, this scarred body.

One thing only was important now—I must get away quietly—he mustn't see me. Knowing I had seen him exposed would be unbearable for him.

Forgetting that I had risen from the stone and it was now behind me, I took a step backwards; then, unable to save myself, I toppled over, twisting as I did so and landing on my side. There was a pain in my elbow and wrist, for my arm had been thrust out to break my fall, but I leaned on it now and I turned my head slowly and looked to where Davie McVeigh was standing facing me. The same distance was between us as before, yet he seemed to be almost breathing down on me. After a brief glance at him, I lowered my head. The front of his body bore the same pattern as the back.

From under my eyelids, I watched his feet moving,

not towards me but towards the belt of trees again. His feet weren't hurrying; their pace was steady. I made an effort to rise, but when I put pressure on my hand the pain was agonizing, and I found myself stretched on my side again. After a moment, I sat up with the aid of my other hand and rested my back against the boulder, gripping my hurt wrist the while. I made no effort to get up and hurry away. I was waiting—the next move would be his. It was only two or three minutes later that I saw him walking towards me with his coat on. I did not look at him when he approached. When he came to a stop, I still did not raise my eyes to his.

'Well!'

The word had a tight sound yet did not give any indication of anger.

I glanced up and found myself stammering, 'I—I came out to see the dawn. I didn't mean—'

'You needn't apologize. I remember you telling me once before that it's a free country. And take that frightened look off your face.'

'I'm—I'm not frightened.'

'You're frightened all the time. Aren't we all?' He turned his face away from mine now and looked over the water. I was surprised at the momentary feeling of resentment that filled me, swamping my pity for the man—resentment that once again he was, as it were, taking the wind out of my sails. I had expected him to rage at me and, in my compassion for him, I had been willing to submit to his rage without rising against it. But here he was turning the tables.

McVeigh was still looking at the lake as he said, 'You are frightened. Oh—' he shook his head slowly '—not of me. You pride yourself that you can see through me, don't you? No, you're not afraid of me, but you're afraid of everything else—don't get up.' He turned and held the palm of his hand towards me. Then he added, 'I can sit down; I've got at least half an hour before the day starts. Have you hurt your hand?'

McVeigh was sitting not more than a foot from me, his legs stretched out from under his coat, his bare feet pointing upwards. I found I was looking at them. There was no contorted skin on them—the skin was natural and the feet were broad and well-shaped.

I said, 'I think I've sprained my wrist.'

'Let's see.'

I did not extend my hand towards him, and, when his fingers touched my wrist, the reaction was the immediate stiffening of my muscles, mostly in the region of my stomach.

He felt this tenseness, I knew, for his fingers remained stationary for a moment and his hard gaze brought my eyes to him. There we sat for some seconds looking at each other. Then he asked quietly, 'What's made you like this? You should never let anything get on top of you to this extent. You should fight it.'

To my amazement, I heard myself saying quietly, 'I am fighting it.'

'Was it because of the break-up?' The muscles were more tense now and I was unable to answer, so he went on quietly, as his fingers moved over the bones of my hands.

'These things happen, they happen to us all—in different ways. The world of people and incidents beats you up, kicks you around, and you've only got one life to answer with.'

His fingers released my wrist as he said, 'There's no bones broken. When you get in, put a strap round it.'

And then he turned his body from me, and, leaning once more against the boulder, he pulled one knee upwards and rested his hands on the top of it. He looked across the water, and I looked across the water, and there was a profound silence between us. The silence grew until it seemed to my mind to become almost a solid thing. It filled the air and spread over the ground with a stillness that quietened the spirit. It was all around me, in me. The essence of that moment will remain with me until I die. Then I remember the atmosphere in the silence changing; it was as if his presence had impregnated it, now forcing an awareness on me. When I became conscious of him, I experienced another strange feeling. I felt that this man and I—this man whom I disliked for most of the qualities he had shown to me—this man and I shared something. It seemed as if we were thinking along the same channels—but what particular channels I, as yet, didn't put a name to.

I came to myself as a single blade of grass flickered; the movement stood out against the stillness like a water spout in a calm sea. My head turned downwards so I could look at the fluttering blade. It was at this moment that my companion began to talk.

McVeigh was still looking over the water as he said, 'When I got this—' he tapped first his shirt front and then his thigh '—I thought it was the finish; I *hoped* it was the finish. When anything big hits us, that's always the natural reaction—to give way before it.'

He paused, and I asked quietly, 'Was it in the war?'

'Sort of—but nothing romantic.' I saw a twist to his lips. 'No dashing in to save my superior officer. No medals. Just a petrol lorry toppling down a bank and catching fire. They found me with my head stuck out of the window—the door had jammed. My boots saved my feet, but they wouldn't have if I had been there much longer.'

'Where did it happen?'

'In Korea. The big war and all the shouting was over. Things like this don't matter often; and then only to the people to whom they happen.'

'I am truly sorry.'

I was looking down towards the grass as I spoke and I felt his head jerk in my direction.

His voice took on that deep satirical quality that verged on laughter as he replied, 'Now, look here, don't go wasting your sympathy on me. I don't want you or anyone else to be sorry for me.'

His voice, his manner, had sent me back to the steep road and the incident with the cars. Hastily, I got to my feet but, before I was standing straight, he was up, too, and, again, we were looking at each other.

I said, 'I'm not sorry for you, I don't think anybody could be sorry for you.'

My meaning was not what my actual words conveyed literally. I suppose I meant he was too big a man to attract pity; his manner spurned pity; yet this wasn't the reaction my words had on him. To my surprise, I saw a look that was almost pain come into his eyes. His lower lip moved in and out twice and his jaw jerked— it was a spasmodic reaction.

Then, his head bouncing once, McVeigh said, 'That's true, that's true.' There was emphasis as he repeated the words. Then he added, 'Well, I've got to get started. Good-bye.'

'Good-bye.' We turned from each other simultaneously and went our separate ways.

The morning had lost its wonder. Although there was no sign of mist, there was now a chill feeling in the air. I was through the belt of trees and nearing the drystone wall when there came over me an impulse for urgency—I wanted to run. If I had asked, where to?— I would have got the reply, 'Home', and home for me spelt Aunt Maggie. I wanted to be near Aunt Maggie, wrapped round by her common-sense, her matter-of-factness. I wanted to touch on her life, a life that had known no unnatural fear.

Yet if I had probed within further and asked why this pressing need, I would have found it was because, deep within me at this moment, although I would not recognize it, was the knowledge of the utter fallibility of impressions, impressions that people gave you of strength. The impression I had first got of Davie McVeigh had been one of strength, perhaps cruel physical strength, but, nevertheless, strength. Now I knew that in that moment of silence when our thoughts had been channelled together, the cores of our beings had recognized, each in the other, the emotion which had dominated our lives—and the emotion was fear. My fear was, and had always been, fear of people and what they might do to me. What they usually did was cast me off in one way or another. My fear had become contorted of late and had acquired strange tangents, but at its root was the fear of particular people and what they could do to me. But what was McVeigh's fear? I did not know—only that it existed.

When I rounded the foot of the hill and saw Aunt Maggie standing at the door in her dressing-gown I ran towards her—actually like a child running home to its mother.

And, like a mother, she greeted me harshly. 'Where on earth have you been at this time of the morning? You had me worried.'

'I couldn't sleep, I went out to see the sunrise. But what's the matter with you?' I was speaking casually now. I was within the ring of security; for the moment, I was without fear. 'You are never up at this time.'

'I've got the toothache.'

'Oh, Aunt Maggie, not again!'

She turned on me now an almost comical look on her face as she chided me, 'You said that to me the other day when I was sick. I didn't want to be sick again, and I don't want the toothache again.'

It seemed a most unsympathetic reaction, but I wanted to laugh. Instead, I said, 'Well, you're having that tooth out, and no more shilly-shallying. You've had it filled until there's no original tooth left.'

Instead of replying, Aunt Maggie probed. 'You look whitish and tired, haven't you slept? Are you cold? You're shivering.'

'Yes, I am a bit cold. I could do with some hot tea.'

'It's all ready.'

A few minutes later, after stirring the wood ash into flame, we sat close to the fire drinking our tea, and apropos of nothing that had been said so far, I made a statement.

'I'm starting a book today,' I said. 'I've got the title. It's called *The Iron Façade*.'

6

It was strange the effect that my new work had on me.
Although, naturally, I camouflaged both the characters
and the surroundings of Lowtherbeck, the essence of
the atmosphere I felt in this place came through in my
writing immediately. But there was one thing which
disturbed me; I found that I had put myself into the
story. Once again, I was probing inwards. I had been
entwined among the characters of my previous three
books. My character then had been that of a sensitive,
poorly-used individual, but now my character was
emerging through these pages as a rather self-centred
individual, and I found I didn't like the person I was
representing.

I didn't like the character, but I couldn't alter her or
remove her from the story, for she seemed an essential
part of it. I knew that the action surrounding this particular character would make her forget herself, as I
wanted to forget myself, but there was something else
I had to bring into her character also. As often, when
building a character in a book, it is the character that
takes charge of the writer instead of the reverse. I
wanted to make this character warm and loving as I
knew myself to be deep within. I wanted to make her
the kind of person to whom people would naturally
turn in times of trouble—a younger edition of Aunt

Maggie. I wanted to make her someone who could forget herself entirely, even to the extent of giving up her whole life for someone else. This was my early intention, but I could not mould this particular character into the shape I had protected. There was an ingredient missing, and I hoped that, as I went on with the story, it would emerge and I would know how to develop her.

When, in the depth of my bitterness, I had poured myself out to Aunt Maggie, saying I must be a frightful person that all these things should happen to me: my mother and father throwing me off, then my husband turning out to be someone else's husband, and his blaming me for it all. He had said, 'Well, take your mind back. I never asked you to marry me; it was you who did the asking.' It was then that Aunt Maggie had consoled me by saying, 'It's their loss for you're a warm, lovable lass. Those that are deceived by your cool model-like exterior have no depths themselves.' It was a portrait of myself as Aunt Maggie saw me that I wanted to set down, but the portrait wouldn't come alive.

I became so engrossed in my novel that during the next two weeks I saw Davie McVeigh only twice, and then only from a distance. When the weather, which had worsened all of a sudden, became permissible, Aunt Maggie did the daily trek to the house for the milk, and, on returning, she nearly always had some comment to make on Flora Cleverly.

One day, my aunt commented, 'That one's so strung up the spring'll snap one of these days. She cannot stand still a minute. But I must hand it to her, she gets through some work. Do you know she does all their washing? She has about eight lines out in the meadow, full of sheets and things. She must have been up bright and early to get that lot done. And there she was in the kitchen baking when I arrived, and that was half-past ten.'

To this particular piece of news, I had replied, 'She's

very likely speaking the truth when she says they can't do without her.'

I had told Aunt Maggie about the conversation I had overheard between Flora Cleverly and Davie McVeigh. . . .

Then one morning Aunt Maggie came into the room whispering hastily. 'He's brought the wood himself, shall I ask him in for a coffee?'

My first reaction was to say *no, no*. Then I placed the onus on my aunt by asking, 'Would you like to?'

'It doesn't matter to me one way or another.' She was still whispering. Then she added, 'Yes, I think I would, if only to prove I'm not early Victorian!'

She returned to the kitchen laughing. She looked and sounded gay. It was one of her young days.

I was using the long refectory table as a desk and I'd hardly risen from it when Davie McVeigh entered the room from the kitchen. I hadn't expected to see him so soon; it was as if he had been standing behind the door. I heard Aunt Maggie's voice and the tail end of her words: 'I'll bring the drink in, in a minute.'

'Am I disturbing you?' McVeigh asked.

'No. Oh, no.' I pushed carelessly at a pile of written work. 'I'm always glad of a break.'

He walked down the centre of the room towards the fire. He did not look at home as he had done on that first evening when he had barged in through the front door, but appeared somewhat ill at ease.

'Are you writing another book?' He was standing on the hearthrug waiting for me to sit down.

'Yes, I'm trying to. It takes some getting into if you've neglected it for a time.'

'That's the same with everything, I think.'

He seated himself now in the high-backed leather chair, and although it was part of the suite, I thought to myself: it's his chair.

He asked abruptly, 'Are you liking it here?'

'Yes. Yes, very much.'

'You're not finding it too lonely?'

'I—we don't mind being alone.'

'Do you mind if I smoke?' He pulled a pipe from his pocket when I answered, 'Of course not.'

When McVeigh had lit the pipe and drawn once or twice on the long stem, he said, 'I was wanting a word with you about Frannie. You'll be wondering why, after I asked you if she could come to the attic, she hasn't been across.'

'Yes, yes. It did make us wonder. I hope she's all right.'

'No, I'm afraid she's not all right. She's hardly been near the house these past weeks. I went across yesterday to see her grannie. The old lady says she's moping. I got her to promise to take her to the doctor's this morning. She's a bitter old stick, is the grannie. I suppose life has made her like that, but it's hard on the child.'

I could find nothing to say to this for Flora Cleverly's suggestion was in my mind again.

Then McVeigh broke the silence by referring to the weather. 'The cold weather has settled in,' he said. 'You won't find it very pleasant in a short while.'

'Oh, I don't mind the cold.'

'I don't think you've experienced our kind of cold.' He was smiling wryly. 'There's been times, even early in December, when we haven't been able to make a path between the cottage and the house—but you'll be gone by then.'

'Yes, yes. I suppose so.'

I felt my eyes widen in surprise when he rose from the chair abruptly and, walking to the window, looked out towards the lake, and after a moment, said quietly, 'I always meant to apologize for the day of the wedding —not for what happened on the road.' His head turned slightly over his shoulder, but he didn't look back at me. 'That was understandable, at least from a driver's point of view. But I mean the evening when that mad lot came across and Alec Bradley—' He stopped now and, turning and facing me, added, 'The truth of it is, I had a drink like the rest and the effect of liquor on me is to turn me into a creator of rhymes, corny rhymes. When I've had a drink I can set anything to rhyme, but, should I try when I'm in my normal state, I find the process difficult and the result laboured. Yet when under—the influence, my verses are fluent and corny.'

I saw that it had taken a great deal for him to speak as he was doing, so I said lightly, 'Oh, I'd forgotten all about it. But tell me, do you write poetry?'

'Poetry—no, it's just this rhyming. My father had a knack too. He filled books with rhymes, sentimental Ella Wheeler Wilcox stuff; yet to look at him, you would never have believed him capable of even that. He was a hard-living, hard-drinking, tough individual but—' He looked downwards now and tapped his pipe against the back of his hand '—endearing for all that.'

'Has he been long dead?'

'He died when I was fourteen; my mother died when I was three.'

And, I thought to myself, Flora Cleverly brought you up and you've hated every moment under her dominance.

Aunt Maggie came bustling in now and the visitor moved forward and took the tray from her and laid it on the corner of the table, well away from my writing.

My Aunt said to him, 'I've been meaning to ask you, Mr McVeigh, did you carve this table and these?' She pointed to the animals on the long shelf.

'Oh, those!' His voice dismissed them lightly. 'Yes. Yes, I used to try my hand at such things in my youth.'

'They're fine pieces of work. And this table is magnificent. Haven't you kept it up?'

'No, no. There's no time now.' He looked towards the carved horse and the hard lines of his broad face seemed to soften as he said quietly, 'I used to spend day after day chipping away at things like that, wood always appealed to me, but as I said—' he turned abruptly round '—there's no time any more.' He smiled and added, 'Thank you,' as he took a cup from Aunt Maggie's hand.

He had just sat down again in the big chair when he excliamed: 'Oh! I forgot. I've some mail for you.' Reaching into his pocket, he drew out two letters which he handed me.

As I took them, I saw from the postmark and the printed address on one envelope it was from my publisher; the other letter, I knew from the writing, was from Alice. It had been sent to my agent's address for Aunt Maggie had agreed with me, without making the reason obvious, that it would be better if we left no postal address.

As Aunt Maggie was now talking to Davie McVeigh and making, as I thought, a successful attempt to prove she did not talk like an early Victorian, I offhandedly opened the letter from Alice. I say 'offhandedly'; Alice was a link with my painful past and, although I wanted no more pain, I felt an eagerness to learn what she had to say.

The beginning of the letter was to the effect that she had been to the house to see me and found only Mrs Bridie there, in the throes of what she called "doing down a bit'. Alice went on to say that she didn't even know we had left Eastbourne.

It was at the beginning of the next paragraph that my heart began to beat at a quicker rate, for it began alarmingly:

What I'm really writing for, Pru, is to warn you. It may not be necessary, but you never know. You see, Ian is out. He got remission on his sentence and he went straight to Mother's, hoping, of course, to find you across the way. Father, I understand, ordered him out.

Then he came to me, feeling sure that I could tell him where you were. He wouldn't believe that I didn't have your address and stated very firmly that he meant to find you. His idea, Pru, is for his wife to divorce him and then to make it up with you. He thinks that once he's divorced he can bring this about. I tried to persuade him otherwise, but it was no use.

I think you had better be on your guard, Pru, wherever you are, because, knowing Ian, I'm sure he'll find ways and means of tracing you. I have no need to emphasize how unscrupulous he can be when he wants anything badly, and of this I'm sure—he wants you very badly at the moment, for, as much as he's capable of loving, he, I think, loves you. But what is vastly more important to him, he needs you if he's going to write, and deep down he knows it.

Two clues he has as to your whereabouts; these are that you are in the North and that you have rented a cottage somewhere. Apparently, he quizzed Mrs Bridie, and if she had known anything more, I'm sure he would have got it out of her. He has the idea that Aunt Maggie will have taken you to her birthplace or somewhere near. He said she has the Northerner's weakness—the homing instinct. But don't let this disturb you unduly, Pru. Yet I felt I ought to warn you.

'Don't let this disturb you unduly.' My heart was racing now. The old fear was filling me again. My limbs were trembling, and I felt sick. I could hear Aunt Maggie talking, but strangely, I couldn't see her, for the room had become blurred, dark. I said something. What it was, I don't know. Then I felt Aunt Maggie's hand gripping my wrist. So hard did she grip that I winced because the sprain in my left wrist was still painful. Her voice was loud around me now, saying, 'Pru! Pru! stop it. Pull yourself together. Come along now, no more of that!—What is it, Pru?'

Nothing that I had been through before had caused me to faint. I had never fainted in my life. Often I wished I could have, just to blot out all feeling. Now, I felt myself retreating rapidly once more away from all contact with people, and, as I went, I heard a voice shouting, 'I won't see him, I won't! I won't!' And then there was a silence.

I seemed to be dragging myself up through layers of black padding, clawing them aside so that I could breathe. At last I was free and I opened my eyes and looked into the face of Aunt Maggie. She was holding a glass to my lips. When she tipped it upwards a stream of warmth zigzagged down my throat. There was warmth at my side too, and I realized I was lying on the hearthrug near the fire, my head resting against something.

'You're all right. There's nothing to worry about.' Aunt Maggie was speaking softly.

What had I been worrying about? I couldn't recall for a moment until Aunt Maggie's next words brought it racing back into my mind.

'You'll see nobody you don't want to see. Now get that firmly into your head. Nobody can get at you here unless they first get past Mr McVeigh and his house. Isn't that so, Mr McVeigh?'

I started as if I had been poked. I had even forgotten the existence of Davie McVeigh, and, when his hands, which had been on my shoulders all the time, steadied me, I lay still once more realizing that he was kneeling on the rug and my head was pillowed on his thigh.

'As your aunt said, you need see no one you don't want to see. I promise you.'

His voice was low and quiet; it was as if McVeigh was talking to Frannie. I made an effort to rise now but found I was unable to do so. Then I felt McVeigh withdraw the support of his leg. The next moment his arms were about me, under my shoulders and my knees, and, for a brief moment, he held me against him, as he carried me to the couch.

As he laid me down, I heard Aunt Maggie say hastily, 'I'll get some rugs.'

My eyes felt heavy and I wanted to close them, but I didn't. When I lifted my gaze upwards, his face was not far from mine. His eyes, glinting with dark green-blue light behind the short lashes were looking deep into mine.

Reaching down, he picked up my hand and held it between his two palms as he said under his breath, 'Don't be afraid, I can't bear to see you afraid—not you.'

As my eyes continued to be held by his, I wanted to ask, 'Why me? Why should I not be afraid?' But I couldn't be bothered. I was tired. Not even the glint in his eyes could hold me any longer. My lids drooped and I shut out his face—and the world. Once again, I was retreating. There was no energy in my body, no purpose in my mind, and I knew that by just allowing myself to drift I could return into complete lethargy—that I would also be hemmed in by the barrier of fear didn't trouble me.

I felt Aunt Maggie's hands tucking the rug around my shoulders, and her voice now had a crisp sound. She was saying, 'You are going to sleep, and, when you wake up, everything will be all right. Do you hear? Pru, do you hear me? Everything will be all right.'

'Yes, Aunt Maggie.'

After a while, I became conscious of soft movements in the room. I was surprised at hearing them, I hadn't gone to sleep. I hadn't retreated. My mind was working again, even calmly. It was, surprisingly, saying to me, 'What can he do? If you were to see him this minute, it would make no difference. He can't force you to live with him. And if we stay here, he'll have to get past Davie McVeigh.'

It was as if Davie McVeigh had heard me thinking, for his voice came to me in a thick whisper from the doorway: 'What is he like, this fellow?'

'Tall, thin—' Aunt Maggie was whispering back. 'About your age, I would say. Very charming manner —as if butter wouldn't melt in his mouth.'

'Yes, that's the sort, the talkers, and they get off with it, don't they?'

'Well, I wouldn't say he got off with it—he was put away for six months. But his sentence must have been reduced.'

There had been no sound for some time, so I thought he had gone, until his whisper came to me again, asking this time: 'Why is it always nice women who are taken in?'

'Search me,' was Aunt Maggie's reply.

When the thought skimmed the haziness of my mind that there wasn't much of the Queen Victoria element about that remark, I realized, with something of surprise, that my attack of nerves had passed. I would not be called upon to spend the next forty-eight hours or even two or three days fighting my trembling limbs and fear-filled mind. Alice's letter had plunged me into the depths, but, like a diver rebounding from the bottom, I had risen to the surface as quickly as I had gone down. This fact left me with a wonderful sense of freedom. I wanted to sit up, even talk. . . .

It was well into the afternoon when I awoke. I had slept solidly for four hours.

That evening Janie came to the cottage. She brought with her two extra pints of milk, a dozen eggs, and a jar of cream.

'Oh, this is very kind,' said Aunt Maggie. 'You must thank Miss Cleverly for me.'

'It was Davie who sent them.'

'Oh! oh, then, you must thank Mr McVeigh.'

Janie turned to me now, where I was sitting near the fire, and asked, 'Are you better?'

'Yes, thank you.'

'Davie says you've got a cold.' She came and stood near me. After scrutinizing me for a moment in her old-fashioned way—I had found Janie to be a very old-fashioned child—she asked, 'It isn't a sniffy one, is it? When I get a cold I run all over.'

When I smiled and said, 'No, it isn't a sniffy one, Janie,' it crossed my mind that it was thoughtful of Davie McVeigh to say I was suffering from a cold.

Janie seated herself on the edge of a chair opposite to me and looked round the room before saying, 'It's always funny to me when other people are living here 'cause I always think of this as Davie's house.'

'He'll have it again shortly—in the winter.'

'Yes—I wasn't being rude.'

'Oh, no, of course not, Janie. I understand what you mean.'

'Doris is coming over tomorrow.'

'Oh, she's back from her honeymoon, then?'

'Yes, they've been back nearly a fortnight. But they live right up yon side of Blanchland, near Hexham, and Jimmy's got a farm—not a big 'un, but he's always busy.'

Aunt Maggie, who was sitting on the couch, asked, 'Were you very fond of your sister?'

'Oh, yes. We got on like a house afire.'

This colloquial saying caused Aunt Maggie to put her head back and laugh. Then she asked, 'And do you like her husband?'

'Oh—Jimmy? He's all right, but he's oldish.'

'Oldish?'

This comment came simultaneously from Aunt Maggie and me for we had both imagined that the young bride we had seen on that particular Saturday had been on her way to a young groom. Then I remembered the girl saying, 'Jimmy'll wait; he's been waiting for years.'

Janie was continuing. 'Well, not really old, you know, but a bit older than Davie.'

'Really!' Aunt Maggie's head was nodding questioningly towards Janie.

'Yes, and if she was going to marry anybody around that age she could have had Davie, couldn't she? She liked Davie, but Davie went away; he went to Australia.

He was only gone a year, but when he came back Jimmy had stepped in—Aunt Flora was all for Jimmy.'

'Mr McVeigh has been in Australia then?'

'Yes.' Janie nodded her head at Aunt Maggie. 'But he couldn't stick it because he hadn't wanted to go in the first place, I think. Aunt Flora had said she could manage, but she couldn't. It was Talbot who wrote and told Davie about things.'

'Talbot?' Aunt Maggie's head was still nodding. Now she asked quietly, 'You're not very fond of Miss Cleverly are you, my dear?'

'Aunt Maggie!' I cried.

My aunt cut off my low censured exclamation with a quick downward movement of her hand as if she were knocking something away from the vicinity of her knee.

'Well—' Janie was looking straight at Aunt Maggie. Now she asked, 'You wouldn't tell her, would you?'

Janie hadn't asked a question; rather she had made a statement: 'You wouldn't tell her, would you?'

'No,' said Aunt Maggie. 'No, I wouldn't tell her anything—nothing about anything.'

I closed my eyes for a second and apologized to Mr Fowler for Aunt Maggie's mangling of the English language.

'Well, then.' Janie picked up the hem of her dress, and, concentrating her attention upon it, she nipped a loose thread between her thumb and forefinger and gave it a tug. When it snapped, she said, 'I never have been fond of her. She's all for Roy. Nobody else matters. She wants Roy to have the place and not Davie. That's why Davie went away—to give him his chance—Roy, I mean. But it didn't work. She's always putting a spoke in Davie's wheel.'

Janie looked at me now and, with the quick change that is the accepted prerogative of extreme youth, she asked, 'You write stories, don't you?'

'Yes, Janie, I write stories.'

'Davie says you're clever.'

Before I could make any comment on this, Janie went on, 'Wordsworth was born near here, at Cockermouth. He wrote poetry. Do you know Cockermouth?'

'Yes, we went there the other day for a drive.'

'Davie says all the good writers come from Cumberland. Do you know what he says?'

I shook my head.

'If they weren't born here, they come here to die. An' John Peel lived here, in Caldbeck. It's not far.'

'You know your county,' said Aunt Maggie now. Then she added, 'I think you'll write stories yourself when you grow up.'

'If I did, I'd write a story about Aunt Flora.' She gave a little giggle. 'She was crossed in love, Talbot says.'

'Was she indeed? Well, well.'

Aunt Maggie's tone conveyed to Janie that she would like to hear more. I wanted to make a clicking sound of disapproval with my tongue, and I knew that Aunt Maggie was aware of this. Although she did not give me the hand signal again, the movement she made with her body, presumably settling herself in the corner of the couch, told me to be quiet.

'So Talbot says Miss Cleverly was crossed in love, does he? Dear, dear.'

'Yes. She was born here you know, in this cottage.'

Janie jerked her head upwards towards the ceiling. 'And two years after, Davie's father was born at the big house. They played together when they were children. Aunt Flora didn't even like my mother playing with them for she was gone on McVeigh, so Talbot says.'

I did not like the child talking this way and was vexed with Aunt Maggie for pumping her, yet this was a bit of surprising news. I did nothing to silence Janie as she went on:

'Talbot said it was all right when they were bairns, but, after Davie's dad came back from college, he wouldn't look at the side she was on, 'cept to be civil to her. Talbot said Aunt Flora never forgave Davie's father for marrying somebody else, but he would never have married her, Talbot said, in a month of Sundays, 'cause McVeigh was so handsome that all the girls were after him.'

She paused, and Aunt Maggie and she exchanged smiles which showed their confidence in each other.

Aunt Maggie said, 'And so you would write a story about all that. And would you give it a happy ending?'

'For Davie, I would. Not for nobody else—oh, except Frannie. But not for her grannie. I don't like her grannie. On market day she was going to take Frannie in to the doctor, but they couldn't find her. And her grannie told Talbot to leave a message at Doctor Beaney's, an' he did an' when the doctor called, Frannie wasn't in. That was after her grannie had locked her upstairs. She had got out of the window and down the drainpipe. It isn't very high—she couldn't have hurt herself very much if she had fallen. . . . Do you like Davie?'

I was grateful that this pointed question had not been put to me. Janie, her little plain face thrust forward, was addressing Aunt Maggie in a lower tone.

Aunt Maggie, I was slightly amused to note, was in a bit of a quandary. Her eyes flicked towards me for a second, then, as if coming to a sudden decision, she made a deep obeisance with her head and said, 'Yes, Janie; yes, I do like Davie. Mind you—' she lifted her finger and wagged it at the child '—I didn't think I would at first, but I've changed my mind.'

'Nobody does at first, but they all change their minds. Except, that is, Aunt Flora—and perhaps Mr Bradley. Alec Bradley and Davie don't get on. That's because Davie was engaged to Mrs Bradley at one time. It was a long time ago—before he went into the army—but when he came back it was off, so she married Mr Bradley.'

I was relieved that Aunt Maggie had the grace not to press further. We looked at each other and then, hitching herself from the couch, she went towards the dresser and, opening a drawer, she took out a tin.

'Do you like walnut toffee, Janie?' she asked.

'Oh, yes, please.'

Janie's tongue was silent for a time while she chewed on Aunt Maggie's favourite sticky walnut toffee. Then, seeming to remember Davie McVeigh's need for her to do the chores, she bade us farewell, but not before she asked me the embarrassing question of whether I had enjoyed having her, and would I like her to come again? This—from a child whom I had taken to be a shy individual. We live and learn, I thought.

When we were alone, I looked coolly at my aunt and remarked, 'You're an inquisitive old woman.'

Aunt Maggie, picking up some knitting from the long wooden shelf, came to the couch and seated herself comfortably before she replied. 'Inquisitive, but not old, Pru—anyway—' she glanced at me, the twinkle deep in her eye now '—you got a packet of information there, didn't you now? So our Miss Flora Cleverly aimed at being mistress of Lowtherbeck! Well, well! She aimed high, didn't she? But I wonder why she liked one child and not the other? They both have the same father.'

'If you wait long enough, doubtless you'll find out.' I stressed the *you*.

'Doubtless,' said Aunt Maggie with another deep obeisance of her head.

Then we laughed, after which we became silent. . . .

I retired early, and, again, it was something concerning the master of Lowtherbeck that erased the harrying thoughts of my own problems from my mind. As sleep overtook me, I was thinking: And when he came back from the war messed up in that awful state, it was to lose his girl to somebody else. He's had it hard, has Davie McVeigh. I was no longer cynical when thinking of him and less and less did I attach to him his string of Christian names. . . .

My attitude towards Davie McVeigh tempered still further as the days went on. In a way, I came to look upon him almost as a sort of protector, a protector against Ian. 'He'd have to get past Mr McVeigh,' Aunt Maggie had said, and now I, too, thought along the same lines. Yet even the barricade he presented couldn't prevent me, at times, from being overpowered by the fear of meeting up with Ian again for, foremost in my mind was the memory of the wild reaction his betrayal had aroused in me.

I had always seen myself as a fundamentally gentle creature, yet there was this mental picture of me flinging myself on Ian and clawing at him with my hands. The violence was absolutely out of character for me— at least, as I saw myself—but it held terrifying possibilities as to what might happen should we meet again. Not that I was afraid now of letting myself go as I had done on that particular day, but the knowledge that the sight of him might arouse that strange aggressive emotion in me again was sufficient to give me frequent, although diminished, bouts of nerves.

So my opinion of Davie McVeigh rose steadily—so much so that, by the Fifth of November, when I recognized that he and I were two of a kind—he ceased to be a barricade between Ian and myself.

The revelation was split, you could say, into two parts: an incident in the morning, followed by another in the afternoon. There were some letters I wanted posted, also an order to be sent in to Talbot, who now obligingly brought in any replenishments we needed on his visits to the farm. It was a very sultry morning, not chilly as you think of November being, but heavy and close. This had been the atmosphere for the past forty-eight hours and I felt that nothing but a storm would lighten it.

I was walking along the hill path that morning, approaching the house by the road down which we had brought the car on that first day we came to Lowtherbeck. As I came up through the kitchen garden out of the shrubbery, I looked towards the house and saw, high up, outlined against the dull sky, the bulky figure of Davie McVeigh. He was doing something to the guttering. Supporting one loose end with one hand, he was hammering in what I took to be a bracket with the other. He was working on the far side of the back of the house where the french windows were, at the corner of the building.

I entered the courtyard from the opposite side, and, when I came to the kitchen door and looked upwards, I could see McVeigh's arm, like a disembodied limb, appearing and disappearing round the edge of the building.

Flora Cleverly was in the kitchen, as was Janie. Janie was sitting at a side table scraping potatoes and she lifted her head quickly and gave me a smile. It had about it a secret quality—we two shared something that Flora Cleverly knew nothing about.

Miss Cleverly greeted me in her usual fashion with, 'Hello. There you are.'

When Flora Cleverly spoke, it did not stop her from working. I had become, over the weeks, fascinated by her seeming tirelessness and her habit of carrying on a conversation while doing two jobs at once. Filling the kettle under the tap with her right hand, she would stack dishes on the draining board with her left, for example. Had I attempted to do this, something definitely would have been broken.

I answered the housekeeper's greeting, then, looking towards Janie I said, 'You're not at school today. Is Guy Fawkes Day a holiday?'

Janie was about to answer when Flora Cleverly put in, 'No. Janie's had a bit of a cold over the week-end. She says she didn't feel like school. But doubtless she'll feel like the Guy Fawkes party tonight. They can always get better for parties.'

Miss Cleverly jerked her head at me as she went on

emptying groceries from a large carton that was standing on the table.

'Do you have a Guy.Fawkes party?' I was looking at Janie again.

'Not here,' said Janie. 'Over at the Ponsonbys'. Mary and Charlie make a big guy and we all take our own crackers. Do you like bonfire parties?' she asked.

'I can't remember ever having been to one, Janie.'

'You haven't missed much.' Again Flora Cleverly was speaking. 'Although—' She paused for just a second as she fingered a coloured box she had lifted out of the stores. Looking down at it she said, 'I used to enjoy them when I was a girl. The bigger the bangs the better I liked them.' She pushed the box across the table now, saying, 'There you are, there's your fireworks.'

'Thanks, Aunt Flora.'

It was at this point that the sound of something falling in the yard, a splintering sound, caused us all to look towards the door and upwards, and brought from Flora Cleverly the remark: 'There's another slate down. He'll have them all off shortly. There'll be no roof left.

On looking back, I am sure it was when the slate dropped into the yard that this enigmatic woman jumped at an opportunity that she thought too good to miss—an opportunity to expose the weakness of a man she hated and to lessen him in my eyes. But it was much later when I worked this out, and, consequently, realized that Flora Cleverly had the power within her to sense forthcoming reactions. Her hate gave her this power. But her power was not omnipotent. On this occasion, the reaction she had foreseen did not occur.

The housekeeper had her hand on the box of fireworks again and there was another almost imperceptible pause in her talking, then she looked at Janie and said, 'Go and try one in the yard.'

'Now?' Janie dropped a potato back into the water.

'Yes. Why not? It will give Miss Dudley and me a bit of a treat; we won't be at the do tonight. Tucked away in bed, I expect.' She turned on me with her tight smile; then, rummaging in the box she pulled out a large, long fire-cracker.

'Ee! not that one.' Janie recoiled a step. 'That's a banger.'

'Well, can't we hear a banger? There are four of them. Talbot must have put them in for good measure.'

'Ee! but I couldn't let off a banger, Aunt Flora. I could a squib.'

'Don't be silly. You just light it and throw it—well, if you won't give us a show, I'll have to do it meself. Where's the matches?'

Janie's face was now shining with excitement, that is, until she reached the yard. Then I watched her eyes lift, as mine did, towards Davie McVeigh. He had evidently moved the ladder around the corner and was now in full view. He was at the top, his head back on his shoulders and his arms reaching up as he screwed a bolt in on a corner bracket. Perhaps it was the stationary figures below him or the flash of the match through the greyness of the morning that brought his eyes towards us. I saw him staring down at Flora Cleverly. For a short time, he was posed like a gnarled fossilized tree, so still was he. I saw his mouth open and his hand lift as if in protest. Then he was startled into movement, but, even before he started his erratic frantic descent down the ladder, Flora Cleverly had lit the fuse and thrown the fire-cracker.

McVeigh must have been about six rungs from the bottom when the fire-cracker, not a yard from the foot of the ladder, exploded with an ear-cracking bang. At the sound, Davie McVeigh's entire body left the ladder, he seemed to fling himself into the air. When he hit the ground, he did not fall but began to stagger like a drunken man.

I knew I had cried out. I was standing with my fingers covering my face up to my eyes. I was aware in this moment that, had the fire-cracker exploded earlier—

say, when he had been near the top of the ladder—the explosion would have automatically caused him to loosen his hold, for, at the sound, he had jumped as if he were leaping clear of something—a mortar shell, for instance.

I wanted to run to him, for he was standing alone—swaying and blinking—but Janie had done that.

Janie had raced to him, crying, 'Davie! Davie! Oh, Davie, it was only a big fire-cracker. Oh, Davie!'

I saw him shake his head once again before thrusting her aside and advancing slowly towards Flora Cleverly like some terrible gigantic creature. She backed towards the granite wall of the house, her tongue still for once.

I heard myself shouting protestingly: 'Mr McVeigh! No! Mr McVeigh. No!

He was about a yard from Flora when he paused only long enough to grind out—and he literally did grind out the words through his closed teeth: 'You! You devil-ridden hell-cat! You!' His arms shot out and he had her pinned by the throat.

At the contact, Flora seemed to come alive, for she kicked and clawed at him; at the same time, I on one side and Janie on the other pulled at him and yelled as we did so, 'Stop it! Stop it!' Even so, I knew that our efforts were as futile as those of two flies attempting to stop a stampeding elephant. Loosening my hold on McVeigh and gazing frantically around the yard for some means of help, I saw, near a big rain barrel that stood underneath a spout, a large wooden bucket full of water. Aunt Maggie had once thrown a glass of water in my face to shock me out of a tantrum. I now heaved up the wooden bucket, which under ordinary circumstances I could hardly have lifted from the ground, and, stumbling forward, I threw the contents upwards and over him, drenching myself in the process.

I jumped away as the bucket clattered to the ground. At the same time I saw Flora Cleverly collapse against the wall, then slowly slide to the ground.

I watched Davie McVeigh shake himself, then slowly push his sodden hair up out of his eyes and over the top of his head. When he looked at me, it was as if he were coming out of a dream, and as if we were all figments of that dream without a trace of reality. Then he moved like a drunken man, aiming, to steady his gait, directly towards the door of the cave. Behind him, tentatively suiting her steps to keep a short distance between them, went Janie.

It wasn't until the door had closed on them both that I turned my trembling attention to Flora Cleverly. She was on her hands and knees now, making an effort to rise. I helped her to her feet, assisted her into the kitchen, and sat her in a chair.

'Can I get you something? Have—have you any brandy?'

Flora Cleverly moved her fingers around her throat, then stretched her neck. Her wrinkled skin was the colour of dirty ivory. She swallowed, then pointing to a cupboard high up on the wall of the kitchen to the right, she muttered, 'My pills.'

I had to stand on a stool before I could open the door of the cupboard. Inside there were a number of small medicine bottles, all holding tablets of different sizes and colours. I took three into my hand and brought them to her. She picked a bottle that held round white tablets, and, after I got her a glass of water, she swallowed two of them.

'Will I make you a cup of tea?'

Flora swallowed again, then said, 'It's made—on the hob.'

After she had sipped at the tea in her pseudo-refined fashion, she looked up at me, straight into my eyes, and said, 'He's mad. I could have him locked up, put away. You witnessed this, didn't you?'

I felt myself suddenly recoil from her. I wanted to step back, but was prevented by the force of her stare.

'This isn't the first time it's happened, but this time

I've got a witness and there'll be marks to show—' she touched her neck gently '—besides what I did to his face.' Her lips came together in a tight thin bitter line. 'I've warned him—I've got him now. I'll ring Doctor Kemp and let him judge Davie's condition.'

As she stroked her neck again, I moved from her, and, speaking very quietly, I said, 'You must remember that it was you who threw the fire-cracker, Miss Cleverly. If he had been further up the ladder, I am sure he would still have jumped. He—he could have broken his neck. What he did was under great stress—emotional reaction.'

'You're for him, aren't you?' There was something frightening in her voice. 'Fascinated like a snake by the great big tough he-man.'

'Miss Cleverly!' My voice was haughty.

'Oh, Miss Dudley, I've seen this all happen before. You'll get your eyes opened before long.'

'I don't need to have my eyes opened, Miss Cleverly. And whatever discord exists between you and Mr McVeigh has nothing to do with me—I'd like you to understand that. And what is more, we won't be here much longer. Our lease is nearly up. Perhaps it's just as well.'

'Yes. Yes, of course. I'm sorry, Miss Dudley. I'm not meself at the moment—that's understandable.' Flora pulled herself upwards and steadied herself against the table. Then, speaking to me over her shoulder, she said, 'You needn't stay; I'll be all right.'

Without another word, I left the kitchen and, taking the short cut, I went back to the cottage, the order for Talbot still in my pocket, as well as the mail.

When I got in, I said to Aunt Maggie, 'Give me something to drink—a brandy and soda or something.'

'A brandy and soda?' Aunt Maggie looked at me through narrowed lids. 'What's happened?'

'Give me a drink first. Then I'll tell you.'

After I had drunk the brandy and soda at a speed that

brandy and soda should never be drunk, I gasped and said, 'Davie McVeigh is terrified of noise, and he nearly throttled Miss Cleverly.'

'Dear God!' said Aunt Maggie. 'What next?'

Then, putting out her hand, she said, 'You're wet, lass.'

'Yes, I had to throw a bucket of water over him.'

'You—what?' She had just seated herself, and my statement brought her immediately to her feet. With her hand pressed against her cheek, she repeated, 'You—*what*?'

When the brandy had steadied me, I related in detail what had happened. I finished by saying, 'I think I'll be glad when we're gone.'

'Will you?'

I had expected Aunt Maggie to say with me, 'Me, too.' But now, resuming her seat once again and stretching her hand out to the blaze, she leant towards the fire as she said, 'You know, I'm sort of sorry for that fellow.'

'But he would have choked her to death!

'A man doesn't do that unless he's been driven to the limit. I never liked that woman from the first time I saw her, and I've liked her less every time I've met her since. And, from what you say, she threw the fire-cracker deliberately.'

'Yes—' I nodded my head slowly '—I'm sure she did that.'

'Well, then, she deserved all she got. She must have known what an effect it would have on him. She's a nasty piece of work, I tell you.'

I rose to my feet now and began to walk around the room, and Aunt Maggie, raising her head, glanced towards me, saying, 'Go and change your dress, you don't want to get cold.'

'I'll have to go out,' I said. 'I didn't post the letters or leave the order.'

She looked towards the window. 'There's going to

be a storm and you don't want to be caught out with the car, do you?' She knew that I didn't like driving in a storm, not even through rain.

'I wasn't thinking of taking the car,' I said. 'We can manage with what we have in the larder, but I must get these letters off. I'll go up to the pillar box at the crossroads.'

In my ramblings. I had found that if, instead of taking the back path to the farmyard, I crossed the field beyond the 'kiosk', as we called our unmodern convenience, climbed one of the innumerable dry-stone walls, and went over yet another field and up a very steep incline, I came out just at the top of the steep track down which I had brought the car on that memorable wedding Saturday. And here, affixed to a telegraph pole, was a letter box; I had used it before on a few occasions.

I said now, 'If I hurry I'll likely make it before the storm breaks.'

'Go and change your dress first.'

'It isn't very wet,' I said. 'It was just splashed—it's nothing. I won't be long.'

'You'll catch—'

'I won't.'

I lifted a light mack off the hook on the back of the kitchen door as I went out and put it on as I walked hastily to the copse, then through it into the open fields. The air was still, the sky was low, so low that there came to my mind a favourite story from my childhood of Henny Penny and Cocky Locky hurrying to tell the King the sky was going to fall. It seemed incongruous that I should think such childish thoughts at this moment, but, looking upwards, I could imagine that the sky was touching the top of the hill.

Long before I reached the summit, I was breathing heavily. Little rivulets of sweat were running down my face, and, as I walked, I heard the first roll of thunder. It was quite near. I'd heard no distant rumbles leading up to it that would have made me think, in Aunt Maggie's idiom, 'Somebody's getting it.' But, by the time I reached the top and the three roads were in sight, I was telling myself I wouldn't make it back home before the rain came.

I had just put the letters in the box when a flash of lightning, streaking across the open fells towards my right, caused me to screw up my eyes and lower my head. Then, right above me, the heavens seemed to split in two. The crash of thunder brought my shoulders hunching and my back bending as if to ward off some gigantic pressure. I turned about now and ran towards the hill.

I could make home, I guessed, in ten minutes. At that moment, I wasn't taking into account any rain. It came with the suddenness of the lightening itself and, strangely, it did not appear to come straight down but struck at me horizontally from the direction of the fells. One minute everything had been so still; now there was turmoil all about me. I could see scarcely a yard ahead, and even this distance was obliterated when my coat whirled upwards like an inverted umbrella. I dizzied round once or twice, thrusting my clothes down, and I suppose it was this that altered my direction. I was running, not away from the road in the direction of the fields and the cottage, but down by the side of it.

I discovered this when I got myself caught up in some brambles. I have described before how this track was overshadowed by trees and heavy with undergrowth and I was now among the low undergrowth. Recognizing this, it came to me that it was better than being in the open fields and that lower down, almost at the foot of the incline, there was an inlet.

I had investigated this one day after seeing Floss galloping, as it were, straight out of the hillside. I'd heard a whistle; then the dog had come bounding out of a large hole. It was, I remembered, some way down the path in a space clear of undergrowth. That's why it had seemed so strange seeing the dog apparently leaping out of the hillside.

The weight of the rain was almost bearing me down to the ground, and it was more by blind groping than by any knowledge of its position that I came upon the aperture. I stood about a yard inside it, leaning heavily against the wall, gasping and spluttering. When my breathing steadied, I straightened up and leant my head back. My eyes were closed; perhaps that was why when I opened them my sight was more accustomed to the dimness and I saw Davie McVeigh.

He was sitting on the ground not two yards from me with his knees up, his elbows on them, and his hands hanging between them. His broad face was turned towards me and it bore the evidence of Flora Cleverly's handiwork.

The bolt hole!

Flora Cleverly's words seemed to fill the small space: *'You were likely in your bolt hole.'* Was this his bolt hole? Yes. And he had bolted to it after the incident in the courtyard.

At the sight of him, my heart had given a quick jump, and, when it slowed, I was about to say, 'It's a dreadful storm,' or some such ordinary remark. But, when I looked at Davie, at his face—all eyes—deep and pain-filled with self-condemnation, I could not utter a word.

I still remained pressed against the wall and he remained sitting in the same position with his knees up. There was only the sound of the rain, yet it seemed distant and far away. As during that morning by the Big Water, a silence enveloped us. In that other silence, I had asked a question; and in this silence, I was getting the answer.

This man was fear-ringed. He wasn't, like me, afraid of people—his fear went deeper. His were intangible fears, the kind of fears I only touched on when I became filled with fear of fear. I recalled a woman I had met when I was having psychiatric treatment. This woman was afraid of the moon; she also felt that if she walked one step forward she would topple over the edge of the earth. Hers was an elemental fear, and it was the kind of fear that Davie McVeigh suffered from—part of it was manifested by his fear of noise.

If I wanted proof of my surmise, I received it almost at that instant, for, crashing through the silence, came a terrific burst of thunder. It broke directly overhead and seemed as if it were rending the hill into splinters. One moment I had been looking down into his up-turned face, the next I saw his head buried in his arms, and I was crying inside myself, 'Oh, no! no!' It seemed such a humiliating thing for a man, a big man, to be afraid of noise, afraid of bangs, afraid of thunder.

'Don't worry, he won't get past McVeigh.' Aunt Maggie's words came back to me. I remembered that what they had implied had brought me a sense of comfort. Nobody could get past this man if he didn't so wish it—that's what I had thought. That was the impression he gave. As the thunder rolled, his head went deeper down between his knees, and, as I watched it droop, there arose in me a feeling, not only of compassion—and this was strong—but of awe and admiration. This man was afraid, innately afraid, yet he showed to the world at large a bold fearless front. Where he thought it was necessary, he struck out and levelled a man to the ground while all the time the mysterious, unfathomable elements of nature were attacking him through his sense of hearing.

I didn't remember moving from the wall, but I had. I was kneeling by his side, and embarrassment overcame me for the merest fraction of a second as I put my arm around his shoulder. His coat was very wet, the result of the wooden bucket of water, and the feeling of proximity was strange, and it must have been so to him, too. My touch must have been like salt in an open wound, for he turned his body half from me. His head was still lowered, and I not only felt, but saw, the shudder that went through him.

As the minutes passed, the thunder gradually rolled away, until silence engulfed us once more. I could not hear even the rain now. I had taken my arm away from him and was sitting on the cold, but dry, earth looking at his bent form when he straightened up. He turned round onto his hips, thrust out his legs and lay back against the wall. I could see his face dimly. He was sweating. He sat looking ahead for quite a while before turning to me. His body was trembling, and, when he spoke, the tremor made his voice shake.

'And—and now you know,' he said.

I shook my head slowly. I found it difficult to answer him. Then I asked, 'What do I know? That you're afraid of noise?'

'Y—yes. I'm a man who's afraid of noise.'

'I'm afraid of many things.'

'It's allowable in a woman.'

I repeated to him what they had said to me when trying to arouse me from my self-pity. 'You're not the only one who suffers like this.'

'I'm—I'm well aware of that.'

'What I meant was—' I was stumbling now '—there's nothing to be ashamed of—nothing.'

It was a moment before he answered. 'Yes, I—I know,' he stammered. 'But I'm such a big fellow phys—physically. "Afraid of noise!" people say. "You—you want to sn—snap out of it, man." '

I now hitched myself back and sat against the wall, near him, but not touching. 'When did it happen?' I asked. 'Before you were hurt?' I could not say burnt.

'All in one go. The l—lorry was caught in cross fire.'' He was stammering less now. 'In the ordinary way, the noise would have been n—nothing, but I suppose I had two skins l—less by that time and it nearly drove me mad.'

I had closed my eyes. I could see his head hanging

through the cab window while mortar shells exploded all about him. Why did people have to suffer such things? There should be a limit to suffering. When his wounds had healed, it should have been the end of it, but, with him, it appeared that he would go down to his grave fearing noise.

I said, 'My fear is of people—not so much what they do to me but what they don't do for me. They don't—' I couldn't say they don't give me 'love', so I substituted 'security'. 'No one has ever given me a feeling of security. People generally think that security means having money and the things that money can buy—it doesn't. You know, there's a certain street in Eastbourne that you'd really call slummy, but it used to attract me like a magnet. The children playing on the pavements always looked happy, and the girls, with their cheap clothes and cheap make-up, looked as if they had the world at their feet—this was simply because most of them belonged to a family. Naturally, there'd be bad hats among them, and I knew that a lot of them drank and fought and that a couple of the men from that street were petty thieves. I knew all about this, yet there was some tie amongst them that I always envied.'

I was surprised to find myself talking to him so easily. I had felt compelled to talk to him, not only to comfort him, but to sooth myself. Yet 'comfort' is not the right word here. It was as if, at last, I was able to explain to myself the complaint that I had always suffered from: simply, the lack of love from my parents—which meant that they had deprived me of security. Added to that deprival, was the betrayal of my love by the man I took to be my husband. The thought came to me that, in talking freely, perhaps I was picking up the reins of maturity. My next action seemed to endorse this.

If anyone had told me three months ago that I would voluntarily put my arm about a man's shoulders, then reach out and take his hand, I would not have bothered to contradict them. Deep within, I would have known

136

the impossibility of such an action and also the futility of making anyone understand the abhorrence with which even such thoughts would fill me. Up to the previous day, I could not have seen myself reaching out my hands to draw this man to his feet—yet this was what I was doing now. I had stood up and, bending over, I was holding out my hands to Davie. He did not take them, but looked up at me, and the muscles of his face were twitching spasmodically, as if he were trying to say something and the words would not come.

When he did not raise his hands to mine, I bent further and took them from his knees and said softly, 'Come on. Aunt Maggie will have a drink ready.' I had spoken as if Aunt Maggie belonged to him as well as to me.

When he got to his feet we were still holding hands. I felt no embarrassment in this, it was almost an elating experience. I could feel the tremor from his flesh passing along my arm. We stood thus, joined not only by our hands and eyes but by our weakness—we were one with our mutual knowledge of fear.

Slowly I withdrew my hands from his, and, turning, went to the opening. The rain had stopped. The threatening sky had lifted, and I could see the smoke from the cottage chimney moving almost vertically upwards above the shrubbery. I turned and looked at him and tried to smile, but I found I couldn't. I couldn't smile into this big broad face, into what was usually a bold face, but was now so drained as to appear almost bloodless. Hesitantly, I moved forward and he with me, and we walked down the sodden hillside, through the equally sodden fields, until we came to the back door of the cottage. And neither of us had spoken a word.

Aunt Maggie was standing waiting, greatly agitated, but she did her utmost to cover her surprise when she saw me emerge from behind the 'kiosk' accompanied by Davie McVeigh.

As soon as I reached her, Aunt Maggie put out her

hand and patted my chest, saying: 'You're sodden. Get those things off. Where have you been? I was worried sick with you out in this. Wasn't that thunder terrib-le?'

Her voice trailed off. She must have sensed, from the drawn look of Davie's face, that something further was amiss for she started to cover up in her quick prattling way. 'I've just made the coffee. I think we all want it laced. You go upstairs and get those things off.' She pushed at me. 'Will you take your coat off, Mr McVeigh? Go in the sitting-room and make yourself comfortable.'

As I stepped from the steep stairs into the bedroom, I heard her voice going on and on, releasing Davie from tension. I had just stripped my wet clothes off when there came to me a gentle whisper from the top of the stairway. I saw Aunt Maggie's head rise above the floor level. She beckoned me and I went towards her.

'What's happened?' she asked, alarmed.

'I'll tell you later,' I whispered back.

'He looks like death.'

'Be nice to him.'

I was surprised that I should have put this request to her and I felt the colour rush to my face.

Aunt Maggie raised her eyebrows quizzically as she whispered, 'I'll do my best.' A few seconds later I heard her talking again.

When I entered the sitting-room, Davie McVeigh was sitting near the fire in his shirtsleeves. He rose hastily to his feet at my approach, and his eyes were still on me when he resumed his seat. I had changed into a lime green dress with a broad scarlet belt; it was a very effective combination and I knew that this particular dress suited me. But I had not worn it for a long time, not, in fact, since before I had become pregnant. Why I had packed it, I don't know, except, perhaps, that it was uncrushable. Certain I was that I didn't pack it with the intention of enhancing my appearance to attract a man.

Aunt Maggie was looking at me, too, and, of a

sudden, I had a panicky feeling that she might make some remark about my wearing the dress. And she did, but it was not a disturbing remark.

All my aunt said was: 'That's better. I'm glad to see you are sensible enough to put on something warm. Now, Mr McVeigh—' she turned to him '—let me fill that cup again. As the song says, "Another little drop won't do you any harm." '

The remark was trite, yet it brought to us a normality, an ease, that was badly needed at this moment.

A flicker of a smile crossed Davie McVeigh's face as he replied, 'You're very kind; I won't say *no*.'

I had asked Aunt Maggie to be nice to him and she was certainly doing her utmost. I cannot recall all she said during the half-hour that we sat by the fire, but it was she who did all the talking, seeming satisfied with monosyllabic replies from Davie and me.

Just before our landlord took his leave, when he was putting on his still damp coat, he asked a direct question, or rather made a statement.

He said, 'Your time is nearly up.' He brought his eyes from Aunt Maggie's and looked at me.

Then his gaze returned to Aunt Maggie as she said, 'Yes—yes, time does fly.'

'Will you be sorry to go?'

Aunt Maggie's mouth opened. She wanted, I know, to look at me, but she kept her eyes directly on his as she answered somewhat hesitantly.

'Yes—yes indeed, we will. Oh, yes, we'll be sorry to go. Won't we, dear?' My aunt turned her round bright eyes in my direction. I had asked her to be nice to Davie, and she was certainly being that—she was lying beautifully. When I turned my glance to him, he seemed to be waiting for it. Was I going to lie, too?

I said, 'I'll be very sorry to leave here.' I made a small gesture with my hand. 'I've been happier here than I've been for a long—long while.'

The room became quiet, a log shifted on the fire and

fell inwards; as I turned to look at it, I was surprised to realize that I hadn't lied.

'I must go. It's been nice sitting here like this.' He was speaking to Aunt Maggie.

'But you're used to sitting here—in this cottage.'

'Not like this, not with company, just talking. Usually I'm doing accounts and working out ways and means. And often I'm so tired I drop off and wake up with the fire dead, and it's the middle of the night.'

Aunt Maggie, determined to keep the conversation on the mundane level, said, 'Now isn't that like a man!' and laughing, she rose and moved towards the door.

I rose to my feet too but I did not accompany them. I knew I was afraid that, were I alone with him, the conversation would not retain its ordinariness, but would revolve around personalities. I felt I could not bear that at the moment. I wanted to be quiet to think. I wanted to know no more about him—at that time, at any rate.

At the doorway, McVeigh turned and, looking back across the room, said, 'Thanks.'

The single word dissolved the veneer which during the last half hour had covered the two startling incidents of the day—it was for my help, at least in the latter of the two episodes—for which he was thanking me.

I could make no reply. He turned away, said a word of good-bye to Aunt Maggie, and then was gone. When Aunt Maggie resumed her seat, I was still standing supporting myself against the mantelpiece and staring down into the fire.

'Well, now, what's all this about?'

I felt her waiting for my answer, for an explanation, but, when I spoke it was not to enlighten her, but to question her. Turning about, I asked, 'Is it really possible for anyone to be absolutely the opposite inside to what they appear outwardly?'

'Well—' Aunt Maggie took up her knitting and her eyebrows were arched as she stared at me. 'You're the writer, you should know that. But aren't we all like Jekyll and Hyde? We've got to be, because if people knew what went on inside some of us, we wouldn't be able to bear it—we'd die of shame. We've got to put up, and live behind, a barricade. And I should say that's what McVeigh's had to do, he's had to build himself a barricade—if he's the one you mean. Well, now, tell me what happened.'

A barricade. Yes, she was right. 'The Iron Façade' so to speak. The title of my new novel was taking on deeper meaning. I looked at Aunt Maggie. She was knitting steadily, her attitude one of waiting. I found I could not pick words to describe what happened between David McVeigh and me during the storm.

'He doesn't like storms,' I said.

Aunt Maggie's eyes came up slowly to meet mine. 'No?'

My aunt waited, and, when I did not supply any further explanation, I watched her eyes narrow—an indication that her mind was working rapidly. I felt the flush rise over my neck and cover my face.

Aunt Maggie had the uncanny knack of previewing my thoughts. She had always seemed, as it were, to hold a key to my subconscious mind, and the knowledgeable look that I saw in her eyes now made me want to protest, not only sharply, but angrily: 'It's nothing like that. How could it possibly be! Don't be silly. I loathe men, all men, and, if I did soften, I could not see myself softening for anyone like Davie McVeigh. Oh, Aunt Maggie, have sense.'

But I said nothing like this. I simply walked to the table, sat down, and in a preoccupied manner, began a new chapter.

7

⁂

Aunt Maggie and I were having tea when we heard the knock. We'd heard no footsteps approaching along the stone path. We exchanged questioning glances before I rose from my seat by the fire and opened the door.

Before me, stood Frannie. A different Frannie. She was smiling, not broadly, just with the corners of her mouth. When she spoke, I found that the change was in her voice, too—not so much the tone of voice as in the stringing together of her words.

She asked, 'Can I get some books, please?' Frannie's voice and manner, though still childish, were different. Before, she would have said, 'Want some books.'

'Yes, of course. Come in, Frannie. We're just having tea. Would you like a cup?'

'Yes, please.' When she came to a stop inside the doorway—this was the Frannie I had come to know, still gauche, still childish—I took her hand and led her towards the fire.

'Why—hello, Frannie!' Aunt Maggie's welcome was sincere. 'Come and sit down. Aren't you cold?'

'No, no, I was runnin'.'

'We haven't seen you for a long time; where have you been?'

At this question from Aunt Maggie, Frannie, sitting on the edge of a chair now, hung her head.

'Here, drink this tea. Would you like a sandwich first, or a piece of cake?'

For answer, Frannie looked up at me and said softly, 'The doctor said I was a good girl.' Apart from the surprising context of this last sentence, she had again used the word 'the', she had not said 'doctor said', but had prefixed the noun with the article *the*.

'Did he, Frannie? So you have been to the doctor's. Have you had a cold?'

'No, 'cause I was hurt.'

'Have this piece of cake.'

I passed Frannie the plate holding the piece of iced sponge-cake, and I watched her eyes brighten as she began to eat it.

'It's nice cake—Grannie took me in Penrith and we had cakes.'

'Really?'

I shook my head in perplexity as I gazed at the child. There was some burden gone from her, some weight. What was it?

'Grannie bought me taffy.'

—I had it! The child had lost her fear of her grannie. That's what had been lifted from her—fear. And what miracles can happen when fear is lifted from a human soul—even in a retarded person—such as this child? Already, she was different, more normal. What had brought about the new relationship between the child and her grannie? The visit to the doctor? The child had said, 'The doctor said I'm a good girl.' Why had her grannie been so eager to get her to the doctor? Because she was acting more strangely than usual; or because she feared there was something wrong with the girl; or had she feared that Frannie was—pregnant?

Aunt Maggie's thoughts must have been moving along the same track as my own, for, inclining her head towards Frannie, she said, 'All your nasty bruises have gone. How did they happen? Did you fall down, Frannie?'

I knew where Aunt Maggie's probing was leading, and I did nothing to check her, for I, too, was interested in knowing what had caused those bruises. Frannie's head was again drooping, but she shook it negatively.

'Did someone hit you? Was it your grannie?' asked Aunt Maggie.

The girls' head came up and her tone was alive in defence of her grandmother as she said, 'No, no, not Grannie. I hadn't smashed nothin'. Grannie hits me when I smash things. It was Mr—'

The name had almost slipped out and, consequently, the child was startled into tilting her plate so the remainder of the cake dropped onto the mat.

'Ee! Ee!'

'Don't worry, Frannie, it's perfectly all right. I'm always dropping cake.' I was picking up the crumbs. 'Don't worry, have a fresh piece.'

I was kneeling now, and I swivelled round to the low table and picked up a fresh piece of cake and put it on her plate, which I placed on her knee. My face was on a level with hers. I smiled at her and she smiled back at me. As she did so, there sprang into my mind a fragment of the conversation I had overheard in the yard between Davie McVeigh and Alec Bradley concerning the cottage where this child and her grandmother lived. I had heard Davie McVeigh ask, 'But why do you want to get them out?' Now it came to me in a flash of revelation why Alec Bradley wanted to get rid of the old woman and the girl.

Slowly I took the girl's hand into mine, and asked, 'It was Mr Bradley who hurt you, wasn't it?'

Her thin bony fingers tried to jerk themselves free; her eyes stretched wide, her mouth dropped into a wordless gape.

'Don't be afraid. It's all right, my child.' Aunt Maggie was on the other side of her now.

Frannie turned her startled gaze towards her and brought out rapidly, 'Ee! Davie—Davie 'll hit him. Ee! No, no!'

'There now. There.' I patted her hand. 'Don't worry about it. Davie won't know.'

Frannie was looking at me again, and she repeated, 'Davie won't know.'

'No, just us—we three. It'll be all right.'

She nodded quickly now. Then, her head drooping, she muttered slowly, 'Mr—Bradley—was—drunk.'

I'll say he was. I was thinking harshly to myself and wishing earnestly that I had Mr Bradley in the room. I would lash him to shreds with my tongue—if nothing else—for, if he had been here at that moment I may not have been accountable for what I would have done. Aunt Maggie had said that the night of the wedding was like a witches' Sabbath, and, from what I could remember of the scene in front of the cottage, Alec Bradley had decidedly led the witches. In his hunt for strange excitement, he evidently had come across this girl, this child-girl whose mind was held in the fortress of childhood, while her body was in the budding cadences of youth.

In Frannie, that night, Alec had seen pleasures to satisfy his stimulated, unbridled passion. I was certain now, with a feeling of surety, that he had tried to seduce this girl. Perhaps she had run out at night and come across the hills to see the dancing and he had stumbled on her.

I surmised that her grannie had found her missing, then later, observing her physical state, feared the worst. Her grannie's suspicions would be emphasized when Frannie was reluctant to be taken to the doctor's. But her reluctance, her refusing to say how she had come about her bruises, I could see now could be attributed to the fact that she did not want Davie McVeigh to know who her assailant had been. Dimly she must have thought that, by keeping the knowledge to herself, she was protecting Davie. I, myself, was very much aware —from what I had witnessed between the two men— that had Davie McVeigh known the truth about the matter, murder would have been done. Whatever Davie McVeigh feared—it wasn't any man. This child, in spite of her backwardness, had deep perception stemming from love.

But why did she love McVeigh?

The question again brought back to my mind Flora Cleverly's question: 'It wouldn't be you who was after the mother, would it?' The recollection I found repugnant. My eyes began to search the girl's face for a resemblance, any resemblance to McVeigh, but I could find none. Yet, that was no proof that she had no blood connection with the man she so blindly and instinctively loved.

'Not tell Davie.'

I found myself blinking. Frannie's words had recalled me to the present, and I said hastily, 'No, my dear. No. Don't worry.'

Frannie had spoken again in the clipped way of a child. But now, seemingly reassured, she asked, 'Can I have my books now?'

'Yes, of course, Frannie. You know where to go.'

She got up from her seat, put her plate on the table, then ran down the length of the room, but, before disappearing into the kitchen, she turned her face towards us and said brightly, 'Grannie says I can have my books home.'

We both nodded at her, smiling the while.

'Grannie's had a great change of heart it seems to me.' Aunt Maggie slanted her gaze up towards me.

'It would seem so.'

'What do you make of it?'

'What do you?'

'Well,' said Aunt Maggie, 'I think the grannie thought

146

that the poor child was pregnant. But, by the sound of it, she's found that the child hasn't been touched and her relief is making her more human.'

'I don't think it was Mr Alec Bradley's fault that she isn't in that condition,' I said bitterly. 'And what if he should attempt it again when he returns. He's still on holiday, isn't he? What then? He could get drunk again.' I was looking down at Aunt Maggie.

'We can't tell Davie McVeigh. That's certain.'

'No, we can't.'

'I think somebody should know though. What about the other one, Roy?'

I paused before I answered; then, with a slow negative shake of my head I said, 'No, no. I don't think he'd be able to keep anything like that to himself.'

'Perhaps you're right. I know!' Aunt Maggie sat upright. 'Talbot. If anybody wanted to ease McVeigh's burden, it would be that long-faced individual. He's the one we should tell. He may be able to convey to Mr Bradley on his return that his escapade, if you can call it such, is known, and that, instead of trying to get rid of the woman and child, he'd better leave them alone.'

My lips twisted as I looked at my aunt. 'You could arrange blackmail lessons, couldn't you, dear?'

'If need be, yes.' She jerked her head at me and we exchanged smiles. Then looking towards the upstairs room, where I could hear Frannie moving about, I said, 'You know, that child's changed.'

'That's what I was thinking. She seems brighter, different.'

'It could be that her mind's starting to move.'

'Could be—perhaps she got a fright. Perhaps that night Alec Bradley did something after all. Good came out of evil. Who knows? If a fright stopped her development, another fright could start it again. Or could it? These things are tricky.'

'Yes, they are. But it would be wonderful if it were

true. Anyway, I'm sure there's a change in her—I can feel it.'

The change in the child was emphasized still further when, five minutes later, coming into the kitchen carrying four books in her arms, she said, 'I've got my *Bambi* books. When I grow up, I'm going to work on the farm, Davie says.'

We both saw her to the door and she turned before entering the trees and waved to us.

Aunt Maggie repeated, 'When she grows up.' She added, 'I've got a feeling she's starting right now. I may be wrong—only time will tell. In any case, we won't be here to see it.'

Aunt Maggie sighed as she turned back into the room, and, as I closed the door, I thought, no, we won't be here to see it.

The following afternoon we set off in the car from Borne Coote. We had talked quite a lot about how we would approach Talbot with the subject of Frannie and Alec Bradley. We planned, after seeing Talbot, to go on a round tour touching the coastline, first through Penrith and on to Carlisle, thence on to Silloth, making our way down to Maryport, or, possibly, as far as St Bee's Head. It would all depend on the time—and if the weather held up, which it promised to do as it seemed very settled after yesterday's storm.

As we drove along the hill path, Aunt Maggie, looking down into the valley, remarked, 'You know, I'm going to miss all this, and more than a little. People just think of Ullswater and Derwentwater and the Lakes when you speak of Cumberland, but there's so much more—places like this, off the beaten track. Sometimes you could imagine you were back at the beginning of things—no wireless, television, planes, or motors.'

'You be thankful there are motors; you wouldn't be going to the coast now if it wasn't for them.'

'Yes, you're right.' I could see Aunt Maggie nodding

agreement in her reflection on the windscreen. She went on, 'But there's one place I do wish we weren't going to, or, at least, that we didn't have to pass—and that's the courtyard. I don't think we've ever once been past there that Cleverly hasn't been at a door, or a window, or some place—watching out. That woman gives the lie to the saying that you can't be in two places at once.'

It was true that we had never once passed the house without glimpsing Flora Cleverly. Perhaps the sound of the car drew her attention, or she just wanted to look at us to see how we were dressed. Whatever her reason, it brought her into evidence when we passed.

But, as I approached the courtyard this morning, I thought: this is one time we're wrong. And I am sure Aunt Maggie was about to make some comment along these lines when, instead, she said under he breath, 'Ah! Ah! Ah! Ah!'

For Flora Cleverly had not only made a quick appearance at the kitchen door, but came running across the courtyard calling to us.

When I pulled the car to a stop, Flora stopped too, but some yards away, and she called, 'Have you a minute?'

'Yes,' I answered, then waited.

'Will you come for a bit?' The housekeeper was backing away as she spoke.

I pulled on the hand brake. Looking at Aunt Maggie, I muttered, 'Are you coming?'

'No, I'll stay here. Go see what she wants.'

When I alighted from the car, Flora Cleverly had almost reached the kitchen door again, and she turned her face towards me, waiting. But she had gone inside before I reached the door and her voice came to me: 'There's someone would like to see you.' I paused on the threshold and my arm went out stiffly towards the stanchion.

'Come in.'

Slowly, I went into the kitchen. My body was rigid, my heart seemed to have stopped beating; there was an icy numbed feeling from my waist upwards. My throat was not only tight, it felt constricted, as if the muscles had solidified. Before I turned my eyes to the right, I knew whom I would see.

He was standing at the far end of the long table. Tall, thin, attractive, the charm still oozing out of him. He looked no different from when I had last seen him. Prison had not left any mark on him. There was a soft almost tender, light in his eyes. Flora Cleverly's voice had been going on all the while but I didn't comprehend what she was saying until my body, demanding breath, forced my mouth open and my ribs to swell as I gulped at the air.

Then I heard Flora Cleverly saying, 'Rosie Talbot said there had been a man asking for someone of your name. He was staying overnight at The Bull, she said, so I went along and looked him up. I thought you would like—'

Ian stepped towards me, speaking my name, and, at that instant, I let out a high scream. I was back where I had started. My body was trembling, I was.hanging onto the table for support, and I was yelling, 'Aunt Maggie! Aunt Maggie!' I was aware of the startled look on Flora Cleverly's face, and I was well aware that I was making a fool of myself. But I could not stop.

If I had truly improved in the past three months, I should have been able to tackle this situation; I should have been able to face this man calmly and to talk to him as one adult to another. But Ian was not an adult—he was an overgrown boy—and, as for myself—would I ever be adult, completely adult?

My mouth was open again ready to shout 'Aunt Maggie!' when I snapped it closed. Regret was already filling me for having acted so childishly.

Ian was talking rapidly now, his cultured tone stabbing each word through me. 'Aunt Maggie or no Aunt Maggie, I'm going to talk to you. I've come a long way. I've been looking for you for weeks. I wouldn't have done that if you had meant nothing, would I? Think—think.'

I was thinking. I was thinking fast. I was addressing the trembling muscles in my body, saying, '*Stop it! stop it! get control of yourself. Show him.*'

I heard a movement behind me in the doorway. Aunt Maggie and someone else—because one set of footsteps moved to the right of me and the other to the left.

Aunt Maggie was now standing by my side. She was staring along the table towards Ian. Her voice sounded very detached as she asked, 'Well? What do you want?'

'I want to talk to my wife.'

The word jolted my body.

Aunt Maggie then said, 'She's not your wife—you know that. Your wife is in Wales looking after your children, I would think—and that is where you should be.'

'I have only one wife—that's Pru, and she knows it.' Ian was staring at me now. 'I'm being divorced, anyway. But divorce or no divorce, I want Pru.'

'Of course, you do—and it's quite obvious why. You'll never earn a living on your own. You've got a damn cheek, you know, to say the least,' said Aunt Maggie.

'How did you get here?' The question came from my left. Davie McVeigh was standing close to me and addressing Ian. I could almost feel the heat from his body.

Ian was looking past me now, and it was some seconds before he answered. 'This lady brought me.' Ian indicated Flora Cleverly with a movement of his long hand.

'You! I told you, didn't I? You mischief-making—'

'It's all right, Mr McVeigh.' My voice sounded flat, even calm. 'It had to happen sometime, I suppose. The sooner the better.'

'I can't see what all the cafuffle is about if he's your husband?' the housekeeper interpolated.

'He's not my husband, Miss Cleverly.' I had turned

my body round and was looking full at this mean-faced woman. 'He already had a wife and two children when he pretended to marry me.'

'Whatever I did, I've paid for. I've spent four months in prison, don't you realize that, Pru?'

Ian's voice had brought me round to face him again. I did realize that he had spent four months in prison, but it evoked no pity in me.

'I don't think that it is too much to ask that I talk to you alone,' he whined.

'There you are wrong—it *is* too much!' Aunt Maggie was speaking again.

Now Ian was looking at her, his pale face showing his dislike of her. 'You mind your own business,' he said to Aunt Maggie. 'You're as much to blame for this as anyone—cuddling and pampering Pru—that's all you've done for years. If you wanted someone to nurse, why didn't you get married yourself years ago?'

I had to put out my hands and hang on to Davie McVeigh to prevent him rounding the table.

'Get out of here!' Davie's voice was menacing.

Ian turned his angered face now towards McVeigh and asked, 'Who are you?'

'I happen to be the master of this house—that's who I am.'

Ian's glance lifted from McVeigh's face to rest on mine; it switched back to McVeigh again. Ian looked at Davie steadily for a moment before bringing his glance finally back to me. He said, with an effort at control. 'I want to talk to you, Pru.'

I could feel both Aunt Maggie and McVeigh about to speak when I put in, 'Very well, you can talk to me. Come outside.'

'Pru!'

'It's all right, Aunt Maggie. It's all right.'

As I spoke to Aunt Maggie, I turned from her, but, in moving, my eyes were caught and held for a fraction by those of Davie McVeigh, which were saying: '*Let me deal with him.*' And some part of me answered, '*If only you would.*'

But there was a voice in my head, a wise voice which had been trained under Aunt Maggie's coaching, and it said: *stand on your own feet. If you don't do it now, you never will. This is neither McVeigh's business, nor yet Aunt Maggie's. You have got to prove to the man who played husband to you that he matters no more, your ability to convince him will affect your future success or failure. Failure will mean that you give way to your nerves. He will return again and again until he breaks you down. Success will mean that, no matter how you feel inside, you will remain outwardly calm, you will convince him that you are calm, that he can no longer affect you.*

I was out in the courtyard; Ian was by my side. He was looking at me. I kept walking until I reached the car; there I stopped and faced him. We were standing quite close now, and the trembling sensation had started low down in the pit of my stomach.

Ian's eyes were searching my face. He did not speak for some minutes; then he said, 'Oh, Pru!'

He had the power to turn my name into a caress. It fell on me like a stroking hand; but the trembling in my stomach increased.

'It's wonderful to see you. I've searched for you for weeks.'

'You've wasted your time.' The tone of my voice gave me courage and I went on. 'Listen to me, Ian. Nothing you can say, nothing you can do—' I paused here, then repeated '—nothing—do you hear me?— nothing you can do will ever make me take up a life with you again.'

'I could make you alter your decision—give me a chance, Pru,' Ian insisted.

I now leaned my head slightly forward and to the side as I said quietly, 'I want you to believe this, Ian. I want you to get this into your head—it will save you a lot of trouble in the future. Now, listen. The very thought of you ever again touching me makes me want to retch—can you understand that?'

I felt at this moment that I was being cruel. As I watched his well-moulded lips compress themselves into a line, I knew a moment of triumph. I had struck home, I had shaken his vanity. I had known for a long while now that the main ingredients that made up this man were charm and vanity. The two essentials for a confidence trickster, and that is what he was—a trickster of women.

His lips curled outwards now as he said, 'Aunt Maggie has done a good job on you; she's toughened you up. She must have worked hard to have achieved so much in so short a time.'

'Aunt Maggie has done no "job" on me, as you call it.'

'Well, if she hasn't, somebody has.' His lip curled further. 'Six months ago you would have been throwing a bout of hysterics, shaking like jelly, or getting fighting mad.'

He was remembering the night when, like a wounded tigress, I had wanted, and tried, to tear him to shreds.

He said now, 'I can't think your steady equilibrium is due to the Cumberland air entirely. It would not have anything to do with the burly landsman back there, would it?' He inclined his head towards the house.

Don't panic, said the voice in my head. *Don't deny it too emphatically. Don't lift your chin or stiffen your back, for he'll see his answer in the signs if you do.*

I said, 'The experiences I had recently will last me for some time. I don't wish to repeat them in any form.'

His lips moved in a twisted smile. 'It was only a thought. Yet, he's not your type, I could never see you going for brawn without brain.'

At this, I felt within me a quick reaction. I found I

was resenting deeply the implication that Davie McVeigh should be classed as a man without brains. Again the voice said, *Steady, steady.*

I spoke now in a tone that surprised even me with its calmness. 'I want to tell you, Ian, that if you try to see me again, or pester me in any way, I will inform my solicitor and instruct him to take the matter to court.'

I saw Ian wince as if he had been flicked by a whip. Whatever his experience in prison had been, he undoubtedly did not want it repeated. His head began to wag now, his shoulders jerked. I knew the signs—this was the nasty side of him.

I forestalled anything he was going to say with: 'Miss Cleverly brought you, perhaps Miss Cleverly will take you back to the village. Good-bye, Ian.'

As I attempted to move away from him he took a step towards me. His face was livid below his dark hair, and he said through clenched teeth, 'You've gone the way of the rest of them. You used to be different; now you're as bitchy as they come.'

I did not answer. I looked at him coldly, then turned about. But as I walked away from him, my legs began to tremble, for I should not have been surprised if his hands had grasped me and he had held me while he poured forth abuse.

I knew Ian was still standing watching me when I reached the kitchen door. I dared not look back, but I almost heaved a sigh of relief when I stepped over the threshold. Aunt Maggie was standing where I had left her; Davie McVeigh was over by the window—he must have been watching us all the while. Although I did not look at Davie. I was aware that he had not turned towards me. Flora Cleverly was not to be seen.

I said quietly to Aunt Maggie, 'We'll go now.'

My aunt said nothing, but walked past and preceded me into the courtyard again. When I reached the yard once more, there was no sign of Ian, but I felt he was still about, standing in some corner watching me. I knew as I walked to the car that Davie McVeigh too was watching me as well.

Seated behind the wheel, I said to Aunt Maggie, 'I can't drive.'

'You drive that car, lass.'

'I daren't, Aunt Maggie. I'm shaking so.'

'There's no sign of it,' she said.

I was about to turn and look at her when I stopped myself and stared ahead through the windscreen. No, there was no sign of it. I might be trembling inside, but I wasn't showing it. I had won. I pushed in the gears, released the brake, and drove the car past the yard and up the steep bank.

When we reached the three roads, I stopped and said to Aunt Maggie, 'I can't go into Borne Coote; I couldn't talk to Talbot now.'

'No lass,, I understand. Let's go straight on to Penrith. We'll see him tomorrow.'

When we reached Penrith, I suggested we should have a drink.

Aunt Maggie agreed. 'And a very good idea an' all. And a bit of lunch with it.'

I did not want to eat, but I forced myself to swallow the food. After the meal was finished, I looked across the table at Aunt Maggie and asked, 'Would you mind if we don't go round the coast?'

'Not a bit.' Then her hand came out and gripped my wrist. 'You did well,' she said softly. 'Splendid. You never need worry again.'

My aunt's kindly tone was almost too much for me; I wanted to drop my head on my arms and cry.

She must have sensed this, for she said, 'Now, now, don't. He's not worth a single thought of yours, never mind your tears. Say to yourself—it's ended finally— for, you know, you were bound to have run across him sometime. I think that's what you've been afraid of, what you've been waiting for—a sort of test.'

She was right as always. I had been waiting for it as a kind of examination, and I had passed my test.

'Let's go—let's go home,' I said.

'You don't want to look round the town?' she asked.

'No,' I said. 'Some other time. Perhaps tomorrow or the next day—there's nearly a week left.'

'Only four days,' she replied.

'We can do a lot in four days,' I said.

We had reached the top of the gully road and I was braking the car for the descent when Aunt Maggie, pointing towards the road that led from the village, exclaimed, 'Stop a minute. Look along there.'

I stopped and looked in the direction she indicated, and saw, staggering towards us, in the far distance, a figure which I made out to be that of Roy McVeigh.

'He's drunk.'

'He certainly isn't sober.' I commented.

'Good lord!' exclaimed Aunt Maggie. 'He'll be in the ditch in a minute.'

As I backed the car onto the main road again, Aunt Maggie asked, 'What are you doing?'

'Going to pick him up.'

'I wonder if he'll thank you. The other one wouldn't —not if he were in this state.'

No, I guess Davie McVeigh would not have thanked any woman for picking him up if he were drunk, but Roy was not Davie.

When I reached the swaying figure, I stopped the car and, leaning out, called, 'Hello! Mr McVeigh.'

'Ah, hall-o, there.' Roy stumbled towards the window and leant heavily on it. 'Hallo, there.' He was nodding at Aunt Maggie now.

'Would you like a lift?'

'Bet your life—been celeratin'. Been celeratin'.' He chewed on the words; then grinned as he finished. 'Got the sack—oh, high jinks 'n low jinks!'

I got out, opened the back door, and assisted him onto the seat, where he sprawled back laughing.

I turned the car once again so we were going down the narrow steep bank towards the house. I could only catch snatches now of Roy's drunken mutterings, but he was talking about us leaving.

'Luckyyou,' Roy was saying, 'leavin' this godforsaken hole. Money to spend—travel. That's it, travel. Luckyyou.'

When I drove in, the courtyard was empty, but, as soon as I shut off the engine, I knew that the kitchen was not empty, for issuing from it came loud angry yelling. And when the shouting penetrated to Roy McVeigh's fuddled brain, he started to laugh. Flopping over sideways into the corner of the car, he spluttered: 'Here we go! Here we go! Up the McVeighs!'

When Roy made no effort to get out, I went around and, opening the car door, extended my hand towards him. Still laughing, he grasped it and eased himself to his feet, but he would have fallen if I had not steadied him. I cast a quick glance towards Aunt Maggie. She got out and took hold of his other arm.

She said briskly, 'Steady up. Come on now. Steady up,' and began to guide him towards the kitchen door.

As I approached nearer, I recognized Davie McVeigh's angry voice so I tried to disengage myself from Roy's hand. But he would have none of it, and, almost swaying with him, I approached the kitchen door apprehensively for the second time that day. As the three of us could not all pass through together, Aunt Maggie released her hold on him, and Roy, stumbling inwards, took me with him. Our precipitous entry brought the eyes of not only Flora Cleverly and Davie McVeigh upon us, but also the terrified gaze of Frannie. She'd had her face buried against McVeigh's waist, and she now turned her tear-blurred eyes in our direction and held her choking breath as she looked at us. In the temporary, yet vibrant, silence that filled the room I led Roy to a chair. After he had dropped into it heavily, he still held on to my hand.

'You good for nothing, lazy—!'

'You leave him alone.'

Flora Cleverly was moving down the long table now and Davie McVeigh shouted back at her: 'You keep out of this. Once and for all, I've warned you, you keep out of this. As for leaving anybody alone, I'm telling you again, you lay a hand on her, just once more, and I'll shoot you up that hill quicker 'n you've gone in your life afore.'

'An' I've told you—' Flora Cleverly was leaning across the table towards him '—if you don't want her mistreated, then keep her away from here.'

'She'll be here as long as I want her to be,' Davie stated flatly.

'Oh, will she, indeed? We're getting somewhere now.' They were talking as if they had the room to themselves. 'I've knocked at the truth before, and now the door's opening, is it?' Flora continued. 'She's got a right here, has she? Because you're the one that fathered her, eh? You're the one that Bill Tarrent was looking for! He beat the daylights out of Minnie to get her to give your name.'

'Shut up! Shut that dirty mouth of yours.'

'Shut up, will I? Oh, no! You've brought this into the open, and now I'm going to give it plenty of air.'

'Aunt Flo-ra!' Roy McVeigh's hand was stretching across the table, trying to reach the enraged woman, but she did not see it. Again, he said, 'Flora! Don't— don't.'

But Flora persisted. 'That's why Cissie Bradley gave you the go-by, eh? She likely knew you were carrying on with Minnie Amble—or Minnie Tarrent as she became just in time—before you joined up. Deny it, if you can—she's yours, isn't she?'

The housekeeper was pointing to Frannie's trembling back. The girl still had her arms round Davie McVeigh's waist, and he had one hand on her shoulder, the other on the top of her head. He was glaring at Flora Cleverly with undisguised hate and was about to speak when Roy, dragging himself to his feet, stumbled towards Flora. When Roy reached her, he pulled her roughly round to him saying, 'No, no. You're wrong. Leave Davie alone.'

'You go and sit down.'

Flora pushed at him offhandedly, for her mind was not on Roy at this moment—it was filled with her loathing of McVeigh. But, in the next second, Roy brought her full attention to him—he turned from her and leaned despondently on the table with both hands. He muttered, 'She's mine.'

'Be quiet! Get out. Don't be such a damn fool.' This was McVeigh speaking.

Roy, lifting his head, but still supporting himself with his hands on the table, looked towards the burly figure of his brother and said, in slow, measured words, 'It's—time—Davie. The truth is rottin' in me. It's time it was out.' Now he lifted one hand up, and half turning his body towards Flora Cleverly, he stated, 'I'm Frannie's father. Now you know, Flora.'

Aunt Maggie was standing beside me, close beside me, gripping my arm. Davie McVeigh was still holding Frannie to him. He had his head bowed and his eyes closed. Roy McVeigh was still managing to support himself drunkenly with one arm on the table. He did this for one second longer, then Flora Cleverly was upon him.

Her hands gripping the collar of his coat, she pulled him upwards as if he were a wooden puppet, and staring into his face, she cried, 'It isn't true! Swear to me—it isn't true. Roy!'

The woman was actually shaking him now. It seemed impossible that such a thin frail woman could have the strength to shake this man. Although he wasn't as big as Davie McVeigh, Roy was of no mean stature.

'Tell me she's his! Tell me!' she cried hysterically.

'She's mine, Flora. She's mine.'

'No, no!' She still had hold of him, but was shaking her head like a golliwog, repeating, 'No, no! It's impossible, you were only a bit of a lad.'

'I was six-teen—sixteen, Flora.'

'Sixteen!' She heaved him once more towards her before flinging him against the table. 'Sixteen!' she cried. 'You couldn't—you wouldn't. I tell you, I won't believe it.'

'What's it got to do with you anyway?'

Davie McVeigh pressed Frannie from him, and, pushing her gently behind him, advanced towards the other side of the table.

Again Davie asked, 'What's it to you? After all it's none of your business. Up to these last three years, you've been paid as a servant—a superior servant in this house, but you've forgotten your place because right from the beginning you've been given too much authority. But Frannie does belong here, she belongs to us both. Roy's her father, and I'm her uncle.'

Flora Cleverly had been leaning across the table looking up into McVeigh's face as he spoke, and she repeated 'Uncle?' And again, 'Uncle?'

Then, straightening herself and putting her hand across her mouth as if struck by some fearful thought, she repeated yet again, 'Uncle?' Her eyes, moving slowly towards the dresser where Frannie now stood, she gazed at the girl as if in horror before she whispered, 'And I'm her grandmother!' As if shocked by her own words, she jumped back and gripped at the sink before yelling, 'Do you hear? I'm her grandmother!' Then: 'No! No! It's not true, it can't be. I won't be.'

When Flora stopped yelling, a silence descended on the kitchen and all eyes were on her. Roy McVeigh, standing with his back to the table now, seemed almost sober, and he would have retreated from Flora if the table had not been in his way, for now she was advancing towards him.

When she was about a yard from him, she stopped

and, looking up into his face, she cried, 'Don't you understand?'

Roy shook his head in bewilderment. Like someone speaking under the influence of a drug, he shook his head and said, 'No, Flora.'

'Not "Flora"—"mother"—I'm your *mother*!'

'Oh—my—God!'

It did not sound like a man speaking; it was more like the whimper of a woman. Strangely, Roy did not deny her accusation, but accepted it with the exclamation: 'Oh, my God!'

'Don't believe her.' McVeigh's voice, crisp and stimulating, brought Roy's dazed countenance round to face him. Again, he said, 'Don't believe her. She wants a hold on you. She's making it up.'

'Making it up, am I? I've made lots of things up in my time, but not this. Your father taught me to make up stories; when we ran wild around these waters, he taught me all I know.'

'You're lying. It was wishful thinking—it's still wishful thinking.'

'You know nothing about it, Davie McVeigh. He would have married me if it hadn't have been for your grandfather. I might have been your mother, too.'

'God forbid!'

I watched Flora's teeth set; they scarcely parted as she went on, ' "God forbid!" you say. Well, let me tell you, I'd have made a better mother than the one that bred you, for she hadn't the guts of a louse. When I went down with him—' she now thumbed in the direction of Roy '—when I went down with him, I told her it was your father's doings and she believed me. She knew he was on the prowl in other quarters, and she never questioned a word I said. She was pregnant herself at the time and she whisked me off to Spain with her—to the very house on the coast where she had spent her honeymoon. And she stayed there; she wouldn't let him come near her. He had made me suffer, but by God I got my own back on him. There was only three days between her confinement and mine. Her child died a few days later, and her with it. I passed mine over as hers—him there.' Flora pointed again at Roy. 'It was easy. An old midwife and a drunken doctor with not a dozen words of English between them.'

'You devil!' Davie exclaimed. 'I could kill you. As for my father—he wouldn't have looked at the side you were on, and you know it.'

'What do you know about it?' She glared at the glowering man opposite her. 'You were a baby then, and he left you with your grannie all your young days.'

'No, I didn't know. But there is someone who did—Talbot. He had your measure from the first. He knew what my father thought—thought about you. He might have had his women on the side, but he made damned sure that you weren't one of them. He loathed you, woman. He only tolerated you afterwards because you ran the house and—' he cast his eyes in Roy's direction '—and saw to him. And it's because of him and what you did for him that I've put up with you all these years—but now, thank God, it's finished.' He pointed. 'Get upstairs, woman, and gather what belongs to you and then leave this house.'

I watched the wrinkles on Flora Cleverly's face move like rippling sand over the bones, and, at that moment, I could have felt sorry for her. That is, until her lip curled back with the action of a snarling cat and she spat at him: 'You're drawing out the last stave that holds this house together. Everything in the past you've touched has gone rotten on you—I've seen to that! And now you'll never pull up. Your land has gone; the house is mortgaged; you've got nothing to raise a penny on. Yes, I'll go, but, unlike you, I'm not without money. An' I'll sit apart and watch you moulder and rot away.'

I saw that Davie McVeigh was trying to control his rage. He was staring, eyes strained wide, towards her when she turned from him and, looking at Roy with a proprietary air, she said, 'Come on.'

Roy was standing away from the table. He shook his head and blinked his eyes; then he turned and looked at the man whom he had always considered his brother. As Davie McVeigh looked back at him, I saw his expression soften. There was a look of sincere pity on his face. It hadn't taken much observation to gather that, in a way, he had despised Roy, but now he was looking at him as if the severance of an apparent blood tie had left him bereft of something. The look on Roy's face was similar.

Roy, although still dazed-looking, appeared to be sober, and, when Flora Cleverly spoke his name, making it a command as she said 'Roy!' he turned his head slowly towards her, and gazing at her a full minute before he spoke, he said quietly, 'I can't come with you.'

'Roy!' The command was high now.

'It's no use.' He dropped his head. 'I tell you, I can't.'

'I'm your mother.'

'That's—that's not my fault. I—I haven't been brought up to look upon you as—as my mother.'

'I've always acted to you as a mother.'

'I can't come with you.' His head was sunk on his chest now.

'Where will you go then?' There was scorn in her words. 'You can't stay here. You have no place here.'

'Are you sure of that?' He raised his head slightly.

'Yes. Yes, I'm sure. Why do you think Talbot's brother, Charlie, left me that money, eh? Because he skedaddled off and wouldn't face up to his responsibilities. Charlie Talbot was your father.' She tossed her head in Davie McVeigh's direction as she ended, 'You are no kin to him. As I said, you don't belong here—come on.'

As Roy's head dropped once again, Davie McVeigh's voice came to him across the table. 'You've a home here as long as you want it, Roy. We've been brought up as brothers, and to all intents and purposes that's what we are—differences or no differences.'

In this moment, something within my breast leapt up and out towards Davie McVeigh. Aunt Maggie must have experienced the same emotion, for the pressure of her hand on my arm tightened until it was painful.

Roy had lifted his head, and the two men stared at each other until their gaze was snapped by Flora Cleverly letting out a sound that rose and ended in a scream. Strangely, she was not screaming at Davie McVeigh, but at Roy.

'You! you fool!' Flora cried. 'Can't you see he's just doing it to get his own back on me? He'll treat you like scum. And what have you here? Nothing. Nothing but work—work and hard tack. And my God, let me tell you, when I'm not here to see to the table, it will be hard tack. Don't be a fool.'

'It's no use, Fl—' Roy hesitated on the name, then said decisively, 'Flora. If I don't stay here, then it'll be somewhere else, but—but wherever it is, it—it can't be with you. I'm sorry because I know—' he turned his eyes away '—I know you've been good to me, yet—yet, I must say this. I think I'd have been a better man today if—if it hadn't been for you.'

'You—you ungrateful swine!'

'I know. I know.'

'I could kill you. Do you hear? I could kill you. And after all I've gone through—all I've done—and then—and then for you to say that. And, on top of everything, for you to deceive me all these years.' Her voice was rising to a high note again. 'And to think that—that—' Flora jerked her head in the direction of Frannie, where the girl was standing tightly pressed against the dresser. '—that can claim relationship with me!'

What happened next took only a matter of seconds, but it jerked us all into horrified action. Flora Cleverly had been standing to the side of the sink. She did not turn her head towards it now, but her hand jerked out, groped at the draining board for a split second, found what it was searching for, a broad blade, taper-edged old vegetable knife, and with all her enraged strength behind it, she threw it in the direction of the dresser. I don't know if I screamed or not—I was horror-stricken —but Aunt Maggie did. The knife had been aimed at the petrified Frannie, but it wedged itself in the out-stretched upper arm of Davie McVeigh.

As I saw the handle quiver and the blood flowing from his wound, I had a frantic desire to turn and fly out of the room—fly away from all this hatred and rage.

'You're mad, woman! You're insane. Get away! Get away!' Aunt Maggie was crying now. She was standing by McVeigh's side, and I was there also, but I couldn't remember moving towards him.

Davie McVeigh had said nothing; after the shock of the impact, he had not even moved. I saw that his face looked ashen white and his left hand trembled slightly as it went to the handle of the knife. With a sharp tug he drew it out of the flesh and his shirt and arm were reddened immediately by the blood gushing from the wound.

It was Aunt Maggie who took charge now. She sat Davie down; she ripped up towels. She turned to Roy who was again shaking so that you could imagine he had fallen back into his drunken stupor, and she brought him to himself by saying sharply, 'Get on the phone! Get the doctor.'

'It's all right; it's nothing, only a flesh wound.'

Aunt Maggie took no notice of Davie McVeigh, but said again, 'Do as I say, and get the doctor. As for you!' She was winding a towel tightly around the upper part of Davie's arm now, and she turned to address Flora Cleverly—but the far side of the kitchen table was astonishingly empty. The door leading to the hall was open and through it came the sound of an upstairs door crashing closed.

'Have you any spirits in the house?' Aunt Maggie was

speaking to McVeigh as she busied herself to staunch the flow of blood.

'In the cabinet in the sitting room.'

Aunt Maggie was about to ask, 'Will you—?' when I hurried out of the kitchen into the drawing room, and, after a little searching, found a bottle, one-third full of whisky. But as I carried it back into the kitchen I thought—tea would have been better.

I poured out a good measure of the spirits and handed the drink to McVeigh. When he took it from me, he did not look at me nor speak, but, putting the glass to his lips, he threw off the drink in one swoop, gave a slight shudder, and closed his eyes as he returned the glass to me.

'The doctor says he'll be here in about fifteen minutes.' I was surprised to find Roy at my side. He was looking down at Davie, and he added, 'Oh, man! Oh, I'm sorry.'

'We'd all be much sorrier if the knife had found its mark.'

The two men were again looking at each other, and I shuddered slightly as I realized that Flora Cleverly's aim, but for Davie's outstretched arm, would have caught Frannie full in the neck, for the girl had been too petrified to move. Thinking of her now, I turned towards the dresser. She was still standing there, seemingly unable to drag herself away from its support.

I went to her and, putting my arm about her, said quietly, 'It's all right. No one's going to hurt you. It's all right.'

Frannie gasped and leant against me.

At this point, Davie McVeigh turned his eyes towards us and asked, 'Will you keep her with you—for the time being?'

All I did was to incline my head in agreement. I knew what he meant by 'for the time being'. What Flora Cleverly had been frustrated in accomplishing once, she was quite capable of attempting a second time.

Now, as if oblivious of us all except the man whom he had always looked upon as his brother, Roy pulled a chair close to McVeigh's, and sat down; their knees were almost touching.

Roy said again, 'Oh, I'm sorry, Davie.' Then lowering his head slightly, he asked, 'Did you know all along about—about us?'

'Forget it—it wasn't your fault.'

'But have you known all along?'

'No. No, I knew nothing about it. I always thought that—that we were brothers and—and, to all intents and purposes, we are.'

'Thanks, man.'

There was an embarrassing silence now, broken by Aunt Maggie ripping more cloth for bandaging.

Then Roy said under his breath, 'I've lost me job; I got the sack. But it's likely all to the good. I'll move on and get something. And I'll—I'll support her. She's mine, and I'll support her.'

'It's a bad time for you to be moving on.' McVeigh was watching Aunt Maggie's hands as he spoke. 'This is my right arm; I'm going to be handicapped with the turning for the next few days.'

'Oh, man, I wouldn't walk out on you; I'll stay as long as you want. I only thought—you would want to get rid of me.'

'Frannie needs an anchor. There's the cottage—we'll talk about it later.'

'Aw, thanks, Davie. Thanks, man. I don't know what to say—only thanks.' His head had drooped further.

McVeigh said briskly, 'The best thing you can do is to go and sleep it off.'

'No, Davie, I'm sober. I've never been more sober in me life.' And getting to his feet and looking in our direction, Roy held out his hand, and said, 'Come on, Frannie.'

The girl, moving slowly from me, caught at Roy's

hand and went with him. Just as they reached the kitchen door, he looked over his shoulder and said, 'I'll take her home and see the grannie. I'll tell her I'm bringing her back here—all right?'

'All right.' McVeigh nodded. 'But be prepared—she won't like it.'

Aunt Maggie said briskly, 'Don't lower that arm, keep it up.' Then she added more softly, 'How are you feeling?'

'All right.'

'Your looks belie you. I wish that doctor would hurry up.'

'He won't thank you for sending for him for this bit of a cut.'

'That remains to be seen.'

McVeigh, turning and looking up at me now, said quietly, with an unsmiling twist to his lips, 'I don't think any more can happen before you leave.'

'I wouldn't be too sure of that.' This came smartly from Aunt Maggie.

McVeigh, turning his head in her direction, said, 'No. No, perhaps I shouldn't.'

There was the sound of a car coming into the courtyard, and the next moment the doctor was in the room. His manner was casual and easygoing.

He began by saying, 'Hello, Davie, what's happened? Had a kick from one of your Shetland ponies?'

McVeigh made no reply. After the doctor had unwound Aunt Maggie's handiwork, he made no comment either except to indicate that Aunt Maggie should open his bag. Then he set to work stitching up the torn flesh.

The procedure was too much for me. The sight of the needle made my stomach heave. I walked to the window and stood looking out.

'There. There now,' the doctor said quietly. 'That's fixed that. Now, perhaps, you'll tell me how you came by it? You know you're lucky, another hair's breadth

169

and it would have been the artery—not saying anything about the main leader.'

'I had a slight accident.'

'That's evident. How did you come by the accident—if it's not asking too much?'

The doctor had gone to the sink now and was washing his hands. When McVeigh did not answer, Aunt Maggie, after taking a deep breath, said, 'It was a knife thrown at him.'

'Yes?' The old man's head came swiftly round to look at her.

'It's got nothing to do with me,' said Aunt Maggie, using the phrase that people adopt when they go all out to make someone else's business their own. 'But, while you're here, I think you should see Miss Cleverly and give her a sedative of some sort.'

'Oh—oh—?' The doctor was shaking his head. 'Flora? Well, well. As to sedatives—' He turned and looked fully at Aunt Maggie. 'She's lived on them for years. Pep pills versus sedatives; this, I suppose, is the result."

He was walking towards Davie now and asked, 'What are you going to do about it?'

'Nothing.'

'Well it hasn't been unexpected; she's been ready to blow her top for a long time. Eaten up inside for years. Where is she now?'

'Upstairs,' said Aunt Maggie.

'I'd better have a word with her.'

'Leave her alone, Doctor, she's going, and the sooner the better.'

'All the same, I think I'll have a word with her if you don't mind, Davie. I think I'd better put it to her quietly that she'd better not try any more tricks. I can talk to her; I've had to do it before.'

When the doctor had left the kitchen, McVeigh got slowly to his feet and, addressing Aunt Maggie, said, 'Thanks; you've been more than kind.'

'Nonsense!' she said briskly. 'We just happened to be here. Now we'll leave you for a time, but I'll be back shortly.'

I noticed she did not say, 'we' would be back. Before I turned to follow her out of the room, I looked at Davie McVeigh who was standing now, supporting himself against the table.

I asked quietly, 'Will you be all right?'

He nodded towards me. 'I'll be all right,' he said. And then, 'I'll see you presently.' It sounded like a promise.

I went out into the yard and followed Aunt Maggie to the car. As we drove to the cottage, we did not exchange any words, but, as soon as we were indoors, she began to bustle about. As she did so she talked.

'Well, I've witnessed some things in me time,' she said, 'but never any like today's do. Flora Cleverly— Roy's mother! She's a devil of a woman that. And Roy —Frannie's father! I wouldn't have believed that! If it had been McVeigh himself—well, yes, I could have swallowed that. But Roy going after a married woman, and him just a lad, and he couldn't have had anything about him really, no real attraction, not like McVeigh. He's a weakling, Roy is. He doesn't take after her; he must have taken after the father who skedaddled off and took the line of least resistance. When you come to think of it, it's very good of McVeigh to take things the way he did, offering to let him stay on.'

I found to my surprise that I was becoming impatient with Aunt Maggie's incessant chatter. I wanted to be quiet to think. I was also surprised in the way I answered her last remark, for I said, 'Well, it's to Davie's advantage to keep him here now, for as he said he can't do much with one hand, turning that mushroom manure takes all of two hands—he's going to need Roy.'

I was not looking at Aunt Maggie as I spoke, but I felt her stop what she was doing and turn her eyes towards me.

171

'What's the matter?' she asked. 'Are you feeling upset?'

'No, no. Of course not.' Then sitting down with a plop on the chair to the side of the hearth, I followed this up with, 'Yes. Yes. Of course, I'm upset.'

She came and stood near me, saying, 'Naturally, you're bound to be with one thing and another. The quicker we get packed up and away the better you'll like it. It's been a day and a half, and no mistake.'

I had turned my face to the fire with my head resting on my hand. 'She could have killed that child,' I said.

'She could also have killed McVeigh. You heard what the doctor said, although I think that it would take more than a knife wound to finish off Davie McVeigh. Still I'm really very sorry for him. Funny things happen in a crisis like this: I think he's made an ally of Roy; and Talbot will certainly see that he gets all the help necessary. It's indoors they are going to be hard put to it. Janie couldn't cope—not a child of ten. Anyway, she's at school. She said they'd have to live on hard tack, and it looks as if they will have to. Still, I suppose they'll get somebody down at Borne Coote to help out. Yet, on the other hand, it isn't everybody who likes cooking and cleaning these days. We are very lucky to have Mrs Bridie, but, of course, she sticks to us because she's a widow and looks upon us as her family.' She sighed and, turning away, said, 'Well, it's their problem. I'm going to make the tea.'

What a day! Everything had happened that could have happened. No, not everything. It was possible that Davie McVeigh could have taken that knife directly in the chest. What if he had? What if he had died? How would I have taken it?

'Don't be silly."

My admonition had been verbal and, actually, I shook my body as if a hand were on my shoulder trying to force some sense into me. My inner voice commented:

'He's got a two-inch wound in the arm. It's stitched. It's only a matter of days before he'll be using it again. So stop it.'

It was quite easy to say '*Stop it*', but not so easy to turn my mind from Davie McVeigh, or to avoid the new knowledge that had sprung at me. As I sat, I kept repeating to myself: '*This is awful—awful. What will I do?*' And I gave myself the answer: '*Pack up and go right now; there's nothing to stop you.*'

But there was—there was Aunt Maggie. I couldn't understand Aunt Maggie's present attitude. I couldn't understand whether she was for or against McVeigh. One minute she was in sympathy with him; the next, she was telling me that the sooner we went the better. If I said to her now, '*Come on, let's get away from this,*' she would more likely than not say, '*What! Don't you think it would look odd under the circumstances? Like rats running away from a sinking ship.*' I could hear her using that exact cliché.

Aunt Maggie came in now carrying the tea tray, and she said, as if there had been no break in the conversation: 'I hope the next one he gets will do something to the house: It could be made into a lovely place if a little money were spent on it.'

I did not turn my head towards my aunt as I said, 'Well, he's not likely to have any money to spend on the house, is he?'

'Oh, I don't know. He told me once he makes a go of the mushroom business, it could be quite profitable.'

'Once,' was all I answered.

On this, Aunt Maggie rounded on me sharply, saying, 'Now, don't be another Flora Cleverly for goodness sake! Have a little faith in the man. Give him a chance.'

I turned my head and looked up.

'All right, all right, Aunt Maggie,' I said. 'Don't shout at me.'

I felt near tears, and, as she turned to the tea tray, she muttered, 'Oh, I'm sorry, lass, I think I'm worked up without knowing it. It's been a day and no mistake.

173

Well, come on. Let's have our tea and forget about the whole business.'

We didn't forget about the whole business.

It was just on dark when there came a knock at the door. I rose hastily from the table where I was attempting to write, and when I opened the door, there stood Janie.

'Hello,' she said.

'Hello, Janie,' I answered. 'Come in.'

'No, I can't stop. I've just brought a message from Davie. He says—he says, will you not come over this night?'

I screwed up my face as I repeated, '*Not* come over?' making sure I had heard aright.

'Yes,'·she nodded. 'That's what Davie says. Flora—Aunt Flora's leaving in the mornin'.' Janie dropped her head. 'She's got a van coming. She's going to take the little tables out of the drawing-room and lots of other things. She says they're hers.'

Aunt Maggie was now standing at the door. She asked, 'And are they?'

'I don't know, but Davie says she can take what she likes so long as she goes.'

'He's a fool.'

Janie made no comment on this, but said, 'He looks sick. Talbot says he should be in his bed.'

'Talbot has come?' I asked.

'Yes, he's in the yard. And Roy's there an' all.' She smiled now. 'Roy's working hard.'

'I'm glad,' I said. And then I asked, 'Where's Frannie?'

'She's at her grannie's, but she's coming to stay with us. Roy said he'll bring her back tomorrow after—after everything is cleared up. I've got to go; I'm helping. Bye-bye.'

'Good-bye, Janie.'

As we turned back into the room, Aunt Maggie said,

'He's mad for letting her stay the night. She could do anything—burn down the place; even do him in.'

'Oh, Aunt Maggie! Talk about me looking at the black side.'

Aunt Maggie patted my arm and laughed. 'Yes, I know. Still, I'm sorry he said we can't go over. I had my mind made up to slip across and make them a meal.'

'You had?'

She looked me full in the face now and repeated, 'I had.'

It was as I said—I really did not know what was going on in Aunt Maggie's mind from minute to minute. Nor was I more enlightened during the evening. When we parted at bedtime, she kissed me on the cheek but she seemed slightly distant.

I lay in bed and looked over the lake. There was a wild moon riding, but its light was fitful, and, at times, it was obscured by great drifts of white cloud. When this happened, it looked as if I were seeing the lake through misted glass. As I lay there, I wondered whether Roy McVeigh, when he took over the cottage, would sit up here and look out on the moonlight. I doubted it. I could see Davie McVeigh quite clearly doing just that, but not Roy. I could even see Frannie looking out into the moonlight; even though unable to comprehend fully its beauty, she would still look at it. There swept over me at this moment a feeling of nostalgia. I was going to miss this place, for here I had felt some sense of security. Over the weeks, I had gathered strength from my surroundings, sufficient to convince Ian that never again would I be affected by him—and that was no small accomplishment.

Following close on this feeling of nostalgia and in direct opposition to it, I began to experience a sense of regret—regret that we had ever come here, for this new emotion that I had now to face up to, and tackle, would colour my future. I was sick of struggling, sick of fighting—I had fought 'nerves' and fear. Was I now going to be called upon to fight—? I wouldn't allow myself to put a name to the emotion I had to fight—I'd had enough of that particular emotion, more than enough. Why had it hit me again? And why, I questioned harshly, had the emotion to be directed towards —Davie McVeigh of all men?

It was a long time later that I felt sleep coming to me. The moon was full on my face and I remembered thinking: they say you'll go mad if you sleep with the moon shining on your face. *'They say what they say; let them say.'* I repeated the quotation to myself.

My lids were drooping when, through the mist, I saw a figure walking from the lake over the lawn towards the cottage. Standing out against the dark bulk of him was the white sling that held his arm immobilized. I saw him stop and look up to my window. I had tried to keep Davie out of my mind. But now I was going to sleep; I was dreaming—I need no longer be on my guard.

In my dream, I knelt up on the bed, thrust open the window, and called to him—he came and held out his arms. There was no evidence of a sling now and, for in dreams the fantastic takes on the form of the natural, I stepped over the sill and jumped down to Davie. But my descent was not rapid; I hovered over him in the air, in the manner of a Michelangelo figure on the ceiling of the Sistine Chapel, until, reaching up, he caught me and pulled me down to him. As we embraced, I laughed and laughed, and then I heard my Aunt Maggie's voice coming from a distance saying, 'Wake up! Wake up, Pru!'

I opened my eyes and there she was, saying, 'Wake up! You're dreaming. Wake up, Pru!'

My mouth still wide in laughter, I stared at her until, remembering the dream and the context of it, to the consternation of both of us, I burst into tears.

Getting into the narrow bed beside me, Aunt Maggie held me tightly, saying, 'There, there!' She did not ask what my dream was about, nor did I tell her; and, so, we went to sleep.

The next morning when we woke in the early dawn, Aunt Maggie almost screamed aloud from the cramp in her arm. I had been lying on her arm most of the night.

It was now about eleven o'clock. I had been for a brisk walk in the direction away from the house. We had had our coffee and I was settled at the table making a vain effort to get on with my story. But, somehow, it had gone dead on me; all my characters seemed to be marking time. I found I could not use the vibrant material of yesterday, not even if I camouflaged it. Something had come unstuck.

I was staring at a half-written page when Aunt Maggie said, 'I think I'll go for a dander. Better take advantage of the sun. I don't suppose it'll last for long.'

When she returned to the room with her coat on and a scarf round her head, I barely stopped myself from saying, '*Don't go near the house.*' It would have been a silly thing to say. I knew Aunt Maggie would not go near the place now until she received word from Davie McVeigh.

'Won't be long.' She nodded at me, smiled, then went out, and I was left alone with my unfinished story.

Now, I asked myself, what did I want to have happen to these two people—these two main characters? Usually, my characters took hold of me and led me along their own paths, but not these two. I had to mould them, and they would do nothing without me. But how was I to mould them from now on—how? I got to my feet and walked towards the fire.

I knew how I would like to deal with the characters, yet I couldn't do it. But why not? Simply because, in touching on these two lives, I was arrested by a kind of shyness. I had not been confronted with these problems when writing my other books, but this book was different. My writing, the critics would say when they read it, had lost its sting. Some would welcome this; some would regret it, no doubt. I sat at the side of the fire and turned my gaze down the long length of the room.

Would Davie come here at times in the winter evenings and keep Roy company? Would he start on his carving again? No. He'd likely be too busy poring over books and accounts, attending to ways and means. I would never look at a mushroom but I would think of him walking the lines in the caves or preparing 'the gold bed'—as he had once laughingly referred to the enormous heap of manure lying under the Dutch barn.

When the clock on the mantelpiece struck twelve, I turned my face to the window. There was no sun now; the sky was heavy again with rain; and I thought: if Aunt Maggie doesn't get back quickly, she's going to get caught in it.

At half past twelve, my aunt still hadn't returned and the rain had started. I went to the door and stood under the porch roof, looking first to the right and then to the left. I didn't know which road she had taken, or by which she would come back. She might have gone round the hill by the Big Water, or through the back way up to the crossroads. She wouldn't, I assured myself again, have gone in the direction of the house. At this thought, my head turned automatically towards the copse. Then I heard the breaking of brushwood underfoot and thought: she *has* been that way, and I added a mental *tut! tut!*

When the figure emerged from the copse, it was not Aunt Maggie but Davie McVeigh. He hesitated a second when he saw me, then came on, and, as he advanced, I tried to recall the dream I'd had the night before. It had been an odd kind of a dream—he'd been in it, and I'd awakened laughing—then I'd cried. But, like all dreams, it had seeped away when exposed to daylight.

'Hello.' Davie was standing, looking down at me.

'Hello. How are you feeling? How is your arm?'

'Oh, all right. Give it another two or three days and it'll be back to normal.'

'Won't you come in?'

I turned and walked into the room, and he followed me and closed the door. I went straight towards the fireplace and stirred up the logs.

I said, 'Aunt Maggie isn't in, she went for a walk. I'm afraid she'll get caught in the rain. I was looking for her.'

When Davie made no comment, I twisted my head round to see him standing a yard or so behind me. Once more I paid attention to the fire, and, as I replaced the poker, I asked, 'Won't you sit down?'

Again there was no response. When I straightened up and turned about, it was to find him standing squarely before me. He was looking into my face and I into his. Why had I ever thought him big, burly, and rough-looking? His eyes were soft; his lips were kind; his hair, at this moment, held an almost irresistible attraction for my hands—like a magnet, it drew them; I wanted to run my fingers through it. I clasped them tightly and became overheated at the thought.

Could this be me? Wasn't once enough? Hadn't I been through all this before—? But no, I hadn't been through this before. I had never felt like this before. Ian's charm had flattered my intellect while he picked my brains. My present feeling did not touch my intellect, but played heavily on my heart.

'We should talk,' Davie said.

What a strange thing to say.

'Should we?' I asked.

What a silly thing to say.

'I'm not much good at charming platitudes.'

'No?'

'No. I'm going to ask you a question; just answer yes or no.'

My eyes were blurry from staring into his face. The pumping of my heart seemed to be forcing that organ

179

up into my windpipe, making breathing difficult. His features were now becoming slightly indistinct as if a thin veil of mist were floating over them. It was like the mist that covered the grass on the morning that I walked to the Big Water.

'Will you have me?'

What had he said? Would I have him? Not, '*I love you, my beautiful,*' as Ian had said. '*I want you; I need you; I can't live without you.*' On, on and on. I, I, I. Nothing like that, just—'Will you have me?' There was a humility about the question that created a sharp pain, like a jab underneath my breast. Where was the big brash individual who had nearly blasted me off the road on that memorable Saturday? There was no trace of him. The man behind the iron façade was a shy, even humble, being, and a man who knew fear. I had knowledge of the fear, but I had not dreamt of the shyness. Nor had I ever imagined him capable of humility—'*Will you have me?*'

I could not get my answer past my throat. I felt myself swaying gently, then, with an inarticulate cry, I was pressed against him. As his good arm went about me, I seemed to sink right into the warm depth of him. For a full minute we stood pressed close, tightly, tightly close, then, slackening his hold slightly, and with a movement of his cheek against my hair, he brought my face round to his. It was a strange moment, that moment before we kissed, and, then, it was not a long kiss, nor passionate—rather it was tender, tender with the promise of an unusual, compelling love that would control our lives. My head dropped back on his arm.

I was gazing up at him when the trembling started in my stomach. But it was not the signal of fear this time, but of laughter, which I tried to check. This was not the moment to laugh. I was back in the dream—in his arms, and laughing. For a moment, I saw perplexity on his face and a look almost of horror, as if I had been playing a game with him. Then the laughter in me changed and

I repeated the performance of last night. A second later, I was sobbing helplessly and we were sitting on the couch, my head buried in his shoulder, and Davie was soothing me as he would have comforted Frannie; only he was using different words.

'Oh, my dear. Darling, darling. Don't, don't. It'll be all right. There's nothing to be afraid of, I'll promise you that. You'll never have need to be afraid of me. I cannot believe that you love me. I don't think you do. I don't expect it—not yet. But it will come. I promise you—don't—don't cry any more.'

'Oh, Davie, Davie, it'll be all right, won't it? Things will work out all right, won't they? I'm—I'm frightened.'

Moving his hand out of the sling, Davie lifted my chin and, looking at me, said quietly, 'I can't speak for you, Pru.'

It was the first time he had used my first name.

'I can only answer for myself,' he continued, 'no matter what has gone bad on me before, this is one thing I know that will work out. There are only a few things we're sure of in life. Death is one. With me, there is another—and this feeling I have for you is it. I know, deep in here.'

Davie brought my hand and laid it so I could feel his hard chest—his seared chest. Again we looked deep into each other's eyes. And, again, his lips dropped to mine.

All I could mutter now was, 'Oh, Davie, Davie.'

Making an effort not to start on another bout of weeping, I tried to return to the commonplace by saying, 'I wonder what Aunt Maggie will say? She should be in at any moment.'

Davie was holding me tightly as he said, 'I don't think she will be.'

'What—what do you mean?'

'Just that she won't be in at any moment. She's busy making the dinner. It'll be ready by now, I should say.'

Davie had turned his head to one side but not before I saw the twinkle in the shaded depth of his eyes.

'Aunt Maggie—making the dinner?'

'Yes.' He was gazing at me again and he began to smile. '*Aunt Maggie* came over about half past eleven. Flora Cleverly and her vanload of what she termed her belongings had just left the yard when your aunt made her appearance. I've an idea she had been watching—and waiting.'

'Aunt Maggie!' My voice was high.

'Yes—Aunt Maggie.' His face was twisted with laughter now. 'She's a remarable woman—Aunt Maggie. She's already reconstructed the kitchen. She's having a new cooker put in, all the old cupboards pulled down, and units put up. She's got all her own furniture mentally placed in the house, and, you'll be happy to know, we are to have a new water system and bathroom.'

I was holding one hand tightly across my lips. All I could do was to shake my head slowly in wonderment.

'Your—or *our* Aunt Maggie is, as I've said, a very remarkable woman. She tells me that, if the business of Flora had not arisen yesterday, she still had no intention of leaving here.' He moved his head to indicate the cottage.

'Oh—?' I bowed my head and bit my lip. Then I said slowly, 'Wait till I see her!'

'Then we'd better go now. The dinner will be waiting, and I wouldn't like to hear what she'll say if it's spoiling.'

Davie drew me to my feet, and, as we made for the door, his arm was about me. He said casually, 'And, oh, by the way, we're going to have another addition to the family—a Mrs Bridie who, Aunt Maggie says, works like a Trojan.'

I stopped. 'Oh, Davie!' I shook my head. 'I'm sorry for you.'

With a pull of his arm, I was caught tightly to him again. 'Go on feeling like that. It's not enough that you give me an aunt, a housekeeper, and—' he paused '—a wife. Go on feeling sorry for me, and I will spend my days wallowing in it.'

'But you said you didn't want anyone to feel sorry for you.'

'And I don't—not *any*one—only you, Mrs David Bernard Michael McVeigh. You remember when I saw you for the first time?'

I put my head back and laughed, a free young laugh. Did I remember? David Bernard Michael McVeigh. *My* David Bernard Michael McVeigh. I put my hands up and ran my fingers through his hair.

'Oh Davie! Davie!' It was the wrong thing to do with Aunt Maggie waiting. . . .